JUDGING AND UNDERSTANDING

Judging and Understanding

Essays on Free Will, Narrative, Meaning and the Ethical Limits of Condemnation

Edited by
PEDRO ALEXIS TABENSKY
Rhodes University, South Africa

ASHGATE

Published by
Ashgate Publishing Limited
Gower House
Croft Road
Aldershot
Hampshire GU11 3HR
England

Ashgate Publishing Company
Suite 420
101 Cherry Street
Burlington, VT 05401-4405
USA

Ashgate website: http://www.ashgate.com

British Library Cataloguing in Publication Data
Judging and understanding : essays on free will, narrative, meaning and the ethical limits of condemnation
    1.Schlink, Bernhard. Reader 2.Judgement (Ethics) 3.Justification (Ethics)
    I.Tabensky, Pedro Alexis, 1964-
    170

Library of Congress Cataloging-in-Publication Data
Judging and understanding : essays on free will, narrative, meaning and the ethical limits of condemnation / edited by Pedro Alexis Tabensky.
        p. cm.
    Includes index.
    ISBN 0-7546-5395-1 (hardcover : alk. paper)
    1. Judgment (Ethics) 2. Understanding—Moral and ethical aspects. I. Tabensky, Pedro Alexis, 1964- II. Title: Judging and understanding.

    BJ1408.5.J82 2006
    170–dc22

2006008829

ISBN-10: 0-7546-5395-1
ISBN-13: 978-0-7546-5395-0

Printed and bound in Great Britain by TJ International Ltd, Padstow, Cornwall.

Contents

Part III The Ethical Function of Condemnation

List of Contributors

Peta Bowden is Senior Lecturer in Philosophy, School of Social Sciences and Humanities, Murdoch University, Australia. Her research interests are in feminist ethics, moral psychology and organizational ethics. Her publications include *Caring: Gender-Sensitive Ethics* (1997) and several papers on the ethics of care. She is currently working on a book on reciprocity in asymmetrical relationships.

Marc Fellman is a Lecturer at University of Notre Dame, Australia. He has taught at various universities in Australia and Japan. His interests include moral philosophy and Holocaust and genocide studies. His most recent article titled 'Memories of the Events Surrounding the Fall of Nanking: The Debate Within Japan and the Role of Testimony in the Framing of National Histories' was published in the *Journal of Language, Culture and Communication* (2005). His current project is a book titled *Moral Complexity and the Holocaust*.

Andrew Gleeson is Lecturer in Philosophy at Adelaide University. He was previously a lecturer at the Australian Catholic University (Brisbane campus). His PhD was from the Australian National University. He has published several papers on ethics, philosophy of mind, and the intersection between them, in journals like *Inquiry* and *Philosophical Investigations*. Much of his work aims at rescuing thought on these topics from the depredations of academic specialization. He is working on a book illustrating this theme.

Ward E. Jones was educated in Berkeley and Oxford. He has lectured in the Department of Philosophy at Rhodes University in South Africa since 1999, and has been the editor of the journal *Philosophical Papers* since 2000. He has published several papers in epistemology and the philosophy of mind, and is editing a book entitled *Ethics in Film*, with Samantha Vice (OUP).

Chandra Kumar completed his doctoral studies at the University of Toronto and is currently a research fellow at Rhodes University, South Africa. Prior to this he has worked in various universities in Canada and South Africa. His interests are in social and political philosophy, metaphysics and epistemology. He is currently working on a book on Foucault, Marxism, and Contemporary Pragmatism. His more recent publications include 'Progress, Freedom, Human Nature, and Critical Theory' in

Imprints and 'Foucault and Rorty on Truth and Ideology: A Pragmatism View from the Left' in *Contemporary Pragmatism*.

Jonathan McKeown-Green completed his PhD at Princeton University in 2002 and currently lectures at the Department of Philosophy, University of Auckland in New Zealand. His interests include the moral and logical underpinnings of moral responsibility, philosophy of language, philosophy of logic and philosophy of music. This year he has written a critical notice on Scott Soames' *Beyond Rigidity*, has forthcoming articles on the Epistemology of Musical Perception and Conceptual Analysis *à la* Frank Jackson, and is currently working on a manuscript on the nature of language and linguistics.

Thaddeus Metz earned his PhD in philosophy from Cornell University in 1997. His research, particularly on Anglo-American philosophical approaches to the meaning of life, but also his work in moral, political, and legal theory grounded on the idea of the dignity of persons, has been widely published in journals such as: *Ethics*, *Philosophy and Public Affairs*, *Law and Philosophy*, *Religious Studies*, *Ratio*, and *American Philosophical Quarterly*. He lectured in the philosophy departments of UCLA, the University of Nebraska, and the University of Missouri, before recently joining the philosophy department at the University of the Witwatersrand, where he is an associate professor.

Kai Nielsen is Emeritus Professor of Philosophy for the University of Calgary, and Adjunct Professor of Philosophy at Concordia University in Montreal. He has published extensively in moral and political philosophy, and the philosophy of religion. His most recent books include *Naturalism without Religion*, *Globalization and Justice*, *Naturalism and Religion* and *Wittgensteinian and Fideism?*; written in critical dialogue with D.Z. Phillips. He is currently writing a book on cosmopolitan justice and starting to research a book on imperialism.

Martha Nussbaum is currently Ernst Freund Distinguished Service Professor of Law and Ethics at the University of Chicago. Her many publications include *Aristotle's De Motu Animalium* (1978), *The Fragility of Goodness: Luck and Ethics in Greek Tragedy and Philosophy* (1986, updated edition 2000), *Love's Knowledge* (1990), *The Therapy of Desire* (1994), *Poetic Justice* (1996), *For Love of Country* (1996), *Cultivating Humanity: A Classical Defense of Reform in Liberal Education* (1997), *Sex and Social Justice* (1998), *Women and Human Development* (2000), *Upheavals of Thought: The Intelligence of Emotions* (2001) and *Hiding from Humanity: Disgust, Shame and the Law* (2004).

Brian Penrose received his PhD in Philosophy in 1991 from Cornell University, having written a thesis on the relationship between liberalism and democracy. A Canadian expatriate, he has been teaching ethics and political philosophy at the University of the Witwatersrand in Johannesburg since 1995. His more recent publications include 'Fairness and Political Obligation', *South African Journal of Philosophy* 23 3 (2004), 'Must the Family be Just?', *Philosophical Papers* 29 3 (Nov. 2000) and 'Mill on Voting as a Public Trust', *South African Journal of Philosophy* 17 2 (1998).

Emma Rooksby has been research fellow at the *Centre for Applied Philosophy and Public Ethics*, based in Canberra, Australia since 2001. She gained a doctorate in philosophy at Murdoch University (Australia). Her research has a number of focuses, including computer ethics, philosophy and literature, and feminist ethics. Recent publications include *E-mail and Ethics* (Routledge, 2002), 'Empathy and Computer-Mediated Communication', (in Mark Wolf (ed.) *Virtual Morality*, Peter Lang, 2003), and 'Moral Theory in the Fiction of Isabelle de Charriere: The Case of Three Women', (*Hypatia*, 2005).

Pedro Alexis Tabensky has recently taken up a post as lecturer in the Department of Philosophy at Rhodes University in South Africa, having worked previously at the Center for the Study of Global Ethics, University of Birmingham in Great Britain. Previously he has worked in Australia and Israel. He is the author of *Happiness: Personhood, Community, Purpose* (Ashgate, 2003) and of several publications in peer reviewed journals. His main areas of interest are ethics and social philosophy. He is currently working on an anthology and a monograph on the roots of evil and on the complex roles evil plays in human living.

Samantha Vice completed her PhD at The University of Reading. She currently lectures at Rhodes University in South Africa. Her recent publications include 'Literature and the Narrative Self' in *Philosophy* (2003), 'On Persons and Immortality' in *The South African Journal of Philosophy* (2004) and 'On the Tedium of the Good' in *Ethical Theory and Moral Practice* (2005). She is also co-editor, with Ward Jones, of *Ethics in Film,* forthcoming for OUP, and is currently working on a festschrift entitled *Reason and Human Value: Essays in Honour of John Cottingham* with Enrique Chávez-Arvizo and Nafsika Athanassoulis.

Richard H. Weisberg is Floersheimer Professor of Constitutional Law at the Cardozo Law School in New York City. He is a General Editor of the journal *Law and Literature* and the author of several books including *Vichy Law and the Holocaust in France* (UK: Harwood, 1996).

Introduction

There is a proverb, well-worn by the friction of time: to understand is to forgive. But the wisdom of the proverb cannot be taken for granted. Age does not guarantee wisdom. Viewed one way it invites compassion and kindness. Viewed another it seems to be a recipe for condoning the abject violations that have on so many occasions brought humanity to its knees. If this proverb were wise, some would argue, then how could we judge people and their deeds in the way that they allegedly ought to be judged? Is not this proverb an invitation to dilute moral vigour, an invitation to ignore the call of justice and to settle for bland indifference to the suffering of victims; an invitation to forfeit moral responsibility and, worst of all, to condone evil; an invitation, perhaps, not to grasp the difference, allegedly the core difference, between victim and perpetrator and to see both as victims; to see us all as creatures at the mercy of circumstances: pathetic and feeble things, slaves of circumstances, perhaps cogs in the machine of cause and effect? Allegedly, this proverb could be used by violators of the moral law in their defence in courts of the land. 'You would have acted in much the same way I did', violators could claim, 'were you in my shoes, under my skin, seeing through my eyes'. Indeed, if we took this proverb to be true, then perhaps there would no longer be a place for holding people to account in the way that we allegedly should. It may seem that moral chaos would ensue, and perhaps even social collapse. Too much understanding may very well bring us to invite vermin – those who have lost their right to form part of the club of humanity – into our homes. 'They are not really bad', we could say, or, relatedly, 'They are not a pretty picture of humanity, but they are, sorrowfully, victims of an unfortunate roll of dice'. What a preposterous scenario! What lack of moral fortitude, some would think. A world of exuberant forgivers would be nothing but a morally barren world of subjects, who, on account of their incapacity properly to condemn, are unable really to understand the meaning of forgiveness. But, on further analysis, would this be the case?

A world where forgiveness was possible would also have to be a world where moral condemnation was possible, or so it may seem. (It is important not to confuse moral condemnation with condemnation of deed or condemnation for pragmatic future-directed reasons.) 'Forgiveness', at least in one of its most widely used senses, the sense that contrasts with moral condemnation, presupposes that people should be punished for their intentional wrongdoings, but not always. 'Your acts were despicable', we could say, 'but we forgive you because we *understand* your history, what pushed you all the way to action'. Leaving aside the issue of who should forgive, for it would be most peculiar if a detached bystander forgave the aggressor, how do we decide when to forgive and when not? Clearly, there must be criteria for doing this, however fleeting and indeterminate. Advocates of the proverb, under one plausible interpretation, are committed to claiming that understanding presupposes that we should always forgive; never condemn. They are committed to claiming that moral condemnation is never warranted for, in principle, there will always be good reasons to forgive; reasons that become manifest, allegedly, after proper understanding. But if it is true that there are no grounds for moral condemnation, then allegedly there are no grounds for forgiveness either, for, to repeat, one must first be warranted in condemning before being able properly to forgive. We have reached the dead end of incoherence, or so it may seem. The proverb, as interpreted here, it seems, is not wise, despite its age.

But, even if it turned out indeed that the proverb was incoherent (and I have said nothing to challenge the coherence of alternative interpretations, including those that construe 'to understand is to forgive' as a descriptive rather than a normative claim) it is still the case that it would in all likelihood not have taken hold of our imagination in the first place were it not for the fact that, at some level, it resonates with basic intuitions (which may be correct independently of the alleged incoherence of the proverb). One such intuition is the inspiration for the present collection of essays. After a particular threshold of understanding of the basic facts leading to a given moral transgression, the more we understand the context and motives leading to crime, the more likely we are to abstain from harsh judgement, condemnatory judgement (and the actions flowing from these sorts of judgements).

I will now offer a general summary of the debate embodied in this collection, a debate aimed at better understanding the tension between judging and understanding, and its normative implications. My focus in this brief introductory section will be on drawing a rough map of the complex weave of views defended and/or denied in this collection rather than a chapter-by-chapter summary of individual contributions (editor's introductions can be found at the beginning of each chapter).

Does understanding, relevantly construed, diminish our urge to condemn individuals? One contributor (Ward E. Jones) discusses the conditions under which the tension between judging and understanding would exist rather than arguing for normative implications of the tension. His focus is on describing the tension and on showing how it may be the case that understanding diminishes our urge to condemn. Some contributors (particularly Thaddeus Metz, Peta Bowden and Emma Rooksby, but also Andrew Gleeson) do not think that there is a tension between judging and understanding (rather, proper understanding will lead to proper judging) or that the tension is part and parcel of our moral understandings and does not diminish our need to condemn (when appropriate). They believe that it may just be that the authors of terrible deeds are so reprehensible, so monstrous, driven by such malicious intent, that increased understanding would only increase our disgust and desire to judge and punish. It may be that in such cases, no level of understanding could bring us to diminish our disgust for perpetrator and their deeds (Andrew Gleeson, particularly, emphasizes this point). Relatedly, another author (Richard Weisberg) believes that, at least in some important cases, understanding may bring about sympathy, but his focus is on sympathy that does not condone. But quite the opposite may also be the case and this view also has its defenders in this collection. Some contributors belonging to this last group (Martha Nussbaum, Brian Penrose, Samantha Vice and Marc Fellman) think that our condemnatory practices must be significantly adjusted but not radically revised, while the remaining members of this group (Pedro Alexis Tabensky, Jonathan McKeown-Green and to some extent Chandra Kumar and Kai Nielsen) reject condemnation (at least the variety implying a commitment to retributive censure, standardly conceived).

Some contributors (particularly Thad Metz, Peta Bowden and Emma Rooksby) argue that judging in word and deed – full-blown retributive judging – is constitutive of a proper understanding of crime such that, if we did not judge in this way, we would not be paying our respects to the victims (and perpetrators) and, relatedly, we would not be able properly to understand the very idea of a serious moral transgression. So, our standard practices of condemnation are constitutive of our understanding of severe wrongdoing. Some contributors (particularly Andrew Gleeson) could agree that we can properly understand only if our reactions towards the authors of crimes are appropriately negative, but they place emphasis on the idea that proper judgement requires that one be sensitive to human fallibility. Related to this view is the somewhat more general view, defended by some contributors (particularly Peta Bowden and Emma Rooksby, but also Thaddeus Metz and Andrew Gleeson) – those sympathetic to Peter Strawson-type arguments defending retributive censure – that our practices of judgement are defined within a complex space of practices, such that recommendations made by some contributors (particularly Pedro Alexis Tabensky and Jonathan McKeown-Green), regarding the elimination of retributive practices, would entail the collapse of the system of practices that constitutes our moral understandings and, crucially, the sorts of lives defined by these understandings.

Some contributors (particularly Martha Nussbaum, Brian Penrose, Pedro Alexis Tabensky and Marc Fellman) acknowledge that we are fallible creatures and think that this is evidence against retributive judging (across the board or to a large extent), but not against the view that acknowledgment and understanding of crime qua crime is constituted by our reactions to crime. But, of course, they will disagree with the camp described above regarding which reactions are appropriate. Some contributors who defend this position (particularly Martha Nussbaum, Brian Penrose and Marc Fellman) argue that, since proper understanding almost always reveals the relevant constraints which play a determining role in the commitment of a misdeed, we will and should almost always or to a large extent be inclined to be merciful towards perpetrators once we properly understand the causes leading to condemnable acts. Proper recognition of our vulnerability to circumstances will, at least in the great majority of cases, tend to lead us to sympathetically identify with perpetrators and sympathetic identification will inspire us to be merciful, to judge in word and deed with leniency, with an understanding of our deep vulnerability to circumstances. After all, it may seem to some that the urge to condemn is dependent upon an assumption of genuine guilt, and someone can be guilty, in the relevant sort of way, only if it was genuinely up to them who they turned out to be. But there is much controversy regarding how the idea of 'up to them' is understood. When, to put the matter in slightly different terms, are individuals genuinely in control of their deeds? Some (particularly Thad Metz), advocates of Frankfurt-style arguments, think that we are genuinely in control, in the relevant sense, independently of whether or not we are the *causa sui* or first cause of action. But other contributors think that the relevant sort of control involves being the *causa sui* of action and that such metaphysical exoticism is untenable (Pedro Alexis Tabensky, Chandra Kumar, Kai Nielsen and Jonathan McKeown-Green). Those advocating this view believe that one cannot both be a compatibilist (much the same applies if one is a pessimist) about free will and advocate retributive censure. It is because of this that some contributors (particularly Jonathan McKeown-Green, but also Pedro Alexis Tabensky) argue that we are as deserving of condemnatory hatred as earthquakes or other natural disasters. One of the contributors who advocate this last position (Pedro Alexis Tabensky) also believes that there are no grounds for mercy given that he believes that mercy presupposes the genuine applicability of retributive judgement. Other contributors (particularly Chandra Kumar but also Kai Nielsen), while advocating the view that we are not deserving of standard retributive censure, either resist or would resist going as far as those advocating the view expressed immediately above. They invite us to re-evaluate standard concepts that are constitutive of the idea of retributive censure (desert, blame, moral responsibility and so on) in the light of pragmatism.

Accepting the tension between judging and understanding does not necessarily, or at least not obviously, mean that there are no grounds for condemnation. It may be that in some cases we will be induced to be merciful or compassionate and in others we will not or it may be (Ward E. Jones allows for this possibility) that the tension does not have normative implications (he argues that it is highly likely that, from the purely psychological point of view, we will be inclined to judge less harshly in the light of greater understanding, but he does not draw any normative implications from this). Allegedly, we will be inclined to be more merciful if we recognize perpetrators to be 'victims of circumstances' or if we can find some way of sympathetically identifying with perpetrators. Which sorts of circumstances make perpetrators into victims or objects of sympathetic identification is an open question. Some contributors (Pedro Alexis Tabensky and arguably Jonathan McKeown-Green) think that all relevant circumstances leading to a crime do so, while others (particularly Martha Nussbaum, Brian Penrose, Samantha Vice, Marc Fellman, Chandra Kumar, Kai Nielsen and Andrew Gleeson) think that only some do. Some (particularly Martha Nussbaum and Pedro Alexis Tabensky) think that the matter can be settled by recognizing that our lives are shaped as narratives, that the unfolding of our lives is largely determined by contingencies that are largely, but not exclusively, out of our control. Another set of contributors (Pedro Alexis Tabensky, Chandra Kumar, Kai Nielsen and Jonathan McKeown-Green) think that our understandings of free will show that, in an important sense, a sense that differs from Frankfurt-style understandings of control, our lives are out of our control and hence important or even radical reforms to our practices of judgement are warranted. Of course, there is a long tradition of moral psychologists who have argued that our best accounts of free will need not have effect on our practices of judgement, and, as mentioned above, most contributors' implicit or explicit allegiances are to this venerable tradition.

Some contributors (particularly Martha Nussbaum, Brian Penrose, Samantha Vice, Marc Fellman, Pedro Alexis Tabensky, Chandra Kumar and Kai Nielsen) think that the tension between judging and understanding means that there is something wrong or even very wrong with our standard judgement practices. We are, for the most part, frail creatures at the mercy of circumstances, pushed around, although not without qualifications, like leaves blown by the wind. A subset of advocates of this position (particularly Martha Nussbaum and to some extent Brian Penrose and Marc Fellman) believe that these conclusions follow from studying the *particular* stories of people's lives, particular narratives. Others (particularly Pedro Alexis Tabensky and to some extent Samantha Vice) believe that this follows from the *general* lessons that emerge from recognition that lives are, at least in crucial respects, shaped like stories. One advocate of the last position (Pedro Alexis Tabensky) believes that understanding lives as narratives entails a compatibilist understanding of free will, albeit a non-standard compatibilist understanding insofar as mainstream compatibilists think of compatibilism as a defence of the standard retributive-practices – implying understanding of moral responsibility in the light of the potential threat of determinism. Tabensky argues that our standard retributive practices cannot be left untouched, but that the required changes to our understandings of moral responsibility do not pose a threat to the idea that we have wills that are free.

One contributor (Samantha Vice) believes that the tension between judging and understanding will incline us to be merciful to others, but believes that the same is not strictly true in the case of self-judgement. She argues that it is easier to let others off the condemnatory hook than it is to let oneself off that same sharp hook (in cases involving extreme violations of the moral law). On the other hand, some contributors (particularly Peta Bowden and Emma Rooksby) do not think that the tension threatens our standard judgement practices in any way, indeed, that it forms part and parcel of our everyday judgement practices. Finally, and as mentioned above, some (particularly Thad Metz and Andrew Gleeson) think that the tension does not actually exist; the more one understands, the better one is able to judge adequately. Who is right? That is for the reader to decide, but this collection, we hope, will help the reader make a decision informed by a realization of the complexity of the problems at hand.

In order to help build a common thread, which could serve as a point of comparison between the different contributions, I asked most contributors to use Bernhard Schlink's novel *The Reader* as a case study, and most have done so. The novel tells the story of Hanna Schmidt, an illiterate ex-Nazi camp-guard complicit in the deaths of hundreds of women in the final days of the war, and Michael Berg, Hanna's teenage lover, ignorant at the time of their relationship, of Hanna's involvement in the war efforts, and a lawyer-to-be who is forced to reconcile his past relationship to Hanna with her deeds (an almost impossible task for him, a task which consumes him). The novel is an ideal case study insofar as, at least according to most contributors who have engaged with the novel (Richard Weisberg is a notable exception), it is, among many other things, a literary exploration of the tension between judging and understanding. I will say no more about the novel here for it is impossible to do full justice to the novel in a short introduction, but the novel is explained in more detail by contributors who have engaged with it.

In this collection I have tried to bring together many of the thinkers whom I have encountered, in conversation and/or through their writing, when working through the issues involved in making sense of the tension between judging and understanding. This collection, if you will, is a record of a long debate, a debate well worth having and which has not been given sufficient attention in the literature. All contributions have been especially commissioned for this collection with the exception of Martha Nussbaum's; a paper which is one of the main inspirations for producing this collection in the first place. 'Equity and Mercy' is a benchmark piece dealing explicitly with the tension between judging and understanding, and this collection would not be complete without her contribution. Additionally, it is a piece that has been discussed both favourably and critically by many of the contributors to this collection (particularly Ward Jones, Samantha Vice, Brian Penrose, Pedro Alexis Tabensky and Andrew Gleeson) and it can be understood as a philosophical defence of Schlink's position. For these reasons, her contribution makes a good first chapter.

In order to help guide the reader through the different chapters I have prepared editor's introductions to each chapter and these can be found at the beginning of each chapter. Because contributions are very different from one another I have found it enormously difficult to divide them into meaningful groups that can help guide the reader. After giving the matter much thought I have decided to divide contributions into three separate sections despite the fact that I do not think that there is an ideal single ordering. Contributions in the first section – 'Narrative, Explanation and Forgiveness: The Limits of Condemnation' – discuss some of the most basic implications of accepting the tension between judging and understanding. Contributions in the second section – 'Free Will, Determinism and Moral Responsibility: Challenging Retributive Judgement' – discuss the tension in light of the free will/determinism debate and argue for the idea that important reforms to our moral practices are warranted. Generally, contributors in the third section – 'The Ethical Function of Condemnation' – discuss the idea either that the tension between judging and understanding does not exist or that it does not pose a threat to our moral understandings (that it is part and parcel of the moral space that defines our lives). Richard Weisberg's contribution in this last section is more of a literary analysis of *The Reader* than a philosophical discussion of the tension, but implied in his analysis is the idea that the tension between judging and understanding does not threaten our ability to condemn. He suggests that, in the light of severe moral transgressions, such as Hanna's in *The Reader*, moral condemnation is warranted even in the light of proper understanding. That is why, despite the fact that his approach to the problem at hand is quite different from all the other contributions, his piece best fits in with the contributions in Section 3.

I would like to thank all those who have been willing to embark on this project with me, for their inspiring contributions and for helping me better understand the issues motivating this collection. I would also like to thank my colleagues at the Centre for the Study of Global Ethics, University of Birmingham, for giving me the space necessary for completing this project. Special thanks must be extended to Bernhard Schlink for his ongoing support and inspiration, and for writing *The Reader* and showing us, through his delicately crafted writing, to what extent the novelist's art can change our ways of seeing things, can improve our vision. Literature has much to teach philosophy.

Finally, I would like to thank my wife, colleague and friend, Sally Matthews, for providing me with her invaluable support and companionship throughout the different stages of this project.

This is a collection which invites us to reconsider central aspects of our moral understandings, but it is not intended only for professional philosophers and advanced philosophy students interested in moral issues. It will also be of interest to legal scholars and professionals interested in jurisprudence, insofar as core dimensions of our legal practices are either called into question or defended in the light of the tension between judging and understanding. Finally, because the issues being dealt with in this collection have wide appeal, insofar as they have an impact on how we understand ourselves, including our relationships to others, this collection will also be of interest to the well-read person who is not an expert in any of the areas mentioned above.

PART I
Narrative, Explanation and Forgiveness: The Limits of Condemnation

Chapter 1

Equity and Mercy

Martha Nussbaum

Editor's Introduction

Following Seneca primarily, Martha Nussbaum argues that there is a tension between judging people for their actions and understanding them, particularly if the judging in question involves condemning in word and deed. The more one understands individuals, the more one understands the storyline of their irreducibly unique lives, the more one comes to realize the extent to which individuals are constrained by their specific circumstances, the more one realizes the limits of agency and culpability. Based on a study that invites us to sensitize ourselves to the narrative structure of our unique lives, a study that privileges *epieikeia* – in Nussbaum's words, 'a gentle art of particular perception, a temper of mind that refuses to demand retribution without knowing the whole story' – over *dike* – impartial or symmetrical justice associated with retributive and deterrence models of judgment – she concludes that the proper judge must be one that is inclined to be merciful (although she does not argue against retribution and deterrence as such). One must seriously, caringly and systematically consider mitigating circumstances insofar as understanding the narrative structure of life reveals that perpetrators of crimes are, to a great extent, yet not necessarily completely, victims of circumstances. Proper justice, for Nussbaum, must exceed retribution; it must do more than merely rectify the balance lost by the crime committed. Brian Penrose and Marc Fellman's contributions reach similar conclusions to Nussbaum's, although the paths they take are significantly different. Ward Jones' contribution, on the other hand, nicely complements Nussbaum's contributions and Pedro Tabensky explicitly takes issue with Nussbaum's argument, while at the same time finding much value in her Seneca-inspired views.

* * *

... we stomp on the rape magazines or we invade where they prostitute us, where we are herded and sold, we ruin their theatres where they have sex on us, we face them, we scream in their fucking faces, we are the women they have made scream when they choose.... We're all the same, cunt is cunt is cunt, we're facsimiles of the ones they done it to, or we are the ones they done it to, and I can't tell him from him from him ... so at night, ghosts, we convene; to spread justice, which stands in for law, which has always been merciless, which is, by its nature, cruel.

Andrea Dworkin, *Mercy*

This second doctrine [of mercy] – counterdoctrine would be a better word – has completely exploded whatever coherence the notion of "guided discretion once had.... The requirement [of mitigation] destroys whatever rationality and predictability the ... requirement [of aggravation] was designed to achieve.

Justice Scalia,
in *Walton v. Arizona*

"O child ... do not cure evil with evil. Many people have preferred the more equitable to the more just."

Herodotus, *History*

I. Mercy and Retribution

I begin with the plot of a novel whose title is *Mercy*.[1] By the author's deliberate design, it is not really a novel, and there is no mercy in it. These facts are connected. To pursue the connection is my plan. The author of this novel, or antinovel, is the feminist writer and antipornography activist Andrea Dworkin. Its narrator is also named Andrea – a name that, as she tells us, means "courage" or "manhood." At the age of nine, Andrea is molested by an anonymous man in a movie theater. At fourteen, she is cut with a knife by a sadistic teenage lover. At eighteen she sleeps with many men for money; she finds a tender black lover but is brutally raped by his roommate. Jailed for antiwar activity, she is sexually abused by prison doctors. She goes to Crete and has a passionate loving relationship with a Greek bartender – but when he discovers that she has been making love casually with many men he rapes her and gives her up. Returning to New York, she lives a marginal life of sex, drink, and drugs. Threatened by a gang one night, she tries to make peace with its leader. He holds her hostage at knifepoint in her own bed. Apparently rescued by a man who turns up at her door, she finds herself raped by her rescuer.

At twenty-two she marries a tender young revolutionary. As soon as they are husband and wife, he finds himself unable to make love without tying her up and hitting her. She leaves him for street life. Some years later, after many other abuses, she takes karate lessons and becomes adept at kicking drunken homeless men to death. We encounter at this point the passage that I quoted as an epigraph to this chapter; it expresses Andrea's angry refusal of mercy, her determination to exact retribution without concern for the identity of the particulars. ("I can't tell him from him from him.") Although one might wonder whether the point is that terrible experiences have corrupted Andrea's perceptions, it appears that her refusal of mercy is endorsed by the novel as a whole.

This novel does not read like a traditional novel because its form expresses the retributive idea that its message preaches. That is, it refuses to perceive any of the

---

1 Andrea Dworkin, *Mercy* (New York: Four Walls, Eight Windows, 1991); *Life and Death* by Andrea Dworkin," *The New Republic*, 1997. *Life and Death* contains a valuable autobiographical essay going over the same events depicted in the novel, to my mind more powerfully.

male offenders – or any other male – as a particular individual, and it refuses to invite the reader into the story of their lives. Like Andrea, it can't tell him from him from him. The reader hears only the solitary voice of the narrator; others exist for her only as sources of her pain. Like the women in the male pornography that Dworkin decries, her males have no history, no psychology, no concrete reasons for action. They are just knives that cut, arms that beat, penises that maim by the very act of penetration. Dworkin's refusal of the traditional novelist's attention to the stories of particular lives seems closely connected with her heroine's refusal to be merciful to any of those lives, with her doctrine that justice is cruel and hard.[2] But the nature of the connection between mercy and a vision of the particular is not yet evident; my hope is to make it evident – and, in the process, to make a case for the moral and legal importance of the novelist's art.

In order to do this, however, I must begin with a historical inquiry into the origins, in the Western tradition, of the close connection between equitable judgment – judgment that attends to the particulars – and mercy, defined by Seneca as "the inclination of the mind toward leniency in exacting punishment. I begin with a puzzle in ancient Greek thought about law and justice. Solving this puzzle requires understanding some features of the archaic idea of justice that turn out to be highly pertinent to Andrea Dworkin's project. This sort of justice is soon criticized, with appeal both to equity and to mercy. After following the arguments of Aristotle and Seneca on this question, I shall return to contemporary issues, using these ideas to make a case for the moral and legal importance of narrative art in several areas of contemporary legal and political relevance, defending the equity/mercy tradition as an alternative both to retributive views of punishment and to some modern deterrence based views.

II. Mercy and Particularity: A Puzzle

There is a puzzle in the evidence for ancient Greek thought about legal and moral reasoning. Two concepts that do not appear to be at all the same are treated as so closely linked as to be aspects of the same concept, and introduced together by one and the same moral term. The moral term is *epieikeia*.[3] The concepts are the two

---

2   We do not find this refusal in some of Dworkin's best essays on sexuality, in particular the essays on Tennessee Williams and James Baldwin in *Intercourse* (New York: The Free Press, 1987), showing that she thinks differently about relationships that unfold in a context of rough social equality. See also the autobiographical essay in *Life and Death*.

3   For an excellent discussion of the term and its philosophical/legal history in Greece and Rome, see Francesco D'Agostino, *Epieikeia: Il Tema Dell'Equità nell'Antichità Greca* (Milan: A. Giuffre, 1973). An excellent study that focuses on fourth-century B.C. oratory and its relationship to Aristotle is John Lawless, *Law, Argument, and Equity in the Speeches of Isaeus*, Ph.D. Dissertation, Brown University, 1991. Both D'Agostino and Lawless have extensive bibliographies. *Epieikeia* is usually translated into Latin by *clementia* – see op. cit. Modern scholars generally render it into German with *Billigkeit*, Italian by *equità*, French by équité or (translating the Latin) *clémence*.

that I have already identified as my theme: the ability to judge in such a way as to respond with sensitivity to all the particulars of a person and situation and the "inclination of the mind" to leniency in punishing – equity, and mercy.[4] From the beginning, the idea of flexible particularized situational judgment is linked with leniency. *Epieikeia*, which originally designates the former, is therefore said to be accompanied by the latter: It is something mild and gentle; something contrasted to the rigid or harsh. The Herodotean father, in my epigraph, contrasts the notion of strict retributive justice with *epieikeia*, at a time when that word was already clearly associated with situational appropriateness.[5] The orator Gorgias, praising the civic character of soldiers fallen in battle, says of them that "on many occasions they preferred the gentle equitable (*to praon epieikes*) to the harshly stubborn just (*tou authadous dikaiou*), and appropriateness of reasoning to the precision of the law, thinking that this is the most divine and most common law, namely to say and not say, to do and to leave undone, the thing required by the situation at the time required by the situation."[6] He too, then, links the ability to do and say the right thing in the situation with a certain mildness or softness; opposed to both is the stubborn and inflexible harshness of law. By this time, the original and real etymology of the word *epieikeia* – from *eikos*, the "plausible" or "appropriate"[7] – is being supplemented by a popular derivation of the term from *eikô*; "yield," "give way." Thus, even in writing the history of the term, Greek thinkers discover a connection between appropriate judgment and leniency.[8]

The puzzle lies, as I have said, in the unexplained connection between appropriate situational judgment and mercy. One might well suppose that a judgment that gets all the situational particulars correct will sometimes set the level of fault high up and sometimes low down, as the situation demands. If the judgment is a penalty-setting judgment, it will sometimes set a heavy penalty and sometimes a light one, again as the situation demands. If the equitable judgment and/or penalty is being contrasted

---

4   Both equity and mercy can be spoken of as attributes of persons, as features of judgments rendered by a person, or as moral abstractions in their own right. Thus a person may be praised as *epieikês*; his or her judgments or decisions display *to epieikes*, or show a respect for *to epieikes*.

5   Herodotus III.53; for discussion, see D'Agostino, *Epieikeia*, 7.

6   Gorgias, *Epitaphios*, fragment Diets-Kranz 82B6. The passage has occasioned much comment and controversy. See D'Agostino, *Epieikeia*, 28–31, for some examples. It seems crucial to understand the passage as pertaining to the civic virtue of the fallen, not their military attributes.

7   See P. Chantraine, *Dictionnaire etymologique de la langue grecque: Histoire des mots*, tome II (Paris 1970), 355. For other references, see D'Agostino, *Epieikeia*, 1–2. *Eikos* is the participle of *eoika*, "seems." (The English word "seemly" is an instructive parallel.) In early poetry, the opposite of the *epieikes* is the *aeikes*, "outrageous," "totally inappropriate," "horrible."

8   In addition to the passages to be discussed later, see Pseudo-Plato, *Definitiones* 412A, the first known definition of *epieikeia*, which defines it as "good order of the reasoning soul with respect to the honorable and shameful," as "the ability to hit on what is appropriate in contracts," and also as "mitigation of that which is just and advantageous."

with a general principle designed beforehand to fit a large number of situations – as is usually the case – we might expect that the equitable will sometimes be more lenient than the generality of the law but sometimes harsher. For, as that not-very-merciful philosopher Plato puts it in his *Laws*, sometimes the offender turns out to be unusually good for an offender of that sort, but sometimes, too, unusually bad.[9] Plato has a modern ally in Justice Scalia, who feels that it is absurd that aggravation and mitigation should be treated asymmetrically in the law. The very same requirements should hold for both and, presumably, once we begin looking at the specific circumstances, we will be about as likely to find grounds for the one as for the other.[10]

But this is not what many Greek and Roman thinkers seem to think. They think that the decision to concern oneself with the particulars is connected with taking up a gentle and lenient cast of mind toward human wrongdoing. They endorse the asymmetry that Justice Scalia finds absurd and incoherent. We must now ask on what grounds, and with what rationality and coherence of their own, they do so.

III. Retribution and Particular Perception

We can make some progress by looking at what *epieikeia* opposes or corrects. We see in our passages a contrast between *epieikeia* as flexible situational judgment and the exceptionless and inflexible mandates of law or rule. We also find these laws or rules described as "harsh," "harshly stubborn," a "cure of evil with evil." This goes to the heart of our puzzle, clearly: For what we need to know is how that sort of justice comes to be seen as *harsh* in its lack of fit to the particulars rather than simply imprecise.

Let us think, then, of the archaic conception of justice. And let us take the first surviving philosophical text to use the notion of justice: For in its metaphorical application of *dikê* to cosmic process, it illustrates very vividly what *dikê*, in human legal and moral matters, was taken to involve. Writing about the cyclical changes of the basic elements into one another – as the hot, the cold, the wet, and the dry succeed one another in the varying combinations that make up the seasons of the year – the sixth century B.C. philosopher Anaximander writes, "They pay penalty and retribution (*dikên kai tisin*) to one another in accordance with the assessment of time."[11]

---

9 Plato, *Laws* 867d, on regulations about bringing an exiled homicide back from exile.

10 Justice Scalia, in *Walton v. Arizona*, 110 S.Ct. 3047 (1990): "Our cases proudly announce that the Constitution effectively prohibits the States from excluding from the sentencing decision *any* aspect of a defendant's character or record or any circumstance surrounding the crime: [for example] that the defendant had a poor and deprived childhood, or that he had a rich and spoiled childhood" (at 3062).

11 Anaximander DK fragment B1, the first surviving verbatim fragment of ancient Greek philosophy. (We know it to be verbatim because Simplicius, who reports it, also comments with some embarrassment about its language, saying "as he said using rather poetic terms.") For an excellent account of Anaximander's idea, and its connection with ideas of justice

What does Anaximander describe? He describes a process in which "encroachments" by one element are made up in exact proportion, over time, by compensatory "encroachments" of the corresponding opposite element. We are, it seems to imagine as the neutral state, a state of balance in which each element has, so to speak, its own – its due sphere, its due representation in the sphere of things. Next the balance is thrown off in that one or more of the elements goes too far, trespasses on the preserve of the other – as, for example, winter is an invasion by the cold and the wet into the due preserve of the warm and the dry. (Thus the root notion of injustice, already in the sixth century, is the notion of *pleonexia*, grasping more than one's due share, the very notion that Plato exploits in the *Republic*, trying to capture its opposite with the notion of "having and doing one's own."[12]) Winter is an imbalance, and for justice or *dikê* to be restored, retribution (*tisis*) must take place, or, in other words, the elements that encroached must "pay justice and retribution" to the ones they squeezed out. What this seems to mean is that a corresponding encroachment in the other direction must take place in order that "the doer should suffer."[13] Summer is the due retribution for the imbalance of winter; mere springtime would not right the balance because cold and wet would not be duly squeezed out in their turn.

In short, this cosmology works with an intuitive idea that derives from the legal and moral sphere. It is the idea that for encroachment and pain inflicted, a compensating pain and encroachment must be performed. The primitive sense of the just – remarkably constant from several ancient cultures to modern intuitions such as those illustrated in our passage from Andrea Dworkin – starts from the notion that a human life (or, here, the life of the cosmos) is a vulnerable thing, a thing that can be invaded, wounded, violated by another's act in many ways. For this penetration, the only remedy that seems appropriate is a counterinvasion, equally deliberate, equally grave. And to right the balance truly, the retribution must be exactly, strictly proportional to the original encroachment. It differs from the original act only in the sequence of time and in the fact that it is response rather than original act – a fact frequently obscured if there is a long sequence of acts and counteracts.

This retributive idea is committed to a certain sort of neglect of the particulars. For Anaximander, it hardly matters whether the snow and rain that get evaporated are in any sense "the same" snow and rain that did the original aggressing. The very question is odd, and Anaximander seems altogether uninterested in the issues of individuation and identity that would enable us to go further with it. Nor are things terribly different in the human legal-moral applications of retributive *dikê*.

---

and equality in law and morals, see Gregory Vlastos, "Equality and Justice in Early Greek Cosmologies," in *Studies in Presocratic Philosophy*, vol. I, ed. David Furley and Reginald Allen (London: Routledge, 1970).

12 See G. Vlastos, "Plato's Theory of Social Justice," in *Interpretations of Plato: A Swarthmore Symposim*, ed. H. North (Leiden: Brill, 1977).

13 *Ton drasanta pathein*, Aeschylus, *Choephoroi*, I. 313. A similar idea is expressed in many places. See, for example, Aeschylus, *Agamemnon* 249, 1564.

For very often the original offender is no longer on the scene, or is inaccessible to the victim: And yet the balance still remains to be righted. What then happens is that a substitute target must be found, some member of the offender's family. The crimes of Atreus are avenged against Agamemnon; Agamemnon's offense burdens Orestes. The law that "the doer must suffer" becomes, in this conception of justice as balanced retribution, the law that for every bad doing some surrogate for the doer must suffer: And, like Andrea Dworkin's narrator, the ancient concept of *dikê* can't "tell him from him from him." A male has raped Andrea: Then another male will get a karate kick. The substitution is usually justified through an intuitive notion that the real offender is "the line of X" or "the house of X," or, in Dworkin, "the gender of X." But this alleged justification entails neglect of the particularity of the so-called offender; it neglects, too, questions of motive and intention that one might think crucial in just sentencing.

A closely related sort of neglect can arise even if the original offender is around to receive the punishment. For suppose that the offender committed an act that is in some sense heinous but did so with extenuating circumstances. (Oedipus committed both parricide and incest, but with an excusable ignorance of crucial factual information.) *Dikê* says: There have been parricide and incest here, and things can never be the same. The balance must be righted. The eyes that saw their mother's naked body must be blinded.[14] Now in this case the doer and the sufferer are the same individual. But notice that Oedipus' particularity is still in a significant sense neglected. For he is being treated the same way, by *dikê*, as a true or voluntary parricide would be treated: And crucial facts about *him*, about his good character, innocent motives, fine intentions, are neglected. But to neglect all this is to neglect *him*: substitution again, though of a more subtle sort.

If we start thinking this way, the asymmetry we asked about naturally begins to arise. For looked at in this way, *dikê* is always harsh and unyielding. Sometimes the harshness is merited; sometimes excessive. But it is rarely too soft – for it begins from the assumption that the doer *should* suffer, that any wrong should be "made up" by a penalty that befits a deliberate wrong. The particulars of the case, more closely inspected, lead in the direction of extenuation or mitigation far more frequently than in the opposite direction. If *dikê* has got the right person, well and good; nothing more need be added. If, however, *dikê* has got hold of the wrong person, a more flexible and particularized judgment will let that person off. So too in the Oedipus-type case: For *dikê* assumes that Oedipus *is* a parricide; there is nothing more we can find out about him that will aggravate his offense. We can and do, on the other hand, find out that in a most relevant sense he is not a parricide because the act he intended and chose was not that act. Once again, the more flexible judgment of *epieikeìa* steps in to say, Be gentle with this man, for we cannot assume without looking further that he really did the awful thing for which strict justice holds him responsible. Getting

---

14 That is the way Oedipus interprets the requirement. There was no religious or secular law that prescribed such a punishment for incest.

the right life and getting the life right are not two separate issues but two aspects of a single process of appropriate scrutiny.

In effect, the asymmetry arises from the fact that the circumstances of human life throw up many and various obstacles to meeting the tough standards of justice; if we set a high standard of good action, the very course of life will often make it difficult for mere human beings to measure up. To put it another way, the asymmetry arises from a certain view about the common or likely causes of wrongdoing: The asymmetrist claims that a certain number of wrongful acts are fully deliberate wrongs and that a certain number are produced by obstacles such as failure of knowledge, mistaken identification, bad education, or the presence of a competing moral claim. There may be some cases of parricide and incest that are produced by an especially or unusually blameworthy degree of hatred or wickedness, going beyond the responsible deliberateness assumed by the law, but the claim is that this is likely to be a smaller class than the Oedipus-type class, given the character of human life and the nature of human motivation.

The world of strict *dikê* is a harsh and symmetrical world in which order and design are preserved with exceptionless clarity. After summer comes fall, after fall comes winter, after day comes the night, and the fact that Agamemnon was not the killer of Thyestes' children is as irrelevant to *dikê* as the fact that the night did not deliberately aggress against the day; the fact that Oedipus acted in ignorance is as irrelevant to *dikê* as the fact that the winter came in ignorance of its crimes against the summer. It is a world in which gods are at home, and in which mortals often fare badly. As a fragment of Sophocles puts it, "The god before whom you come ... knows neither equity nor grace (*oute toupieikes oute tên charin*), but only cares for strict and simple justice (*tên haplôs dikên*),"[15] The world of *epieikeia* or equity, by contrast, is a world of imperfect human efforts and complex obstacles to doing well; a world in which humans sometimes deliberately do wrong but sometimes also get tripped up by ignorance, passion, poverty, bad education, circumstantial constraints of various sort; a world in which bad things are sometimes simply bad, sometimes extremely bad – but sometimes, and more often, when one goes into them, somewhat less bad, given the obstacles the person faced on the way to acting properly. *Epieikeia* is a gentle art of particular perception, a temper of mind that refuses to demand retribution without understanding the whole story; it responds to Oedipus' demand to be seen for the person he is.

IV. Equity and Justice: Aristotle

So far we are still dealing with a contrast between the equitable and the just. Justice itself is still understood as strict retribution, and therefore the equitable, insofar as it recognizes features of the particular case that the strict law does not cover, stands

---

15 Sophocles fr. 770 (Pearson). See D'Agostino, *Epieikeia*, 8–10 for other related passages.

in opposition to the just. But justice or *dikê* is by the fifth century a venerated moral norm, associated in general with the idea of giving to each his or her due. We would expect, then, as the conflict between equity and strict retributive justice assumed prominence, an attempt to forge a new conception of justice, one that incorporates the insights of equity. This project was pursued to some extent by Plato, in his late works the *Statesman* and the *Laws*.[16] Even more significant for our purposes, it was pursued, albeit unsystematically, by the Attic orators, in their actual arguments about particular cases in front of citizen juries.[17] But it was Aristotle who made the major contribution.

Aristotle's discussion of the equitable in the *Nicomachean Ethics* (*EN*) occurs within his account of justice. It begins with an apparent dilemma. The *epieikes*, he says, is neither strictly the same as the just nor altogether different in kind (*Nicomachean Ethics* 1137a33–4). On the one hand, it looks as if it would be strange to separate *epieikeia* from justice. For we praise both people and their judgments for the quality of *epieikeia*, recognizing it as a normatively good thing. But in that case, it will be odd if it turns out to be altogether opposed to the just. Then we would either have to say that justice is not a normatively good quality, or withdraw our normative claims for *epieikeia* (1137a34–b8).[18] Aristotle's solution to the dilemma is that equity is a kind of justice, but a kind that is superior to and frequently opposed to another sort, namely, strict legal justice (1137b8–34). It may be regarded as a "correcting" and "completing" of legal justice.[19]

The reason for this opposition, he continues, is that the law must speak in general terms and therefore must err in two ways: both leaving gaps that must be filled up by particular judgments, and sometimes even getting things wrong. Aristotle says that this is not the fault of the lawgiver but in the very nature of human ethical life: The "matter of the practical" can be grasped only crudely by rules given in advance and adequately only by a flexible judgment suited to the complexities of the case. He uses a famous image. The good architect does not measure a complicated structure

---

16 See *Statesman* 294A–95A; *Laws* 757E, 867D, 876A–E, 925D–926D. Like Aristotle, Plato recognizes the importance of *epieikeia* both in the judgment of whether or not a certain offense was committed and in the assessment of penalties. He suggests that laws are written deliberately in such a way as to leave gaps to be filled in by the judgment of juries. He compares the prescriptions of law to the general instructions that an athletic trainer has to give when he cannot deal with each pupil one by one – and also to a trainer or a medical doctor who has to go out of town and therefore leaves instructions that cannot anticipate all the circumstances that may arise. This being so, it is in the spirit of law that when one *does* look into the particular case, one will modify the prescription to suit the differing conditions.

17 See Lawless, *Speeches of Isaeus*, bibliography; for some particulars, see op. cit.

18 Strictly speaking, there is another possibility: that they are both valuable norms that pervasively conflict in their requirements. Aristotle does recognize contingent conflicts of obligation, but not this sort of more deep seated value conflict.

19 *Epanorthôma* suggests both things: The image is of straightening up something that has fallen over or gone crooked a bit. So the suggestion is that equity is putting law into the condition to which it aspires in the first place.

(e.g., a fluted column) with a straight edge. Or, if he did, he would get a woefully inadequate measurement. Instead, he uses a flexible strip of metal that "bends to the shape of the stone and is not fixed" (1137b3–32). Even so, particular judgments, superior in flexibility to the general dictates of law, bend round to suit the case.[20]

Aristotle ends the discussion with some remarks that seem ill-suited to their context. But by now we should be prepared to understand how they fit in:

> It is also clear from this [sc. account of the equitable] what sort of person the equitable person is. For a person who chooses and does such things, and who is not zealous for strict judgment in the direction of the worse, but is inclined to mitigation, even though he can invoke the law on his side – such a person is equitable, and this trait of character is equity, being a kind of justice and not a distinct trait of character. (1137b34–1138a3)

Here Aristotle alludes to and endorses the tradition that links perception of the particular with mitigation. By now we can see on what grounds he does so. But he makes a new contribution: for he insists that this is the way a truly *just* person is: In keeping with his insistence throughout his ethical and political writings that justice, as a virtue of character, is a peculiarly human virtue, one that gods neither possess nor comprehend,[21] and indeed would think "ridiculous" (*EN* 1178b11), he now gives the just a definition suited to an imperfect human life.

In the *Rhetoric* discussion of *epieikeia*, having given a very similar account of the equitable as that which corrects or supplements – and thereby fulfills – the written law, he adds a somewhat more detailed account of equitable assessment, telling us that the equitable person is characterized by a forgiving attitude to "human things." He uses the word *suggnômê*, "judging with," which typically suggests the idea of forgiveness, in a way that connects it etymologically with the idea of sharing the other person's point of view.[22] He links this ability with particular perception, and both of these with the ability to classify actions in accordance with the agent's

---

20 On the role of this passage in Aristotle's ethical theory generally, see Martha C. Nussbaum, "The Discernment of Perception: An Aristotelian Model for Public and Private Rationality," in *Love's Knowledge: Essays on Philosophy and Literature* (New York: Oxford University Press, 1990). There I discuss in greater detail Aristotle's reasons for thinking that general rules cannot be sufficient for the complexities of particular cases.

21 See *Nicomachean Ethics* VII.I on ethical excellence in general; *Politics* I.I on the social excellences, and *EN* X.8, 1178a9–b18, on virtue and justice as purely human and not divine.

22 See Kenneth J. Dover, "Father, Sons and Forgiveness," *Illinois Classical Studies* 16 (1991), 773–82. Dover shows that *suggnômé* is a category of judgment or opinion about what has been done, and is persistently opposed to a revenge taking attitude, often in the context of a view about the origins of error as in obstacles common in human life, rather than in essential evil. A characteristic passage, discussed by Dover, is Xenophon *Cyrus* 3.2.38–40, where a wrongly sentenced man, about to be executed, asks the son of his enemy to forgive his father, since "[h]e does this not from ill will (*kakonoia*) but from ignorance (*agnoia*), and all the wrong that people do from ignorance I regard as action under constraint." Cyrus, hearing this story, agrees that the father's fault is only human, and urges forgiveness on the son.

motives and intentions (1374b2–10[23]). Elsewhere, Aristotle links *suggnômê* closely with sympathy or compassion (*eleos*), an attitude he defines as requiring the thought that one's own possibilities are in significant ways shared with those of the person one contemplates, and that this person was overwhelmed by obstacles not of his own making.[24]

The logic of these connections seems to be as follows. To perceive the particular really accurately, one must not simply be concerned with retribution.[25] One must, in addition, "judge *with*" the agent who has done the alleged wrong. One must, that is, see things from that person's point of view – for only then will one begin to comprehend what obstacles that person faced as he or she tried to act. In that sense, it takes *suggnômê* to deliver a "correct discrimination" of the equitable. And when one looks at the person's case with *suggnômê*, certain distinctions that do not play a part in the archaic conception of *dikê* assume a remarkable salience. Equity, like the sympathetic spectatorship of the tragic audience, accepts Oedipus' plea that the ignorant and nonvoluntary nature of his act be duly acknowledged; it acknowledges, too, the terrible dilemmas faced by characters such as Agamemnon, Antigone, and Creon, the terrible badness of all their options. Recognizing the burden of these "human things," the equitable judge is inclined not to be "zealous for strict judgment in the direction of the worse" but to prefer merciful mitigation.

I have already illustrated Aristotle's argument by speaking about tragedy and tragic spectatorship. And because I shall go on to develop my own account of the equitable with reference to literature, it seems well worth pointing out that Aristotle's account of *suggnômê* and *epieikeia* in these passages has close links with his theory of tragedy. For in his theory, the spectator forms bonds of both sympathy and identification with the tragic hero.[26] This means that "judging with" is built into the drama itself, into the way in which the form solicits attention. If I see Oedipus as one whom I might be, I will be concerned to understand how and why his predicament came about; I will focus on all those features of motive and agency, those aspects of the unfortunate operations of chance, that I would judge important were I in a similar plight myself. I would ask *how* and *why* all this came about – and ask not from a vantage point of lofty superiority but seeing his tragedy as something "such

---

23 Cf. also *EN* 1143a19–20, connecting *suggnômé* and equity, and both with perception of the particular; cf. also *EN* 1110a24–5, 1111a1–2, on *suggnômé* in tragic situations.

24 For the link between *suggnômé* and *eleos*, see, for example, *EN* 1109b32, 1111a1. On *eleos* and obstacles, see *Rhetoric* II.8. Dover similarly, in describing tragic occasions for *suggnômé*, writes that it is frequently accompanied by the thought that the person did wrong through some error such as "[i]gnorance; duress; poverty, alcohol, lust, provocation ... the mortal propensity to err."

25 As Aristotle evidently is, in his account of "corrective justice," in *EN* V.

26 See Stephen Halliwell, *Aristotle's Poetics* (London: Duckworth, 1986); and "Pleasure, Understanding, and Emotion in *Aristotle's Poetics*," in *Essays on Aristotle's Poetics*, ed. A. Rorty (Princeton: Princeton University Press, 1992), 241–60.

as might happen" in human life, in my own life.[27] Tragedy is thus a school of equity, and therefore of mercy. If I prove unable to occupy the equitable attitude, I will not even enjoy tragedy: For its proper pleasure requires emotions of pity and fear that only *suggnômê* makes possible.

Aristotle's attitude to law and equity was not simply a theoretical fiction. There is evidence that it both shaped legal practice and, even more clearly, built on an already developed and developing tradition of Athenian legal thought.[28] We have, of course, almost no records of the actual *outcomes* of jury trials, and no record at all of the deliberation of jurors. The process did not encourage lengthy or communal deliberation, as each juror cast a separate vote after hearing the various arguments, apparently without much mutual consultation.[29] We do, however, have many examples of persuasive speeches delivered to such juries. And because the orator's reputation rested on his ability to persuade a jury of average citizens, chosen by lot, we can rely on these speeches for evidence of widespread popular beliefs about legal and ethical concepts. These speeches show the orators relying on a concept of law and even of justice that is very much like the one that Aristotle renders explicit and systematic. Thus litigants frequently call for a justice tailored to the circumstances of their own case, and they frequently use the expression *ta dikaia* ("those things that are just") in that sense.[30] And they often proceed as if the written law is understood to be a set of guidelines with gaps, to be filled in, or corrected, by equity argumentation.[31] In this process, frequent appeal is made to the juror's sense of fairness, as if, once the particular circumstances of the case are understood, they can be expected to see that justice *consists in* an equitable determination.

---

27 See *Poetics*, chap. 9, and the excellent discussion in Halliwell, "Pleasure." Aristotle remarks that neither pity nor fear will be experienced by a person who believes that he or she is above the uncertainties of life and can suffer no serious reversal. See *Rhetoric* 1382b30–32, 1385b21–2, 31: He calls this state of mind a *hubristiké diathesis*, an "overweening disposition."

28 Among the legal/ rhetorical figures to be mentioned, Lysias predates Aristotle, and is active in the late fifth century; both Isaeus and Isocrates are contemporaries of Aristotle, and their period of activity overlaps with the likely period of composition of Aristotle's *Rhetoric*, which is prior to Aristotle's first departure from Athens in 347. Isaeus' earliest and latest works, for example, can be dated approximately to 389 and 344/3 B.C.

29 On all this, see Lawless, with copious references to sources ancient and modern.

30 See Michael Hillgruber, *Die zehnte Rede des Lysias: Einleitung, Text und Kommentar mit einem Anhang über die Gesetzesinterpretation bei den attischen Rednern* (Berlin and New York: Walter de Gruyter, 1988), 116–7. Hillgruber cites passages in the orators where an appeal to to *dikaia* is used to persuade the dikasts that obedience to the letter of the law is not required by their oath. These passages are: Andocides I.31, Lysias 15.8, Demosthenes 21.4, 21.212, 23.194, 24.775 [Dem.] 58.61. Lawless, 78, discusses this material and adds Isaeus 1.40 to the list.

31 See K. Seeliger, "Zur Charackteristik des Isaios," *Jahrb, für Philologie* 113 (1876), 673–9, translated in Lawless: "The principle of equity is almost always maintained, while the letter of the law is not infrequently circumvented, however much the orator is accustomed to holding his opponents to it."

This is a deep insight, and one that I support. For it seems wrong to make a simple *contrast* between justice and equity,[32] suggesting that we have to choose between the one and the other. Nor, in a deep sense, do we have to choose between equity and the rule of law as understandings of what justice demands. The point of the rule of law is to bring us as close as possible to what equity would discern in a variety of cases, given the dangers of carelessness, bias, and arbitrariness endemic to any totally discretionary procedure. But no such rules can be precise or sensitive enough, and when they have manifestly erred, it is justice itself, not a departure from justice, to use equity's flexible standard.

V. Equity and Mercy: Seneca

We are still not all the way to a doctrine of mercy. For what Aristotle recommends is a precise attention to the circumstance of offense and offender, both in ascertaining whether or not there is any guilt and in assessing the penalty if there is. He is prepared to let people off the hook if it can be shown that their wrongdoing is unintentional, or to judge them more lightly if it is the result of something less than full deliberate badness. But the point of this is to separate out the fully and truly guilty from those who superficially resemble them. In effect, we are given a more precise classification of offenses, a classification that takes intention and motive into account. But once a particular offense is correctly classified, the offender is punished exactly in proportion to the actual offense.

By contrast to the archaic conception of justice, this is indeed merciful, but it does not suffice, I think, for all that we mean by mercy – which seems to involve a gentleness going *beyond* due proportion, even to the deliberate offender. With his emphasis on sympathetic understanding, Aristotle is on his way to this idea. And he insists that the virtuous disposition in the area of retributive anger is best named "gentleness" (using the same word that Gorgias had used in connection with *epieikeia*). He stresses that "the gentle person is not given to retribution [*timôretikos*], but is rather inclined to sympathetic understanding [*suggnômonikos*]" (*EN* 1126a2–3). But retribution will still play an important role where the circumstances demand it. For "people who do not get retributively angry[33] at those at whom they should look like fools.... For they seem to have no perception and no feeling of pain ... and to allow oneself and one's loved ones to be kicked around, and overlook it, is slavish" (1126a4–8). The demand to avoid the slavish is certain to play a role in the public world of the law, as well as in the private world of the family. This demand

---

32 For examples of such contrasts, see Richard Posner, *Law and Literature* (Cambridge: Harvard University Press, 1988), 108 ff., to be discussed in a later section.

33 I am translating *orgizesthai* this way because Aristotle defines *orgê* as a desire for retribution, on account of the pain of a believed slight.

makes Aristotelian *suggnômê* stop short of mercy. For the full development of that idea, we must wait for Roman Stoicism, and for Seneca.[34]

Stoic moral theory accepts and builds on the Aristotelian insight that rules and precepts are useful only as guidelines in both private and public thought. Any fully adequate moral or legal judgment must be built on a full grasp of all the particular circumstances of the situation, including the motives and intentions of the agent. Like Aristotle, Stoics are fond of using an analogy between medicine and ethics to illustrate this point: General ethical or legal rules are about as useful as are medical rules and precepts – which is to say, useful as outlines, but no substitute for a resourceful confrontation with all the circumstances of the case. Both the Greek and the later Roman Stoics stress the fact that an act is a fully correct and moral act, what they call a *katorthôma*, only if it is done with the appropriate motives and the appropriate knowledge; a *kathêkon* or (in Latin) *officium* is an act of (merely) the right general type, without consideration of the agent's thoughts and motivations. Rules can tell you what the *kathêkonta* are, but to get all the way to a full *katorthôma* you need to become a certain sort of person. The same goes in reverse for bad actions. This means that the Aristotelian idea of justice as equity is already built into the moral schema from the beginning; it will automatically influence the classification of offenses in public reasoning and in the law.[35]

The Greek Stoics stop there, and in their moral rigor they explicitly reject any application of *epieikeia* that goes beyond the careful classification of offenses. The soul of the good Stoic judge is a hard soul that protects itself from all impulses that might sway it from the strict path of virtue and duty. "All wise men," they announce, "are harshly rigorous [*austêroi*]."[36] They "never permit their soul to give way or to be caught by any pleasure or pain."[37] And this hardness cordons them off from any yielding response to the defects of another person. The wise man, they announce, does not forgive those who err, and he never waives the punishment required in the law. An unyielding judge, the Stoic will do exactly what strict justice requires. In this connection, *epieikeia* is explicitly rejected: He will never waive the punishment that is mandated for that particular type of offense.[38]

---

34 I have discussed Seneca's views on mercy in "Seneca on Anger in Public Life," *The Therapy of Desire: Theory and Practice in Hellenistic Ethics* (Princeton: Princeton University Press, 1994), chap. 11.

35 One possible difference: Aristotle's ethical schema makes a big distinction between *adikêmata*, for which it is necessary to have a bad *character*, and lesser wrongdoings that will be classified as among the blameworthy *hamartêmata*; the latter class will include bad acts done from weakness of will with respect to some passion. Stoic moral theory is harsher toward the passions, treating them as types of false judgment that it is always in an agent's power to refuse. Thus the distinction between *akrasia* and wrongdoing from bad character is significantly weakened, if not altogether eroded.

36 Diogenes Laertius VII. 117 = *Stoicorum Veterum Fragmenta* (*SVF*) 111.637.

37 Clement, *Strom*. VII.7 = *SVF* 111.639.

38 *SVF* III.640.

Many Greek Stoic texts show us this attitude of detachment and hardness to offenders, an attitude far removed from the Aristotelian norm of *suggnômê*. One can see this emerge with particular clarity in the treatment of tragedy, which Stoics are permitted to watch, provided that they watch it from a vantage point of secure critical detachment – like Odysseus, they say, lashed to the mast so that he can hear, but not be swayed by, the sirens' song.[39] From this secure vantage point they view the disasters and vulnerabilities of ordinary mortals with amusement, and even scorn, defining tragedy as what happens "when chance events befall fools."[40] To Oedipus, the wise man says, "'Slave, where are your crowns, where your diadem?'" To Medea, the wise man says, "'Stop wanting your husband, and there is not one of the things you want that will fail to happen.'"[41] There is no inevitability in tragedy: For if one has the proper moral views there is no contingency in the world that can bring one low.[42]

Here Seneca steps in, perceiving a serious tension in the Greek Stoic position. On the one hand, Stoicism is deeply committed to the Aristotelian position that good moral assessment, like good medical assessment, is searchingly particular, devoted to a deep and internal understanding of each concrete case. On the other hand, the Stoic norm of critical detachment withholds psychological understanding, treating deep and complex predicaments as easily avoidable mistakes, simply refusing to see the obstacles to good action from the erring agent's own viewpoint.

Seneca opts for the medical side of this dilemma, offering a complex account of the origins of human wrongdoing that leads to a new view of the proper response to wrongdoing. Seneca begins his argument in *On Anger* as an Aristotelian would, asking the judge to look at all the circumstances of the offense (I.19.5–8). At this point he still seem to be a symmetrist, urging that sometimes a closer look makes the person look better, and sometimes worse. But he then continues his reflections, in the second book, in a manner that makes our asymmetry open up. People who do bad things – even when they act from bad motives – are not, he insists, simply making a foolish and easily corrigible error. They are yielding to pressures that lie very deep in the fabric of human life. Many of these pressures are social. Before a child is capable of the critical exercise of reason, he or she has internalized a socially taught scheme of values that is in many ways diseased, giving rise to diseased passions: the excessive love of money and honor, angers connected with slights to one's honor; excessive attachment to sex, and especially to romanticized conceptions of the sexual

---

39 Plutarch, *On How the Young Person Should Listen to Poetry*, 15CD. I argue that this work represents some of the contents of Chrysippus' lost work of the same title, in M. C. Nussbaum, "Poetry and the Passions: Two Stoic Views," in *Passions & Perceptions*, ed. J. Brunschwig and M. Nussbaum (Cambridge: Cambridge University Press, 1993), 97–149.

40 Epictetus, *Diss.* 2.26.31; though a Roman Stoic, Epictetus is loyal to the Greek Stoics.

41 Epictetus, 1.24.16–18, 2.17.19–22.

42 The proper view is that virtue by itself is sufficient for *eudaimonia*.

act and the sexual partner; anger and violence connected with sexual jealousy; the list goes on and on.[43]

These cultural forces are in error, and in that sense someone who is in their grip is indeed a "fool," as Epictetus holds. But there is not much point in giving a little sermon to Medea as to a docile child; for such errors, taught from an early age, take over the soul, and can be eradicated, if at all, only by a lifetime of zealous and obsessive self-examination. And, furthermore, Seneca suggests that anger and the desire to inflict pain – the worst, in his opinion, of the errors of the soul – are not in any simple way just the result of a corrigible error, even at the social level. He firmly commits himself to the view that they do not result from innate instinct. On the other hand, they "omit no time of life, exempt no race of human beings" (*De Ira* III.22).

In a crucial passage, Seneca says that the wise person is not surprised at the omnipresence of aggression and injustice, "since he has examined thoroughly the circumstances of human life" (*condicio humanae vitae*, II.10). Circumstances, then, and not innate propensities, are at the origins of vice. And when the wise person looks at these circumstances clearly, he finds that they make it extremely difficult not to err. The world into which human beings are born is a rough place, one that confronts them with threats to their safety on every side. If they remain attached to their safety and to the resources that are necessary to protect it – as is natural and rational – that very attachment to the world will almost certainly, in time, lead to competitive or retaliatory aggression. For when goods are in short supply and people are attached to them, they compete for them. Thus aggression and violence grow not so much inside our nature as from an interaction between nature and conditions that is prior to and more deeply rooted than any specific form of society.

Seneca now uses this view as the basis for his argument against retributive anger and in favor of mercy. Given the omnipresence of aggression and wrongdoing, he now argues, if we look at the lives of others with the attitudes typical of the retributive tradition of justice – even in its modified particularistic form – if, that is, we are determined to fix a penalty precisely proportionate to the nature of the particular wrongdoing, then we will never cease to be retributive and to inflict punishment, for everything we see will upset us. But this retributive attitude, even when in some sense justified, is not without its consequences for the human spirit. For a person who notes and reacts to every injustice, and who becomes preoccupied with assigning just punishments, becomes, in the end, oddly similar to the raging ungentle people against whom he reacts. Retributive anger hardens the spirit, turning it against the humanity it sees. And in turning against humanity, in evincing the rage and hardness of the angry, one then becomes perilously close to the callous wrongdoers who arouse rage in the first place. Thus in Seneca's examples we find acts of horrifying vindictivenes and cruelty committed by people whose anger is in the first place justified, according to a precise assessment of the nature of the crime. Sulla's acts of retribution were initially directed against legitimate enemies; they ended in the murder of innocent

---

43 Most of my argument in this passage is based on the *De Ira* (*On Anger*), though there are many similar passages in other works.

children (II.34). Caligula was justified in his anger over the imprisonment of his mother, and yet this led him to cruelty and destruction. Cambyses had just cause of battle against the Ethiopians, but in his obsession with revenge he led his men on a fatal campaign that ended in cannibalism (III.20). Andrea Dworkin's heroine would be right at home here, for she reacts in some sense appropriately to real wrongs but becomes in the process an engine of revenge, indifferent to the face of humanity.[44]

Seneca's famous counterproposal, announced at the very end of *On Anger*, is that we should "cultivate humanity" (*colamus humanitatem*, III.43). He elsewhere describes this as the proposal to "give a pardon to the human species" (II.10). It is this attitude that he now calls by the name of mercy – translating Greek *epieikeia* with the Latin word *clementia*. Rejecting the austerity and rigor of the Greek Stoic, he makes a sympathetic participatory attitude central to the norm of good judging. Senecan *clementia* does not fail to pass judgment on wrongdoing; this is continually stressed. Seneca does not hold that the circumstances of human life remove moral and legal responsibility for bad acts. We may still convict defendants who fulfill some basic conditions of rationality in action. But, looking at the circumstances of human life, one comes to understand how such things have happened.[45] And this "medical" understanding leads to mercy.

Clementia, mercy, is even defined in a manner that makes its difference from Greek Stoic harshness evident: For it is an "inclination of the soul to mildness in exacting penalties," and also "that which turns its course away this side of that which could be justly determined" (*Clem.* II.3). The Greek Stoic soul, by contrast, never bends aside, never inclines away from hardness. The somewhat more gentle Aristotelian soul does bend, but inconstantly, conscious always that it is slavish to allow oneself and one's loved ones to be kicked around. Given that Seneca defines mercy as the opposite of cruelty, and given that cruelty is held to be a frequent outgrowth of retributive anger, we can say, putting all this together, that mercy, *clementia*, is opposed at one and the same time both to strictness in exacting penalties and also to retributive anger, as if that strictness does indeed lie very close to anger in the heart. As Seneca says, "It is a fault to punish a fault in full" (*culpa est totam persequi culpam*, *Clem.* II.7, fragment).[46]

One might, of course, adopt this attitude as a practical strategy to keep the self pure from anger, without endorsing it as *just* or *correct* toward the offender.

---

44 Insofar as she punishes people who are totally innocent of crime, she is not even a good Greek Stoic judge, for whom the particulars of the crime and offender must be correct. But the Greek Stoic would say that once some basic criteria of responsibility are met, a tough punishment is in order without a search for mitigating factors; and here her judicial procedure is like theirs.

45 Cf. K. Dover, *Greek Popular Morality in the Time of Plato and Aristotle* (Oxford: Clarendon Press, 1974), 270–2.

46 Unlike Aristotle, Seneca does not endorse *pity* or compassion as a correct response to the misfortunes of human life: for in his view, to do so would be to give too little credit to the person's own will and dignity, and, frequently, too much importance to external events.

Seneca sometimes appears to oscillate between these two positions, because he can commend the practical strategy even to those who do not accept his position about correctness. But in the end his position clearly is that it is right and correct to assign punishments in accordance with mercy, both because of what it means for oneself and because of what it says about and to the offender.

The merciful attitude, as Seneca develops it, entails regarding each particular case as a complex narrative of human effort in a world full of obstacles. The merciful judge will not fail to judge the guilt of the offender, but she will also see the many obstacles this offender faced on the way to being just – as a member of a culture, a gender, a city or country, and, above all, as a member of the human species, facing the obstacles characteristic of human life in a world of scarcity and accident. The starting point is a general view of human life and its difficulties, but the search for mitigating factors must at every point be searchingly particular. The narrative/medical attitude asks the judge to imagine what it was like to have been that particular offender, facing those particular obstacles with the resources of that history. Seneca's bet is that once one performs this imaginative exercise one will cease to have the strict retributive attitude to the punishment of the offender. One will be inclined, in fact, to gentleness and the waiving of the strict punishment mandated in the law. And the punishments that one does assign will be chosen, on the whole, not for their retributive function but for their power to improve the life of the defendant.[47]

This merciful attitude requires, and rests on, a new attitude to the self. The retributive attitude has a we/them mentality, in which judges set themselves against offenders, looking at their actions as if from a lofty height and preparing to find satisfaction in their pain. The good Senecan judge, by contrast, has both identification and sympathetic understanding. Accordingly, a central element in Seneca's prescription for the judge is that he should remind himself at every turn that he himself is capable of the failings he reproves in others. "If we want to be fair judges of all things, let us persuade ourselves of this first: that none of us is without fault. For it is from this point above all that retributive anger arises: 'I did nothing wrong,' and 'I did nothing.' No, rather, you don't admit to anything" (II.28).

This part of Seneca's argument reaches its conclusion in a remarkable passage in which Seneca confronts himself with the attitude of merciful judgment that he also recommends, describing his own daily practice of self-examination in forensic language that links it to his public recommendations:

> A person will cease from retributive anger and be more moderate if he knows that every day he has to come before himself as judge. What therefore is more wonderful than this habit of unfolding the entire day? How fine is the sleep that follows this acknowledgment of oneself, how serene, how deep and free, when the mind has been either praised or admonished, and as its own hidden investigator and assessor has gained knowledge of

---

47 One should not ignore the fact that some ameliorative punishments, according to Seneca, can be extremely harsh. Indeed, in a peculiar move, he defends capital punishment itself as in the interest of the punished, given that a longer bad life is better than a shorter one: he compares it to merciful euthanasia.

its own character? I avail myself of this power, and plead my cause daily before myself. When the light has been removed from sight, and my wife, long since aware of this habit of mine, has fallen silent, I examine my entire day and measure my deeds and words. I hide nothing from myself, I pass over nothing. For why should I fear anything from my own errors, when I can say, "See that you don't do that again, this time I pardon you." (III.36)

Seeing the complexity and fallibility of his own acts, seeing those acts as the product of a complex web of highly particular connections among original impulses, the circumstances of life, and the complicated psychological reactions life elicits from the mind, he learns to view others, too, as people whose errors emerge from a complex narrative history. Seneca's claim is that he will then moderate his retributive zeal toward the punishment of their injustices and intensify his commitment to mutual aid.

This part of Seneca's work seems very private. But there is no doubt that the primary aim of this work, and of the later *De Clementia* as well, is the amelioration of public life and public judgment. The *De Ira* was written at the start of the reign of the emperor Claudius. It responds to a well known speech by Claudius on the subject of anger and irascibility and obviously contains advice for the new regime.[48] Moreover, its explicit addressee and interlocutor is Novatus, Seneca's own brother, an aspiring orator and public man. Thus its entire argumentative structure is built around the idea of showing a public judge that the retributive attitude is unsuitable for good judging. As for the *De Clementia*, its explicit addressee is none other than the new emperor Nero Caesar himself, and its explicit task is to persuade this young man to use his immense power in merciful, rather than retributive, ways. The private material provides the basis for a new sort of public and judicial life.

VI. Mercy and the Literary Imagination

But instead of pursuing this history further, I want now to suggest some implications of these ideas for contemporary political and legal issues. First I shall develop a general thesis; then I shall apply it to some particular questions. The general thesis concerns the connection between the merciful attitude and the literary imagination. The Greco-Roman tradition already made a close connection between equity and narrative. The person who "reads" a complex case in the manner of the reader of a narrative or the spectator at a drama is put in contact – by the structure of the forms themselves, as they solicit the reader's or spectator's attention – with two features of the equitable: its attentiveness to particularity and its capacity for sympathetic understanding. But this means that the spectator or reader, if he or she reads well, is already prepared for equity and, in turn, for mercy.

---

48 See J. Fillion-Lahille, *Le De Ira de Sénèque* (Paris, 1984), and the summary of the evidence in Nussbaum, *Therapy*, chap. 11.

I could illustrate these points about the relationship between form and content in many ways. Instead I want to choose just two examples, which show with particular clarity the connection between mercy and the art of the novelist. For the novel has been in recent times an especially vigorous popular literary form. And it goes beyond tragic drama in its formal commitment to following complex life histories, looking at the minute details of motive and intention and their social formation – all that Seneca would have the good judge examine. This means that the novel, even more than tragic drama, is an artificial construction of mercy.

My first example is from Charles Dickens's *David Copperfield*.[49] James Steerforth, we know, is a bad person, one who deserves blame for some very serious bad actions. He humiliates the kind teacher, Mr. Mell; he uses his charm to get power over those younger and weaker than himself; he uses his wealth to escape discipline and criticism. And, above all, he destroys the life of Em'ly, who falls in love with him – betraying, in the process, both David's trusting friendship and the simple kindness of the Peggotty family. These bad actions are seen and judged by Agnes Wickfield in the straightforward way characteristic of the strict moral code that is her guide in life. A reader of religious books rather than of novels and stories, Agnes has no interest in the psychology of Steerforth's acts, or in seeing them from his point of view. She simply judges him, and judges him harshly, calling him David's "bad angel," and urging David (even before the serious crime) to have no further association with him. (It is a subtle point in the novel that moralism here allies itself with and provides a screen for the operations of jealousy: For Agnes resents the romantic hold that Steerforth has over David and uses her moral condemnation to get revenge.) David's view is more complex.

The novel – a novel represented as written by David some years after the event, during a tranquil marriage to Agnes – does present its reader with Agnes's moral judgment of Steerforth and the reasons for that judgment. The reader is led, at times – even as David shows himself being led – into the strict moral point of view, and is inclined at such times to judge Steerforth harshly. But these times are moments within the novel; they are not the overall attitude with which the novel leaves us. David tells and shows the reader that the novelist's imagination is of a certain sort – very different, in fact, from the moral imagination of Agnes. And this imagination leads to a different way of judging.

The central characteristic of the narrative imagination, as David depicts it, is that it preserves as a legacy from childhood an ability to attend closely to the particulars and to respond to them in a close and accurate manner. Like our ancient tradition, David immediately goes on to link this "power of observation" with gentleness: Adults who retain it retain also "a certain freshness, and gentleness, and capacity of being pleased, which are also an inheritance they have preserved from their childhood (61)."[50] The nature of the connection is apparent in the manner in which

---

49 These issues are discussed in more detail in "Steerforth's Arm," in *Love's Knowledge*.

50 All citations from the novel are taken from the Penguin edition, ed. Trevor Blount (Harmondsworth: Penguin, 1966).

the character David sees Steerforth, and in which the mature novelist David depicts him for the reader's imagination.[51] For, as I say, we do become aware of Steerforth's crimes. But we see them as episodes in the life of an extremely complicated character, who has enormous ability, awesome powers of attraction, great kindness and beneficence to his friends – and an extremely unfortunate family history. We do judge Steerforth's arrogance, duplicity, and self destructiveness. But we know also, as readers of the novel, that he grew up with no father to guide him, and with the misguided and uncritical affection of a willful and doting mother who indulged his every whim. We know, too, that his position and wealth compounded this ill fortune, exempting him for too long from the necessity to discipline his character and to cooperate with others. We are led to see his crimes as deliberate in the immediate sense required by strict legal and even moral judgment, but we also know that behind these crimes is a tangled history that might have been otherwise, a history that was not fully chosen by Steerforth himself. We imagine that with a different childhood Steerforth might have made an altogether different use of his abilities – might have had, in short, a different character. Like Seneca's reader, we are led to see character itself as something formed in society and in the family, something for which strict morality rightly holds individuals responsible, but something over which, in the end, individuals do not have full control.[52]

The result of all this is mercy. Just before Steerforth leaves to run off with Em'ly – in, then, the last conversation he has with David – we have the following exchange:

> "Daisy, if anything should ever separate us, you must think of me at my best, old boy. Come! Let us make that bargain. Think of me at my best, if circumstances should ever part us!"
>
> "You have no best to me, Steerforth," said I, "and no worst. You are always equally loved, and cherished in my heart." (497)

David keeps the bargain, loving Steerforth with the unconditional attention and concern of his narratorial heart. When, years later, the tempest washes Steerforth's body ashore and he recognizes it, David exclaims:

---

51 These are not precisely the same, because the mature novelist has achieved an integration of the erotic and the moral that eludes the character earlier on.

52 Compare the ideas on moral responsibility developed in Susan Wolf, *Freedom Within Reason* (New York: Oxford University Press, 1990). Wolf holds – like the ancient tradition described here – that there is an asymmetry between praise and blame, that it is legitimate to commend people for achievements that are in large part the outgrowth of early education and social factors but not legitimate to blame them when such forces have made them into bad characters who are unable to respond to reason. In Wolf's view, as in mine, this asymmetry will sometimes mean not holding individuals responsible for their bad acts. Unlike her, however, I make a distinction between culpability and punishment, holding that a defendant's life story may give reasons for mitigating punishment even when requirements for culpability are met.

"No need, O Steerforth, to have said, when we last spoke together, in that hour which I so little deemed to be our parting-hour – no need to have said, "Think of meat my best!" I had done that ever; and could I change now, looking on this sight!" (866)

Just as the character David suspends punitive judgment on Steerforth's acts, so the imagination of the narrator – and of the reader – is led to turn aside, substituting for punishment an understanding of Steerforth's life story. David makes it very clear that the activity of novel writing causes him to relive this moment of mercy,[53] and that its "freshness and gentleness" can be expected to be, as well, its reader's experience. In this sense the novel is about itself, and the characteristic moral stance of its own production and reception. That stance is the stance of equity, and of mercy.

My second example is contemporary. In 1992, the novelist Joyce Carol Oates visited my seminar at Brown to speak about the moral and political dimensions of her fiction. As we discussed her recent novel *Because It Is Bitter and Because It Is My Heart*, a student, silent until then, burst in with a heated denunciation of Oates's character Leslie, a well-meaning but ineffectual liberal photographer. Isn't his life a complete failure really? Isn't he contemptible for his inability to do anything significant out of his antiracist intentions? Isn't he to be blamed for not more successfully combatting racism, in his family and in his society? Oates was silent for a time, her eyes peering up from behind her round glasses. Then she answered slowly, in her high, clear girlish voice. "That's not the way I see it, really." She then went on to narrate the story of Leslie's life, the efforts he had made, the formidable social and psychological obstacles in the way of his achieving more, politically, than he had – speaking of him as of a friend whose life inhabited her own imagination and whom, on that account, she could not altogether dismiss or condemn. Here, I believe, was mercy; and, lying very close to it, the root of the novelist's art. The novel's structure is a structure of *suggnômê* – of the penetration of the life of another into one's own imagination and heart. It is a form of imaginative and emotional receptivity, in which the reader, following the author's lead, comes to be inhabited by the tangled complexities and struggles of other concrete lives.[54] Novels do not withhold all moral judgment, and they contain villains as well as heroes. But for any character with whom the form invites our participatory identification, the motives for mercy are engendered in the structure of literary perception itself.

---

53 See especially, shortly preceding the discovery of Steerforth's death: "As plainly as I behold what happened, I will try to write it down. I do not recall it, but see it done; for it happens again before me" (855).

54 Of course, the novelist's stance is traditionally linked with compassion, as well as with mercy. Sometimes, that is, the response will be to sympathize with the plight of a character without blaming, whereas in other cases there may be both blame and a merciful punishment. The line is, and should be, difficult to draw, for the factors that make mercy appropriate also begin to cast doubt on full moral responsibility. (In other cases, of course, there is not even a prima facie offense, and therefore we will have pity without mercy.)

VII. Mercy and Legal Thought

Now to contemporary implications.

Until now, I have been talking about a moral ideal, which has evident implications for publicly promulgated norms of human behavior, and for public conduct in areas in which there is latitude for judicial discretion. I have suggested that in many ways this norm fulfills and completes a conception of justice which lies, itself, at the basis of the rule of law: For it was to prevent incomplete, defective, and biased discretionary reasoning that the rule of law was introduced and defended. But at this point and for this reason caution is in order; for the moral ideal should not be too simply converted into a norm for a legal system. First of all, a legal system has to look out for the likelihood that the moral ideal will not always be perfectly realized, and it should protect against abuses that moral arbitrariness and bias can engender. This suggests a large role for codified requirements in areas in which one cannot guarantee that the equity ideal will be well implemented; the equity tradition supports this. Second, a system of law must look to social consequences as well as to the just judgment on particular offenders; thus it may need to balance an interest in the deterrent role of punishments against the equity tradition's interest in punishments that suit the agent. Both the balance between codification and discretion and the balance between equity and deterrence are enormously complex matters, with which my analysis here cannot fully grapple. What I do wish to offer here are some representative suggestions of what the equity tradition has to offer us, as we think about these issues.

A model of judicial reasoning

In other recent work,[55] I have been developing the idea that legal, and especially judicial, reasoning can be modeled on the reasoning of the concerned reader of a novel.[56] Following in some respects the lead of Adam Smith, in *The Theory of Moral Sentiments*,[57] I argue that the experience of the concerned reader is an artificial construction of ideal moral and judicial spectatorship, with respect both to particularity of attention and to the sort and range of emotions that will and will not be felt. Identifying with a wide range of characters from different social circumstances, and concerning oneself in each case with the entire complex history of their efforts, the reader comes to have emotions both sympathetic and participatory toward the things that they do and suffer. These emotions will be based on a highly particularized perception of the character's situation. On the other hand, because the reader is not herself a character in the story, except in the Henry Jamesian sense of being a "participator by a fond attention,"[58] she will lack emotions relating to her

---

55 The development of this idea begins in "The Discernment of Perception," in *Love's Knowledge*; it continues in *Poetic Justice* (Boston: Beacon Press, 1996).

56 Or the spectator at a play. I discuss some reasons for focusing above all on the novel in *Poetic Justice*, chap. 1.

57 Discussed in "Steerforth's Arm," in *Love's Knowledge*.

58 The citation is from the opening pages of *The Princess Casamassima*.

own concrete placement in the situation with regard to which she is asked to judge; her judgments will thus, I argue, be both sympathetically emotional and, in the most appropriate sense, neutral.

My current inquiry into mercy takes the model one step further, where judgment on the wrongdoing of others is concerned, going, with this step, beyond Smith's rather austere construction of emotional spectatorship. For it construes the participatory emotion of the literary imagination as emotion that will frequently lead to mercy, even when a judgment of culpability has been made. And this merciful attitude derives directly, we can now see, from the literary mind's keen interest in all the particulars, a fact not much stressed by Smith in his account of the literary (perhaps because he focuses on classical drama, in which the concrete circumstances of daily life are not always so clearly in view). My literary judge sees defendants as inhabitants of a complex web of circumstances, circumstances which often, in their totality, justify mitigation of blame and/or punishment.[59]

This attitude on the part of my ideal judge is unashamedly mentalistic. It does not hesitate to use, and to use centrally, the notions of intention, choice, reflection, deliberation, and character that are part of a nonreductive intentionalist psychology. Like the novel, it treats the inner world of the defendant as a deep and complex place, and it instructs the judge to investigate that depth. This approach is opposed, in spirit if not always in outcome, to an approach to the offender articulated in some well-known writings of Justice Holmes and recently further developed by Richard Posner.[60] According to this approach, the offender should be treated as a thing with

---

59 John Roemer suggests the following important point: Insofar as my literary judge treats many of a person's abilities, talents, and achievements as products of circumstances beyond his or her control, this reinforces and deepens the novel's commitment to egalitarianism. (In "The Literary Imagination" I had argued that the novel is already egalitarian in asking us to identify successively with members of different social classes, and to see their needs, without being aware of where, in the social scheme we are to choose, we ourselves will be.) For we will then see the talents and dispositions in virtue of which people earn their greater or lesser social rewards as not really theirs by desert, or not fully so, given the large role played by social advantages and other external circumstances in getting to these dispositions; and we will be more inclined to treat them as social resources that are subject to allocation as are other resources. (Not, obviously, in the sense that we will take A's talents from A and give them to B; but we will regard A's talents as like a certain level of wealth, on account of which we may require A to give back more to society in other ways.) On all this, see Roemer, "Equality of Talent," *Economics and Philosophy* I (1985), 151–86; "Equality of Resources Implies Equality of Welfare," *The Quarterly Journal of Economics* (November 1986), 751–83; "A Pragmatic Theory of Responsibility for the Egalitarian Planner," *Philosophy and Public Affairs* 22 (1993), 146–66.

60 The most important sources for Holmes's view are "The Path of the Law" and "The Common Law," now printed (the latter in extracts) in *The Essential Holmes*, ed. Richard A. Posner (hereafter Posner ed.) (Chicago: University of Chicago Press, 1992), 160–77, 237–64. For Posner's views, see *The Problems of Jurisprudence* (Cambridge, MA: Harvard University Press, 1990), chap. 5.

no insides to be scrutinized from the internal viewpoint – but simply as a machine, whose likely behavior, as a result of a given judgment or punishment, we attempt, as judges, to predict.[61] The sole proper concern of punishment becomes deterrence; as law becomes more sophisticated, and our predictive ability improves, states of mind play a smaller and smaller role in judgment.

Holmes's defense of this idea takes an interesting form, from our point of view. For it begins from an extremely perceptive description and criticism of the retributive idea of judgment and punishment.[62] His own deterrence-based view is advanced as an alternative – he seems to think it the only plausible one – to retributivism; and much of the argument's force comes from the connection of the positive recommendation with the effective negative critique. The trouble begins when he conflates the retributive idea with the idea of looking to the wrongdoer's state of mind, implying that an interest in the "insides" invariably brings retributivism with it.[63] As we have seen, matters are far more complicated, both historically and philosophically. It is, I think, in order to extricate judging from the retributive view – felt by Holmes, rightly, to be based on metaphysical and religious notions of balance and proportion and to be an outgrowth of passions that we should not encourage in society[64] – that he feels himself bound to oppose all mentalistic and intention based notions of punishing. In "The Common Law," Holmes argues that so far from considering "the condition of a man's heart or conscience" in making a judgment, we should focus on external standards that are altogether independent of motive and intention. And here he insists on the very sort of strict assessment, without mitigation, that the entire mercy tradition opposes:

> [The external standards] do not merely require that every man should get as near as he can to the best conduct possible for him. They require him at his own peril to come up to a certain height. They take no account of incapacities, unless the weakness is so marked as to fall into well-known exceptions, such as infancy or madness. They assume that every man is as able as every other to behave as they command. If they fall on any one class harder than on another, it is on the weakest. (253)

---

61 Posner commenting on Holmes's view, with approval: "We would deal with criminals as we deal with unreasonably dangerous machines.... [I]nstead of treating dangerous objects as people, he was proposing to treat dangerous people as objects" (168).

62 See especially "The Common Law," Posner ed. 247–53. Holmes does not mention the ancient Greek debate; he focuses on Hegel's account of retributivism.

63 See, for example, Posner ed., 247: "The desire for vengeance imports an opinion that its object is actually and personally to blame. It takes an internal standard, not an objective or external one, and condemns its victim by that."

64 Holmes notes that the retributive view of the criminal law has been held by such eminent figures as Bishop Butler and Jeremy Bentham. He then quotes, without comment, Sir James Stephen's view that "[t]he criminal law stands to the passion of revenge in much the same relation as marriage to the sexual appetite" (248). Presumably this means that it allows for the satisfaction of this passion in an institutionalized and civilized form, not that it causes the passion's decline.

But from our viewpoint, this dichotomy between intentionalism and retributivism leaves out the real opponent of retributivism, both historical and philosophical – simply putting in its place a strict external assessment that looks suspiciously like the old Anaximandrean *diké* in modern secular dress, despite its evident differences.

Posner follows Holmes's view in most essential respects, developing it in much more detail, with appeal to modern behaviorist theories of mind. Like Holmes, Posner is motivated above all by the wish to describe an alternative to retributivism, which he criticizes eloquently, with appeal to both history and literature.[65] His argument is highly complex and cannot even be accurately summarized, much less appropriately criticized, in the space available here. What is most important for our purposes is that Posner makes explicit the fact that his behaviorist view of the criminal law requires rejecting – for legal purposes – the Kantian idea that people are to be treated as ends rather than means. It requires, in fact, treating them as objects that, through their behavior, generate either good or bad social consequences. This, we can easily see, is profoundly opposed to the stance of the literary judge, who may differ from some Kantians in her focus on particular circumstances but who certainly makes the Kantian insight about human beings central to her entire project. Posner also makes it clear that the case for his account of the external standards to be applied stands or falls with the case for behaviorism (perhaps eliminative materialism as well?) as an adequate and reasonably complete theory of human behavior. Because I think it is fair to say that the best current work in the philosophy of mind and in cognitive psychology – like the best work on mind in classical antiquity – finds serious flaws in the behaviorist and reductionist views, this explicitness in Posner makes the vulnerable point in the Holmes/Posner argument especially plain. On the other hand, unlike Holmes, Posner does not seem to claim that the behaviorist view is the only available alternative to retributivist views of punishment. He shows an awareness, in fact, of the mercy tradition – strikingly enough, not in the chapter dealing with the criminal law but in his chapter dealing with "Literary and Feminist Perspectives."[66] He shows some sympathy with this tradition, arguing that what the law should really seek is an appropriate balance between strict legal justice and a flexible and merciful discretion.[67] He is, however, pessimistic about the role that latitude for mercy is likely to play in actual cases, holding that a discretionary approach on the part of judges will frequently be harsher to defendants – especially minority defendants – than will an approach based on strict rules.[68] This is a valuable insight, and I shall return to it shortly. But first I must conclude the story, where Holmes is concerned.

---

65 See especially Posner, *Law and Literature: A Misunderstood Relation* (Cambridge, MA: Harvard University Press, 1988), 25–70.

66 Posner, *Problems of Jurisprudence*, 393–419. See also Posner, *Law and Literature*, 105–15.

67 Posner, *Law and Literature* 108–15.

68 There is another reason for Posner's skepticism about mercy: He feels that it implies a kind of interfering scrutiny of the "insides" that sits uneasily with the libertarian hands off attitude to government intervention he has long defended. I think this is wrong: Wanting

Holmes's "The Common Law" was written in 1881, "The Path of the Law" (where Holmes argues for a related view[69]) in 1897. It is worthy of note that toward the end of his life, in a remarkable letter, Holmes appears to endorse the mercy tradition as a result of his reading of Roman philosophy. Writing on March 28, 1924, to his friend Harold Laski,[70] Holmes begins by speaking of the large impression made on him by Seneca's "cosmopolitan humanity"; he suggests (correctly) that this notion came to Christianity, from Roman philosophy, rather than vice versa. He confirms the impression by reading Plutarch, in order to get the Greek perspective. After making an obligatory shocking remark that "the literature of the past is a bore" – he vigorously praises Tacitus. Then, appended to the account of his Roman reading, comes the arresting insight: "Before I leave you for the day and drop the subject let me repeat if I have said it before that I think the biggest thing in antiquity is 'Father forgive them – they know not what they do.' There is the modern transcending of amoral judgment in the most dramatic of settings...."

It is not terribly clear to what extent Holmes means to connect this remark about Jesus with his observations concerning the debt owed by Christianity to Roman thought. My argument has shown that he certainly could do so, with justice. Nor is it clear how, or whether, he would apply his insight to concrete issues in the law. What is clear is that by this time in his life Holmes has recognized that the transcendence of strict moralism that he has recommended throughout his career need not be captured through a reliance on external behavioral standards. It seems to him to be most appropriately captured in the "dramatic setting" in which Jesus takes up, toward his enemies, the attitude of Senecan mercy.[71] I think that he is right.[72]

In short, to depart from a retributivism that is brutal in its neglect of human complexity, we do not need to embrace a deterrence-only view that treats people as means to society's ends, aggregating their good and ill without regard to what is appropriate for each. The deterrence view is all too close to the retributive view it opposes[73] in its resolute refusal to examine the particularities of motive, intention, and story; in its treatment of people as place holders in a larger social or cosmic calculus. A merciful judge need not neglect issues of deterrence, but she is above all committed to an empathetic scrutiny of the "insides" of the individual life.

---

to know the relevant facts in no way entails additional curtailment of individual liberty of choice.

69 Here he advances his famous "bad man" theory of the law: In order to figure out the deterrent aspect of punishment correctly, the judge should think, in each case, of what a bad person, completely insensitive to legal or moral requirement except in calculating personal costs and benefits, would do in response to a particular set of legal practices. Thus he endorses the basic strictness in assessing penalties that gave rise to our asymmetry in the ancient tradition.

70 Posner ed., 59–60.

71 Senecan influence on Christianity begins with the work of writers such as Clement of Alexandria and Augustine. I mean to point to a resemblance which is later developed in explicitly Stoic terms.

72 For the distinction between forgiveness and mercy, see my previous discussion of Seneca; a good modern discussion is in Jean Hampton and Jeffrie Murphy, *Forgiveness and Mercy* (Cambridge: Cambridge University Press, 1988). The attitude of Jesus toward sinners

Mercy and the criminal law

The implications of the mercy tradition for issues in the criminal law are many and complex. The criminal law has long had a profound commitment to Aristotelianism – that is, to the proposition that we should in most cases take cognizance of the accused person's motives and intentions in determining guilt or innocence and in fixing the level of wrongdoing. This Aristotelian tradition treats people as, on the whole, the authors of their own characters. Thus a genuinely angry person will be able to claim "reasonable provocation," and thus get a reduction, for example, from first degree murder to manslaughter, only if he or she can show that the anger that produced the crime was that of a "reasonable person." As one Pennsylvania court expressed this idea, when confronted with a defendant who made a plea of unusual irascibility, "Suppose then we admit testimony that the defendant is quick tempered, violent and revengeful; what then? Are these an excuse for, or do they even mitigate crime? Certainly not, for they result from a want of self discipline; a neglect of self culture that is inexcusable."[74] This demand for appropriate "self-culture" leads, in general, to the rejection of pleas for mitigation or exculpation when the defendant acted out of motives that are not thought to be part of a good character. Thus racial hatred, however deeply and sincerely felt, will not be regarded as mitigating a crime and may even appropriately be regarded as an aggravating feature.[75]

Is the law, then, Aristotelian rather than Senecan? Once bad character is on the scene, is there no room for mercy? What does it say where we have reason to believe, with Seneca, that people form their characters in circumstances that may deform their aspirations? Consider Bigger Thomas, the hero of Richard Wright's novel *Native Son*, an impoverished and undereducated African American who eventually commits two violent criminal acts, at least one of which (the killing of his lover Bessie) is clearly a murder. Throughout the novel, Wright prevents us from having easy sympathy for Bigger by showing him as someone whose emotions are deformed and inappropriate. At the same time, Wright makes us feel discomfort with our urge to condemn Bigger by showing us in detail how his character and emotions have been shaped by both poverty and racism, how shame at the color of his skin,

---

appears to be more one of mercy than of forgiveness: For sinners will certainly be condemned and punished, not let off the hook.

73 And in many cases it is harsher than the retributivist view, because a deterrence based view often punishes attempts at crime that do not succeed; and a relatively minor crime may be punished harshly if there is reason to think the offender a dangerous repeat offender.

74 *Small v. Commonwealth*, 91 Pa. 304, 306, 308 (1879). See generally Dan M. Kahan and Martha C. Nussbaum, "Two Conceptions of Emotion in Criminal Law," *Columbia Law Review* 96 (1996), 269–374.

75 See Kahan and Nussbaum on the relationship of changing social norms to these ideals of appropriateness. Of particular interest is the contested area of homophobic killings, where some courts have refused as a matter of law to admit evidence of strong hatred and disgust as potentially mitigating, and others have in fact judged them to be mitigating factors.

fear of the dominant white community, and rage at his unequal and immobilized situation all interact in the daily events of Bigger's life. We are led to think that he did not have the degree of control over his character development that we usually do, given the extremely closed and unequal situation in which he lives. If we look at his crime as Aristotle recommends, we will find him guilty and refuse to ask further questions. But Seneca, like the novelist's vision, prompts a deeper inquiry; admitting his culpability, we are urged to see with sympathy the road that led him to become a person of this sort.

In fact, the criminal law is Senecan as well as Aristotelian. In determining an offender's guilt or innocence and the grade of her offense, the law evaluates her actions, including her motives and character; at this point the law is usually unconcerned with how the defendant came to be the way she is. But during the sentencing process the law has traditionally permitted the story of the defendant's character formation to come before the judge or jury, in all its narrative complexity, in such a way as to manifest any factors that might, once presented, give rise to sympathetic assessment and to a merciful mitigation of punishment. Indeed, a long tradition has held that we owe it to the dignity and humanity of the defendant to make this individualized inquiry. This tradition was well articulated in a 1976 capital-sentencing case:

> A process that accords no significance to relevant facets of the character and record of the individual offender or the circumstances of the particular offense excludes from consideration in fixing the ultimate punishment of death the possibility of compassionate or mitigating factors stemming from the diverse frailties of humankind. It treats all persons convicted of a designated offense not as uniquely individual human beings, but as members of a faceless, undifferentiated mass to be subjected to the blind infliction of the penalty of death.[76]

Woodson does not explicitly say that the tradition is asymmetrical, as in Seneca. But we can see that it is by focusing on a pair of more recent cases involving the death penalty, which raise issues of mitigation and aggravation in connection with discretionary sentencing. One is *Walton v. Arizona*[77]; the other is *California v. Brown*.[78] At stake are the role to be played by discretion in deciding capital cases and the criteria to be used in analyzing the aggravating and mitigating features of the case. Walton was convicted by a jury of first degree murder and sentenced to death

---

76 *Woodson v. North Carolina*, 428 U.S. 280, 304 (1976) (opinion of Stewart, Powell, and Stevens, J.J.).

77 110 S. Ct. 3047 (1990)

78 479 U.S. 538 (1987). For discussion of both of these cases I am indebted to Ronald J. Allen, "Evidence, Inference, Rules, and Judgment in Constitutional Adjudication: The Intriguing Case of *Walton v. Arizona*," *Journal of Criminal Law and Criminology* 81 (1991), 727–59. For later thoughts about the role of logic in judicial inference, see Allen, "The Double Jeopardy Clause, Constitutional Interpretation and the Limits of Formal Logic," *Valparaiso University Law Review* 26 (1991), 281–310.

by the judge, in accordance with an Arizona statute that requires the judge first to ascertain whether at least one aggravating circumstances is present – in this case two were found[79] – and then to consider all the alleged mitigating circumstances advanced by the defendant, imposing a death sentence if he finds "no mitigating circumstances sufficiently substantial to call for mercy." The defendant is required to establish a mitigating circumstance by the preponderance of the evidence – and it was this that was the central issue in Walton's appeal. Because previous Supreme Court decisions had rejected a requirement of unanimity for mitigation,[80] Walton contended that the preponderance of the evidence test was also unconstitutional. His claim was rejected by a plurality of the court. My concern is not so much with the result as with some interesting issues that emerge from the opinions.

First, it is plain that the Arizona system, which the decision in effect upholds, establishes a lexical ordering in which a finding of aggravation – which must be based on criteria explicitly enumerated in the law – is used to classify an offense as a potential death-penalty offense; mitigation is then considered afterwards, in a discretionary manner. In other words, the whole range of potentially mitigating circumstances will be brought forward only when it has already been established that an offense falls into a certain class of extremely serious offenses. And discretionary concern for the entirety of the defendant's history will enter the picture only in the mitigation phase. Justice Stevens comments on this feature in his dissenting opinion, arguing that once the scope of capital punishment is so reduced, the risk of arbitrariness in sentencing is sufficiently reduced as well to permit very broad discretion and individuated decision making with the remaining class. This seems to be a correct and valuable observation. Indeed, the mercy tradition stresses that merciful judgment can be given only when there is time to learn the whole history of the life in question, with great complexity, and also inclination to do so in a sympathetic manner, without biases of class or race. The tradition wholeheartedly endorses decision making by codified requirement when these requirements cannot be met. (Here Posner's warnings about arbitrariness in equity seem perfectly appropriate, and they are reflected in the move away from unguided discretion represented by the Federal Sentencing Guidelines.[81]) We should not, however, say, as Stevens seems to, that the main function of such criteria is to reduce the *number* of cases that are eligible for the death penalty. What

---

79 The murder was committed in an "especially heinous, cruel or depraved manner," and it was committed for pecuniary gain. Note that even here, in the nondiscretionary and codified portion of the judgment, intentional notions are prominently used.

80 *Mills v. Maryland*, 486 U.S. 367 (1988); and *McKoy v. North Carolina*, 110 S. Ct. 1229 (1990).

81 I have not committed myself here on the ideal scope for discretion in other areas of the law. This is an issue I feel I need to study further before making concrete claims. I focus on the capital cases because they have been the focus of an especially interesting debate about mercy, in which the penalty setting phase has a special weight. But I think that a similar approach could be tried in another group of cases to which a finding of aggravation is pertinent, namely hate crimes. Here I think one would want to describe the grounds for aggravation very explicitly and systematically, either by setting up a special class of crimes or

they do is, of course, more substantial: They eliminate from the death eligible group many cases for which death would *clearly* not be an *appropriate* penalty, leaving the judge free to turn his or her attention to those that are more problematic, requiring a more fine tuned deliberation.[82]

A second significant feature, and a more problematic one, is the plurality's unquestioning acceptance of the preponderance of the evidence test – which, as Allen has shown here and elsewhere, has grave defects when we are dealing with a case having multiple relevant features.[83] For suppose a defendant advances three grounds for mitigation, each of which is established to a .25 probability, and therefore to be thrown out under Arizona's rule. The probability that at least one of the factors is true, assuming they are independent,[84] is, as Allen shows, .58. If each of three factors is proved to a probability of .4, the probability that at least one is true is .78. On the other hand, if the defendant proves just one of the mitigating factors with a probability of .51 and the others with probability 0, he is successful, even though the probability that the decision is correct is in fact lower here than in the previous cases. And so forth.[85] The law asks the judge to treat each feature one by one, in total isolation from any other. But human lives, as the literary judge would see, consist of complex webs of circumstances, which must be considered as a whole.

This same problem is present in Justice Scalia's scathing attack on the whole notion of mitigation. For Scalia thinks it absurd that we should have codified criteria for aggravation, apply these, *and then* look with unguided discretion to see whether a mitigating factor is present. If the criteria for aggravation are enumerated in the law, so too should be the criteria for mitigation. Only this explicitness and this symmetry can prevent total irrationality. Scalia here ignores the possibility – which Stevens recognizes – that the functions of aggravation criteria and of mitigation are not parallel: Aggravation places the offense in the class to which mitigation is

---

in the guidelines for sentencing. Once one had determined that the particular offense was of this particularly severe kind, one could then consider whether the defendant's youth, family background, and so forth gave any grounds for mitigation.

82 See Allen, "*Walton*," 741. I agree with this point against Stevens but disagree with an earlier one. Allen argues that "the primary thrust of [Stevens's] argument ... is for categorical rather than discretionary sentencing" (736). This seems to me inaccurate: It is, instead, a statement about the conditions under which discretionary sentencing can be well done.

83 See also Allen, "A Reconceptualization of Civil Trials," in *Probability and Inference in the Law of Evidence*, ed. P. Tillers and E. D. Green (Dordrecht: Kluwer, 1988), 21–60.

84 See Allen, "*Walton*," 734–5. This is the assumption that the current test in effect makes. If they are not independent, this probabilistic analysis does not follow, but there is also, then, no justification at all for treating them in isolation from one another, the conclusion for which I am arguing.

85 One might also point out that different jurors might be convinced by different factors, as long as they are treated as isolated units; thus one could have a situation in which all jurors agree that there is at least one mitigating factor present, but, if they disagree enough about which one that is, the defendant's attempt fails. I owe this point to Cy Wasserstrom.

relevant.[86] And, furthermore, in ridiculing the entire notion of discretionary mercy, Scalia adamantly refuses the forms of perception that we have associated with the literary attitude. That is, he treats mitigating factors as isolated units, unconnected either to one another or to the whole of a life. It is in this way that he can arrive at the conclusion that unbridled discretion will (absurdly) be permitted to treat traits that are polar opposites as, both of them, mitigating; for example, "that the defendant had a poor and deprived childhood, or that he had a rich and spoiled childhood."[87] His assumption is that both of these cannot be mitigating, and that it is a sign of the absurdity of the current state of things that they might both be so treated. But the alleged absurdity arises only because he has severed these traits from the web of circumstances in which they actually figure. In connection with other circumstances, either a trait or its opposite might, in fact, be mitigating.[88] This, in Allen's argument and in mine, is the reason why categories for mitigation should not be codified in advance, for it will be impossible for such a code to anticipate adequately the countless ways in which factors interweave and bear on one an other in human reality. Telling the whole story, with all the particulars,[89] is the only way to get at that.[90]

In reality, of course, the mercy tradition has serious reservations about the whole idea of capital punishment. Although some of its major exponents, including Seneca, endorsed it, they did so on the basis of very peculiar arguments comparing it to euthanasia (see n. 47). If we reject these arguments, we are left, I think, with no support for capital punishment from within that tradition and strong reasons to reject retributivist justifications. Indeed, the tradition strongly suggests that such punishments are always cruel and excessive. The question would then have to be whether the deterrence value of such punishments by itself justifies their perpetuation, despite their moral inappropriateness, and the deterrence-based argument has never been made out in a fully compelling way.

---

86 Here the similarity to the ancient tradition is striking especially to Seneca's insistence on separating the determination of guilt, and its level, from the assignment of (merciful) punishment.

87 110 S. Ct. at 3062.

88 See Allen, "*Walton*," 739, also 742: "Any particular fact is of very little consequence standing alone. The web of facts is what matters." In *David Copperfield* we see a very clear example of a rich and spoiled childhood as a mitigating factor: Steerforth has no opportunity to learn moral self-restraint and is encouraged to use his talent and charm in a reckless manner.

89 I am not claiming that knowledge of the whole story should never give rise to aggravation of punishment, and by focusing on capital cases I have left undiscussed a number of lesser cases in which such thinking might figure. Consider, for example, *United States v. Lallemand*, discussed loc. cit.

90 Another point against Scalia is the structure of the pardon power: A governor can pardon a criminal but not increase a criminal's sentence or condemn someone who was acquitted. Indeed, asymmetry is built into the entirety of the criminal justice system, in the requirement to prove guilt beyond a reasonable doubt, in the safeguards surrounding the admissibility of confessions, and so forth.

California v. Brown raises a different issue: the issue of jury instruction, where emotion is concerned.[91] The Court reviewed a state jury instruction stipulating that the jury in a capital case (in the sentencing phase) "must not be swayed by mere sentiment, conjecture, sympathy, passion, prejudice, public opinion or public feeling." From the point of view of our account of literary judging, this instruction is a peculiar and inappropriate mixture. For the juror as "judicious spectator" and merciful reader would indeed disregard conjecture, prejudice, public opinion, and public feeling. On the other hand, sentiment, passion, and sympathy would be a prominent part of the appropriate (and rational) deliberative process, where those sentiments are based in the juror's "reading" of the defendant's history, as presented in the evidence. It would of course be right to leave aside any sentiment having to do with one's own involvement in the outcome – but we assume that nobody with a personal interest in the outcome would end up on the jury in any case. It would also be correct to leave aside any mere gut reaction to the defendant's appearance, demeanor, or clothing – anything that could not be made a part of the "story" one tells about the case, giving reasons. But the vast majority of the passional reactions of a juror hearing a case of this kind will be based on the story that is told: In this sense, the law gives extremely bad advice.[92] The Court, however, approved the instruction, concluding that "A reasonable juror would ... understand the instruction ... as a directive to ignore only the sort of sympathy that would be totally divorced from the evidence adduced during the penalty phase."[93] On the one hand, this seems to me a perfectly reasonable way of articulating the boundaries of appropriate and inappropriate sympathy. On the other hand, the likelihood is so high that the sentiments of the juror would be of the appropriate, rather than the inappropriate, sort – for what else but the story told them do they have to consider? – that approving the regulation creates a misleading impression that some large and rather dangerous class of passions is being excluded.[94] The other opinions in the case confirm the general impression of confusion about and suspicion of the passions. Thus Justice O'Connor argues that "the sentence imposed at the penalty stage should reflect a reasoned *moral* response to the defendant's background, character,

---

91 Note that for a juror, the case at issue is likely to be a rare event, and thus there is reason to think that jury deliberations will be free from at least some of the problems of callousness and shortness of time that may limit the advisability of discretion in cases involving judges. On the other hand, the limits of juror sympathy with people who are unlike themselves remains a clear difficulty, and this is why I sympathize, to the extent that I do, with parts of the warning in the California juror instruction.

92 Compare the advice given to the prospective juror in the state of Massachusetts, in the "Juror's Creed" printed in the *Trial Juror's Handbook*: "I am a JUROR. I am a seeker of truth ... I must lay aside all bias and prejudice. I must be led by my intelligence and not by my emotions...."

93 *California v. Brown*, 479 U.S. at 542–3.

94 Thus I agree in part with Allen, "*Walton*," 747 – although I do think it reasonable to stipulate this restriction on sentiment, and believe that it is possible to think of cases where sentiments would be of the inappropriate sort.

and crime rather than mere sympathy or emotion." She goes on to state that "the individualized assessment of the appropriateness of the death penalty is a moral inquiry into the culpability of the defendant, and not an emotional response to the mitigating evidence."[95] This contrast between morality and sympathy is a nest of confusions, as our argument by now should have shown. Justice Brennan, too, holds that "mere sympathy" must be left to one side – though he does hold (dissenting) that the instruction prohibits the juror from considering exactly what it should consider, and although he does demonstrate with a wealth of examples that the instruction has been frequently abused by prosecutors, who convince juries that they should disregard all sympathy.[96] Justice Blackmun does somewhat better with the concepts, defending the juror's ability to respond with mercy as "a particularly valuable aspect of the capital sentencing procedure." But he, too, contrasts rationality with mercy, even in the process of defending the latter: "While the sentencer's decision to accord life to a defendant at times might be a rational or moral one, it also may arise from the defendant's appeal to the sentencer's sympathy or mercy, human qualities that are undeniably emotional in nature."[97] The confusion persists: In a more recent case, the Court now speaks even more suspiciously and pejoratively of the juror's emotions, contrasting them with the "actual evidence regarding the crime and the defendant"[98] – as if these were not the source of and basis for these emotions.

In short, the insights of the mercy tradition can take us a long way in understanding what is well and not well done in recent Supreme Court writings about sentencing. It can help us to defend the asymmetry between mitigation and aggravation that prevailed in *Walton*, as well as *Walton*'s moderate defense of discretion. But it leads to severe criticism of the categories of analysis deployed in the juror instruction cases, which employ defective conceptions of the rational.

It is important, however, to notice that, even in the midst of conceptual confusion, the Court is unhesitatingly Senecan about the penalty phase. All the opinions in *California v. Brown* agree that we owe it to the defendant to hear the whole story and to look for mitigating factors; they disagree only about whether the instruction, as written, is likely to mislead.

Legal mercy is not and should not be the same as mercy in the moral life. According to Seneca, if we look hard enough at any case of individual wrongdoing we are likely to discover factors that lead to mercy. His plausible view about the causes of human error makes it likely that we will find ignorance, or bad cultural and parental influence, or some type of suffering and deprivation, behind any bad act. But in the law we set the penalties for bad acts in a way that presupposes a norm of

---

95 479 U.S. at 545.

96 Ibid. at 548–50.

97 Ibid. at 561–3. Thus I do not agree with Allen that Blackmun "gets it right" (750). Allen, like Blackmun, is willing to give the normative term "rational" to the opposition, granting that merciful sentiment is not rational. Why not? It is based on judgments that are (if the deliberative process is well executed) both true and justified by the evidence.

98 *Saffle v. Parks*, 110 S. Ct. 1257 (1990), at 1261.

"self-culture" and a sense of what conditions normally enable the requisite amount of self-culture. (If we are Senecan about the normal case, this will give us reasons to resist extremely harsh penalties generally, or to favor those that are likely to reform and educate.) What we are looking for in the penalty phase, then, is the atypical case – the person who, like Bigger Thomas, has suffered an unusual degree of either cultural or personal deprivation and whose process of character formation therefore seems unusually deformed. In giving mercy to such a defendant we recognize that all citizens in our society do not have equal opportunities to become good; to see this is to see something true about our world, and to acknowledge incentives to change it.

It has recently been argued that those who admit the narrative voice of the defendant in a criminal trial must, in all consistency, admit the narrative voice of the victim, in the form of a "victim impact" statement.[99] Is this true? The claim is that if the defendant has a chance to bid for the sympathy of the judge or jury, the victim should have an equal chance – and the victim is often no longer around to tell his or her own story. It is simply arbitrary politics to admit the one story and to exclude the other.

This argument is not convincing. A criminal trial is about the defendant and the crime he or she has committed. The question before the court is what the defendant did; the function of narrative is to illuminate the character and origins of that deed. What has to be decided is not what to do about the victim but what to do about the defendant. Everything about the victim that is relevant to the crime is already included in the evidence – including not only the immediate impact of the defendant's actions on the victim but also such further consequences as whether the victim ultimately died. For this we do not need a victim impact statement. Furthermore, in the penalty phase of a trial the sentencing guidelines direct the judge's or jury's attention to certain further facts about the victim. In sentencing a defendant convicted of blackmail, for example, the judge is instructed by the Federal Sentencing Guidelines to consider whether he or she preyed on an "unusually vulnerable victim."[100] This seems relevant to assessing the defendant's crime because it sheds light on the level of malice involved in the crime. But why should we go beyond this? There is no requirement that narratives be symmetrical in the sense that Gewirtz suggests because a criminal trial is not symmetrical: It is focused from the start on the fate of the defendant.[101]

What more might we hope to gain from the victim impact statement? Such statements typically shed light on the upstanding nature of the victim, and they elicit

---

99 See Paul Gewirtz, "Victims and Voyeurs," in *Law's Stories: Narrative and Rhetoric in the Law*, ed. Peter Brooks and Paul Gewirtz (New Haven: Yale University Press, 1996), 135–61.

100 See *United States v. Lallemand*, 989 F.2d 936 (7th Cir. 1993), where Judge Posner argues that a married homosexual is an "unusually vulnerable victim," given the current level of prejudice against gays in American society.

101 See Susan Bandes, "Empathy, Narrative, and Victim Impact Statements," *University of Chicago Law Review* 63 (1996), 361–412.

sympathy in ways closely related to the victim's social class and character, treating the well-placed and the homeless or outcast victim differently. They also focus on the pain and suffering of children or relatives – thus skewing the process in favor of people who happen to have families and against those who are alone. In both of these ways the process treats victims unequally, in a manner that is repugnant to our democratic traditions, according to which the rich and the poor, the married and the unmarried, the well housed and the homeless, should stand as equals before the law. Nor is it fair that a defendant should fare worse because he happens to kill a rich person: Such bias is endemic in criminal trials anyway, and it should be the business of the legal system to counteract it, not to magnify it.

Susan Bandes has raised a further issue in her excellent article, "Empathy, Narrative, and Victim Impact Statements." In the penalty phase of a criminal trial, it is usually difficult for the judge or jury to have sympathetic understanding of the defendant, who has not only been convicted of a serious offense but is likely to be from a different socioeconomic milieu from that of the jurors. By contrast, "the feeling of identification with the victim of a crime often comes naturally," because most people readily fear being in similar circumstances.[102] The introduction of victim impact statements does not simply add one more voice, thus completing the jury's understanding. More often, it provides a distraction from the difficult task of understanding the defendant, diverting the jury into a perspective on the events that is much easier for them to assume and that may block their attempt to understand the defendant. As Bandes concludes, "It is the defendant who is at a disadvantage, and who needs rules and structures to enable the jury to make the empathetic connection with him" (403). I conclude, with Bandes, that we should admit all evidence about the victim that is relevant to establishing what happened and what the defendant did – and then no more. In the penalty phase, the jury or judge should turn to the difficult task of understanding the character of the criminal, because the penalty phase is about his fate. The additional information imported by victim impact statements seems to function primarily by giving vent to the passion for revenge against such offenders, and it is this passion that, as I have argued, the criminal justice system should seek to counteract.

Feminist political thought

It is now time to return to Andrea Dworkin, and to feminism. Dworkin's novel *Mercy* has been in the background throughout this chapter, providing us with a striking modern example of the strict retributivist position, and showing us how the retributive imagination is opposed to the literary imagination. But Dworkin's book is, after all, called a novel. And so one might well wonder how I can so easily say that the novel as form is a construction of mercy.

---

102 Ibid., 400 (citing psychological literature).

The problem is only apparent. For Andrea Dworkin's "novel" is formally not a novel but an antinovel. By the author's deliberate design, it does not invite its reader to occupy the positions of its characters, seeing their motivations with sympathy and with concern for the entire web of circumstances out of which their actions grew. It does not invite its reader to be emotionally receptive. In the case of its central figure it does do this to a limited degree. But this figure is such a solipsistic self-absorbed persona that to identify with her is to enter a sealed world of a peculiar sort, a world in and from which the actions of others appeal only as external movement, without discernible motive. And as for the men who people the novel, the reader is enjoined to view them as the narrator views them – as machines that produce pain. We are forbidden to have an interest in their character, origins, motives, points of view. We are forbidden all sympathy and even all curiosity. We are refused perception of the particular – for, as in the male pornography that Dworkin's activism opposes,[103] her male characters are not particulars but generic objects. In effect, we are refused novelistic readership.

Indeed, the very form of Dworkin's work causes us, as readers, to inhabit the retributive frame of mind and to refuse mercy. The inclination to mercy is present in the text only as a fool's inclination toward collaboration and slavery. When the narrator, entering her new profession as a karate-killer of homeless men, enunciates "the political principle which went as follows: It is very important for women to kill men,"[104] a voice within the text suggests the explanations that might lead to mercy. As the return of the narrator quickly makes clear, this is meant to be a parody voice, a fool's voice, the voice of a collaborator with the enemy:

> He didn't mean it; or he didn't do it, not really, or not fully, or not knowing, or not intending; he didn't understand; or he couldn't help it; or he won't again; certainly he will try not to; unless; well; he just can't help it; be patient; he needs help; sympathy; over time. Yes, her ass is grass but you can't expect miracles, it takes time, she wasn't perfect either you know; he needs time, education, help, support; yeah, she's dead meat; but you can't expect someone to change right away, overnight, besides she wasn't perfect, was she, he needs time, help, support, education; well, yeah, he was out of control; listen, she's lucky it wasn't worse, I'm not covering it up or saying what he did was right, but she's not perfect, believe me, and he had a terrible mother; yeah, I know, you had to scrape her off the ground; but you know, she wasn't perfect either, he's got a problem; he's human, he's got a problem. (329)

---

103 James Lindgren, "Defining Pornography," *University of Pennsylvania Law Review* 141 (1993), 1153–1275, has shown that none of the standard definitions of pornography work very well in separating feminist fiction from pornography if (as MacKinnon has urged – see chap. 8, this volume) the test is applied to passages taken out of context of the whole work. MacKinnon's and Dworkin's definition worked better than others in one test to separate Dworkin's own fiction from pornography, but only because Lindgren selected a rare Dworkin passage in which the woman is in control of what happens and is not subordinated. When he chose a nonconsensual episode from *Mercy*, it was judged more pornographic (by the Dworkin/MacKinnon definition) than other materials in the test (1201–2, 1242–3).

104 *Mercy*, 328.

The only alternative to the retributive attitude, Dworkin implies, is an attitude of foolish and hideous capitulation. According to Dworkin, the style of perception characteristic of the novel is in league with evil.

There are some reasons to think this a psychologically accurate portrayal of the ways in which women who are repeatedly brutalized by men lose the ability to see particularity and to give and receive love; as the novel's amorphous sentences show, they may even lose the ability to grasp causal connections and temporal sequence.[105] Read in that way, the novel would be profoundly tragic, for it would tell us that there are things that happen to people that do in fact destroy the world.[106] But it remains unclear whether this is the spirit in which the novel is written. Its double ending, in which Andrea both immolates herself and dedicates herself to revenge on homeless men, does not clarify the stance of the authorial presence, and a plausible reading of the text as it stands is that the projects of revenge are endorsed as an appropriate, rather than a tragic, response to the evils that Andrea has suffered. Probably it is supposed to be both, and the tragedy lies in the fact that women are in a position where only the retributive response is appropriate, if one does not commit suicide. But such a despairing depiction of our situation obscures prospects of progress and reconciliation that we need to be able to contemplate if we are to take political action to right these wrongs.

Because the emotional and political stance of the novel as a whole remains so unclear, the novel seems to me not entirely successful. And yet it is in another way an important book – for it brings to the surface for scrutiny the strict retributive attitude that animates some portions of our moral and legal tradition and allows us to see this attitude as a reasonable response to terrible wrongs. Dworkin is correct in stressing the pervasiveness of male violence against women, and correct, too, in insisting that to deny and conceal these wrongs is to condemn women of the present and future to continued bodily and psychological suffering. She is correct in protesting loudly against these wrongs and in refusing to say that they are not wrongs. The only remedy, Dworkin (or at least her heroine) suggests (if one does not commit suicide), is to refuse all sympathy and all particular perception, moving over to a conception of justice so resolute in its denial of particularity that it resembles Anaximandrean *dikê* more than it resembles most modern retributive schemes. The narrator announces, "None of them's innocent and who cares? I fucking don't care." And it is Dworkin's position, repeatedly announced in the novel as in her essays, that the social norms of the American heterosexual male are in some ways those of a rapist, and that, to the extent that society endorses these norms, rape is not abnormal but "normal" heterosexual intercourse. This does not mean that there are no individual exceptions, but it does mean that the norm itself is guilty *and* that it is

---

105 Miriam Hallbauer, a University of Chicago law student who worked with battered women who had committed crimes of violence against their abusers, wrote an impressive paper demonstrating these connections, from which I have learned much.

106 See, in this connection, Elaine Scarry, *The Body in Pain: The Making and Unmaking of the World* (New York: Oxford University Press, 1985).

appropriate to act politically against that generalized target. In this sense, there really is no difference between him and him, and to refuse to see this is to collaborate with evil.

But Dworkin is wrong. Retributivism is not the only alternative to cowardly denial and capitulation.[107] Seneca's *On Anger* is hardly a work that denies evil where it exists: Indeed, it is a work almost as relentlessly obsessed with narrating tales of evil as is Dworkin's work. Like Dworkin's work, it insists on the pervasiveness of evil, the enormous difficulty of eradicating it, the necessity of bringing it to judgment. Mercy is not acquittal. In what, then, does its great difference from Dworkin's work consist? In two things, I think. First of all, it does not exempt itself. It takes the Dworkin parody line, "She wasn't perfect either," very seriously, urging that all human beings are the products of social and natural conditions that are, in certain ways, subversive of justice and love, that need slow, patient resistance. And this interest in self-scrutiny already gives it a certain gentleness, forces it out of the we/them mentality characteristic of retributivism. Second, it is really interested in the obstacles to goodness that Dworkin's narrator mocks and dismisses – the social obstacles, deeply internalized, that cannot be changed in an instant, the other more circumstantial and particular obstacles that stand between individuals and justice to those they love. It judges these social forces and commits itself to changing them, but, when judgment on the individual is concerned, it yields in mercy before the difficulty of life. And if you really open your imagination and heart to admit the life story of someone else, it becomes far more difficult to finish that person off with a karate kick. In short, the text constructs a reader who, while judging justly, remains capable of love.

Feminist thought should retain those complex capacities: It should not ignore the evidence, or fail to say that injustice is injustice, evil evil[108] – but, drawing on the resources of the novelist's art, it should remain capable of *suggnômê* and therefore of *clementia*.

Toward the end of his address to Nero Caesar, Seneca asks the young man a pointed question: "What ... would living be if lions and bears held the power, if serpents and all the most destructive animals were given power over us?" (*Clem.* I.26.3) These serpents, lions, and bears, as Seneca well knows, inhabit our souls – in the form of our jealous angers, our competitiveness, our retributive harshness.[109] These

---

107 One might argue that Dworkin's style of retributivism, even if not morally precise, has strategic value, in publicizing the pervasiveness of harms done to women. There is some truth in this. See chap. 9, this volume. But there are dangers: In equating justice with a permanent state of hostility, Dworkin obscures possibilities for progress and education.

108 Contrast Dworkin, *Mercy*, 334, where, in an epilogue entitled "Not Andrea," a liberal feminist attacks Andrea Dworkin as "a prime example, of course, of the simple-minded demagogue who promotes the proposition that bad things are bad."

109 For Seneca's use of this animal imagery elsewhere, see Nussbaum, "Serpents in the Soul: A Reading of Seneca's Medea," in Nussbaum, *Therapy*, chap. 12. On related imagery in Lucretius, see Nussbaum, *Therapy*, chap. 7.

animals are as they are because they are incapable of receiving another creature's life story into their imagination and responding to that history with gentleness. But those serpents, lions, and bears in the mind still play a part today, almost two thousand years after Seneca's treatise was written, in determining the shape of our legal institutions – as the merciful attitude to punishment still comes in for ridicule, as the notion of deliberation based on sentiment still gets repudiated and misunderstood, as a simple form of retributivism has an increasing influence on our legal and political life. With Seneca, I argue that we should oppose the ascendancy of these more obtuse animals[110] and, while judging the wrong to be wrong, still cultivate the perceptions and capacities of mercy.

---

110 Cf. also *De Clementia* I.17.1: "No animal has a more troublesome temperament, none needs to be handled with greater skill, than the human being; and to none should mercy more be shown."

Chapter 2

Explanation and Condemnation

Ward E. Jones

Editor's Introduction

Ward E. Jones discusses explanatory strategies endorsed by Raimond Gaita and Martha Nussbaum that allegedly weaken our need to condemn in order to make explicit what sorts of things would have to be true for the proverb "*tout comprendre, c'est tout pardonner*" ("to understand all is to forgive all")' to contain at least the seed of truth. In Jones's words, 'It is a philosophical and legal truism that what kind of explanation we offer of [someone's] behaviour will affect the kind of judgement that we make of [that person] in virtue of that behaviour, but *which* explanatory strategies have *which* effects, and why?' Jones's focus is on condemnatory attitudes rather than on condemnation itself, for his concern is to analyse some of the modes of understanding that would incline us to lessen the strength of the reactive attitude of condemnation. Following Socrates, Gaita argues that evil emerges out of ignorance and he thinks that understanding this should incline us to judge perpetrators less harshly than we otherwise would. Nussbaum, on the other hand, following Seneca, argues that sensitivity to human vulnerability to adverse circumstances will incline us to be more merciful towards perpetrators than we would otherwise be. Jones, without committing himself to either explanatory strategy, gives us reasons for thinking that, if we adopt their explanatory strategies, then the attitudes towards condemnation that they recommend would follow. So, it does seem that at least with regard to some possibly better forms of understanding, understanding is in tension with condemnatory judgement.

* * *

The origin of the French proverb '*tout comprendre, c'est tout pardonner*' ('to understand all is to forgive all') is uncertain. Its earliest known appearance in exactly these words is in a Russian novel, Tolstoy's *War and Peace*.[1] The proverb is sometimes attributed to Madame de Staël, but she had written something slightly different: '*tout comprendre rend très-indulgent*' ('understanding everything makes one very charitable').[2] De Staël may have been inspired by Goethe, who twenty

---

1   Leo Tolstoy, 1868, Chapter 28.
2   *Corinne*, 1807.

years earlier had written '*was wir verstehen, das können wir nicht tadeln*' ('what we understand we cannot reproach').[3]

My suspicion is that, like all good proverbs, this one – along with its earlier historical variants – contains an important truth, hidden in both simplification and exaggeration. As a first stab – which we will subsequently need to modify – we can say that this proverb and its variants all make the following claim:

> [T]   There is a tension between, on the one hand, understanding or explaining someone's wrongdoing, and, on the other, condemning her for it.

I take [T] to be a contingent claim about our moral psychology, and as such must in the end be supported or falsified by empirical work.[4] However, just as in any other area of our contingent moral psychology, there is room here for non-empirical discussion. In particular, a certain amount of theoretical work is required to find a plausible way of describing the phenomenon at hand. It is a philosophical and legal truism that what kind of explanation we offer of Jones's behaviour will affect the kind of judgement that we make of Jones in virtue of that behaviour, but *which* explanatory strategies have *which* effects, and why?

This paper is intended as a start on the descriptive project of finding a more precise statement of [T], as well as its sources. In the first half of this paper, I will argue that the tension is this: *improving* one's understanding of someone's wrongdoing is likely to result in an abating of our *negative moral sentiments* towards the wrongdoer. Drawing from work by Raimond Gaita and Martha Nussbaum, I will outline two ways in which understanding of moral wrongdoing can be improved. While I will not defend either account of moral wrongdoing, I will argue that we can expect both ways of improving an explanation of a wrongdoing to lessen the explainer's condemnatory attitudes towards a wrongdoer.

1. The Tension: Understanding and the Reactive Attitudes

I take it that any tension that exists between understanding and condemnation is a tension between attitudes: one or more of the ways in which we gain an *understanding* of someone's wrongdoing lead us away from having an unequivocal or unambiguous *condemnatory attitude* towards her for what she has done.

On the one side of the tension is understanding. *Explaining* and *understanding* are interdependent notions: to explain ϕ to someone (including oneself) is to attempt to increase her understanding of ϕ. A successful explanation increases someone's understanding of ϕ by informing her of some aspect of why ϕ occurred. I will be concerned solely with explanations of human behaviour, although the phenomenon

---

3   *Torquato Tasso*, 1790.

4   Other writers in this collection take the tension to be a normative phenomenon, e.g., that the more one understands, the less *reason* one has to condemn.

at hand may be applicable to nonhuman behaviour, or to mental states like beliefs, desires, or intentions.

On the other side of the tension are the various emotional attitudes that we have in response to another person's wrongdoing. A number of writers, beginning in recent years with P.F. Strawson, have emphasized the ethical importance of our emotional responses to another person's behaviour – the so-called 'reactive attitudes' or 'moral sentiments'.[5] A condemnatory moral sentiment is an emotion that arises when a moral expectation that we have of someone is violated. When the violator is myself, I may feel *guilt*, *shame*, or *remorse*; when the violator is someone else, I may feel *indignation* or *disapprobation*.

My condemnatory emotion towards you incorporates a *moral judgement* of you for what you have done. As R. Jay Wallace writes:

> The reactive emotions have the backward-looking focus characteristic of the attitude of blame, and their connection with moral expectations one accepts properly situates blame in the nexus of moral obligation, right, and wrong.[6]

When, for example, I feel indignation towards you given something you have done, the content of that emotion both (i) is targeted at you as *responsible* for the wrongdoing and (ii) involves a *moral criticism* of you.

While we might be able to *imagine* creatures who judge without feeling the condemnatory attitudes, our disposition to the condemnatory emotions is a central feature of our moral lives. As William Neblett writes, in his discussion of indignation,

> Feeling (other-regarding) feelings of indignation over injustices suffered by others is a symptom of sympathetic concern for others, and in general, of a special sensitivity to matters of morals. Feeling (self-regarding) feelings of indignation over wrongs we ourselves suffer is central to a proper sense of dignity and self-respect.

And later, he adds,

> Certainly, an individual absent of all moral anger and indignation must be indifferent to the existence of moral evil, must be absent of all moral sensitivity.[7]

Condemnatory attitudes like indignation represent one mode of identifying someone as accountable for a moral transgression; without them, our ethical personalities would be very different indeed.

---

5 'Freedom and Resentment', 1962, reprinted in Gary Watson (ed.) *Free Will*, Oxford: Oxford University Press, 1982, pp. 59–80.

6 *Responsibility and the Moral Sentiments*, Cambridge, MA: Harvard University Press, 1996, pp. 82–3.

7 'Indignation: A case study in the role of feelings in morals', *Metaphilosophy*, 10, April 1979, p. 139 and p. 140.

As I conceive of them, the condemnatory attitudes are laid out on a spectrum of strength, in terms of how strongly they lead us to want to *act towards* the wrongdoer before us. At their weakest, they do not lead us to respond in anyway before the wrongdoer; I will simply *feel* indignation, disapprobation, or some form of righteous anger towards the perpetrator. This may or may not include an inclination to see the wrongdoer suffer; for some reason or another, I may not feel that the wrongdoer's suffering is appropriate or justified in the light of her wrongdoing. Stronger condemnatory attitudes will incline me to verbally reproach, rebuke, or otherwise censure the wrongdoer. At its strongest, a condemnatory attitude may lead me to make *restitutional* demands of the wrongdoer; I may desire an apology or compensation from her, or I may support her imprisonment or physical punishment. Jeffrie Murphy describes such an emotion, which he calls 'retributive hatred':

> The desire to hurt another, to bring him low, is … sometimes, I suggest, … motivated by feelings that are at least partly *retributive* in nature – e.g., feelings that another person's current level of well-being is undeserved or ill-gotten (perhaps at one's own expense) and that a reduction in that well-being will simply represent his getting his just deserts.[8]

The sort of condemnatory attitude that Murphy describes is *essentially* retributive, and has clear behavioural manifestations. My feeling retributive hatred towards you would involve my undertaking or supporting some form of punishment on your behalf.[9]

Like all mental states, the condemnatory attitudes are at least partly constituted by their manifestations in our behaviour or other mental states, and so I will not distinguish in this paper between the weakening of the manifestations (behavioural or otherwise) of the attitude and the weakening of the attitude itself.

2. *Verstehen* Explanations: Reasons and Identification

Our question is whether there are any explanations of a person's wrongdoing such that when I accept them my condemnatory attitudes are likely to weaken. A basic and undefended assumption of this paper is that there are two ways in which we can explain someone's behaviour, which I will designate using the German words '*erklären*' and '*verstehen*'.[10]

An *erklären* explanation of someone's behaviour involves showing – in accordance with science – that the behaviour instantiates some sort of generalization.

---

8   Jean Hampton and Jeffrie Murphy, *Forgiveness and Mercy*, Cambirdge: Cambridge University Press, 1988, p. 89.

9   My conception of condemnation—allowing as it does for condemnation without action or the desire for suffering—is looser than that found in other contributions to this collection.

10 The philosophical and sociological use of *verstehen* and *erklären*—and related concepts—to pick out two different modes of explanation, stretches back to Wilhelm Dilthey and Max Weber.

Not all *erklären* explanations involve causes; there are *erklären* explanations that cite non-causal correlations. Imagine, for example, someone who adds orange juice to milk, and then explains the result by claiming that the juice of all orange-coloured fruit curdles milk, knowing full well that it is not the *orangeness* of the fruit that causes the curdling of the milk.[11] What makes this person's explanation *erklären* is that it depends upon a generalization; he explains what happens by showing how it instantiates the way of the world.

A *verstehen* explanation of Jones's behaviour, on the other hand, works by making Jones's behaviour appropriate from his point of view; it appeals to what appear to be Jones's own reasons for doing what he did. Just because an explanation cites reasons, however, does not in and of itself make it *verstehen*. The differentiating component of *verstehen* explanations is their lack of dependence upon generalizations. While *erklären* explanations need generalizations, *verstehen* explanations get nothing from them; any generalization that *could* meaningfully be added to a *verstehen* explanation – like 'people tend to act in accordance with their desires' – will be a truism, and thus will add no explanatory power to the explanation.

For some explanatory statements, it will not be clear where they fall in the dichotomy between *verstehen* and *erklären*. On the one hand, when someone says, 'Jones φ-ed because he is selfish', is he saying that 'Jones *tends* to perform selfish acts, and that explains why he performed the selfish act φ' (i.e., an *erklären* explanation), or is he saying something like 'Jones was seeking his own benefit when he φ-ed' (i.e., a *verstehen* explanation)? We would need to know more about the speaker, the hearer, and the context of their interaction, in order to know which interpretation is correct. On the other hand, and as we will see below, an explanation may have both *erklären* and *verstehen* features. However, even in such 'mixed' explanations, *erklären* and *verstehen* elements contribute their explanatory power in very different ways. Introducing an *erklären* element into an explanation of a piece of behaviour works by showing that some aspect of the behaviour instantiates a pattern, while introducing a *verstehen* element works by showing that the behaviour was undertaken because it was, from the agent's point of view, reasonable or appropriate, and does not depend upon any pattern in the world.

I will look at each of these explanatory strategies in turn. In this and the next section, I will focus on *verstehen* explanations, and in Section 4, I will return to explanations with *erklären* elements.

Verstehen explanations and rationalization

Those who write on explanations in the *verstehen* category tend to emphasize one of two characteristics that such explanations apparently possess. Some writers present *verstehen* explanations as 'rationalizing'; offering a *verstehen* explanation

---

11 This example comes from Fred Dretske and Berent Enç's 'Causal Theories of Knowing', *Midwest Studies in Philosophy*, Peter French et al. (eds), Minneapolis: University of Minnesota Press, 1984.

of someone's behaviour involves showing that the actor behaved as he did because he had a reason to do so. Other writers present *verstehen* explanations as involving a process of 'identification' or 'replication'; offering a *verstehen* explanation of someone's behaviour involves seeing the behaviour from the actor's own point of view.[12] I am not here concerned with defending either rationalization or identification as a necessary aspect of *verstehen* explanations. Rather, I will be concerned with showing that *neither* apparent aspect of *verstehen* explanations would, by itself, lead us to expect there to be a tension between offering a *verstehen* explanation of someone's wrongdoing and at the same time condemning her for it.

Many accounts of *verstehen qua rationalizing* explanations claim that such explanations present the agent as behaving because there is some sense in which it is *suitable* or *fitting* for him to do so. This view of mental state explanations has been prominent in influential work from Donald Davidson, Daniel Dennett, and John McDowell. McDowell, for example, claims that propositional attitudes 'have their proper home' in rationalizing explanations, that is, in 'explanations in which things are made intelligible by being revealed to be, or to approximate to being, as they rationally ought to be'.[13] Explicitly contrasting *verstehen* explanations with *erklären* explanations, Phillip Pettit writes that the former include

> ... a norm at which [an agent] aimed, rather than just a datum about how [she behaves] ... the explanandum [is] made intelligible, not by being shown to exemplify the world's regular mode of operation, but by being depicted as something that had to happen if the [agent] was to continue to satisfy the principle that represents its norm.[14]

Each of these writers emphasizes that *verstehen* explanations treat an agent as behaving in such a way because he had reason to do so.

Conceiving of *verstehen* explanations as rationalizing has the consequence that they have a positive partiality inherent in them. In a rationalizing explanation, an agent is said to have behaved in such a way because he *should* – in a minimal sense – have behaved as he did. The qualification 'in a minimal sense' must be added, because an explainer who gives a rationalizing explanation of Jones's behaviour need not *endorse* Jones's behaviour; she need not agree that Jones ought to have behaved as he did. Nonetheless, the explainer must make some sort of positive evaluation of the behaviour. Rationalizing explanations work precisely by showing that the agent's behaviour was, from her point of view, proper.

Bernhard Schlink emphasizes this aspect of *verstehen* explanations in order to diagnose the tension between explaining and condemning. *Verstehen*, Schlink declares, has enough 'positive normative connotation ... to make condemning

---

12 Some writers, like Jane Heal, emphasize both of these features.

13 'Functionalism and Anomalous Monism', in *Perspectives on Actions and Events: The Philosophy of Donald Davidson*, Ernest LePore and Brian McLaughlin (eds), Oxford: Basil Blackwell, 1986, p. 389.

14 'Broad-minded Explanation and Psychology', in *Subject, Thought, and Context*, in Philip Pettit and John McDowell (eds), Oxford: Oxford University Press, 1986, p. 38.

difficult'.[15] The thought here is that the positive partiality inherent in rationalizing explanations, while leaving the explainer plenty of room for *praising* Jones for his behaviour, does not seem to leave as much room for *condemning* Jones; this is because, in the process of offering a rationalizing explanation of Jones's behaviour, we have already established that he saw himself as having a reason to do what he did. Schlink writes that 'once we understand that another person's behaviour *makes sense* in light of our own normative considerations, it becomes, of course, hard to judge his or her behaviour'.[16] As the lens through which we see Jones's action, rationalizing explanations seem to give a head start to a positive judgement of Jones, while a basis from which to reproach Jones looks harder to come by. This, Schlink suggests, is the source of tension [T].

While there seems to be a positive assessment built into *verstehen* explanations, I do not think that this can be the source of our tension. To see this, imagine an agent, Jones, who performs an action, ϕ, which we judge to be a wrongdoing. Perhaps the simplest explanation of Jones's ϕ-ing would portray him as, simply and straightforwardly, *intending* to commit a wrong: Jones's ϕ-ing was a malicious committing of harm. Note that this explanation of Jones's action is a rationalizing explanation, as it presents Jones as intending or desiring harm, and then acting in such a way as to bring that harm about. It recognizes that Jones acted in such a way as to fulfil his (malicious) desires. I will refer to explanations which present an actor as intentionally malicious as '*verstehen*$_M$ explanations'. *Verstehen*$_M$ explanations claim that in full awareness of what he was doing, an agent sought and acted so as to bring about harm.

Verstehen$_M$ explanations are a counterexample to Schlink's suggestion that rationalizing explanations *simpliciter* are in tension with condemnation, for there seems to be no tension whatsoever between offering a basic *verstehen*$_M$ explanation of someone's action and feeling condemnatory emotions towards her. There is nothing in a *verstehen*$_M$ explanation that either detracts from our thinking that the agent is responsible for her action or which would lead us to be compassionate with her. On the contrary, a straightforward *verstehen*$_M$ explanation states that the agent is both responsible and malicious; indeed, that is *all* that a *verstehen*$_M$ explanation tells us, so there is nothing within such an explanation to lessen our condemnatory feelings. So, *pace* Schlink, there is nothing in a rationalizing explanation *per se* that is in tension with condemnation.

Verstehen explanations and identification

Perhaps the other alleged aspect of *verstehen* explanations – as involving 'identification' with the agent – will lead us to predict a tension between understanding

---

15 'Why Understanding?', a public lecture given at the Goethe Institute, Johannesburg, in November 2004. I thank Bernard for sharing a copy of this lecture with me.

16 Schlink, 'Why Understanding?', Section II, emphasis added. Although Schlink uses the neutral word 'judge', it is clear from his paper that by this he means *negative* judgement.

and condemnation. The idea here is that a *verstehen* explanation involves adopting, to some extent, the agent's own attitudes and thought processes. Jane Heal describes the process – which she calls 'replication' – thus: 'I place myself in what I take to be [the agent's] initial state by imagining the world as it would appear from his point of view and I then deliberate, reason and reflect to see what decision emerges.'[17] And Robert Gordon writes that, in essence, the explainer predicts or explains what the agent does by herself 'deciding what to do'.[18] According to this conception of *verstehen*, the *verstehen* explainer explains by having *herself* run through the agent's decision process.

Is the process of identifying with a wrongdoer in tension with condemning her? Again, *verstehen*$_M$ explanations seem to provide us with a counterexample to this suggestion. I can adopt your point of view in my *verstehen*$_M$ explanation of your wrongdoing. That is, I can imagine having your malicious desires, and imagine being confronted with the situation that was in front of you before you committed your wrongdoing. Then, I can deliberate with those desires and perceptions, and decide to commit the same action that you did. Doing so would be a replication of your decision process. However, my running through this replication process does not seem to detract from my inclination to condemn you for your malicious act. I understand why, from your own point of view, you have acted as you did, but it is far from obvious that my doing so will weaken my condemnatory attitudes towards you.

Brian Penrose, a defender of the identification view, writes that 'when we consider what we *would* have done, most of us, I think, find it hard to say with any confidence that we would have [acted] any differently' from a wrongdoer; Penrose adds that an explainer's recognition that he would have done the same as the wrongdoer Jones will weaken his condemnation of Jones.[19] I do not find the second claim obvious; is it really true that my thinking 'there but for the grace of God go I' will weaken my condemnation of a wrongdoer? Even if I agree with Penrose that it would, however, the existence of *verstehen*$_M$ explanations throws significant doubt on Penrose's first thought, namely that understanding a wrongdoing leads me to doubt whether I would have acted differently in the wrongdoer's situation. In a *verstehen*$_M$ explanation, I attribute malicious desires to a wrongdoing agent, and in doing so I discover reasons for her doing what she did. However, it is obvious that I can attribute malicious desires to another agent *without attributing them to myself*. And if this is true, then it follows that I can offer a *verstehen*$_M$ explanation of someone's wrongdoing without thinking that I would have done the same thing in the same situation. If one's explanation of

---

17 'Replication and Functionalism', in Martin Davies and Tony Stone (eds), *Folk Psychology*, Oxford: Blackwell, 1995, p. 47. Originally in J. Butterfield (ed.) *Language, Mind, and Logic*, Cambridge: Cambridge University Press, 1986.

18 Robert M. Gordon, 'Sympathy, Simulation, and the Impartial Spectator', *Ethics* 105, July 1995, p. 733.

19 'Understanding "Understanding" in *The Reader*', Chapter 3 in this volume, Section I.

a wrongdoing is based on desires the wrongdoer has but one does not, then one can explain a wrongdoing while at the same time thinking that in the same situation one would have acted differently. I can learn a great deal about a wrongdoer, in short, while not thinking that I am relevantly like her to have performed the same action.

Improved understanding and the tension

As we have seen, *verstehen*$_M$ explanations provide us with a counterexample to the thought that either rationalizing or identifying with a wrongdoer is in tension with feeling condemnatory attitudes towards her. More importantly, however, *verstehen*$_M$ explanations, which are perfectly *familiar* and *usable* explanations, show us that if there is a tension between understanding and condemnation, it is not *just any* instance of understanding which will create that tension. Rather, the tension must lie between having *improved* understanding – e.g., compared to that achieved with a *verstehen*$_M$ explanation – and condemnatory attitudes; the *better* we understand, the more likely our condemnatory attitudes will weaken. That is, we must change the phenomenon we are looking for into one that is essentially normative:

> [T$_N$] While there may be no tension between accepting a *verstehen*$_M$ explanation of someone's behaviour and condemning her for it, having a *better* understanding of her immoral behaviour will lessen one's condemnatory emotions towards her.[20]

Thus, in order to capture any tension between understanding and condemnation, we need to find ways in which we can improve upon a *verstehen*$_M$ explanation, and we need then to determine whether it is plausible that the condemnatory attitude(s) that we feel towards the agent in virtue of what she has done will be weakened by any of these explanatory improvements. In the next two sections, I will examine two views of the nature of wrongdoing; each gives us a standard according to which one explanation will be better than another, and each, I will suggest, gives us reason to think that my accepting a better explanation of a wrongdoing may indeed weaken my condemnatory attitudes towards a wrongdoer.

3. *Verstehen*$_I$ Explanations: Wrongdoing and Ignorance

Some *verstehen* explanations present Jones's wrongdoing as not being a matter of malicious intent, but rather as the result of Jones's ignorance. Jones threw away Rachael's latest poem, but he did not know that the poem was scrawled on the crumpled piece of paper on the floor. In such cases, Jones's ignorance is seen to *excuse* him – although, as we will see, perhaps not completely – from being guilty of a malicious act. Wallace writes:

---

20 This conception of the tension fits better with two of the quotations with which I began this paper, which make reference to understanding 'all' (*'tout comprendre'*).

> Suppose I do something that happens to be of a kind x [e.g., bring about a harm]. The first class of excuses [i.e., inadvertence, mistake, and accident], defeats a presumption that I did x intentionally, by showing that I did not know that I would be doing something of kind x at all when I chose to do whatever it was that turned out to be of kind x.[21]

The inclusion of this kind of excusing condition portrays the agent's harming not as a consequence of his malicious intent, but the result of an epistemic failure: Jones did not know that his φ-ing might or would result in harm.

Ignorance *verstehen* explanations, or *verstehen*$_1$ explanations, make reference not to Jones's reasons for harming (for he may have had none), but to Jones's reasons for doing something else altogether; perhaps Jones wholly intended to throw the piece of paper away as a part of his larger activity of cleaning the house. Thus, *verstehen*$_1$ explanations *are* a kind of *verstehen* explanation. However, a *verstehen*$_1$ explanation recognizes that Jones did not know (with certainty in some cases, or at all in others) that the harm would result. Jones was not malicious in the harm he brought about; Jones's throwing away Rachael's poem was not intentional.

Introducing the presence of ignorance *may* mean that Jones does not deserve any condemnation; perhaps Jones took every sensible precaution against such harm from occurring, or perhaps he could not have expected such harm to have resulted from his action. But in other cases the presence of ignorance will not let Jones completely off the hook, as Wallace reminds us:

> [Ignorance] may not be accepted [as an excuse] if the ignorance that makes what one did unintentional is itself culpable. In that case, it will be taken not as a valid excuse, but evidence for one of a different family of faults that includes negligence, carelessness, [and] forgetfulness …[22]

Jones did not know that the piece of paper he threw away contained Rachael's latest poem, but he *should* have known that a piece of paper on the floor in her room could be important, or he *should* have checked that there was nothing on the piece of paper before he threw it away. So, while it is true that introducing Jones's ignorance into our explanation of his action leads us to recognize that harming was not something Jones desired or did intentionally, we may reproach him nonetheless: perhaps he should have known that harm could result from his action (i.e., he was culpably ignorant) or perhaps he did know that such harm was *possible*, but he did not take this possibility into account (i.e., he was negligent).

Importantly, even if it does not get Jones completely off the hook, introducing the presence of ignorance changes what otherwise might look to be a malicious action into one that is not malicious. If Rachael thinks that Jones is guilty of negligence or culpable ignorance, then she may feel he deserves her resentment or reproach. However, her resentment will be *less* than it would be were she to believe a *verstehen*$_M$ explanation of Jones's throwing her poem away. In the latter case, Rachael will see

---

21 Wallace, *Responsibility and the Moral Sentiments*, pp. 136–7.
22 Wallace, *Responsibility and the Moral Sentiments*, p. 138.

Jones's action as expressive of an ill will towards her; she will see him as having sought to cause her harm. However, changing her mind to a *verstehen*$_I$ explanation would remove Rachael's thought that Jones had any ill will towards her. So, by attributing an element of ignorance to Jones – that is, by changing her *verstehen*$_M$ explanation into a *verstehen*$_I$ explanation – Rachael's condemnatory attitude towards Jones for what he has done is likely to weaken.

Verstehen explanations of wrongdoings can be divided into *verstehen*$_M$ explanations, in which the agent is said to have intentionally committed a malicious act, and *verstehen*$_I$ explanations, in which the agent is said to have been negligent or ignorant.[23] Furthermore, I have suggested that the latter are going to arouse less strong condemnation – and perhaps no condemnation at all – than the former. If this is right, then we now have one place in which switching from one kind of understanding to another lessens condemnatory attitudes: while *verstehen*$_M$ explanations are not in tension with condemnation, introducing ignorance into our portrayal of an agent's wrongdoing, it seems, is likely to decrease condemnation.

Gaita: the ignorance at the bottom of maliciousness

Drawing a simple division between two categories of *verstehen*$_M$ and *verstehen*$_I$ explanations, and showing that the latter will arouse less condemnation than the former, however, does not establish that [T$_N$] is correct. [T$_N$] says that a *better* explanation leads to weaker condemnatory attitudes. We have established that *verstehen*$_I$ explanations lead to weaker condemnatory attitudes, but we have not yet established that *verstehen*$_I$ explanations are to be preferred over *verstehen*$_M$ explanations.

Raimond Gaita pursues a train of thought, associated with Socrates, that would make *verstehen*$_M$ explanations less desirable than *verstehen*$_I$ explanations.[24] Gaita argues that an act that is apparently malicious will in reality be an act that is done in ignorance of what one is doing. The ignorance Gaita has in mind here is an evaluative ignorance, a lack of understanding of the value of human beings; one could not, he thinks, wholly comprehend 'the preciousness of each individual human being' and at the same time intend to bring about harm to one. Discussing the example of the sadist, someone who 'clear-sightedly' treats evil as an object of 'fascination and desire', Gaita writes:

> Sadists appear to have a refined sense of human dignity and they take self-conscious pleasure in its violation. But that is quite evidently consistent with the Socratic thought that the sense of human dignity that gives pleasure to their cruelty is a false semblance of a genuine understanding of it. If Socrates is right, then the sadist fails fully to understand what he does, just as the ordinary brute does.[25]

---

23 I do not claim that these two categories exhaust all *verstehen* explanations.

24 'Evil Beyond Vice', the second chapter of his *A Common Humanity: Thinking About Love and Truth and Justice* (London: Routledge, 2000).

25 Gaita, *A Common Humanity*, p. 43.

If this is right, then a *verstehen*$_M$ explanation of an act, one which presents the agent as intentionally acting so as to bring about harm, should in reality be a *verstehen*$_I$ explanation, one that acknowledges the agent's ignorance. Following Gaita's Socratic line of thought would mean that we tend to opt for *verstehen*$_I$ explanations as being 'deeper' than *verstehen*$_M$ explanations. The malicious wrongdoer is such because he has not gained or appreciated a fundamental kind of moral or evaluative understanding.

Gaita emphasizes that

> ... this failure of understanding is not of a kind that would interest a court. It would not enable one to enter a plea of diminished responsibility for a crime.[26]

He is right, of course. The sort of ignorance he is describing is not a straightforward excusing condition. The sort of *verstehen*$_I$ explanation he has in mind will not mean that we wholly excuse an agent from responsibility for wrongdoing. Nonetheless, it remains true that seeing the wrongdoer in this light tempers our condemnation of him. This is not merely because – as Gaita is at pains to point out – such understanding serves as a reminder that *we* must treat the wrongdoer himself as precious, but also because it moves the agent's wrongdoing into the realm of a 'lack' in his epistemic character. Accepting a *verstehen*$_I$ explanation in place of a *verstehen*$_M$ explanation involves a change of focus, from malicious intent to epistemic lack, and it is not implausible to think that this change of focus would tend to diminish our urge to condemn him. Such an explanation directs our attention to the type of person the wrongdoer has *not* become, rather than upon the action he has performed. We come to see the agent's wrongdoing as a matter of epistemic shortcoming. As this is the change of view lying behind the whole range of ignorance excuses, it is plausible to think that adopting *verstehen*$_I$ explanatory strategy in lieu of *verstehen*$_M$ strategy will to some extent weaken our condemnatory attitudes towards wrongdoers.

If Gaita is right, then a better understanding of wrongdoing is to be found through a *verstehen*$_I$ strategy than a *verstehen*$_M$ strategy. And as we have seen, there is reason to think that this better strategy tends to weaken our condemnatory reactions to the wrongdoer, that using it will lead us towards weaker condemnatory attitudes than we may otherwise have felt.

While I will not here undertake to defend Gaita's ignorance view of wrongdoing, it seems to me that this is precisely the sort of consideration that we need to support [T$_N$], for it gets us to the claim that better understanding is in tension with condemnation. If we were to *correctly* understand how intentional harms happen, says Gaita, we would see them as at bottom a matter of ignorance, and our condemnatory feelings would weaken as a matter of course.

---

26 Gaita, *A Common Humanity*, p. 43.

4. *Erklären* Explanations

In an *erklären* explanation, a piece of behaviour is explained as being an instantiation of a generalization. Jones, it is said, behaved in a B-like way, because Jones was characterized by C (e.g., has a certain genetic configuration, or a mental illness, or was abused as a child), and people who are characterized by C tend behave in B-like ways. The property of *being-characterized-by-C* tends to be accompanied by the property of *behaving-in-a-B-like-way*. Early in his lecture, Schlink suggests that we could offer an *erklären* explanation of someone's behaviour and still condemn it: 'After having dealt with empirical facts and nothing but empirical facts, we are free to judge and, if appropriate, to condemn.'[27] An *erklären* explanation, Schlink suggests, is not in tension with condemnation.

At the limit of *erklären* explanations, at least, this is not right. To see someone's behaviour *solely* as an instantiation of a generalization is not to see it *as an action*, as something that an agent does intentionally, in pursuit of a goal or in adherence to a norm. But to see a piece of behaviour in this way is not yet to see it in light of which it can be judged at all. It is only when we see the behaviour as being undertaken in fulfilment of some norm or goal, and not just *as a part of the way of the world*, that we have a position from which to speak of the behaviour as appropriate or unsuitable, as good or bad. When we take a solely *erklären* view of a piece of behaviour, it tends to lose its status as something in the light of which anyone deserves judgement, condemnation, or praise. An *erklären*-explicable piece of behaviour is not, by that fact, in the space of reasons, and, accordingly, if I accept a wholly-*erklären* explanation of Jones's behaviour, then I am not likely to feel any condemnatory attitudes towards him. We need to see someone through *verstehen* lens before we feel the moral sentiments towards her.[28]

More commonly, however, an explanation will not be *wholly erklären*, but will be a *verstehen* explanation with *erklären* elements. That is, the explanation will be a *verstehen* explanation in which the agent's action is seen as being causally influenced by non-rational factors. For example, imagine explaining why a teenager hits his little brother. We may offer a simple *verstehen*$_M$ explanation of the teenager's action: he simply wanted to hurt his little brother to see him cry. But perhaps we know more about him. Perhaps we know that he is often hit in a similar way by his father, and we think that such treatment is likely to have causally influenced his own treatment of others. Or, perhaps we know that he has a genetic make-up which makes him susceptible to impulsive behaviour. The result of adding either bit of information would be a mixed *verstehen*/*erklären* explanation, one which includes both kinds of explanatory elements. It is in these sorts of examples – in which intentional actions are influenced by other factors – that we see that there must be no clear boundary

---

27 Schlink, 'Why Understanding?', Section II.

28 The thought of this paragraph has a long pedigree, but the early influential twentieth-century statements of it include G.E.M. Anscombe's *Intention*, Oxford: Blackwell, 1957; Stuart Hamphire's *Thought and Action*, London: Chatto and Windus, 1959; as well as Strawson's 'Freedom and Resentment', 1962.

between *verstehen* and *erklären* explanations of actions. The former often include elements of the latter.

So, while it is clear that accepting a wholly *erklären* explanation will not bring about condemnation, we need to look at 'mixed' explanations, *verstehen* explanations with *erklären* elements, in order to see (1) whether adding *erklären* elements can be seen as an improvement on other explanations, and (2) whether adding *erklären* elements to an explanation will tend to reduce the condemnatory attitudes of those who accept that explanation.

Nussbaum: the necessity of non-rational determination

One of the core points of Nussbaum's 'Equity and Mercy', as I read it, is that the more one examines an individual who commits a wrongdoing, the more one comes to appreciate the role that non-rational determinants play in determining what he has done. In her sympathetic interpretation of Seneca, Nussbaum writes, 'People who do bad things ... are yielding to pressures – many of them social – that lie deep in the fabric of human life',[29] and thus,

> ... the wise person is not surprised at the omnipresence of aggression and injustice, 'since he has examined thoroughly the circumstances of human life' [Seneca, *On Anger*, II.10]. Circumstances ... are at the origins of vice. And when the wise person looks at these circumstances clearly, he finds that they make it extremely difficult not to err. ... Thus aggression and violence grow not so much inside us as from an interaction between our nature and external conditions ...[30]

Nussbaum is here endorsing a phenomenon that most of us will find familiar: looking to a person's upbringing, circumstances, and context can lead us to discover aspects of her past and present context that play a role in determining her behaviour on any one occasion. Importantly, this determination is not a rational determination. Nussbaum's phrases 'yielding to pressures' and 'an interaction between our nature and external conditions' do not describe an agent following reasons; they describe non-rational correlations between our behaviour and the world. To appeal to this sort of determinant in the explanation of someone's behaviour is to introduce *erklären* elements into that explanation.

Nussbaum is not specific about the nature of non-rational determinants of behaviour, nor does she tell us the mechanisms by which they work. I suspect that these omissions are intentional. What determinants I introduce into my explanations will depend upon the 'theory' of behavioural forces with which I work.[31] Some of the generalizations in such a theory will describe *social* influences, like 'in the midst

---

29 Nussbaum, 'Equity and Mercy', (Ch. 1, this volume, p. 17, in *Sex and Social Justice*, Ch. 6, p. 164).

30 Nussbaum, 'Equity and Mercy', (Ch. 1, this volume, p. 18, orig. p. 165).

31 Such a theory may be worked out in detail (e.g., if you are a professional psychologist or sociologist), or it may be held only in vague brushstrokes.

of peer pressure or a crowd, an agent may do things that she would otherwise have avoided as wrong'. Others will be *psychological* or *biological*, as in 'if an agent is under great stress then she is more likely to act in an impulsive, unthinking, or callous way towards other persons' or 'if S was abused as a child, then she is more likely to behave in a callous or less caring way towards other persons'.[32] Indeed, we have every reason to think that our knowledge of the non-rational processes affecting behaviour will continue to change and grow; as, for example, we come to have more *genetic* knowledge of ourselves, we may begin to incorporate such knowledge into our explanations of each other's behaviour.

Whether or not any of the particular generalizations concerning the non-rational determination of behaviour are correct is irrelevant to the points that Nussbaum wants us to take from her discussion. First, she wants us to see that it is inevitable that as one delves deeply into an agent's life, one will come across features of her action for which the agent has no reasons. At some level of description, an agent will be influenced by emotions and tendencies to behaviour which are not, from her point of view, rational or suitable. While a *verstehen* explanation may, in a particular context, be sufficient, an expanded *verstehen* explanation will eventually become a mixed *verstehen*/*erklären* explanation. At some point as I fill out the portrayal of a wrongdoer, I will no longer be able to offer a purely *verstehen* explanation of her behaviour. As I add more and more details in my explanation of the agent's behaviour, I will inevitably make recourse to non-rational determination, and at this point my explanation will become partly *erklären*.

Nussbaum also wants to convince us that, all else being equal, a mixed explanation is going to be a *better* explanation than a purely *verstehen* explanation. As she writes, 'good moral assessment, like good medical assessment, is searchingly particular, devoted to a deep ... understanding of each concrete case'.[33] The mixed *erklären*/*verstehen* explanation is one that 'the wise person' accepts. Lying behind this claim is a view of wrongdoing: 'People who do bad things ... are yielding to pressures', she writes, 'circumstances ... are at the origins of vice.'[34] Just as Gaita thinks that wrongdoing is, at bottom, the result of a certain kind of ignorance, Nussbaum thinks that wrongdoing is *at least partly* the result of non-rational pressures; a more particular explanation of wrongdoing, including *erklären* elements, is going to more accurately represent how the agent came to commit the harm, than one that is wholly and simplistically *verstehen*.

As in my discussion of Gaita in the previous section, I am not here concerned to defend Nussbaum's view of wrongdoing. Rather, I want to return to the question

---

32 Nussbaum speaks about influences in both categories; she writes, for example, of our 'socially taught scheme of values' giving rise to 'diseased passions', like 'excessive attachment to sex' and 'anger and violence connected with sexual jealousy' ['Equity and Mercy', Ch. 1, this volume, pp. 17-18, orig. p. 164].

33 Nussbaum, 'Equity and Mercy', (Ch. 1, this volume, p. 17, orig. p. 164). I have removed the words 'and internal' from this sentence, having discussed identification in the previous section.

34 Nussbaum, 'Equity and Mercy', (Ch. 1, this volume, p. 18, orig. pp. 164–65).

of whether the change of agential explication that Nussbaum advocates will lead to the weakening of my condemnatory attitudes towards her. There are two reasons why one might think that such elements will do so; only one, I will argue, is a good reason.

Non-rational determination and responsibility

Ignorance, we saw in Section 3, is one condition under which we excuse an agent from responsibility. We also excuse an agent in the face of behaviour that she did not initiate and could not prevent. Recognizing this second kind of excuse may lead to the following line of thought. Non-rational determination involves a loss of *control* over one's behaviour; the *passivity* of an agent's behaviour, we might say, is incompatible with her being held responsible for that behaviour. In so far as an explainer sees an agent's behaviour as influenced by non-rational elements, so far will she see the agent's behaviour as having been out of her control. But to see a piece of behaviour as, to some extent, out of one's control is to see it, to that same extent, as not being an action which belongs to the agent. The more I see non-rational elements influencing an agent's behaviour, the less I see her as responsible for that behaviour. Accordingly, and as a result, as I come to see that particular and non-rational causes have influenced an agent's behaviour, my moral sentiments towards her will be weakened.

This line of thought is related to that behind the traditional problem of free will. The *thesis of causal determinism* – which says that any event, including any action of mine, will have been inevitable given the state of the world at some previous time – inspires an image in which we are mere *liaisons* of change, in that while an event may not have arisen without us, we will not hold an originating place in its being carried out. But if such motions are already determined to occur – as the thesis of causal determination tells us – it is perplexing how I can be seen as something that is a source of my bodily movements, for the intuitions associated with the practice of excusing an agent in the face of passivity suggest that seeing someone as an agent of an action involves taking her to be non-passively involved in change. Thus the traditional problem of agency: how, in the face of determinism, can I be picked out as locus of responsibility for any change?

P.F. Strawson famously pointed out that a commitment to the thesis of causal determinism will not block the moral sentiments; even if I believe determinism, I will still respond with emotions like resentment and indignation in the face of wrongdoing.[35] Strawson is surely right in this. However, his point about the inefficacy of the *generalized* thesis of causal determinism upon our moral emotions towards individuals does not change the possibility that when I come to think that particular and non-rational causes have influenced a particular agent's behaviour, this image of the agent's passivity emerges with a force, one might think, that can weaken our moral sentiments. Seeing an individual wrongdoer as having been socially,

---

35 Strawson, 'Freedom and Resentment'.

psychologically, or genetically influenced to behave in the way in which she did, will affect our moral responses to her in a way that the general thesis of determinism cannot. In short, the suggestion that I am now considering is that as we add *erklären* elements to our explanation of a wrongdoing, the agent begins to have less and less salience in our portrayal, and with that disappearance goes our condemnatory attitudes.

This is certainly a sensible suggestion, but it is not right. It is important that the *erklären* feature under consideration here *influences but does not necessitate* the agent's bringing about harm. If it did necessitate her behaviour, then there would be a wholly *erklären* explanation of the behaviour. In this case the wrongdoer would be off the hook completely; she would thereby be shown not to have been in control of her behaviour *at all*. However, we are here concerned with *adding erklären elements* to an account of someone's wrongdoing, that is, we are concerned with non-rational *influences* upon behaviour. Such influences may not, and in many cases will not, be seen as entailing a loss of control. In the situation in which Jones was susceptible to a non-rational influence leading him to wrongdoing, the question is bound to arise as to whether Jones could have prevented himself from acting in the way in which he did. And if we cannot see why this person did not 'control herself' in the face of such an influence, then we may not be inclined to condemn her less.

The American lawyer Alan M. Dershowitz advocates a non-excusing response to many non-rational influences on behaviour in his book *The Abuse Excuse, and Other Cop-Outs, Sob Stories, and Evasions of Responsibility*. For example, Dershowitz disagrees with the 1991 acquittal of a woman (from the charge of assaulting a police officer) on the basis that she was suffering from premenstrual syndrome (PMS), writing:

> Though some women who are irritable and hostile during the premenstrual period of their cycle may well suffer from PMS, the vast majority of women who suffer from PMS do not behave the outrageous way the [woman] in this case did. ... She ought to take responsibility for her own actions.[36]

The last sentence in this passage indicates that while Dershowitz appreciates that PMS can influence a woman's behaviour, he assumes that its influence is controllable, that is, that PMS does not entail its sufferer's complete loss of control. Because of this, he argues, we must condemn behaviour under the influence of PMS no less than that which is under no such influence.

In 'Equity and Mercy', Martha Nussbaum is concerned to have us recognize that erring agents face what she calls *obstacles* to good action.[37] Perhaps the wrongdoer was under great stress, perhaps she was jealously in love, perhaps she was not shown compassion as a child, or perhaps she has a genetic tendency to impulsive behaviour. As the passage from Dershowitz shows, it is not obvious that my recognizing your

---

36 *The Abuse Excuse*, Boston: Little, Brown and Company, 1994, p. 55.

37 'Equity and Mercy' (Ch. 1, this volume, p. 17, orig. p. 164).

obstacles will lessen my condemnatory feelings towards you. Importantly, this is true even *if I have faced the same obstacles*. As Michael Stocker writes,

> ... consider jurors who learn of the difficulties and temptations the defendant faced and remembered that they also faced similar difficulties and temptations. This may increase leniency and mitigation; perhaps these people are moved by thoughts such as: 'There but for the grace of God go I.' But some people become harsher the more they see others as similar to them. Here we might think of those who remember – fiercely, perhaps with pride, perhaps with indignation – that they struggled and overcame their own difficulties without any excuses. They now *demand* the same high performance from others ...[38]

Jones's personal experience with the obstacles that a wrongdoer has faced will not necessarily weaken his condemnation of her, because the process of identifying with her involves Jones's bringing his own past to bear in his judgement of her. Such baggage may mean that Jones, as explainer, feels more condemnation towards the wrongdoer, rather than less.

I introduce the above passages from Dershowitz and Stocker not because I endorse either Dershowitz's view or the view of Stocker's demanding jurors. Rather, I see both as illustrating that non-rational influences upon behaviour may not, and in many cases will not, detract from our moral condemnation of the agent. While it may be true that non-rational *necessitation* of Jones's behaviour *completely* excuses him from condemnation, it does not follow that a non-rational *influence* on Jones's behaviour *partially* excuses him from condemnation.[39]

Pity, compassion, and ambivalence

My condemnatory attitudes towards a wrongdoer will not weaken with my recognition of *just any* non-rational influences. However, it seems likely that they will weaken if the recognition of those influences lead me to have emotions towards the wrongdoer that *conflict* with condemnatory attitudes. If Jones's *erklären* explanation of a wrongdoing leads him to feel pity or compassion towards the wrongdoer, then it is to be expected that his condemnation of the wrongdoer will not be as unambiguous as it would otherwise have been.

We expect conflicting *beliefs* not to exist side-by-side. A rational believer will give up one of a pair of contrasting beliefs, or suspend judgement on both. In contrast, conflicting emotions can exist side-by-side, without any loss of rationality on the part of the emotive agent. In 'Ambivalence and the Logic of Emotion', Patricia Greenspan imagines the following familiar situation:

---

38 'Responsibility and the Abuse Excuse', *Social Philosophy and Policy*, 16(2), 1999, pp. 189–90.

39 For philosophical discussion of this point, see the papers collected in Part II of *Genetics and Criminal Behavior*, David Wasserman and Robert Wachbroit (eds), Cambridge: Cambridge University Press, 2001, especially contributions by Marcia Baron, Patricia Greenspan, and David Wasserman.

Suppose that a friend and I are in competition for some honorific position ... What emotions might I feel, not toward my rival himself, but toward the fact that he turns out to win? I think we might plausibly hold, in some conceivable cases, that I have mixed feelings. I feel both pleased (at least to some extent) and pained – happy 'for' him (as we say) – since I know that he deserves the honour and has been hoping for it, but unhappy on my own account, since my own desire has been frustrated.[40]

Situations like this will be recognizable to all of us, not only in our public careers but in our relationships; think of your feelings towards an ex-partner who excitedly announces to you that he or she is getting married. In such cases, our emotions may be, as Greenspan puts it, 'ambivalent' or 'mixed'; we may find ourselves 'in two minds'. Emotional ambivalence is reflected in our behaviour. We may pause, for example, before congratulating our colleague or ex-partner, or we may be less enthusiastic in our expression of happiness for him.

It is possible to experience a similar ambivalence with our condemnatory attitudes. Condemnatory attitudes conflict with *conciliatory* attitudes like pity, empathy, and sympathy. While the former lead us towards reproach, retribution or punishment, the latter lead us towards amenability, consolation, forgiveness, or mercy. The two kinds of emotions pull in opposite directions. It is clear, however, that both condemnatory and conciliatory attitudes can be held towards the same subject at the same time. When they do so, we can see that the condemnatory attitudes may be weakened by the co-existence of conciliatory attitudes and the contrary feelings and behaviour to which these conciliatory attitudes incline me.

I suspect that this may be the moral psychological feature driving much of 'Equity and Mercy'. As we have seen, Nussbaum's conception of an improved *erklären* explanation involves focus on the 'obstacles' that each of us faces in our lives. Such an explanation provides us with a story, of an agent and her wrongdoing, which involves events that *happened to* her. Sometimes, as we develop a picture of a wrongdoing agent, we will begin to feel conciliatory attitudes towards her. Our feeling pity or compassion will, of course, depend upon what the picture shows us as having happened to the agent. We are perhaps most likely to pity her if she was herself the victim of abuse, malicious wrongdoing, or neglect, but our empathy or sympathy can arise in the face of other facts about her as well; perhaps someone she loved greatly died, or perhaps she has been the victim of a natural happening or some significant piece of bad luck. In the face of such knowledge about a wrongdoer, we may come to feel an emotional ambivalence towards her. On the one hand, we will feel condemnatory emotions towards her in the face of the fact that she intentionally harmed someone else, but on the other hand, we will feel conciliatory emotions towards her in the face of something we have learned about her life.

Perhaps I can pity a person and still wholly condemn her, if I think that what I pity her for has *nothing* to do with what I condemn her for. However, and more often, we will incorporate pity-inducing features of a wrongdoer's life into our

---

40 In A.O. Rorty (ed.), *Explaining Emotions*, Berkeley, CA: University of California Press, 1980, p. 228.

understanding of the agent's behaviour. I take, for example, Jones's childhood abuse to contribute to his tendency to violent action as an adult. The result is a clash between my emotions over Jones's violent behaviour: I feel pity towards him in virtue of his suffering abuse, and yet I also feel condemnation towards him in virtue of his harmful behaviour. An influence upon Jones's behaviour, his past abuse, is something that brings about my compassion. Thus, adding *certain* kinds of *erklären* elements to an explanation of wrongdoing will lead us to feel, at the same time, both conciliatory and condemnatory attitudes towards the wrongdoer, with the overall result that the latter, or the *effects* of the latter, are weakened.

Much of 'Equity and Mercy' is concerned with narratives and their presentation of wrongdoers, and Nussbaum is explicit in endorsing narratives that lead to conciliatory attitudes. At the end of the paper, she describes the sort of explanation she sanctions:

> It is really interested in the obstacles to goodness … It judges these social forces … but, where judgement on the individual is concerned, it yields in mercy before the difficulty of life. This means that it can be in its form a powerful work of narrative art. If you really open your imagination and heart to admit the life story of someone else, it becomes far more difficult to finish that person off with a karate kick. In short, the text constructs a reader who, while judging justly, remains capable of love.[41]

I am suggesting that the best way to understand the reader Nussbaum describes in the final sentence of this passage is 'emotionally ambivalent', caught between feeling as if she should condemn the wrongdoer, on the one hand, and 'loving' her, on the other.

Nussbaum predicts that some narrative art will embody the sort of explanation that she endorses, a prediction that is borne out perhaps most strikingly in narratives that are concerned to portray real wrongdoers. Several biographical films in recent years have presented the lives of real wrongdoers in such a way that while we have no inclination to excuse the wrongdoer, many viewers do find themselves with conciliatory attitudes towards him or her. *Dance With A Stranger* (dir. Mike Newell, 1985), *Dead Man Walking* (dir. Tim Robbins, 1995), and *Monster* (dir. Patty Jenkins, 2003) portray non-excusing, detailed accounts of intentional wrongdoings – all three films are about murderers. It is, of course, by no means necessary that a viewer will respond to these narratives with emotional ambivalence, but I suspect that such a response was the aim of some or all of the writers and directors involved. Nussbaum, I suspect, would approve of all of these films; they each bear the mark of their makers' compassion for their subjects.[42]

---

41 Nussbaum, 'Equity and Mercy', (Ch. 1, this volume, p. 41, orig. p. 183).

42 Bernard Schlink portrays such an emotional tension in his novel *The Reader*. Watching Hanna's trial, Michael feels an intense contempt for her wrongdoing, but as he comes to realize the effect that her illiteracy has had on her, this contempt becomes mixed with a pity towards her. Above all else, *The Reader* is about the pitiable circumstances involved in human wrongdoing, and the mixed emotions that we can feel when we are learn about them.

5. Conclusion

I have been concerned with the nature of, and the possible sources of, a tension between understanding a wrongdoing and condemning an agent for it. In Section 2, I claimed that *verstehen*$_M$ explanations – which are not in tension with condemning a wrongdoer – provide evidence for concluding that if there is a tension, then it lies not between *any* explanation and condemnatory attitudes, but between *better* explanations and condemnatory attitudes. In order to discover candidates for a 'better explanation of a wrongdoing', I turned in the next two sections to look at two conceptions of wrongdoing; any theory of wrongdoing is going to give us a standard by which to judge an explanation of a wrongdoing as better or worse.

First, we saw that Raimond Gaita argues that ignorance is at the bottom of malicious wrongdoing; this entails that *verstehen*$_I$ explanations are better than *verstehen*$_M$ explanations. Secondly, we saw that Martha Nussbaum argues that wrongdoing will, at least partly, be the result of non-rational influences; this entails that explanations of wrongdoings that include certain *erklären* elements will be better than those that do not.[43] The work of both authors suggest that a purely *verstehen*$_M$ explanation is in an important way incomplete, that an understanding that allows us to see an act as malicious is necessarily oversimplified. Neither author, however, defends a purely *erklären* explanation of wrongdoing. On Gaita's picture of wrongdoing, I have suggested, a *verstehen*$_I$ explanation will be an improvement over a *verstehen*$_M$ one, while on Nussbaum's picture of wrongdoing, *verstehen* explanations will be improved by introducing *erklären* elements.

Although I have defended neither Gaita's nor Nussbaum's conception of wrongdoing, I find it plausible that accepting certain explanations of either kind will result in my experiencing weakened condemnation. Were I to follow Gaita, and change my view of wrongdoers from seeing them as malicious to seeing them as ignorant, it seems likely that it this will, indeed, bring about a weakening of my condemnatory attitudes towards them. Were I to follow Nussbaum, and incorporate the circumstances of wrongdoers' lives into my explanation of their wrongdoings, it seems likely that my doing so will similarly result in my pity, empathy, or sympathy towards them; such emotions would, I suspect, weaken my condemnatory attitudes towards wrongdoers. Both of these claims are conjectures, however, and empirical work will be needed to establish that either tendency to weaker condemnation holds.

My conclusion is, in sum, a conditional whose consequent is speculative: *if* either Gaita's or Nussbaum's respective views of wrongdoing is correct, then it *looks* as if there is a tension between having better understanding of someone's wrongdoing and holding condemnatory attitudes towards her.

I began with a French proverb and its variants. I have not yet established that they hold any truth, but if I have been right in this paper, then we know a bit more about

---

43 I take it that these two views of wrongdoing are not mutually exclusive, but I will not defend this here.

what we need to establish in order to discover what truth, if any, this proverb and its variants contain, and why.[44]

44 Thanks to Thad Metz, Mac Rebennack, Pedro Tabensky, Samantha Vice, and the members of an audience at the University of Oklahoma.

Chapter 3

Understanding 'Understanding' in *The Reader*

Brian Penrose

Editor's Introduction

In Brian Penrose's words, '*properly understood*, there is something noble and good about "understanding", and base, oversimplified, and often mean-spirited about "judging"'. But, how should we properly understand 'understanding' and 'judging' in this context? Using *The Reader* as a case study, Penrose concludes that the relevant sort of understanding is a state that lessens our need to judge harshly. Understanding, in this sense, is a kind of sympathetic identification with the perpetrator; Hanna, in the case of *The Reader*. When sympathetic identification fails, when we are unable to put ourselves in the shoes of a perpetrator, we are more easily able to judge, in the relevant sense. Judging, in this sense, performs the opposite function to understanding; it stops us from putting ourselves in the shoes of a perpetrator. So, understood thus, there is indeed a tension between judging and understanding. However, that we are invited by *The Reader* to sympathetically put ourselves into Hanna's shoes does not mean that, if we take up the invitation, we would be unable to judge Hanna for her crimes. We are able to judge her and her deeds negatively, while at the same time sympathetically acknowledging that it is not unlikely that we would have acted similarly in analogous circumstances. The mere fact that we could have acted like her in analogous circumstances does not mean that no crime has been committed, but it does predispose us not to be so harsh in our affective reaction to the crime. The reason we can simultaneously condemn and sympathetically identify, without contradiction, is that two different understandings of 'understanding' are at stake. We can recognize that Hanna did something terrible and judge her accordingly: 'Hanna', we could say, 'has committed a condemnable act and these acts reflect basic condemnable character flaws'. But, at the same time, we can claim that 'I cannot be completely certain that I would not have acted as Hanna did were I in her shoes. She did something terrible, but I can identify with the vulnerabilities that led her to do what she did.' Notice also that this second variety of understanding, understanding entailing sympathetic identification, depends on the first variety, for we must be able to recognize an act or person as condemnable in order to understand in the second sense. Ward Jones's and Marc Fellman's contributions reach conclusions which are relevantly similar to Penrose's.

* * *

One of several philosophically fascinating themes in Bernhard Schlink's *The Reader* is the tension experienced by its protagonist, Michael Berg, between what Pedro Tabensky has called 'judging' and 'understanding'.[1] This tension is most clearly and concisely captured in the following passage:

> I wanted simultaneously to understand Hanna's crime and to condemn it. But it was too terrible for that. When I tried to understand it, I had the feeling I was failing to condemn it as it must be condemned. When I condemned it as it must be condemned, there was no room for understanding. ... I could not resolve this. I wanted to pose myself both tasks – understanding and condemnation.[2]

In particular, as this passage makes clear, it is *condemnatory* judging that is in tension with 'understanding'. Michael's condemnation of Hanna for her having joined the SS in World War II some years previously, and having participated in one particular episode of apparently monstrous cruelty during the war, dissipates in light of various pieces of knowledge and insight that he gains about her, and her circumstances, in the course of her trial for her role in this episode. This 'understanding' makes it impossible for him to 'judge' or 'condemn' her for what she's done, and when he 'condemns' her, the 'understanding' vanishes.

The novel does not merely explore this tension; it also takes a favourable normative stance to such dissipation of condemnatory judgement, and in his presentation at a conference devoted to discussion of this tension, Schlink, himself, confirmed this reading of *The Reader*.[3] But this normative attitude was not universally held amongst the conference participants, however, and it is clear, in any case, that a number of eminently reasonable normative questions arise in considering this tension. Among the sorts of worries that arose, either in essays or in discussion, were these: *should* we try to understand someone–Hanna, say–when they have done horrible things. Won't we lose our critical moral faculties and allow wrongdoing to go unpunished, or even unacknowledged as wrongdoing. Won't we come to think things are 'okay' when, morally speaking, they're anything but 'okay'? Perhaps there are moral *requirements* upon us to judge those things that should be judged, and *not* to understand them.[4]

My own view is similar to *The Reader*'s on the normative questions. I share the sense which I take the book to encourage, that, *properly understood*, there is something noble and good about 'understanding', and base, oversimplified, mean-spirited,

---

1   My initial interest in this topic dates back to a paper that Tabensky presented in February 2003 at the University of Pretoria, in which he uses these terms. Two descendants of that paper are 'Judging and Understanding', *Law and Literature*, 16(2), 2004, pp. 207–28, and his contribution to the present volume.

2   Bernhard Schlink, *The Reader*, Carol Brown Janeway (trans.), London: Phoenix House, 1997, p. 156.

3   'Why Understanding?', presented at a conference held at the Goethe Institute, Johannesburg in November, 2004.

4   I allude to and discuss some published critiques of *The Reader*'s and Schlink's normative attitude toward judging and understanding in Section III below.

and sometimes even cowardly about 'judging'.[5] And whether such an assessment of 'understanding' is plausible and defensible is, I think, a normative question of great interest and importance. But my purpose in what follows is somewhat more pedestrian. For in thinking on and off about 'judging and understanding' since my initial exchange with Tabensky, I've found myself tripping over the question of just what 'judging' and 'understanding' *are* exactly. On the one hand, they seem to be kinds of things we *do*: Michael Berg *tries* to understand Hanna, and when he succeeds, he *fails* to condemn her actions as he thinks they ought to be condemned. Judging is to *pass* judgement on something, to *formulate* a (moral) belief about something. Judging and understanding are characterized as 'tasks' in the quotation with which we began. 'Understanding' is a way of *coming* to understand. And it is this sense of the words–call it the 'action sense'–which underlies the normative worries I mentioned above.

This essay undertakes to expose and unpack a second sense of the words 'judging' and 'understanding'. In this sense, 'judging' and 'understanding' are not things we *do*, but *attitudinal states* in which we can find ourselves, or, arguably, undertake to place ourselves in. To attempt to understand a wrongdoer and his/her deeds can lead us *into* this attitudinal state of understanding (which I'll henceforth abbreviate as [U]), and we can ask those normative questions raised earlier about whether we ought to try to do that. But while I'll suggest in passing that this is less normatively problematic than those who worry about too much 'understanding' and not enough 'judging' might think, my main occupations will be to tease this second sense of 'understanding' out of *The Reader* and to give it a bit of philosophical location.

There are three main sections to my discussion. I will begin in the next section by looking at a few passages from *The Reader* which, in different ways, bring out the tension and the phenomenon of 'understanding', understood (as it were) as [U]. The second section locates [U] in the context of Peter Strawson's famous discussion of the reactive attitudes. In the third section I will develop and extend some of the observations made in Sections I and II, look at other instances of [U], and connect it to the idea of 'moral complexity'. In so doing I hope to deepen our understanding of 'understanding', and expose some possible misunderstandings of what I take to be Schlink's interest in the tension between judging and understanding.

I

In scrutinizing novels and other art works there is always a danger of over-analysing, of what Wordsworth called 'killing to dissect'. The passage above with which I began is edited, omitting a reference to Michael's need to not betray Hanna all over

---

5   These are my words, not Schlink's. If I'm wrong to attribute this sort of view to *The Reader*, then one can just think of this as one of *my* intuitions about the two ideas. I do think there's plentiful evidence in *The Reader* to support my reading of it, and some will emerge below. But space prevents me from trying to argue for this case here, and it will not be my point to try to do so.

again. There can be no doubt that [U], and its relation to condemnatory 'judging', is interwoven with other features of the novel. Most obviously, of course, is the romantic history of Michael and Hanna, the various feelings Michael still has for Hanna, or consciously doesn't have, and so on. There is also a recurring thread touching on the inter-generational misunderstanding and recrimination which occurred in post-war Germany running throughout *The Reader*. In addition, Michael worries in various places about what amounts to the problem of collective responsibility for the Nazi atrocities. And there is an embedded critique of law, legal thinking, and legal punishment. These various threads interweave with and inform one another in subtle ways, and to that is owed a not insubstantial part of the novel's beauty and complexity.

But since *The Reader* is the source of our current interest in [U], I see no alternative but to make it our first stop in trying to understand what [U] is. Thus, I want to abstract away from its other aspects, and in doing so, I'm aware that I may to some extent be killing to dissect. Before proceeding, however, it is worth noting one point that will facilitate the process of teasing the phenomenon of [U] out of the text of *The Reader*. In the passage cited above, it is *Michael* that finds himself struggling to maintain condemnation in the face of [U], and vice versa. But *we, as readers*, are meant, I think, to experience a similar struggle for ourselves. Our awareness of Hanna's dark past emerges with Michael's awareness, and in the same sharp contrast, felt by Michael, to Hanna-the-lover that we experience with Michael earlier in the novel. So the tension between condemnatory judging and [U] is not merely chronicled or reported therein, but presented in such a way as to allow us to share it directly. We can thus use our own experience of [U] as readers of *The Reader* to help ourselves understand what it is.[6]

These points noted, I want to focus now on two salient clusters of things upon which Michael (and we) pass judgement, and which in distinct though overlapping ways are undermined for Michael (and us) by [U]. The first concerns one of the two main charges Hanna faces: her actions (or, better, her omissions) on the night of the church fire: her refraining from unlocking the doors, rescuing the people in the burning church, and so forth.[7] As the details emerge of what she's refrained from

---

6   An inconvenient upshot of relying on 'our' own reactions to Hanna is that not all readers of the novel will share them, or share them in the same way. Those, for instance, who do not share my positive normative attitude to [U] may not find references in the text below to 'our' reactions to different pieces of information terribly helpful *for them*. Since I *do* have (what I take to be) [U]-like responses though, and since I think that we are *meant* to have them, given Schlink's positive attitude about them, I will continue to speak in terms of how 'we' react when faced with certain portions of text of *The Reader*, what 'our' reactions are, and so forth. This may put those who don't view [U] as favourably as I do at some sort of expository disadvantage, but I don't think it ultimately begs any of the normative questions I alluded to in my introduction.

7   The other main charge was that Hanna had participated in selecting women from the work camp she helped run to be sent back to Auschwitz, where, it was known, they would almost certainly be killed. See *The Reader*, p. 105.

doing that night, and in sharp contrast to the Hanna we've been introduced to in Part I of the book, most of us find ourselves condemning Hanna to some considerable degree. How could she let these people burn (or suffocate) to death, especially given that there was a key? Who could be so callous and monstrous not to take action? What kind of person could she be?

In the face of this, we are presented with Hanna's testimony about the events of that night. It will be helpful to quote this passage (henceforth 'Passage 1') at some length. In response to the judge's question, 'What did you do?', Hanna says the following.

> 'We didn't know what to do. It all happened so fast, with the priest's house burning and the church spire, and the men and the cart were there one minute and gone the next, and suddenly we were alone with the women in the church. They left behind some weapons, but we didn't know how to use them, and even if we had, what good would it have done, since we were only a handful of women? How could we have guarded all those women? A line like that is very long, even if you keep it as tight together as possible, and to guard such a long column, you need far more people than we had.' Hanna paused. 'Then the screaming began and got worse and worse. If we had opened the doors and they had all come rushing out ...'.
>
> The judge waited a moment. 'Were you afraid? Were you afraid the prisoners would overpower you?'
>
> 'That they would ... no, but how could we have restored order? There would have been chaos, and we had no way to handle that. And if they'd tried to escape ...'.
>
> Once again the judge waited, but Hanna didn't finish the sentence. 'Were you afraid that if they escaped, you would be arrested, convicted, shot?'
>
> 'We couldn't just let them escape! We were responsible for them ... I mean, we had guarded them the whole time, in the camp and on the march, that was the point, that we had to guard them and not let them escape. That's why we didn't know what to do. We also had no idea how many of the women would survive the next few days. So many had died already, and the ones who were still alive were so weak ...'.[8]

Frustrated and desperate, Hanna concludes all of this by asking the judge–tellingly, and not for the first time–'what would you have done?'[9]

On the first occasion on which Hanna asks the judge this we get the sense that this is not an entirely inappropriate question. But then, and again at the second asking, the judge doesn't respond. Now consider the passage, in the voice of Michael Berg as narrator of the novel, which immediately follows ('Passage 2').

> Not that it was impossible to imagine the confusion and helplessness Hanna described. The night, the cold, the snow, the fire, the screaming of the women in the church, the sudden departure of the people who had commanded and escorted the female guards–how could the situation have been easy? But could an acknowledgment that the situation had been hard be any mitigation for what the defendants had done or not done?[10]

---

8   Ibid., pp. 126–7.
9   Ibid., p. 127.
10 Ibid., p. 128.

Two things interest me about this passage with regard to understanding [U]. To begin, think about the question about mitigation with which Passage 2 ends. The answer here is clearly supposed to be 'no'. It's clearly going to be 'no' in a legal sense; indeed, the very intelligibility of legally passing judgment on people in response to their wrongs, as retributive theory would have us do, seems to be yet another underlying question in the novel. But 'mitigation' has a non-legal meaning here as well, I think. It means roughly 'relaxation, or abandonment of the original judgement of wrongness', in this case the wrongness of Hanna's inaction on the night of the fire. So whatever effect this passage has, or is meant to have on us, it's not that Hanna was to be excused, or that her omission wasn't morally wrong. It's meant to be something distinct from that.

This difference is also reflected in the disparity between Hanna's testimony, and that of the other accused. Book II, Ch. Nine begins with the judge asking 'why did you not unlock the doors?', of each of the various defendants. Here's Michael-the-narrator's description of their answers (Passage 3):

> One after the other, they gave the same answer. They couldn't unlock the doors, Why? They had been wounded when the bombs hit the priest's house. Or they had been in shock as a result of the bombardment. Or they had been busy after the bombs hit, with the wounded guard contingent, pulling them out of the rubble, bandaging them, taking care of them. They had not thought about the church, had not seen the fire in the church, had not heard the screams from the church.[11]

Hanna's own answer begins along analogous lines, though as we've seen, those lines are quickly abandoned. Reports the narrator: "'We were ... we had ....'" Hanna was groping for the answer. "There was no alternative."'[12] In contrast to Hanna's account in Passage 1, these *are* claims of a lack of moral responsibility for what had happened, if not legally, then in some moral sense involving innocence against condemnatory judgement. Whether they ring true or not is another question, though I think they don't, and are intended not to. But what's significant, I think, is not their ring of truth or absence of it, but that even if true, they miss a certain point. The point is that even if they're false, the question of condemnatory judgement is more complicated than either the law, or we as condemners, typically allow.

And that's the second thing I find interesting about Passages 1 and 2 above, and why they're relevant to understanding [U]. The narrator says, 'Not that it was impossible to imagine the confusion and helplessness Hanna described.', and then leads us through his own imaginings (Passage 2), which, presumably, are not that different from our own. And this imagining is what diminishes or dissolves, even if incompletely, our initial condemnatory judgement of Hanna for her inaction. We are invited (particularly in Passage 1) to put ourselves in Hanna's shoes.[13] We are forced

---

11 Ibid., p. 123.

12 Ibid., p. 125.

13 More strongly, given Schlink's favourable attitude to [U], I think we are *expected* to put ourselves in Hanna's shoes here, since I think he *wants* us to experience it ourselves. But

to ask ourselves the question of what we, ourselves, would have done had we been in Hanna's situation. And that's a question distinct from the question of what we *should* have done. And it is different again from the question which the other witnesses (in Passage 3) raise for us, in effect, namely what we *could* have done? When we consider what we *would* have done, most of us, I think, find it hard to say with any confidence that we would have acted any differently than Hanna did.

And this, I think, breaks down a kind of moral barrier between us and Hanna, a moral barrier that is essential to our initial condemnatory judgement. We find ourselves relating to her in a different, more connected way, and it is distinct from both excusing her (because she couldn't help it) and feeling her justified in her action (because there was nothing wrong with it). (When we find ourselves doubting that we *would* have done differently than her, we do not thereby find ourselves doubting that we *should* have done so if we could.)

So we have here one instance of [U] as it appears in *The Reader*, and a mechanism by which it is achieved: the detailed and honest identification with Hanna in the horrifying situation that it actually was. The other example I want to isolate pertains to a second cluster of things about which our condemnation becomes undermined. This cluster concerns more general worries about Hanna, what she's like, her attitude to herself and her actions, and things of that kind. Her decision to join the SS rather than take another job is one element of this cluster. So is her later-revealed failure to have read the charges properly, to have raised objections to things she has signed at appropriate times, and her overruled insistence on having the daughter's book read into the trial proceedings.[14] These things make us worry that, at the very least, she's callous and uncaring, contemptuous about the legal proceedings and thus of the significance of the things she's charged with, and this, of course, gives rise to condemnatory judgement on our part as well. We find ourselves in the grip of some sort of condemnatory feelings towards her, perhaps quite intensely.

The example I have in mind is the remarkable passage where Hanna's illiteracy is revealed. Here's the passage, again in Michael's voice (Passage 4):

Hanna could neither read nor write.

That was why she had had people read to her. That was why she had let me do all the writing and reading on our bicycle trip and why she had lost control that morning in the hotel when she found my note, realized I would assume she knew what it said, and was afraid she'd be exposed. That was why she had avoided being promoted by the tram company; as a conductor she could conceal her weakness, but it would have become obvious when she was being trained to become a driver. That was also why she had refused the promotion at Siemens and become a camp guard. That was why she had admitted to writing the report in order to escape a confrontation with a handwriting expert. Had she talked herself into a corner at the trial for the same reason? Because she couldn't read the daughter's book or the indictment, couldn't see the openings that would allow her

---

this is not essential to the point being made in the text.

14 The daughter alluded to here is one of two survivors of the night in question, who had published a book on the events. See *The Reader*, p. 104.

to build a defence, and thus could not prepare herself accordingly? Was that why she sent her chosen wards to Auschwitz? To silence them in case they had noticed something? And was that why she always chose the weak ones in the first place?[15]

One interesting feature of this passage, which I won't dwell on, is that it begins with a number of revelations about why Hanna had done this or that, and concludes with a number of questions that are less certain. Her illiteracy was 'why', for instance, she had turned down the job at Siemens and become an SS guard instead. And the narrator *wonders* whether, for example, it also explains her talking herself into a corner at the trial, but is less certain than he is about the previous items on the list. Independently of that, some of the things she's done that look differently in light of her illiteracy do not involve matters which have raised our condemnatory hackles. (Though of course their significance for Michael, given his previous relationship with Hanna, is different than for us.) So where there is no condemnatory judgement on our part, [U] does not enter the picture.

But some of the things Hanna had done do lead us to condemn her or her actions, in particular her decision to join the SS rather than take a job at Siemens, and her seemingly contemptuous behaviour at, and attitude towards, her trial, both of which suggest to us a gross lack of moral concern on Hanna's part for her own previous actions. But upon learning that Hanna is illiterate, this changes. Our condemnatory judgements of Hanna which make up the second cluster that I distinguished earlier become diminished. They lose their condemnatory bite, perhaps not entirely, but to some substantial extent at least. We find ourselves in a kind of evaluative ambivalence, not unlike that which Hanna's description of the church-burning night leaves us in. And again, that state does not amount to one in which we think she is either excused, in either the legal or moral sense that she couldn't have done otherwise than she did, or justified, in the sense that there was nothing morally wrong with her choices. We don't find ourselves thinking, for instance, that it wasn't wrong to join the SS, rather than take a job at Siemens. Our evaluation of her and her actions may be lesser; there may be an element of mitigation, just as Michael wants the judge to see that 'she was guilty, but not as guilty as it appeared'.[16] But even if that's true, it's also substantially beside the point. We *feel* differently about whatever remains wrong than we do without the knowledge of her illiteracy, and the imaginative leap to what it must have been like to be her in those various situations that that knowledge inspires. To borrow a phrase that Michael uses in a slightly different context, we find ourselves 'oddly moved'.[17] And to be thus 'oddly moved' is to find ourselves in the state of [U] itself, or so it seems to me.

---

15 *The Reader*, p. 131.
16 Ibid., p. 136.
17 Ibid., p. 133.

II

Thus far I have been trying to tease the phenomenon of [U] out of the actual text of *The Reader* as part of my project of understanding it as an attitudinal state, as distinct from something we do or undertake. I will return to some of the tentative suggestions made above about what that state is (and is not), and about how we arrive at it below. Now, however, I wish briefly to approach this question from a different direction. And it will help us at this point, I think, to look a little more closely at [U]'s complement, condemnatory judging, and to make explicit some features of [U] that have thus far been more or less implicit.[18]

So what is 'judging'? It seems to me that there are two ways in which this idea could be understood. First, there's a sense to which I've already alluded in suggesting that our coming to 'understand' Hanna and her situation does not amount to the abandonment of a moral judgement which we had previously held. 'Judging' in this first sense is the cognitive assent to the claim, 'that was wrong'. Non-cognitivists about moral language may bristle at this perhaps. They think that despite grammatically superficial similarities to non-moral descriptive claims, moral claims are actually not really claims at all, but expressions, prescriptions, projections or something more complex of that sort. But since cognitivism is a possible position, this sense of 'judgement' is a *possible* sense of 'judgement'. So the first way we might understand 'judging' is in this cognitivist way. To judge is to formulate assent to a claim to such and such an effect, and in the case of condemnation, to the effect that such and such is wrong, despicable, monstrous, or whatever.

But I hope it's clear that judging in the dichotomy of judging and [U] is not this. I said, in looking at the first cluster of cases of understanding in *The Reader* that while condemnatory judgement dissolves or diminishes as we put ourselves in Hanna's shoes, our cognitive assent to the claim 'that was wrong' does not. 'Judgement' and 'judging' in that sense is a *conative, attitudinal* or *emotional* state of some sort. It's a way of *feeling* about something, in this case a condemnatory *feeling* or *attitude* towards Hanna, and/or what she's done when she misbehaves in court, or declines to unlock the burning church. And it's that *feeling* or *attitude* which is what dissolves to a greater or lesser degree as we come to 'understand' in the sense we walked through in Section I.

Now being clear about this gives us another in, as it were, to exploring the question of what [U] is. Because it seems clear that 'judging' in the relevant sense (which I'll henceforth refer to as [J]) is an instance of what Peter Strawson has famously called the 'reactive attitudes'.[19] And since [J], I want to suggest, *is* a reactive attitude, and [U] is some sort of dissipation or suspension of [J], the discussions by Strawson

---

18 Condemnatory judging, of course, is only one kind of judging, and some of what I want to say here applies to judging more generically while some does not. I do not think, however, that anything turns on this difference.

19 Peter Strawson, 'Freedom and Resentment', in Gary Watson (ed.), *Free Will*, Oxford: Oxford University Press, 1982, pp. 59–80. Strawson's essay was first published in 1962, but references to it will be to the anthologized version in Watson.

and others about the ways in which reactive attitudes become diminished, altered or suspended might be of some help to us in locating [U].[20]

Strawson introduces his discussion of the reactive attitudes as follows:

> I want to speak ... of ... the non-detached attitudes and reactions of people directly involved in transactions with each other; of the attitudes and reactions of offended parties and beneficiaries; of such things as gratitude, resentment, forgiveness, love, and hurt feelings.[21]

To fill this in a bit, think of the feeling we get when we learn that we have been slandered behind our backs by someone who we have considered a friend. Or the feeling that we get when someone gives us a gift, something that we have particularly wanted, say, and the giving of which is a manifestation of a particular concern and recognition of our special wants and needs. Contrast the feeling we get, to adapt an example of Strawson's, when someone steps on our hand accidentally, with that we get when someone has done it on purpose. Or the feeling we get when someone pays us a sincere compliment. All of these are examples of the reactive attitudes; they're conative, emotional or attitudinal responses to something that someone has done to or for us. And as Strawson notes, the having of them is, or seems to be, about as basic a feature of human life, and our ways of representing or understanding it, as there could be.

Now clearly these 'second-person' examples with which Strawson explains the idea are not the only kind of reactive attitudes. Strawson goes on to discuss both third-person examples, and first-person examples, which have been nicely summarized by Gary Watson. The reactive attitudes, he says,

> ... permit a threefold classification. Personal reactive attitudes regarding others' treatment of one (resentment, gratitude, etc.); vicarious analogues of these, regarding others' treatment of others (indignation and approbation); self-reactive attitudes regarding one's own treatment of others (and oneself?) (guilt, shame, moral self-esteem, feeling obligated).[22]

Now it seems clear that [J], too, admits of such a three-fold classification, and this would be in keeping with my sense that we can think of [J] as a kind of reactive attitude. And for purposes of coming to grips with [U] and its relation to [J], it is the 'third-person' category of 'vicarious analogues' that is our concern. For I take it that the condemnatory feelings we have towards Hanna, which are dissipated as we step

---

20 Unlike my more general remarks about 'judging' above, [J] should be taken to refer particularly to the sort of condemnatory judging or judgemental state that involves moral condemnation.

21 Strawson, *op. cit.*, p. 62.

22 Gary Watson, 'Responsibility and the Limits of Evil: Variations on a Strawsonian Theme', in John Martin Fischer and Mark Ravizza (eds), *Perspectives on Moral Responsibility*, Ithaca: Cornell University Press, 1993, pp. 119–48, p. 122. The essay was originally published in 1987.

into her shoes or learn about her illiteracy, are analogous, even similar, to Watson's (and Strawson's) example of indignation. As such, and thus located, Strawsonian queries into the dissipation of the person-to-person reactive attitudes like resentment and gratitude will apply, *mutatis mutandis*, to what we want to say about indignation and, particularly, [J]-like condemnation.

Now as Watson notes, reactive attitudes 'are not mere effusions of feeling, unaffected by facts'.[23] They have 'internal criteria, since they are reactions to the moral qualities exemplified by an individual's attitudes and conduct'.[24] They 'depend on an interpretation of conduct'.[25] How do they do so?

Strawson distinguishes two classes of cases in which the reactive attitudes do not seem 'natural, or reasonable, or appropriate', in which that is, the 'internal criteria' of the reactive attitudes are not met. One class is affiliated with expressions like, 'He didn't mean to', 'He hadn't realized', 'He didn't know.' or as he puts it, '"He couldn't help it" when this is supported by such phrases as "He was pushed", "He had to do it", "It was the only way", "They left him no alternative", etc.'[26] Watson notes that these are widely regarded as acceptable 'excusing' conditions, and I'll follow him in referring to these as 'Type-1 pleas'. They imply nothing about the agent as an inappropriate source of the relevant reactive attitudes, and they focus on a particular action token under particular circumstances, or the 'injury', as Strawson puts it, to which the action has led. Watson adds that this type of plea has a good deal in common with what we would ordinarily think of as 'justification', but helpfully notes that 'in general, an excuse shows that *one* was not to blame, whereas a justification shows that one was not to *blame*' (p.123).

Unlike these 'Type-1' pleas which merit a relaxation of the reactive attitudes, 'Type-2' pleas *do* undermine the status of the agent, temporarily or locally as in Strawson's first subclass of such pleas, or permanently or globally as in his second. The first subclass are characterized by claims like 'He wasn't himself', or 'He's been under great strain lately', the second by characterizations like, 'He's only a child', 'His mind has been systematically perverted', or 'That's purely compulsive behaviour on his part'.[27] Here, as I say, the status of the agent him or herself is open to – perhaps calls for – reconsideration. We're not sure that the person in question is in the right sort of relationship to us to properly underwrite the propriety of the reactive attitudes. These pleas, in Strawson's words, 'invite us to view the agent himself in a different light from the light in which we should normally view one who has acted as he has acted'.[28]

Our acceptance of pleas of either of these sorts is the typical way in which our being in the grips of a reactive attitude is diminished. Van der Merwe insults us,

---

23 Ibid.
24 Ibid.
25 Ibid.
26 Strawson, *op. cit.*, p. 64.
27 Ibid., p. 65.
28 Ibid.

or someone else, and our feeling of condemnation towards him dissipates as we learn that 'he didn't mean to', or that 'he hasn't been himself lately', or that 'he has the mental age of a three-year-old'. Or someone gives us a bad cheque – just what reactive attitude we come to have might depend to some extent on who it is, whether it's a friend, or a stranger we're selling a piece of furniture to – but we then learn that 'she didn't know', or 'she's been under great strain lately' or 'that's purely compulsive behaviour on her part'.

But what about [U]? Where does *it* fit into this picture? It seems to me that we should think of it as what we might call a 'Type-3' plea, or rather, the *result* of one.[29] I've tried to suggest that it fits nicely into Strawson's framework, in virtue of being the diminishment of a type of reactive attitude (namely [J]). But it seems to me to be a different *kind* of diminishment, resulting from different *sorts* of considerations than those involved in either Type-1 or Type-2 pleas.

We can see this latter point by briefly reconsidering our re-evaluation of Hanna discussed in Section I. It seems clear to me that our 'understanding' of Hanna is not the result of a Type-2 plea. No part of our coming to 'understand' her actions on the night of the fire, or her joining the SS, or her behaviour in the courtroom, results from our coming to doubt her capacity for *agency*, whether temporarily, as in Strawson's first sub-class of Type-2 cases, or permanently, as in his second subclass. It could have, if, for instance, what we had learned about Hanna was not that she was illiterate, but that she had been massively and perpetually abused as a child, such that any kind of self-esteem or self-worth she might once have had had been beaten out of her. With that information, we might wonder whether Hanna was really the sort of person towards whom we should even be having a reactive attitude, the sort of person that merits condemnatory feelings for what she's done, or at all.[30]

But this isn't at all what happens, for us or for Michael, in either of the clusters of [J]-like condemnation discussed in Section I. If [U] is to be found in either of Strawson's two categories, it must be in the first, Type-1, category of excuses or justifications. It must be that while she's a morally responsible agent, either, to adapt the phrase from Watson that I cited earlier, *she*'s not to blame for what she's done, or she's not to *blame* for what she's done.

But this doesn't seem right to me either. There *is* a sense in which I think [U] undermines our desire or capacity to blame Hanna, a sense present when we are condemning her. A desire to blame, or consider particularly worthy of blame, is an

---

29 We would need to use the word 'plea' loosely here, since [U] is arrived at not by any 'pleading' or argument necessarily (though 'she was illiterate' might count), but by the process of identification and imagining, as discussed in Section I.

30 This, in fact, is what I do wonder about the case of Robert Alton Harris, a double murderer whose case is discussed in some detail by Watson. Harris murdered two teenagers in cold blood, laughed about it, and ate one of their unfinished hamburgers later on. But when we learn the staggeringly awful facts about Harris's upbringing, and see how, as his sister later says, 'all the love was beaten out of that boy', I wonder whether this doesn't amount to a sort of Type-2 plea of some sort. See Watson, 'Responsibility and the Limits of Evil', especially pp. 131–7.

important element of [J] and one which lessens as we come to 'understand'. But this dissipation of blame (in the [J] sense) is distinct from Watson's, which involves the realization that someone hasn't, in fact, done anything wrong, and *that*, I've suggested, is not what happens with [U] in *The Reader*. But what I want to emphasize here is that [U] in *The Reader*, even allowing that it involves a diminishment of a desire or capacity to blame, is not at all like Strawson's paradigmatic instances of Type-1 pleas. It's *not* that 'She didn't mean to', that 'she hadn't realized', that 'she didn't know' or that 'she couldn't help it'. Where we find Type-1 pleas in the parts of *The Reader* we have looked at is in the contrasting testimonies of the other defendants, those cited in Passage 3 above. Remember how these go: they *couldn't* unlock the doors to the church because they were wounded, or in shock, or had been busy or hadn't thought about the church in all the confusion. We don't feel any diminishment of a reactive attitude towards these defendants – come to 'understand' them – not because they're the wrong kinds of pleas but because we don't believe them. (Indeed, speaking for myself, I find myself in the grip of a negative reactive attitude towards these defendants precisely for so pathetically trotting out such pleas when they were so palpably implausible.)

So that contrast I pointed to earlier, between, on the one hand, the excuses of the other defendants and, indeed, Hanna's own opening salvo that 'there was no alternative' and, on the other hand, the 'understanding' process that Michael and we undergo through imaginatively putting ourselves in Hanna's shoes, is, I think just this contrast between Type-1 pleas, and those associated with [U]. While 'understanding' functions *like* a Type-1 plea, it *isn't* a Type-1 plea. So for that reason, it seems, within the framework of Strawson's reactive attitudes, it marks out what we might think of as a Type-3 plea.

III

I want now to approach the question of how we should think of [U] from a third direction. Our starting point here is an exchange between Jeremiah Conway and John MacKinnon on *The Reader*.[31] Conway's essay uses *The Reader* and its tension between (what I've been calling) 'judging' and 'understanding' as a basis for critically testing an account by Martha Nussbaum of 'compassion'. He sees it as a kind of counterexample to Nussbaum's view.[32] In particular, he wants to contest the idea

---

31 Jeremiah P. Conway, 'Compassion and Moral Condemnation: An Analysis of *The Reader*', *Philosophy and Literature*, 23(2), 1999, pp. 284–301, and John E. MacKinnon, 'Crime, Compassion and *The Reader*', *Philosophy and Literature*, 27(1), 2003, pp. 1–20. For more of MacKinnon's take on *The Reader*, see also his 'Law and Tenderness in Bernhard Schlink's *The Reader*', *Law and Literature*, 16(2), 2004, pp.179–201.

32 Conway's discussion of Nussbaum's account of compassion refers to her *Cultivating Humanity*, Cambridge: Cambridge University Press, 1997, and *Poetic Justice*, Boston: Beacon Press, 1995. For a more recent and lengthy discussion, see Part II of Martha C. Nussbaum, *Upheavals of Thought: The Intelligence of Emotions*, Cambridge: Cambridge University

that compassion requires the belief that the person for whom we feel compassion 'is suffering "some significant pain or misfortune in a way for which that person is not, or not fully, to blame".'[33] In other words, on Nussbaum's Aristotelian account (or Conway's understanding of it), we don't feel compassion for someone whose suffering is their own fault. In agreeing that Nussbaum's view accords with common sense and usage, he agrees that 'we tend not to feel compassion for those who suffer because of their own carelessness, avoidable ignorance, or reckless behaviour'.[34] But, he thinks, this sort of exclusion, whether by Nussbaum or by 'established patterns of feeling' is problematic.[35] And, he says, '[t]he problematic nature of this kind of exclusion resides at the heart of *The Reader* ....'[36]

What follows then is an account of the book, and how it supports this point. In particular, he touches on a number of points not unlike some of my own above, and says insightful things about our complicated feelings for Hanna, including the tension between judging and understanding. Most important is the observation that in dissipating [J], [U] does not back away from judgement in the cognitive sense to the effect that Hanna has acted wrongly. Whether we regard her as anything as strong as a 'moral criminal'[37] might be debated, but the state of [U] I've been discussing does not deny the wrongness of her deeds, or the weakness of her character. '[T]he novel,' Conway rightly observes,

> ...never backs off the judgment that Hanna acted knowingly and wrongly. It never finds excuses for her deeds, Michael never contests, for example, the eighteen-year sentence that Hanna receives. The story acknowledges Hanna's moral guilt and finds room for compassion nonetheless. It intimates that moral condemnation is possible without distancing criminals from us so greatly that we fail to recognize ourselves in their midst.'[38]

Returning to his issue with Nussbaum's account of compassion, he adds that '[The novel] maintains, as Nussbaum does not, that compassion is possible, indeed necessary, for the moral criminal.'[39]

John MacKinnon disagrees. Maintaining that Conway's reading of *The Reader* is 'untenable', he suggests that

---

Press, 2001, especially Ch. 6. I should add that in saying that Conway sees *The Reader* as providing a counterexample to Nussbaum's account, I don't mean to attribute to him the view that the novel is *intended* to serve as such a counterexample.

33 Conway, 'Compassion and Moral Condemnation', p. 285, quoting Nussbaum, *Cultivating Humanity*, pp. 90–91.

34 Conway, 'Compassion and Moral Condemnation', p. 286.

35 Ibid.

36 Ibid.

37 Ibid., p. 298.

38 Ibid. Notice that Conway here alludes to the effects on us of recognizing that we, too, could have been as morally negligent in the fire, and perhaps in our behaviour in the trial, as Hanna had been. I'll return to the point of 'distancing criminals' below.

39 Ibid., pp. 298–9.

Schlink raises questions throughout the novel about Hanna's responsibility in order to support a claim not just of collective, but of universal guilt, and that whatever compassion one is able to muster for Hanna is prompted by the repeated representations he makes on her behalf. Accordingly, her case is presented in such a way as to be accommodated with perfect ease by Nussbaum's account of compassion.[40]

On MacKinnon's view, '*The Reader* is ... concerned to establish the circumstances of Hanna's life as mitigating her crime.'[41] In contrast to the sorts of points I made in sections I and II, MacKinnon sees the novel as *inter alia* defending Hanna, if perhaps obliquely. While rightly noting that we are meant to question the moral difference between Hanna and ourselves once we've attended empathetically to the situations she's found (and put) herself in, and once we've absorbed facts, like her illiteracy, that are unknown to us when we're in the grips of the reactive attitude [J], MacKinnon takes this a step further. Because, on his interpretation, 'certain propensities [are] common to all human beings, perpetrators and victims alike', MacKinnon asserts that 'we are no doubt intended to conclude that the need to provide [a moral] accounting is no more pressing for Hanna than it is for any of us'.[42] On his interpretation of the novel's message, '[t]he only thing that separates Hanna from either Michael or his father, a Nazi officer from the judge, the Nazis themselves from "second generation" Germans, is circumstance'.[43] While questioning Conway's interpretation of Nussbaum's compassion condition with which he, Conway, is taking issue,[44] the bulk of MacKinnon's critique of Conway hangs on his differing interpretation of the novel. 'In order for us to count the case of Hanna Schmitz as a counterexample to Nussbaum's view of compassion', he writes, 'we must, with Conway, deny that *The Reader* is concerned about mitigation, or that the novel aims to illuminate the conditions under which Hanna's crimes, and those of people like her, can be reasonably mitigated.'[45] Hanna is not a counterexample to the requirement that we feel only compassion for those whose suffering is not their fault because, to put it a bit crudely, Hanna's plight is *not*, in *The Reader*, her fault.

I'll come to my main reason for pointing to this exchange a little later. First, though, I want to use some of the insights and confusions in these essays to elaborate on and clarify some of the points raised in sections I and II, and to introduce the idea of moral complexity as distinct from straightforward 'mitigation'. [U] is a tricky and difficult-to-capture idea, but MacKinnon seems to me to have grotesquely misread *The Reader* and lost touch with it completely. While no part of my point is to *defend* my reading of it, Andrew Nagorski's suggestion that 'it's too simplistic to write off the crimes of former concentration-camp guards as the work of monsters, never recognizing that they belonged to the human race' seems much closer to Schlink's

---

40 MacKinnon, 'Crime, Compassion and the Reader', p. 2.
41 Ibid.
42 Ibid., p. 8.
43 Ibid., p. 13.
44 Ibid., pp. 13–14.
45 Ibid., p. 14.

intentions.[46] As Schlink himself is quoted as saying in the same article, recognizing and wrestling with that complexity 'doesn't mean not condemning or that it's any less awful what they did'.[47] To treat Hanna's illiteracy, or the sympathetic treatment of her 'what would you have done?' question as attempts or pleas for some sort of ordinary *mitigation*, as MacKinnon does, seems to me hopelessly wrong. It's to treat the processes by which our softening of [J] as either a Type-1 or Type-2 plea, which I suggested in the previous section is not the kind of thing it is.

What MacKinnon's reading lacks, it seems to me, is any recognition of, and taste for 'moral complexity'.[48] Moral complexity is often thought of as the complexity of *assessing* wrongdoing (or 'rightdoing', virtue, vice, etc.). That is, it's sometimes difficult to say, once the facts are in, *whether*, or *how*, or *to what extent* a particular thing is wrong (to confine ourselves to wrongdoing). This is closely related to difficulties in identifying properly just *what it is* that one has *done* or *not done*. Let's return to Passages 1 and 2 for a moment. A feature of imaginatively occupying Hanna's shoes, as absorbing these passages properly require us to do, is that we start to wonder about the *nature* of Hanna's omission. It seems like a *different kind* of omission, and arguably a less morally severe one, than if it had occurred in a 'cool hour', without the chaos and confusion described in Passage 1. I put this feature to one side in discussing Passages 1 and 2 earlier, focusing more on the divergence between our continued preparedness to cognitively judge Hanna's omission as wrong while at the same time experiencing the dissipation of our condemnatory state [J]. But this cognitive recognition of 'moral complexity' is part of the effect of these passages as well. While still maintaining that Hanna has acted *wrongly* (through omission), we see a moral distinction between not unlocking the church in a calm situation and not unlocking the church in her particular chaotic circumstances. We notice, and incorporate into our moral assessment, the particularities of the situation and thus there's a shift of descriptive characterization of the *nature* of the wrongful act (or omission).[49]

While I doubt that moral complexity in this sense is *always* a feature of Type-3 pleas, I suspect it often is. Consider the other aspect of *The Reader* on which I chose to focus in Section I, the discovery and its attitudinal impact on us of the revelation of Hanna's illiteracy. It does not, I suggested, lead us to 'excuse' or 'justify', say, Hanna's choice to join the SS, or to make the choices she does in her trial. But

---

46 Andrew Nagorski, 'A World In Shades of Gray', *Newsweek International*, 12 Nov. 2001, p. 61.

47 Ibid.

48 For another striking example of the same shortcoming, at least with regard to *The Reader*, see Cynthia Ozick's otherwise interesting essay, 'The Rights of History and the Rights of Imagination', in *Quarrel and Quandry*, New York: Alfred E. Knopf, 2000, pp. 103–19, and originally published in *Commentary*, 27, March, 1999, pp. 22–7. For an interesting discussion of *The Reader* with an eye to Ozick's criticisms, see Jeffrey I. Roth, "Reading and Misreading *The Reader*', *Law and Literature*, 16(2), 2004, pp.163–77.

49 This is an important theme in a number of Nussbaum's writings on *legal* assessment of wrongdoing. I discuss briefly one such discussion below.

it does seem to complicate our characterization of what that choice *is*. While still tainted by her obstinacy, and an over-evaluation of the shame involved in having her illiteracy revealed, there can be little doubt that her choice to join the SS looks and feels very different to us as an object for moral evaluation once the fact of her illiteracy is revealed, than it does before that evaluation. The choice is morally more complicated than we at first acknowledge, and contributes to our attitudinal shift away from [J] and towards [U]. It's clear, I think, that we still regard her as having chosen morally wrongly, and maintain that the shame notwithstanding, she should have revealed her illiteracy and declined to join the SS. But at the same time, our condemnatory [J] state dissipates on recognition of the true nature of the choice, the 'moral complexity' inherent in the facts of the matter.

This is, I suppose, a kind of 'mitigation' and as such MacKinnon might appear to be not as far off the mark as I've suggested. But even here, it's worth noting that it's 'mitigation' in a distinct sense. 'Mitigation' in MacKinnon's sense, like that inherent in Type-1 pleas involves a dissipation of our evaluative condemnatory state with the nature of the condemned act held constant. It doesn't involve in any meaningful way the idea or recognition of moral complexity. Our understanding of the nature of the deed is largely unchanged, but we excuse or justify it upon taking in the Type-1 plea that accompanies it. Here, perhaps as part of the nature of a Type-3 plea, our understanding of the nature of the deed itself changes. As suggested above, the nature of Hanna's omission to unlock the church appears to us to be a different kind of omission once we allow ourselves to see things from her perspective.

In addition to the cognitive moral complexity just discussed, though, there's a kind of attitudinal or conative complexity as well. Type-1 and Type-2 pleas – for example, the Type-1 pleas offered by the other defendants (in Passage 3) – keep our cognitive and attitudinal assessments aligned, as it were. With the acceptance of either sort of plea, we cease to experience [J] *and* we abandon (or substantially modify) our assessment of the act as wrong. [J] and judging wrong in the cognitive sense go hand in hand, in those more typical kinds of plea acceptance. [U], if what I've been saying is right, is different. What I suggested might be a Type-3 plea, seems to involve these coming apart. We have one, the cognitive evaluation of wrongness (even if softened or modified), but the dissipation of the other, the [J]-like attitude. We see an act (or omission) as wrong, but rather than feeling condemnatory, outraged, morally contemptuous or whatever, we find ourselves, or can find ourselves, 'oddly moved', to return to that phrase from *The Reader* that I appealed to in section I. Type-3 pleas seem to involve this sort of disconnect between what we think, and how we feel. And [U], which I suggested in section II, is the attitudinal upshot of Type-3 pleas, seems to be characterized in part by our experience of this disconnect. If we can refer to this as a kind of moral complexity, it seems to be a second sort of moral complexity that is part of the fabric of [U].

There are many instances of this kind of complexity I think, as distinct from the moral simplicities of straightforward guilt or innocence (if these, particularly the former, actually exist). One which struck me when I read it concerned a video-taped and widely broadcast incident in Fallujah in late 2004 wherein an American soldier shot dead a defenceless and unarmed man at point blank range in a mosque. As with our initial acquaintance with Hanna's actions and omissions, we judge this to be grossly wrong and find ourselves in the condemnatory state [J].[50] But like Schlink and Conway (and me), the journalist Rosie DiManno thinks this is too quick. Writing in the *Toronto Star*, DiManno begins her piece thus:

> Looks like a cold-blooded execution to me.
>
> But then I'm not a weary and scared infantryman who's been inching through the sniper-infested labyrinth of Falluja for over a week, shot in the face just the day before, and watched a member of my platoon get blown to bits while tending to the booby-trapped body of a dead insurgent. ...
>
> What was his state of mind? Was he suffering from combat strain or merely in possession of an itchy trigger finger and corroded humanity? Did he have reasonable cause given personal exposure to the urban battlefield tactics in Falluja, for believing the Iraqi was faking injury and posed a legitimate threat?
>
> This much American troops know from bitter experience: Insurgents routinely dress as and mix in among civilians, use mosques as launching pads for their attacks, and conduct suicide bombings after arranging themselves as victims of grievous injury, thereby luring the enemy close and vulnerable. More shredded bodies for your bang.[51]

Some of the features DiManno mentions here might constitute, singly or collectively, the making of a Type-1 plea/s, and she refers to some of them as 'potentially *mitigating* factors' in the formal investigation that was to be conducted into the incident. But DiManno, like Schlink with Hanna, is fundamentally asking us not to excuse the soldier, but to understand him in the context in which he found himself. She's recognizing moral complexity of both sorts discussed above, and her opponents here are those who respond with the righteous indignation and expressions of moral outrage characteristic of at least one form of [J]. But unlike the sorts of people mentioned in the previous footnote, she is hardly condoning, excusing or justifying his doing what he did. She clearly thinks that this was wrong, that the soldier shouldn't have done it, and that investigating his actions is completely appropriate. But we should also not be so quick to demonize him as a cold-blooded murderer as many people were busy doing from the comfort of their homes and offices at the time. And, reminiscent of the process by which Passages 1 and 2 provoke [U] in us, she urges that we 'try to imagine the thought process of that ... shooter, the unidentified Marine in the Falluja mosque'.[52]

---

50 Some people didn't, of course. Some people seem to think (falsely) that moral considerations don't apply to combat situations at all. Others insisted at the time (sometimes correctly, but in any case irrelevantly) that fastening on this episode, as the media and critics of the war did, was politically motivated by anti-Iraq invasion sentiments and inferred (invalidly) that while 'unfortunate' the soldier's action wasn't 'wrong'.

51 Rosie DiManno, 'Try to imagine the way U.S. Marine was thinking', *Toronto Star*, www.thestar.com, 17 Nov. 2004.

52 Ibid.

Another much more sustained example which I'll only mention briefly is Pumla Gobodo-Madikizela's fascinating book on her conversations with South African *apartheid* assassin and murderer, Eugene de Kock.[53] The book's central issue is not one of 'judging' and 'understanding'; it is more centrally concerned, as its title implies, with 'forgiveness' which while located in similar terrain to that of 'understanding', is importantly distinct from it. Nevertheless, the pursuit of 'understanding', and its moral dangers to which I alluded at the outset, are ever present here, and the difficulties of characterizing it emerge here as well. One might think, in fact, that despite its title, this book is really a sustained exercise in what I called at the outset, 'understanding' in the action sense, with the author finding herself in something like the 'oddly moved' state which Michael describes. Here it is the person himself that is more the object of attention, rather than this or that particular act, though obviously it's in virtue of things de Kock *did* that raise issues of 'judging' and 'understanding' *him*.[54] And, obviously, while I've been focusing on our understanding of things Hanna did and omitted to do, the issue of how we should feel about *her* are never far away.

Gobodo-Madikizela frequently wrestles with variants of the normative questions about 'understanding' (in the action sense) that I mentioned at the outset. Simon Sebag Montefiore, the author of a recent book on Stalin, alludes to such variants when he bemoans the fact that '[e]very time a new book or film on Hitler appears ... there is an uproar that he is being inappropriately humanized'.[55] He alludes (in agreement) to the cautionary noted sounded in *The New Yorker*'s review of his Stalin book: 'Any biography of a tyrant runs the risk of humanizing its subject to the point of appearing to mitigate his crimes.'[56] And Gobodo-Madikizela worries a great deal about very similar issues. 'To what extent', she writes,

> does the attempt to understand 'explain away' the behaviour of murderers? When we locate causes 'out there' – in societies and in structures of authority – does this not implicitly make violent acts more acceptable to the mind? Does understanding not send an implicit message of mercy born out of compassion for the murderer in view of the circumstances found to have influenced his behaviour?[57]

Montefiore's response is disappointingly instrumental, even if sound. Gobodo-Madikizela, by contrast, responds, in effect, by appealing to moral complexity and embracing [U]. She agrees with Christopher Browning that 'understanding [in the

---

53 Pumla Gobodo-Madikizela, *A Human Being Died That Night: A Story of Forgiveness*, Cape Town: David Philip, 2003.

54 For one exception to this, which is reminiscent in its effects on us of the effects of being put into Hanna's situation in Passages 1 and 2, see de Kock's first person account of one particular raid in which he participated, see Ibid., p. 76.

55 Simon Sebag Monefiore, 'Intimate detail on tyrants throws their cold-hearted brutality into sharper relief', *Sunday Independent* (South Africa), 6 June 2004, p. 24.

56 Ibid.

57 Goboda-Madikizela, *op. cit.*, p. 16.

action sense] implies an attempt to empathize' but also, like Browning, rejects, (in Browning's words) 'the old clichés that to explain is to excuse, to understand is to forgive'.[58] The 'old clichés' fail to see the distinction between understanding and condoning or excusing, the Type-1 (or 2) plea and the Type-3 plea, the acceptance of moral monsters with 'understanding' them. She recognizes the 'shades of gray' which both inform, and are informed by, [U].

Another feature of [U] which permeates Gobodo-Madikizela's study, and which is intimately bound up with the recognition of, and sensitivity to moral complexity is 'the tension, contradiction, and complexity that are forever present when one comes face-to-face with the coexistence of good and evil in human beings'.[59] And 'human beings', of course, includes us. 'One factor pulling us toward empathy rather than antipathy', she rightly observes, 'is that in the final analysis, perpetrators are human like us.'[60]

Part of what's distinctive about [U], I think, can be teased out of a feature of this observation. MacKinnon regards *The Reader* as suggesting that morally, we're all on a par, and there's a sense in which this is true and a sense in which it's not. It's the sense in which it's not true that MacKinnon fastens on. He's right, of course, to think (as I think he's implying) that unlike Hanna, we haven't joined the SS and sent Jews to their deaths. Unlike DiManno's soldier, we haven't shot anyone dead in cold blood. And unlike DeKock, we haven't murdered hundreds of people in defence of an evil regime. But MacKinnon doesn't give enough attention, as Gobodo-Madikizela does, to the sense in which it's true. Part of the reason for this, I think, is that as with so many other subtleties in *The Reader*, he over-simplifies things. Consider Hanna's 'What would you have done?' question, and the way it functions in leading our condemnatory [J]-state to dissolve to some extent. MacKinnon regards the point of this question as to suggest with a kind of inappropriate confidence, that we *would* have done as Hanna did. '[I]f we imagine ourselves into Hanna's mind and circumstance, ... [Schlink urges], we can only conclude that we too *would* have acted as she did' (emphasis added).[61] But if we interpret Hanna's question, not as an *assertion* about what we would do, but rather, as I think Schlink wants it to be interpreted, as an invitation to *wonder* what we would do, things are much murkier. When discussing this question in Section I, I said that our condemnatory stance diminishes because we can't be sure that we wouldn't act as she had done.

---

58 Ibid. The quotation is from Christopher Browning, *Ordinary Men: Reserve Police Battalion 101 and the Final Solution in Poland*, New York: Harper Perennial, 1993, p. xx.

59 Ibid., p. 17.

60 Ibid., p. 149.

61 MacKinnon, 'Crime, Compassion and *The Reader*', p. 3. Other instances of this reading of Hanna's question can be found elsewhere in his essay, for example on pp. 8 and 9. Daniel Stern also misreads this question in my view. Calling Hanna's query '[t]he classic argument in bad faith', Stern responds, 'Don't answer for me. Not until I am tested and found wanting ....' See Daniel Stern, 'Some Notes toward a Response to *The Reader*', *Law and Literature*, 16(2), 2004, pp. 203–5.

This illuminates a feature of [U] in the following way. For it seems as though part of what characterizes [J] is a sense of difference, of moral distinction, of separation and otherness. The condemnatory stance is a finger-pointing one. It says that you're guilty, and I'm not, and I'm entitled to condemn you from this position of moral superiority. But as with the other complexities involved in [U], things aren't that simple when we honestly put ourselves in the position of Hanna, or DiManno's soldier, or de Kock. While we haven't done what any of them have done, we're guilty of a frightfully unwarranted confidence if we think ourselves incapable of it. [J] involves a kind of moral hubris which thinking about what we would have done with some honesty and depth dissolves, if only partially and incompletely. [U] involves a corresponding moral humility, and in that sense, we're acknowledging our shared humanity with perpetrators.

Much of Gobodo-Madikizela's explicit explorations of this 'equality' between perpetrators and others occurs, as mentioned above, in her attempt to understand the psychological bases of forgiveness, and thus are not directly relevant to our purposes here. But, as Schlink himself insisted in his conference paper, this breaking down of otherness is an important aspect of [U]. Not anything goes, of course. Few people are Hitlers, Stalins or de Kocks. But most of us have it in us to do at least some of the things they did, and Conway, Montefiore and Nagorski are right, I think, that visions of these people without a full sense of their capacity for pain, and their various virtues, are over-simplifications. So, I think, are MacKinnon's Hanna and MacKinnon's Schlink.

But all of this said, however, let me now return briefly to MacKinnon's debate with Conway about *The Reader* and compassion. I think MacKinnon may have a point against Conway in their debate about whether Hanna and our connection to her constitutes an exception to Nussbaum's account of compassion. But the reason is not MacKinnon's reason, which as I noted earlier, relies largely on his distinct and less plausible reading of *The Reader* than that of Conway. As I've been suggesting, on that score I think Conway has it largely right. But as a final attempt to try to locate and understand [U], I want to suggest that where Conway goes wrong is in thinking that 'compassion' is the relevant 'emotion' or attitudinal state. It's close, of course, and [U] surely overlaps with aspects of compassion. And he's right to see close affinities between what he finds in *The Reader* and some of Nussbaum's work. But he might be pointing to the wrong piece of Nussbaum's work. Perhaps we ought to look, instead, at her discussion of Senecan 'mercy', particularly in her essay, 'Equity and Mercy'.[62]

Nussbaum's essay is ultimately about 'the connection between mercy and a vision of the particular'.[63] In the course of her discussion she touches on a number of deeply

---

62 Martha C. Nussbaum, 'Equity and Mercy', in *Sex and Social Justice*, Oxford: Oxford University Press, 1999, pp. 154–83. A previous version of this essay was published, bearing the same title, in *Philosophy & Public Affairs*, 22(2), 1993 pp. 83–125 and is reprinted as Chapter 1, this volume, pp. 3–42. Subsequent references will be to the version in this collection.

63 Nussbaum, 'Equity and Mercy', p. 5.

interesting questions about law, the authorial point of view, literature more generally, and contemporary feminism; her take on many of these topics will be familiar to those who have spent time studying her work. She begins, though, with a lengthy but fascinating historical exploration of what she calls, 'equitable judgement – judgement that attends to the particulars'.[64] And after leading us through the evolution of this idea in Greek and Roman philosophy, she shows how it becomes deeply informed by mercy, appealing to Seneca's account of mercy, defined, she says, as 'the inclination of the mind toward leniency in exacting punishment'.[65]

Now 'mercy' is not really our topic here, though it's a related phenomenon in some obvious ways. Mercy concerns how we respond in action to a wrong-doing, and in particular, how we respond with regard to punishment or retribution. What interests me, rather, is the relevant 'inclination of the mind', that inclination which is, as she says, 'toward leniency in exacting punishment'. For it seems to me not only distinct from Conway's and MacKinnon's 'compassion', but similar in a number of ways to [U]. Only here, instead of an inclination towards leniency in punishment, we have something like a diminishment of the desire (and capacity) to condemn.[66]

It's worth noting, in the first place, that when Nussbaum is analysing 'compassion' (at least in the works of hers on which Conway relies), she's analysing a notion derived from the Aristotelian view of *eleos*.[67] But the portions of Nussbaum's 'Equity and Mercy' paper on which I want to focus with an eye to [U] and *The Reader* draw me to phrases of hers which she connects to the Greek word *suggnômê*. I don't read or know Greek so it would obviously be inappropriate for me to pronounce on the distinction between those two Greek terms. But when Nussbaum discusses things that I find reminiscent of [U] as manifested in *The Reader*, it's *suggnômê* (or something like it), not *eleos*, that is being appealed to.[68] This leads me to think, by way of suggestion, that where Conway has gone wrong, *if* he has, is in seeing the *The Reader*'s exploration of [U] as an exploration of 'compassion'. It's for that reason, perhaps, as distinct from MacKinnon's, that *The Reader* isn't a counterexample to Nussbaum's analysis of 'compassion'. It's because it's about [U], not compassion. Still, this is speculative, and in any case it doesn't follow from this, nor am I suggesting, that [U] is a rendering of *suggnômê*. Only that the sorts of things Nussbaum says in connection with it seem to me close in certain respects to [U] in ways to which 'compassion' is less close. So let's turn to what matters *here*, to Nussbaum's discussion of Seneca.

The distinction I'm interested in is one between what Nussbaum calls the 'merciful *attitude*' (my emphasis) and the 'retributive *attitude*' (again, my

---

64 Ibid.

65 Ibid.

66 Such a diminishment could, of course, *result* in a merciful response.

67 Conway, 'Compassion and Moral Condemnation', p. 301.

68 For a brief discussion of the similarities and differences between *eleos* and *suggnômê*, see Nussbaum, *op. cit.*, pp. 12, 13.

emphasis).[69] Nussbaum's discussion is couched in terms of the legal context, where we're interested, for *legal* purposes, in how a judge should understand a wrong, and how he/she should punish it. But now, substituting, say 'judgers' or 'condemners' for Nussbaum's 'judges', consider this passage:

> The retributive attitude has a we/them mentality, in which judges set themselves against offenders, looking at their actions as if from a lofty height and preparing to find satisfaction in their pain. The good Senecan judge, by contrast, has both identification and sympathetic understanding . Accordingly, a central element in Seneca's prescription for the judge is that he should remind himself at every turn that he himself is capable of the failings he reproves in others.[70]

Whether we *should* do this, of course, is one of the normative questions that I've been trying to put to one side as much possible to concentrate on diagnostic matters. But *what* we're meant to do bears striking similarities to what, I think, *The Reader* asks us to do with regard to Hanna. I haven't said that [J] necessarily involves finding satisfaction in anyone's pain, though I think it frequently does. But it does possess the 'we/them' mentality that I teased out of Gobodo-Madikizela's discussion, and so does the state we're in as we condemn Hanna and of which [U] is a dissipation. That attitude yields to one in which we recognize that we ourselves are 'capable of the failings that [we] reprove in others', others such as Hanna, or DiManno's soldier, or, arguably, even de Kock.

Similarly, the merciful attitude, (which Nussbaum characterizes as a 'medical/narrative attitude'), 'asks the judge to imagine what it was like to have been that particular offender, facing those particular obstacles with the resources of that history. Seneca's bet is that once one performs this imaginative exercise one will cease to have the strict retributive attitude to the punishment of the offender.'[71] Or, I would want to add, the condemnatory attitude [J]. Passages 1 and 2 of *The Reader*, and, indeed, Passage 4 in the illiteracy context, ask *us* to imagine what it would have been like to be that particular offender – Hanna – facing the particular obstacles of that evening with the resources of *her* history. [U], a diminishment of the condemnatory stance embodied in [J], is the result. While not *exactly* Nussbaum's 'merciful attitude' perhaps, it's close, it seems to me. And, to reiterate, closer than Conway's 'compassion'.

Nussbaum also discusses, as she has often in her work, the role of the literary, and in particular the novel itself, in shaping perception and judgement. In one particular passage, she recounts a visit to a class of hers (Nussbaum's) by the novelist Joyce Carol Oates. At one point in the course of a discussion of an Oates novel, one normally quiet student launches into a condemnatory critique of one of the characters. As Nussbaum reports on the episode, Oates's response involved an exploration of various of the character's traits, efforts, circumstances that led her to

---

69 See, especially, Ibid., Section 5, pp. 15–21.
70 Ibid., p. 20.
71 Ibid.

see the character in a less condemnatory way, 'as of a friend whose life inhabited her own imagination and whom, on that account, she could not altogether dismiss or condemn'.[72] In the student, we have an instance of [J], the condemnatory 'reactive attitude' towards the character; with Oates, we have a different perspective, one characteristic of [U]. Nussbaum connects the threads of this phenomenon with the 'novelist's art' as follows:

> Here [in Oates's response to the student] ... was mercy; and, lying very close to it, the root of the novelist's art. The novel's structure is a structure of *suggnômê* – of the penetration of the life of another into one's own imagination and heart. It is a form of imaginative and emotional receptivity, in which the reader, following the author's lead, comes to be inhabited by the tangled complexities and struggles of other concrete lives. Novels do not withhold all moral judgement, and they contain villains as well as heroes. But for any character with whom the form invites our participatory identification, the motives for mercy are engendered in the structure of literary perception itself.[73]

My point here is neither to agree nor disagree with Nussbaum's view about the connection between *suggnômê* and the nature of the novel, though if she's right, not only the sorts of passages I cited from *The Reader* do the work of dissipating [J] and nurturing [U], but the very fact that it's a novel of the relevant kind does so as well. Again, it's the state that (on Nussbaum's view) novelistic integration with a character *engenders* that matters for my purposes. It's not, as I've suggested, compassion precisely. It's much more like [U], an odd (in the case of morally unappealing characters) inability to judge (cognitively) with a condemnatory attitude, from the standpoint, as Nussbaum sometimes puts it, of 'retributive anger'. One is made aware of the first sort of moral complexity I discussed earlier, and [U], and maybe *suggnômê*, are instances of the second kind. If I'm right, *The Reader* is not a counterexample to Nussbaum's account of compassion, not because it involves Type-1 pleas on Hanna's behalf, but because it's not quite compassion that is involved. It's [U]. And while I haven't explicitly explored the differences, my hope is that the passages from Nussbaum I've cited above give us both some feel for the difference, and, in conjunction with the other instances of [U] I've discussed in this section, a richer sense of just what [U] is exactly.

IV

In trying to come to understand 'understanding', I have not attempted any sort of careful analysis of this idea. I very much doubt that I'm capable of arriving at anything satisfactory, but in any case, many such philosophical analyses of these kinds of concepts strike me as either just wrong, or as squeezing all interest out of the concept in the process. Rather, I've undertaken a rather woollier 'exploration' of 'understanding', in the attitudinal sense I've been calling '[U]'. I've tried to tease

---

72 Ibid., p. 24.
73 Ibid.

it out of *The Reader* by focusing on some passages where it seems to arise, and I've tried to locate it alongside other, more typical, ways in which we find reactive attitudes being weakened and dissipated. In the final section I tried to develop points initiated earlier by linking it up with moral complexity, and our recognition of it, noting other examples of it, pointing to its connection with a recognition of our own fallibility and our consequent connection to wrongdoers, rather than separation from them. I also tried to suggest that it's distinct from notions like compassion despite obvious overlap with them.

None of this either settles or (I hope) begs the kinds of normative questions to which I alluded at the outset. While I've tried to avoid begging them, my sympathies regarding them should be clear. But I have certainly not argued for a sympathetic treatment of understanding in the action sense, nor for the virtue of an understanding disposition. And as such, I've made no attempt to settle these normative questions.

I do think, though, that some of them dissolve, to some extent, once we get a clearer sense of what understanding, in both the action sense, and the attitudinal sense [U], is. One commentator has described the state characterized by Michael in the quotation with which I began as a 'sympathy that does not condone'.[74] While I don't think 'sympathy' is quite right – and I'm not sure we really *have* a term that is quite right other than, perhaps, 'understanding' itself – the idea that [U] does not condone has been one I've stressed throughout. As such, worries about moral complacency or blindness, diminishment of our moral critical faculties, and the like dissipate considerably, or so it seems to me. If I'm right, the sense in which Michael finds himself unable to condemn Hanna as he comes to understand is not these potentially worrisome ones. Rather, he is unable to feel or find himself in the grip of the reactive attitude [J], to muster righteous indignation towards Hanna's deeds or separate her as a wrongdoer from himself as a perfectly potential wrongdoer. All this is for the best in my view. In her concluding paragraph, Nussbaum writes that '[f]eminist thought ... should not ignore the evidence, or fail to say that injustice is injustice, evil evil – but ... it should remain capable of *suggnômê* ....'[75] I want to say the same about [U] and the inescapable practice of moral evaluation. We cannot and should not surrender our evaluative capacities or will. We mustn't fail to say that horrific moral failures are horrific moral failures, or cowardly decisions are cowardly decisions. But unlike Hanna's finger-pointing co-defendants in *The Reader*, and as urged by the novel itself, we must remain capable of understanding, without which, in my view, such judgements lose much of their moral worth. It's meritorious to find oneself incapable of condemnation in Michael's sense, so that our condemnatory judgements, when we make them, come from a place of humanity and humility.[76]

---

74   Richard H. Weisberg, 'A Sympathy That Does not Condone: Notes in Summation on Schlink's *The Reader*', *Law and Literature*, 16(2), 2004, pp. 229–35.

75   Nussbaum, *op. cit.*, p. 41.

76   Initial work on this essay began while I was on sabbatical leave from the University of the Witwatersrand. I wish to thank the University for granting me that leave, and for its very generous Anderson-Capelli grant during that time. I also wish to thank all the participants at

the conference on 'judging and understanding' held in November 2004 at the Goethe Institute in Johannesburg, as well as Pedro Tabensky for organizing it and the Goethe Institute for hosting it. In particular, conversations with, or essays by, Pedro Tabensky, Bernhard Schlink, Samantha Vice, Ward Jones, Thaddeus Metz and Peta Bowden have helped me think about these issues tremendously.

Chapter 4

Living with the Self: Self-Judgement and Self-Understanding[1]

Samantha Vice

Editor's Introduction

Samantha Vice defends the plausibility of the 'relation between understanding and mercy'. However, although in general terms, but not completely, she agrees with Nussbaum, who thinks that understanding others should incline us to be merciful, she is less comfortable with the idea of being merciful to oneself, particularly when one has committed as serious a transgression as Hanna did. Her concern is less with the alleged moral obscenity of letting oneself off the moral hook too easily, but with the limits of the possibility of self-forgiveness. Although Vice acknowledges that in the case of less serious transgressions one may, without great effort, be able to treat oneself mercifully, in the case of serious violations this is far more difficult, no matter how well one understands how it is that one came to do what one did. The asymmetry occurs, Vice argues, as a consequence of the relative difficulty in adopting an impersonal stance on oneself. From the impartial point of view one can observe how others have acted reprehensibly as a consequence of a specific set of unfortunate circumstances, expressive of the vulnerability to circumstances that typifies the human situation, but when it is one's turn to asses one's own deeply reprehensible deeds, adopting this position is almost if not completely impossible. The impersonal stance requires that one see oneself 'against a framework of knowledge of the human condition' and one must be able to let 'that play a role in one's evaluation' and being able to do this 'will lead understanding on to mercy'. Although there is a relation between understanding and mercy, understanding as such is not sufficient for mercy. One must be able to assess one's heinous moves from the impartial point of view – a quasi or total impossibility.

* * *

1   Research for this paper was partly undertaken while an Andrew Mellon Fellow at Rhodes University. Many people have commented on the paper through its phases and I am grateful to all. My thanks go especially to Ward Jones for many helpful discussions, and to David Martens and Pedro Tabensky for insightful comments on an earlier draft. Thanks, too, to John Cottingham, Dylan Futter and Elisa Galgut.

1. Introduction

There is a long tradition to the idea that the more one comes to understand the particularities of another person's character and circumstances, the less inclined one will be to judge her too harshly. As Martha Nussbaum has shown, the view that 'flexible particularized situational judgement is linked with leniency' can be traced back to ancient Greek and Roman writers.[2] While one's just evaluation may still be negative, knowledge of particulars seems to dissipate the urge to condemn, as well as the appropriateness of doing so. This connection between understanding and mercy is perceptively explored in Bernard Schlink's novel, *The Reader*, which shows the difficulty in trying to accommodate impulses towards both understanding and condemnation. In a passage which could act as the motto for this collection, Michael says, 'I wanted to pose myself both tasks – understanding and condemnation. But it was impossible to do both.'[3] Michael's struggle to accommodate his intimate history with Hanna alongside his new knowledge of her again suggests that mercy rather than condemnation accompanies understanding.

The first aim of this paper is to understand and defend the plausibility of this relation between understanding and mercy. Taking Nussbaum's argument in 'Equity and Mercy' as my starting point, I will argue that, suitably interpreted, the idea does present us with both an ethical ideal and an account of what for the most part happens when we understand a person. That is, as a descriptive claim it is correct about what generally happens and it sets a praiseworthy ideal given the complexity and frailty of human life. Whether it is something we are always comfortable with and whether the understanding is always possible are difficult questions, as Schlink's novel shows.

This first task, however, is only a preliminary to the second. My main concern is to explore whether the connection holds equally for one's relation to self. Would self-understanding generally lead one to be less harshly judgemental towards one's own crimes? In particular, I am interested in those who have done something deeply immoral – someone like Hanna – for this is the realm in which questions of mercy become relevant. However, despite the novel's revelation of her illiteracy, neither we nor Michael reach any really adequate understanding of Hanna, and so I take as my examples men implicated in the same kind of crimes: Albert Speer, the most able, intelligent and remorseful of Hitler's ministers; and Franz Stangl, Kommandant of the camps Treblinka and Sobibor. And for this, I am relying on Gita Sereny's extraordinary studies of these men.[4] My point is not that certain crimes are beyond the pale, and that therefore the relation between understanding and mercy is over-stressed from any perspective. There is something to this, as I shall suggest later, but my main concern is to show the limits of mercy from the first-person perspective.

---

2   Nussbaum, 'Equity and Mercy', Ch. 1, this volume, p. 6.

3   Schlink, *The Reader*, p. 156.

4   Sereny, *Albert Speer: His Battle with Truth*; and *Into That Darkness*, respectively. Stangl died in prison in 1971, shortly after finally admitting guilt to Sereny. Speer lived a productive life after his twenty years in prison, untiringly and publicly denouncing Hitler's regime, although only very late admitting knowledge of the final solution. He died in 1981.

These portraits are useful for my purposes in a number of ways: Firstly, my concern is put in stark relief by the immensity of these men's crimes, so they provide good test cases for the scope of mercy. Secondly however, and more interesting, are their evasions and the images used to describe their relation to themselves, which, I shall argue, provide a clue to the differences between self- and other-evaluation. Finally, Sereny presents us with records of actual exercises in self-reflection. It is, for instance, 'Speer's profound malaise with his own conscience, his "battle with his soul"' throughout his life, that animates and directs Sereny's powerful study.[5]

The intuition that I wish to support is that the relation between understanding and mercy will not hold in the same way for cases of self-understanding, and so there is an asymmetry between understanding others and understanding the self. Coming to understand oneself will, it seems to me, make one's crimes appear overwhelming, will bring with it, as Raimond Gaita writes, 'a shocked realisation of the meaning of what one has done'. Remorse might properly 'haunt' one all one's life, 'blighting it'.[6] While I will concentrate on serious moral wrong-doing, I will argue that the explanation for this asymmetry is a general feature of persons. Furthermore, I shall argue that this asymmetry is how it ought to be. To be a person is to have a relation to oneself that explains and justifies the asymmetry, and we cannot wish it away without also wishing away a central aspect of personhood.

Before exploring this, my use of the terms 'condemnation' and 'mercy' should be noted.[7] As already suggested, both terms apply only to serious and actual cases of wrong-doing. They refer to possible responses – emotional, intellectual, punitive – that accompany a correct evaluation that there was wrong-doing. The standard usage of 'mercy' links it with the mitigation of punishment out of pity for the wrongdoer, and as such, mercy is properly shown only towards those over whom we have some power.[8] Nussbaum similarly understands mercy as leniency regarding punishment which would otherwise be deserved. It is an 'inclination of the soul to mildness in exacting penalties' as Seneca writes;[9] we punish less than we judge the act deserves.

Of course, this sense of mercy will not quite do the work with respect to the self except metaphorically, and yet it is not nonsensical to speak of showing mercy towards oneself. I thus propose to use the term in a way that includes the sense of

---

5   *Albert Speer*, p. 13.

6   Gaita, *A Common Humanity*, p. 31.

7   My use of these terms is perhaps more specialized than others in this collection. As it will become clear, I take mercy and condemnation to be *particular kinds of* positive or negative responses to the knowledge of a wrong-doing, rather than positive or negative responses *per se*, or, in the case of condemnation, the recognition *per se* of a crime.

8   See, for example, Jeffrie G. Murphy and Jean Hampton, *Forgiveness and Mercy*, p. 158. I thank John Cottingham for bringing this point to my attention.

9   Seneca, *De Clementia* II.3, quoted in Nussbaum, 'Equity and Mercy', Ch. 1, this volume, p. 19, orig. p. 166. Though this characterization makes mercy separate from, and supererogatory to, justice, with the Stoics it eventually became part of justice proper. I return to this in section 3.

leniency in punishment, but that extends it in a way that allows for self-directed mercy. This extension seems justified by the larger concerns of this project: of exploring the kind of responses – gentle or harsh – appropriate to knowledge of a person and his crimes.[10] We show leniency in punishing *because* we pity the wrong-doer, so mercy is most fundamentally a response to the person rather than the deed. We respond in a gentler way to the person, a way compatible with (and indeed requiring) judging his act very harshly indeed. This wider sense is best brought out in contrast to condemnation. The root of condemning, Roger Wertheimer writes, 'is in damning ... declaring a wish for a fate: that its object suffer'; it is 'final and decisive.'[11] In contrast, mercy allows the possibility of redemption; it acknowledges wrong-doing, but does not allow the act to be decisive in judging the person. The person is not forever stained by the wrong-doing, irrevocably placed outside the moral community. This account of mercy therefore assumes that I can respond mercifully to a person, and so in a sense 'show mercy', even if I have no power over him and even if my thoughts will have no consequence for his fate. Mercy will therefore be a wider-ranging virtuous disposition of gentleness and inclusion than is suggested by concentrating on leniency in punishing. As such, it can be shown towards myself. I can think myself marked and damaged forever, with no claim to the respect of others or myself, or I can think myself capable of, and more importantly, *worthy* of the work of redemption.[12] This attitude will then open and prepare the way for self-forgiveness.

As I understand it, then, both mercy and condemnation are primarily responses to persons, which follow a justly negative judgement of an action; and they are attitudes displaying gentleness or harshness regarding punishment and the person herself. In this wider sense, both can be directed towards others or the self. As I shall argue, there are indeed dissimilarities between self-directed and other-directed mercy. One difference can be immediately noted: other-directed mercy (and condemnation) does not necessarily depend upon the agent doing or acknowledging anything about her crime. One can show mercy regardless of whether that person has acknowledged guilt, felt shame or attempted reparation. This does not seem to be the case for mercy towards the self, where at least recognition, but usually some kind of restorative work, seems essential. The knowledge that other-directed mercy requires if Nussbaum and Schlink are correct, is therefore not *self*-knowledge on the part of the person towards whom mercy is shown.[13]

---

10 Those objecting to my wider notion of mercy should bear this context in mind, and, if necessary, take 'mercy' as shorthand for a variety of such gentle responses.

11 Wertheimer, 'Constraining Condemning', pp. 492 and 493.

12 On the relation between self-forgiveness and self-respect, see Margaret R. Holmgren, 'Self-Forgiveness and Responsible Moral Agency', and Robin S. Dillon, 'Self-Forgiveness and Self-Respect'.

13 The need for self-directed attention also characterizes self-forgiveness. Holmgren discusses the process of addressing our own wrongs that is required for genuine and morally appropriate self-forgiveness in 'Self-Forgiveness and Responsible Moral Agency'. It may be possible – for very good people – to forgive or show mercy towards others who have no

As a final preliminary point, note that the claim under consideration is not that understanding in the relevant sense is *necessary* for any mercy at all.[14] It may be possible to be merciful towards someone one knows little about, or towards whom this kind of understanding does not even play a role in one's response – parents' reaction to their children's crimes is perhaps an example. The argument, rather, is that if we do reach understanding, mercy rather than harshness will in fact typically result. And it is this claim, particularly as it applies to the evaluation of one's self, that I want to explore.[15]

2. Images of the Self

The plausibility of claiming an asymmetry between self- and other-evaluation depends partially on the plausibility of claiming a general relation between understanding and mercy.[16] I begin exploring this in Section 3, but in order to persuade you to enter the discussion at all, note, briefly, the difficulty of reaching self-knowledge and the contortions we often go through in order to avoid it. In the cases of Speer and especially Stangl, we see this taken to tortuous lengths. That these men needed to go to such lengths and that they were in some sense horrified by their own actions, shows that they were at least minimally moral and keeps them within the sphere of the human. They were not, in short, monsters, a conclusion some will find more comforting than others. Such strategies, along with the painful emotions of guilt, shame and remorse are indications of the difficulties attending self-knowledge. These are different in kind from the undoubted difficulties attending merciful evaluation of another. We seek knowledge in the hope that it will exonerate others; we flee self-knowledge because we fear it will destroy any excuses.

In order to focus the discussion, a few passages from Sereny's studies will prove useful. In the first passage, Sereny says of Stangl: 'Except for a monster, no man who *actually participated* in such events ... can concede guilt and yet ... "consent to remain alive".'[17] The second concerns Speer: 'Speer's lies ... are a demonstration of his ever-increasing need to schematize his life into an alignment of feelings and fears

---

tendency or capacity for this kind of work, but generally some recognition and change from others is also required before forgiveness is possible.

14 There is nothing in Nussbaum's 'Equity and Mercy', for instance, that suggests the stronger claim about the necessity of understanding for mercy.

15 Apart from some brief remarks in Section 4, I leave aside the debate surrounding free will and determinism, which is often thought crucial to the issue of judging and understanding others (see, for example, Pedro Tabensky's contribution to this volume, Chapter 6). My concern is phenomenological, with how people experience and respond to themselves and others, and this can remain unaffected by one's metaphysical views.

16 For ease of reference I will use the terms *self-evaluation* and *other-evaluation* to capture aspects of both understanding and responding to others and self, where the latter responses include (but are, of course, not restricted to) mercy and condemnation.

17 *Into That Darkness*, p. 39.

he could live with. "How can a man admit more and go on living?" said his daughter Hilde.'[18] The final passage is taken from a letter from Speer to Hilde, then seventeen, written in 1953 from Spandau prison:

> You ask ... about the Nazis ... You ask how could an intelligent person go along with such a thing ... Let me say the hardest bit first: unless one wants, cowardly, to avoid confronting the truth, one has to say that there can be no excuse; there is no justification. It is in that sense that I am convinced of my own guilt. There are things, you see, for which one has to carry the blame, *even if purely factually one might find excuses*: the immensity of the crimes precludes any attempt at self-justification ...[19]

There are two related ideas from these passages to hold on to: The first is that there are certain things about ourselves that, if we acknowledged them, would make us unable to continue living without radical self-estrangement. Our self-respect and very identity are so bound up with certain values that betraying them would, in a sense, be the death of the self. When we have done something so terrible we flee rather than face up to the knowledge. The second idea is that from one's own perspective, certain actions must be acknowledged as coming from one's own responsible agency if they are acknowledged at all. Possible mitigating factors – what Speer calls 'purely factual' considerations – are irrelevant and this renders any attempt at self-justification or mercy impossible. I will argue that the relation to the self expressed in the first idea informs this second phenomenon. But I want to begin with the second point and work back to the first, for my main claim is that there is indeed the asymmetry between self- and other-evaluation that Speer's letter at least suggests. That is, in order to understand why we cannot acknowledge mitigating circumstances in our own case which we would acknowledge in the case of others, we need to understand just why self-knowledge can be so destructive of the self that one comes to know. This task requires that two things be established. The first is that there is the relation between understanding and mercy that the asymmetry assumes. This is explored in the following section. The second is that this relation does not hold, or holds in a different way, in the case of self-evaluation – the task of sections 4 and 5.

3. Understanding Another

In this section, I wish to render as plausible as possible the claim that understanding another dissipates both the urge to condemn and the appropriateness of doing so. The starting-point is the thought that providing a full explanation and evaluation of a person's action requires knowledge of the particularities of her character and situation. The idea is that knowledge of such particulars will lead to mercy rather than harshness towards the person, even when our judgement of the worth of the

---

18 *Albert Speer*, p. 407.
19 Quoted in ibid., pp. 19–20 (my emphasis).

action remains negative. What then are these 'particularities', that in trying to explain a person's action would bring us to judge her more leniently, and how do they generate mercy?

Let us explore what happens when we try to explain a person's action, assuming that our concern is ethical as much as epistemological. We begin from a disinterestedly curious stance, motivated by the desire to evaluate justly. Very quickly, we find ourselves investigating the person and not just the external circumstances of the action. We ask, typically, for the reasons for the action or omission,[20] which would take us on to the beliefs and desires of the agent: from what mental states could acts of that sort issue? How did she rationalize her actions? In order to understand this fully, we would need to know something about her character: what kind of person is she, that she could have those desires or beliefs and allow them to influence her in those ways? Was this action typical of her? What did *she* think of her reasons? With what emotions did she view the situation? Is she prone to them and to acting upon them? What is her basic personality type, the largely already-set traits from which character issues? These questions would lead us to consider the person's history and circumstances: How did she become the person she is today, capable in whatever manner of doing this? We would look at her upbringing, her family situation, her education, the socio-political climate against which she was formed.[21] Along with this character-based exploration, we would investigate the circumstances under which a person acted: More generally, in what climate of ideas did she live? More particularly, did she act under duress? Was she ill or under immense stress? The investigation thus moves from the external action, through the motivations and character of the person, out again to the larger milieu in which she moves; and from the external features of the action to aspects of agency and responsibility. To understand a person's actions fully we need to know things both about her directly, and facts that aren't about her at all, but which influenced her development into the individual she is, or provided the setting for the action we wish to explain.[22]

---

20 I will speak from now on simply of actions. Omissions, however, are in many ways more interesting from the perspective of the agent, because they leave room for more (and interesting) kinds of rationalization. Ultimately it is a person's choices that we are interested in here, whether those choices led to actions or failures to act. On this, see R. Jay Wallace, *Responsibility and the Moral Sentiments*, p. 128f.

21 Sereny's goal is partly to find answers to these questions during her interviews. Her desire to be just is manifest throughout her studies, despite her suspicion or dislike of her subjects. She writes of Stangl, for instance, that it was essential to understand him 'as far as possible unemotionally and with an open mind', and that it was 'important ... to assess the circumstances which led up to his involvement, for once not from our point of view, but from his' (*Into That Darkness*, p. 13).

22 This is well recognized by Sereny. She writes that her aim in writing *Albert Speer* was to understand the man, and that it 'would have been impossible to achieve this if I had only viewed him in isolation, out of context with the environment in which he lived' (*Albert Speer*, p. 14).

Very often, the particularities we discover will provide *excusing* or *exempting* conditions, to use familiar terminology. An excuse grants that an action is morally wrong, but provides reasons for thinking the person did not really do the action after all.[23] Something about the circumstances means that she did not do it intentionally – she was pushed, or accidentally bumped, or suffered a seizure, which, it is thought, is not really to act at all. Exemptions, on the other hand, are less localized; they 'make it inappropriate to hold the agent accountable more generally'.[24] Examples include childhood, extreme stress and deprivation, psychopathology, behaviour control. In short, if the particularities we come to know about a person provide us with excusing or exempting conditions, then it is not surprising that condemnation would be inappropriate, for there was no guilt to begin with. Precisely because of this, however, such cases are not those most relevant here. Mercy and condemnation are responses that occur along with the judgement that a person *was* responsible, that her action *was* heinous. We are not merciful if we don't condemn someone who meant no wrong. Any interesting connection between understanding and mercy cannot therefore depend on knowledge of excuses or exemptions. Nussbaum's reconstruction of the Stoical position in 'Equity and Mercy' is helpful to make sense of just what this connection could be.

Nussbaum is also most concerned with a mitigating condition that operates once guilt has been established and her explanation for this is indebted to Seneca. According to him, people who do bad things are 'yielding to pressures that lie very deep in the fabric of human life'.[25] The merciful judge will see the guilt of the offender, but, writes Nussbaum, 'she will also see the many obstacles this offender faced … as a member of a culture, a gender, a city or country, and, above all, as a member of the human species, facing the obstacles characteristic of human life in a world of scarcity and accident.'[26] Given this, mercy ultimately becomes something required by full justice, rather than supererogatory.[27]

---

23 See R. Jay Wallace, *Responsibility and the Moral Sentiments*, p. 120. My understanding of these notions in this section is indebted to Wallace.

24 Ibid., p. 154.

25 'Equity and Mercy', p. 164, this volume, p. 17.

26 Ibid., p. 166, this volume, p. 20. Interestingly, Seneca thinks that this attitude can be taken up equally towards oneself as towards others, and displays this attitude to wonderful effect in his writing – apparent counter-examples to my asymmetry thesis. As I argue later, it *is* indeed possible to view oneself in this way. However, maintaining such a stance towards the self, as the Stoics apparently managed to do, would require a massive disruption of one's value structure and a radical reorganization of one's sense of self and others – precisely the programme recommended by the Stoics. Whether we should follow them is doubtful, given that so much of what we value would have to be renounced. See Nussbaum's fine discussion of the Stoics in *The Therapy of Desire*.

27 See, for example, 'Equity and Mercy', p. 170, this volume, p. 25: 'I have suggested that in many ways this norm [of mercy] fulfills and completes a conception of justice which lies, itself, at the basis of the rule of law.'

What seems to be doing the work now is not, however, understanding of the *particulars* of each individual, but knowledge of the general human condition. These two ideas are distinct, but Nussbaum, endorsing Seneca's position, writes that while the 'starting point [for the merciful judge's investigations] is a general view of human life and its difficulties ... the search for mitigating factors must at every point be searchingly particular'.[28] The connection between these two ideas is not clear, but is perhaps something like this: The judge imagines what it is like to be the offender, with his particular history and situation – the Aristotelian idea of *suggnômê* or 'judging with' is just such an exercise.[29] Placing himself in the position of another, he realizes that his own, similar frailties could easily have led him to do the same in those circumstances, and he will therefore be inclined towards gentleness. This identification itself depends upon thinking of humans as prone to making such mistakes, and of the world as encouraging them.

Despite Nussbaum's insistence on the importance of particularity, however, it seems that the merciful attitude resulting from this imaginative exercise still operates ultimately from knowledge of the human condition. The particularities we learn about a person lessen condemnation against a framework of knowledge of the general state of human existence. Humans are such, and the world they move in is such, that it is understandable that people would be influenced in the wrong direction. We hold this thought together with the judgement that their actions are often deeply immoral, so opening a space for mercy or condemnation. This step towards what I will call the *impersonal* or *objective stance* is crucial for the relation between understanding and mercy to hold even generally. For consider that it is only against such a background that the unpleasant 'particularities' that will typically characterize a person and her crime can be viewed at all mercifully. Knowledge of a person's ingrained malice or irascibility; that she is naturally insensitive or overwhelmingly self-centred – in themselves these factors do not seem to mitigate a person's offence, and yet very often these are precisely the kind of facts that our investigations will reveal. Only with knowledge of the human condition as a framework will we feel less inclined to hold even this knowledge against her. So the kind of understanding Nussbaum has in mind cannot stop at understanding character, formative influences and the circumstances of the particular action if it is to lead to mercy. Rather, it must continue on to the general conditions of human existence, and it is this that does the work for mercy. We are shown that the fallibility of the person under investigation is typical, that in these respects he is unique probably only in the degree and configuration of his weaknesses. And once we realize this, we can place ourselves in that person's position and realize that we are alike in being, simply, human. The surprising conclusion is that particularity, which is so central to

---

28 Ibid., this volume, p. 20, orig. p. 166.
29 Nussbaum discusses this at ibid., this volume, p. 13, orig. p. 161.

Nussbaum's larger ethical vision,[30] is less fundamental than generality in creating the connection between understanding and mercy.

This, I think, is the most plausible way of establishing a relation between understanding and mercy. The relation will not hold universally. On the one hand, some people may lack the imaginative or emotional resources ever to identify with another. On the other hand, people may be so wicked or so motiveless in their iniquity that the thought that we too are somehow capable of their atrocities will be too abstract to help us. It is just possible that some people may be uniquely wicked, so that our imaginative exercises repel rather than incline us to mercy, although it is doubtful that such people would be held morally responsible at all: sanity and morality have some intimate connection. However, the limitations posed by immense atrocities do not render the general relation between understanding and mercy too weak to be interesting. And if the human condition really *is* so fragile, the circumstances of the world really so harsh, and people in general banal rather than extraordinary in their crimes, then imaginative engagement and mercy are indeed ideals for which to strive.

I have been speaking so far of the third-person perspective on another, but my main interest was, after all, to ask after the first-person perspective: will the relevant knowledge of one's own particularities and shared humanity lead one to be merciful towards oneself when one has done wrong?

4. Understanding Oneself

Recall Speer's remark to Hilde: 'There are things … for which one has to carry the blame, even if purely factually one might find excuses.' By 'purely factually' I presume he means knowledge acquired from some objective or impartial perspective, the knowledge of Nussbaum's ideal judge, or, he might hope, of Sereny herself. And assume, as his acceptance of blame throughout suggests, that he means excuses only in a loose sense, that he acknowledges guilt. Of course, there will also be present, as there are for every person, the circumstances explored earlier – formative and situational influences, and the simple fact of being born human and imperfect in a world that provides obstacles to goodness at every turn.

Now there is no reason to think that we cannot acquire knowledge of ourselves with the same content as knowledge others can gain of us. Through self-reflection we bring these facts to our awareness in order to understand their significance in relation to our lives as a whole, just as we could for another. If the argument so far is correct, knowing another in this way will generally incline us to mercy, even if his crimes are terrible. However, this knowledge does not have the same force when Stangl and Speer regard themselves. We see throughout Sereny's studies that they are not, nor can they be, dispassionate or merciful about their guilt once they have acknowledged it. Moreover, this seems appropriate. Why is this?

---

30 See Nussbaum's *Love's Knowledge* for essays on the importance of particularity for ethics.

If it is possible to evaluate Stangl and Speer mercifully, then it is an interesting question why these men cannot do so towards themselves.[31] That their crimes were so terrible is certainly important, and I shall return to this. However, this is not the only or the full explanation, as we see if we ask how the evaluative process would work from the agent's perspective. Once he comes to know certain things about himself, or brings them to his awareness to explore, what happens next? Having the facts – that he had certain weaknesses; was prone to finding dubious rationalizations; that he had an abused or emotionally deprived childhood and that his moral growth was stunted as a result; that he found himself as an adult in a socio-political climate that encouraged certain views and actions; that he is, after all, merely human – knowing all this, can he view himself in a manner likely to lessen self-condemnation?

My claim now is that the closer to my core sense of identity the particularities revealed by self-exploration, the more difficult it will be to view them dispassionately, from the wider humane perspective earlier discussed. From the observer's position, disinterested yet sympathetic understanding brings perspective; the person is seen in his place, he is made sense of from the broader climate that is not him, but which must be grasped in order to grasp him. The observer can, in a sense, step back to get the full, panoptic view. In undertaking self-examination, however, one comes fundamentally to know *oneself* more immediately and fully, not primarily to know something *about* oneself. By this rather opaque distinction I mean something like the following:[32] The thought is that coming to understand oneself will bring *one's self* more fully into the picture, at closer range. One stands before one's own awareness in all one's smallness and moral grubbiness, and it is not another, but one's very self standing, inescapably, there. Because who one essentially is takes up the horizon of awareness, there is no space to move around and judge oneself tenderly or dispassionately. Regarding another, one has a distance that in principle allows one to choose the stance from

---

31 I am supposing that understanding Speer and Stangl does render utter condemnation difficult to maintain, despite our proper revulsion. Many will disagree and this is understandable, especially in the terrible case of Stangl. However, in this relation relies much of the undoubted force of Sereny's studies, which is difficult to understand otherwise. Once again, this does not mean we judge their *actions* less harshly and we certainly do think their self-condemnation appropriate; we just do not think these men irredeemable monsters. The war may indeed have bred or encouraged such monsters, but Sereny's work (and Hannah Arendt's seminal *Eichmann in Jerusalem*) rather shows us the dubious upbringings, petty moral weaknesses, and steady moral decline typical of the perpetrators. They were not bred in a vacuum. On this, see Sereny's Epilogue to *Into That Darkness*.

32 It has been suggested that the distinction in this paragraph maps the distinction between acquaintance knowledge and propositional knowledge (David Martens, in correspondence). This sounds promising, though not all acquaintance knowledge will face the problems I explore here. My concern is with aspects of the self which are constitutive of one's ethical identity, not any aspects with which we might conceivably be acquainted. Martens suggests that the ideal position would be one in which a person had both kinds of knowledge. In the cases of serious wrong-doing that interest me, however, this will be very difficult to achieve, but possible after long work. I discuss this in the following section.

which to approach her: merciful, condemnatory, contemptuous. In one's own case, however, self-exploration makes one more than ever *here*, brimming to the edges of one's awareness, a terrible generosity of presence. If one has any moral decency, a stance cannot be chosen; the confrontation with the self that performed an action so deeply opposed to standards one in some sense adheres to,[33] will make it immediately impossible to be merciful towards oneself. This will be especially true when, as in the case of Speer and especially Stangl, one has spent years of one's life avoiding this knowledge – finally faced, it would prove overwhelming.

Less metaphorically, my point concerns the ethical identity of the person, which I am calling the 'self'. In this normative sense, the self is essentially constituted by what we care about and value, and by our moral qualities. In self-reflection, along with knowledge of one's history, previously unknown or unexplored aspects of this normative identity are brought to one's attention. One may become aware of the quality of one's choices and desires, one's overall mode of interacting with the world, one's dominating vices. It is understandable that if one's ideal self-conception does not match the reality discovered through self-reflection, one's sense of self would become fractured – especially when the essential *I* is vicious, yet a sense of responsibility is nevertheless retained. I am thus not claiming that any kind of personal knowledge will prove so destabilizing, that in discovering anything about ourselves we will react in this way. My interest lies with constitutive (and in these cases, as yet unendorsed) aspects of a person's ethical identity.

What we therefore see in these cases is that self-knowledge seems to compel condemnation, despite the self-evaluator sharing something crucial with the disinterested observer – the content of understanding, the particularities of the individual involved. This is more than a logical point about the identity of subject and object in self-evaluation and, as I will discuss shortly, a measure of objectivity regarding oneself is certainly possible and often required. The point is, rather, evaluative: for a minimally moral agent, it is practically impossible to abstract away from certain facts about oneself once one becomes aware of them, for they are fundamentally opposed to values that one in some sense accepts and that define one's identity.

But, it might be immediately objected, why can't awareness of myself *as* frail moral creature or *as* person damaged in childhood or simply *as* someone as weak as anyone else similarly fill my awareness and bring along mercy? Granted, knowing my character as one notable for malice or greed, realizing the sordidness of my motivations, quite rightly would not lessen condemnation, but why not knowledge of my formative influences or of the human condition, just as in the case of another? These are, after all, just as much a part of the whole person as are the ethical qualities constituting what I call the self. Well, one can up to a point, as I shall explore later, but for now there are two things to note: First, consider the practical difficulty of thinking oneself determined, whatever one's beliefs on the matter. I cannot – practically

---

33 Speer and Stangl's acceptance is demonstrated by their evasions, their consuming guilt, their paying lip-service to moral codes of conduct.

cannot, as an agent – consider myself determined by elements of my history. They are a part of me, to be sure, and I can certainly come to realize their deep importance in making me the person I am, but once I am aware of them, I must allow a gap between them and my choices, a gap in which *I* move, permitting or preventing their influence. To think that my background could mitigate responsibility and guilt would be to renounce agency and authority over myself: I am no longer answerable to others for who I am and what I do. To be in this position is no longer to be a moral agent among others; it is to forgo citizenship of the moral kingdom.[34] And second, when I am able to consider my weaknesses as those merely typical of humanity, this cannot be used as mitigation if it leads one to terrible acts. To be morally mature is precisely not to be overwhelmed by ordinary weaknesses to commit extraordinary (or ordinary) crimes.

In the process of self-exploration, therefore, I come to understand a self for whom I am answerable, for whom the question is always possible, of whether or not I should allow my history and formative influences, once brought to awareness, simply to influence me further, at least without struggle. In this respect there is liberation in coming to self-knowledge, for no longer do such facts work darkly. I now have some control over them, even if that control is demonstrated in renouncing and trying, however arduous the task, to eradicate them. This would be the end of a long process of self-reflection and work, however, of which I shall have more to say in the following section. The immediate consequence of self-understanding, as I have argued, would be an *inability* to be dispassionate about one's faults. The ideal judge is able and generously willing to place a person in a wider context, and to see her as typical in respect of her faults, as just more sad evidence of the human lot. In contrast, I have argued that a person cannot in the first instance take up this impersonal stance towards himself, because any movement towards it would be halted by self-disgust. The overwhelming awareness of one's ethical identity would make it impossible to consider oneself in context, or to judge one's faults dispassionately. What does the work in any move from understanding to mercy, therefore, is not the content or goals of understanding alone but the possibility of taking up this impersonal stance towards the agent.

The logic of familiar emotions like guilt and shame supports the argument so far.[35] These emotions are 'self-referential', directed in the first instance towards one's self rather than one's action. The phenomenology of shame is that of wishing to disappear,

---

34 For a position that would disagree with this, see Pedro Tabensky's contribution (Chapter [Ch.] 6, this volume). Tabensky has argued (in correspondence) that one can nevertheless have authority over oneself insofar as one values oneself and the reason one instantiates. It is unclear to me how Tabensky's determinism is compatible with identifying oneself as the author of one's actions, in the sense of being the one called upon to account for one's actions before others, whether or not one regards the relevant actions as valuable. It is also unclear how one can consider oneself an agent, rather than an aesthetic object, while valuing one's good or bad actions or character, without taking responsibility for them to some degree.

35 I am here relying on Gabriele Taylor, *Pride, Shame, and Guilt* and Bernard Williams, *Shame and Necessity*.

not to be seen naked in one's depravity by others, or even more terribly, oneself. In the case of guilt, one judges oneself to have done something morally forbidden, and thus to deserve punishment. Once again, the focus is one's self, but because guilt is a more localized emotion than shame, and one's entire self is not degraded, some hope remains for self-restoration. In these contexts, the image of being able to live with oneself easily arises. How, knowing one's self to have fallen so terribly below one's own standards, is it possible to continue living as that self? The image of *facing up to* or *hiding from* the self is equally ubiquitous here[36] and shame is closely related to notions of audience. In learning about our own 'particularities', we face ourselves and become aware of *who we are*, rather than simply of *what we did*, and this can be a terrible realization.[37] If mercy is primarily a response to the person, as I earlier suggested, and the terrible deed so contrary to my self-conception issued from *this* person – myself – how can shame be overcome and mercy be possible?

Despite the uncomfortable consequences attending the asymmetry between self- and other-evaluation, however, it is difficult to wish it away without also wishing away a defining aspect of moral agency. To the descriptive claim about what typically occurs, should again be added the normative claim that this is, indeed, as it should be. We are creatures partly constituted by the moral emotions, which structure and prescribe our responses to ourselves and others. Not feeling shame when appropriate, having no integrity to lose, a self one can face no matter one's deeds – this places one without rather than within the moral community.

So my claim is that the stance of dispassionate impartiality that does the work for mercy regarding others is immediately unavailable for a person judging her own crimes. From the perspective of an agent with any moral sense, the realization that it was through her agency and character that a terrible deed was committed seems likely to augment condemnation rather than dispel it, in a way that makes the considerations of Nussbaum's ideal judge irrelevant. It is therefore this fundamental, entirely unsurprising first-personal relation to the self that hinders the possibility of being merciful towards oneself, and that grounds my opening intuition of an asymmetry between self- and other-evaluation.

5. The Possibility of Merciful Self-Evaluation

From the immediate confrontation of a person with her self, I now move on to what might happen next. I have been speaking so far of the impossibility of being the merciful judge towards ourselves that we ought to be towards others. But in fact we *can* be objective towards ourselves, and many people can in the end view themselves mercifully. There is thus strictly speaking no impossibility here at all, even if there

---

36 E.g. see Sereny, *Into That Darkness*, p. 135.

37 A nice illustration is found in ibid., p. 129. Sereny writes that what Stangl was most concerned about 'were what one might call the lesser manifestations of moral corruption in himself … what he did rather than what he was. It was his 'deeds' – his relatively mild deeds – he was at great pains to deny or rationalize rather than his total personality change'.

is a practical difficulty built into the structure of personhood. How, then, can my account explain self-directed mercy and dispassionate self-knowledge? In order to answer this, I will explore the conditions and limits of the movement characteristic of the merciful judge in self-evaluation. I will end by suggesting that when self-directed mercy is appropriately achieved, it will not be on the same grounds as mercy towards others.

Detached self-reflection is required by most people at some stage of life. It is possible to bring those particularities I have discussed to one's awareness, and to reflect upon them in the way one would if they characterized another person. When the smooth links within one's mental life, or between mental life and action, have broken down, or when one has avoided full awareness of who the person is who has done shameful things, viewing oneself as if one were in effect another person will be necessary for appreciating how one arrived at this point. Richard Moran explores how in therapy, for instance, we can look within to discover, based on evidence from our behaviour and mental states, what it is we actually think or feel. From such a third-personal or 'theoretical' position, however, a person cannot '*speak for* her feelings ... for she admits no authority over them'.[38] Her beliefs and emotions, and her awareness of them, are detached from her sense of the reasons supporting them. The value of this kind of relation to the self is thus instrumental, a means towards achieving the normal self-relation in which one is able to speak for, or *avow*, one's beliefs and feelings, rather than report that they are based on detective work one could equally well do for others.[39] For many people, incorporation and acceptance will be relatively easily accomplished and they will continue with life, a life in which they don't view themselves as therapeutic objects to be probed and placed in perspective. For others this might be more difficult to achieve because of the immensity of the crimes or the deep damage done to the self. Saying that 'theoretical' knowledge has instrumental value is therefore not to deny that it is very important, and indeed required for most of us at some point. However, it is a condition of self-directed mercy that one incorporate the knowledge gained from the theoretical perspective, construct a coherent view of the self and be able to live as that newly constructed self. If it is to be experienced as truly *self*-directed mercy, rather than as mercy towards some entity felt to be only theoretically identical with one's experienced self, one must work through the third-person perspective on one's 'particularities' back to first-person avowal or assimilation of them. It is only then that self-forgiveness, self-acceptance or mercy become possible.

Eventually, by considering oneself from a theoretical perspective, even the worst of us may be able to view herself up to a point as Nussbaum's impartial judge would

---

38 Moran, *Authority and Estrangement*, p. 39. Moran's 'theoretical stance' has much in common with my notion of the impersonal stance, though because of Moran's different concerns, it lacks notion's connection to evaluation and judgement. I am indebted to Moran's fine discussion of self-knowledge for my understanding of possible relations to the self in this section.

39 On reporting one's mental states, see ibid., e.g. p. 86.

– 'up to a point' for the following, by now familiar, reasons: If one's upbringing and milieu were vicious, one may be able to take this into consideration and think of oneself more tenderly. In cases where such considerations do not excuse or exempt, it might also be possible to consider one's everyday, petty weakness as those typical of humanity in general, and the comfort this affords may be justified. From here one can return relatively easily to the first-person lived perspective. However, it does not seem that appreciation of general human frailty will do the work in serious wrong-doing that it does when evaluating others. For it seems difficult to regard one's own serious crimes and vices as in some sense mitigated by the thought that all humans have the capacity for being quite grotesquely immoral.

Never to be escaped from the point of view of a subject is the question of his responsibility for allowing those factors to influence him at the time of action. 'Not all people, after all, did as I did. What was it about *me* that made me so susceptible, that permitted malign influences to move me to action?' And if one has progressed enough to do the work required to understand oneself in the first place, it seems difficult to see how such a newly-moral person would consider the impersonal point-of-view of some ideal judge as at all relevant for how to respond to his own appalling crimes.[40]

In the previous section, I argued that the impersonal stance could not be achieved towards oneself *in the first instance* of acquiring self-knowledge. Such knowledge would make the contextualizing of the self and one's crimes, which generates mercy in the evaluation of others, immediately impossible. It was then admitted in this section that through reflection and work on the self, a measure of impartiality can be later attained through taking up what Moran calls the theoretical position towards the self. But my claim now is that there is a limit to this movement, at least in the kind of cases under consideration, the cases relevant to mercy. The force typically generated by considering another person against a more general framework is rendered ineffectual from the first-person perspective. If my argument is correct, and if mercy as an appropriate response to serious wrong-doing is dependent upon such a move, then mercy, or at least this way of reaching mercy, is not available from the first-person perspective. Just how far back one can effectively step within the impersonal stance, so to speak, is partially dependent on the seriousness of the crime and the quality of any residual moral sensibility. Indeed, as I suggested at the end of Section 3, this may be true of the evaluation of others. In those cases, however, the relation between understanding and mercy holds for the most part, as it must if talk of mercy is to have any force, and even if extraordinary crimes or imaginative and sympathetic incapacity may conceivably cause the relation to break down. In self-evaluation, by contrast, the final kind of understanding that typically gives rise to mercy towards others will not be achieved, because the identity-constituting role of values prevents human nature from proving mitigating.

---

40 Seneca once again provides a counter-example to my claim. And once again, I admit the logical possibility of such a stance, but refer readers to my response in footnote 26 above.

We still need to know how mercy towards the self is to be explained, given that it happens and is often felt to be justified. My suggestion is that what is required is not further understanding or an impersonal perspective, but *conversion*, with all the connotations of rebirth, rejuvenation and penitence attending that notion. In his first few years at Spandau, for instance, Speer attempted just such a conversion: from being 'morally extinguished' he strove to 'become a different man',[41] not by neglecting his past or excusing his crimes, but by confronting them, admitting guilt[42] and trying to change the self that had so disastrously led him to this point. In *The Reader*, this is arguably what Hanna attempts in prison, by overcoming her secret shame of illiteracy, reading about the war and bequeathing money to a survivor of the church fire. Finally, there is Sereny's judgement on Stangl's death, all the more poignant because of her instinctual aversion to the man: '… I think he died when he did because he had finally, however briefly, faced himself and told the truth; it was a monumental effort to reach that fleeting moment when he became the man he should have been.'[43]

This way of understanding the possibility of mercy towards the self relates nicely to the emotions of guilt and shame. If shame is the sense of not being able to live with the self, conversion will be the moral attempt to escape shame – or better, to dispel it – by becoming a new and better self. When the crimes are so terrible, shame for what *that* self did may be impossible to alleviate and the only way of moving beyond that debilitating emotion would be to leave that self behind, become someone of whom shame is no longer the appropriate response. Mercy would thus be a complex response: It would require self-knowledge and full – deep – acknowledgement of the moral rift one brought about. It would require the appreciation and incorporation or avowal of a new set of values, and the sincere and steady attempt to break old habits of thought, feeling and action. It would require the simultaneous awareness of past crimes with the thought, essential to mercy, that the person is not irredeemable, in virtue of ongoing effort and some actual change. One's history and one's possible future are held together in this awareness. Mercy towards the self is thus something to be worked for and earned, rather than, as it seems to be regarding others, something required by justice once we understand human nature and our world. It may, in fact, never be achieved.

The possibility of mercy here is also partly dependent upon the person turning away from her own consuming guilt and shame, to attend to the victims of her actions. In fact, the phenomenology of guilt and shame suggests that as long as a person is only entangled in those emotions, gentle evaluation from the self or others would be both difficult to achieve and perhaps inappropriate. To see this, contrast these two emotions with remorse. Remorse, according to Gabriele Taylor, is more

---

41 Sereny, *Albert Speer*, pp. 10 and 23.

42 Problematically, he admitted guilt only up to a point. Personal knowledge of the final solution and responsibility in a personal capacity for that (rather than as a member of the group responsible) were denied until close to his death.

43 *Into That Darkness*, p. 366.

'outward looking' than the other two because it 'concentrates on the deed rather than on the agent as he who has done the deed'.[44] One attempts to make amends, not primarily to be able to live with the self again, but in order to undo what has been done as far as possible. I suggest that there would be a place for remorse once one has avowed those parts of the self discovered by taking up the theoretical stance. The move from the self-directed emotions to the other-directed emotion of remorse could accompany the move from Moran's theoretical perspective back to first-personal avowal. Perhaps paradoxically, this move to the first-personal perspective then removes the self from one's purview, so that one can concentrate on the action and its victims. One sees the world, not merely one's self. And this seems right, for concentrating on the wrong of one's action and attempting to make whatever amends possible are the correct foci of attention to warrant gentler responses. One wishes a person to be fully aware of the damage done to another, not just the damage done to his self.

6. Conclusion

The main task of this paper has been to establish two claims: that there is an asymmetry between self- and other-evaluation, and that understanding alone is not sufficient to guarantee mercy, from either the first- or second-person perspective. Understanding with the same content will not have the same results from the two perspectives; rather, it is the possibility of being impersonal towards a person, of seeing her against a framework of knowledge of the human condition, and being willing to let that play a role in one's evaluation, that will lead understanding on to mercy. I argued that there are limits to the extent such considerations can have force from the first-person perspective, the reason for which lies deeply in what it is to be a person, in the normal relation to the self that is constitutive of moral agency and identity.

In conclusion, I wish to suggest briefly another limitation regarding mercy, this time returning to our starting-point of evaluating others. For the purpose of equitable evaluation, it seems that there ought to be a limit to the extent of our identification with others.[45] If we take up too intimately their perspective, their reasoning, their vision of the world, we may lose our ability objectively to evaluate them, and lose that distance between people in which equity and mercy move – the distance I argued we lack from the first-person perspective. The dangers of too-close identification are (at least) two-fold: Firstly, we could find ourselves viewing the world and employing rationalizations just as that person did, and our ability to evaluate negatively when

---

44 *Pride, Shame, and Guilt*, pp. 100 and 98.

45 There are weaker and stronger forms of identification, namely, identifying oneself as being in X's position; and identifying oneself as being X in X's position. My point applies to both kinds.

required could come under pressure.[46] Secondly, and more to the point, if we attempt to place ourselves in the position of another who has reached self-knowledge and acknowledged serious wrong-doing, we might become equally engulfed by guilt and shame *for* that person, and think it as justified as that person would. Knowledge that there are things we couldn't live with having done would accompany the imaginative exercise. In short, too literal identification will have the consequence that evaluating others will become occluded by one's self again, the opposite to what identification was meant to achieve.

Of course, there are practical and logical limits to identifying with another, and identification to such a degree that one retains no sense of *not* being that person, or not really being in her position, is highly unlikely. But still, this seems to raise a worry for theories that take identification or sympathy with another as a normative ideal, in whatever respect.[47] We are shown again, from a different direction, that it is not the content of understanding that does the work in merciful evaluation, but rather understanding achieved from a certain stance. The need for maintaining objectivity towards others, and the difficulty of maintaining it towards oneself both, however, seem to work to the advantage of justice.

---

46 On this worry, see Robert Gordon, 'Sympathy, Simulation, and the Impartial Spectator'. Gordon is concerned with this worry in the context of simulation theory, a theory of explaining and predicting the behaviour of others.

47 There are certainly implications for simulation theories that work on the personal level of description.

Chapter 5

The Case for Moral Complexity

Marc Fellman

Editor's Introduction

Via an alternative route to the one taken by Nussbaum, Marc Fellman reaches similar conclusions to hers, but the focus of his concerns is somewhat different. He too is a particularist, focusing his attention on how to morally respond to specific others, how to be responsible to them, given their specific circumstances, adverse circumstances in particular. How we respond to others both expresses and determines our moral understandings. His primary case study is the Holocaust and, relatedly, the relationship between Hanna and Michael in *The Reader*. One crucial way of determining how to respond, including how to judge, involves the imaginative exercise of putting ourselves in another's shoes. Doing this, Fellman believes, will allow us to be more compassionate or, in Nussbaum's preferred vocabulary, merciful. Fellman spends some time showing us how the complex weave of practices of responding to others often leads us, to put things in Walzer's preferred terms, to get dirty hands; to be forced to do something bad in order to bring a good about. Of course, the case of perpetrators of the Holocaust is somewhat different. Their primary aims were deeply reprehensible. But complexity, which includes our vulnerability to circumstances that invite us to respond in certain ways, often lead to moral failings, even failings that overwhelm our capacity to understand. Our recognition of this complexity, of the moral complexity of living humanly, should incline us to judge with care, even in the light of the moral enormity of the Holocaust. Michael's complex relationship with Hanna paradigmatically embodies the complexity involved in our moral understandings of serious wrongdoing, understanding which involves judgement, but not merely judgement. Brian Penrose and Ward Jones' contributions nicely complement Fellman's piece.

* * *

There is a passage in Bernhard Schlink's *The Reader*[1] in which the problem of the tension between judging and understanding is crystallized. It arrives at a moment in the story when the central character, Michael, comes to the conclusion that simultaneously understanding and condemning the crimes that his former lover had

---

1 Bernhard Schlink, *The Reader*, London; Phoenix, 1998.

committed was possibly an impossible task. For Michael, and in particular because of his past relationship with the former camp guard, Hanna, it is as if the tension itself resists being accommodated, or even accorded a satisfactory coherency, within his moral worldview.

I hope to shed some light on Michael's predicament by situating the tension between judging and understanding, as it is understood in *The Reader*, within the context of a discussion on another powerful tension, that between moral complexity and moral enormity in Holocaust experiences. That is to say, I think that there are some interesting parallels between the two tensions. An important claim with respect to my argument is that the Holocaust more broadly, though not unlike Michael's personal quandary, represents a genuine moral problem. On the one hand, the Holocaust appears to encapsulate the paradigm case of evil while it is also the case that the Holocaust is a modern, human phenomenon, the very complexity of which can have the effect of placing into question our capacity in such matters as judgement. Put another way, enormity analyses, that is analyses that foreground the moral enormity of the Holocaust, demand that we judge and ascribe responsibility, yet, for equally urgent reasons complexity analyses compel us to understand the whys and wherefores of human actions.

First, I will expand on the form of the problem of the tension between enormity and complexity, whilst paying particular attention to establishing the presence and parameters of moral complexity within both individual moral experiences of the Holocaust and the Holocaust itself as a defining event. My core concern here is to establish to what extent there is a tension between moral complexity and enormity.

Specifically, I will argue that moral complexity is informed, in large part, by a variety of understandings of responsibility. My claim will be that it is the various understandings of, and issues arising from, responsibility, that are of prime importance to understanding both moral complexity itself and the tension that arises between complexity and enormity analyses. By responsibility I mean both particular individuals' senses of responsibility as well as more generalized conceptualizations. To clarify, I will elaborate on the ways of understanding responsibility that I think contribute to the idea that moral complexity is a core element of accounts of the Holocaust. It is in the context of discussions of responsibility that I make the link between the twin tensions of complexity and enormity and judging and understanding.

As a way of visualizing the relationship between moral complexity and responsibility I additionally propose the idea of a 'weave' as a means of structuring the various understandings of responsibility.

I justify my attention on complexity analyses of the Holocaust because this aspect of the tension seems more difficult to defend in the face of the moral horror that usually characterizes it.

Moral Enormity and the Imperative to Judge

An invitation into the sort of general awe encountered in the face of enormity evaluations of the Holocaust is conveyed when Lawrence Langer writes,

> ...how can we inscribe...[narratives of Holocaust experiences]...in the historical or artistic narratives that later will try to reduce to some semblance of order or pattern the spontaneous defilement implicit in such deeds? Where shall we record it in the scroll of human discourse? How can we enrol such atrocities in the human community...Well, we can't: we require a scroll of *in*human discourse to contain them; we need a definition of the *in*human community...[2]

I happen to disagree with Langer's view that such acts as those referred to by him occurred, in some sense, in an *inhuman* universe. On the contrary, part of what contributes to their incomprehensibility is precisely the fact that they occurred in *our* universe and were committed by people with the same sorts of strengths and weaknesses most of us possess. That said I also think that Langer's sentiment does convey the power of the horror felt upon encountering Holocaust accounts. In a vein similar to Langer, Douglas Lackey writes:

> The evils of the Holocaust are so numerous, so diverse, and so extreme that at first sight it seems presumptuous to judge them at all, much less than to judge them by ordinary moral norms. Judgement requires comprehension and transcendence, and comprehension and transcendence of these events seems almost beyond human power. The ordinary moral categories feel too pale and narrow to do justice to our sense of condemnation...[3]

The sort of comprehension implied by Lackey is in itself difficult enough but when moral enormity is accompanied by moral complexity as a component of rendering morally intelligible, particular events and experiences, then the task is especially problematic. The combination of moral enormity and moral complexity with regard to the way the Holocaust was and continues to be understood, brings with it particular difficulties. The requirement of condemnation serves to restrict the capacity to comprehend the multiple moral dimensions that are a feature of this complex of events. Or to put it another way, the sort of enormity analyses often associated with the Holocaust can have the effect of obscuring the ways in which this same phenomenon is also morally complex. Of course, the opposite can also be the case. Misguided attention to the presence of complexity analyses can have the effect of diluting the moral enormity of such experiences.

Part of the challenge lies in understanding the extent of the problem presented by the tension. Moral enormity, for instance, appears to imply straightforward accounts

---

2   Lawrence Langer, *Pre-empting the Holocaust*, New Haven: Yale University Press, 1998, p. 2.

3   Douglas Lackey, 'Extraordinary Evil or Common Malevolence: Evaluating the Jewish Holocaust', in Brenda Almond and Donald Hill (eds), *Applied Philosophy, Morals and Metaphysics in Contemporary Debates*, London: Routledge, 1991, p. 141.

of the way moral life is assessed. Moral complexity, on the other hand, suggests that moral life is anything but amenable to straightforward ways of understanding what is at issue. I intend to demonstrate that an important hurdle lies in the attempt to understand what the nature of the relationship between enormity and complexity may yield for an understanding of both Holocaust experiences and Michael's personal moral quandary in *The Reader*.

One particularly interesting aspect of the tension between complexity and enormity analyses concerns the issue of the distinction between understanding and judgement. This is an issue often alluded to in accounts that stress moral enormity and includes the concern that experiences such as those typified by the Holocaust threaten to overwhelm understanding. Mary Midgley, in her book *Wickedness*[4] evokes just such a distinction in the context of a discussion of the factors influencing human behaviour. She writes:

> Infection can bring on fever, but only in creatures with a suitable circulatory system. Like fever, spite, resentment, envy, avarice, cruelty, meanness, hatred and the rest are themselves complex states, and they produce complex activities. Outside events may indeed bring them on, but, like other malfunctions, they would not develop if we were not prone to them.[5]

Midgley's analogy entices us to pursue its implications for what they may reveal about individual human behaviour and the factors influencing such behaviour. For Midgley, a key requirement of understanding why we act the way we do is being able to recognize that eliciting both social and individual causes is required for properly explaining human wickedness. Midgely's aim is to enquire into the question as to why people treat others and sometimes even themselves abominably. She wants to be able to understand why, as she puts it '...[people] constantly cause avoidable suffering'.[6] As I indicated above this is never going to be straightforward. One difficulty concerns the distinction between what she refers to as individual and public wickedness. The exact significance of the distinction becomes evident when the discussion moves to an examination of the issues surrounding responsibility and, in particular, judgement. Midgley recognizes that some actions are categorically wrong. But she is less clear about how the perpetrators of such actions are to be placed in a discussion of responsibility.

Midgley is well aware that judgement is sometimes necessary but she also recognizes the complexities and difficulties that judgement entails. Such complexities very often render, at the very least, certain sorts of judgement problematic. Midgley's attempt at resolving the problem of judgement is interesting. She continues her discussion with the claim that moral judgements function to 'orient' us as we plot our way on the path that is moral life. In other words, moral judgements are a necessary precondition for making sense of our own behaviour as well as the

---

4   Mary Midgley, *Wickedness*, London: Routlege and Kegan Paul, 1985.

5   Ibid., p. 3.

6   Ibid., p. 2.

behaviour of others. However, Midgley is careful to point out that the requirement to judge is not a licence, as she puts it, to stone people. Rather, it is an important part of understanding the behaviour of others, but understanding can have the effect of tempering judgement and make us less prone to judging harshly. Extrapolating from Midgley's position, I believe judging to be an important social practice and indeed that the tension is internal to the practice. The tension, though, can make moral life more difficult and indeed complex. So, while judgement is an important component of moral understanding, it ranks as only one component among others.

I would want to add that whilst I find this aspect of Midgely's argument plausible, there is enough evidence to indicate that people are likely to conceive of responsibility as entailing obligations for which a person is morally accountable. Standardly, emphasis is on the fulfilment or violation of those responsibilities, deserving of praise or blame, rather than understanding what a particular individual might take to be his or her responsibility. This view is supported by the currency of such terms as 'retributive justice' and the proliferation in both Eastern and Western cultures of a mentality of harsher penalties, increasing incarceration rates and expanding police forces.

Midgely of course, is not unaware of the significance of judgement as a function of moral understanding. She writes:

General scepticism about the possibility of moral judgement, though it may look like a piece of neutral, formal analysis, cannot fail to act as propaganda in this contest of attitudes. It must make us lose confidence in our power of thinking about moral issues involving individuals – including ourselves. Yet this power is absolutely necessary to us.[7]

Judgement for Midgely, is a necessary part of what it means to be a 'responsible agent'. This is a significant point because, as I argue, moral judgements are a necessary part of the way we arrive at moral understanding. Many situations are not able to be reckoned with responsibly without incorporating matters of judgement. There is a need though to distinguish between certain forms of judgement. To clarify, I may in one situation judge a person or their actions without holding them accountable in any significant sense. On the other hand, there are other sorts of situations requiring other sorts of judgements that, whilst entailing accountability, are also more problematic in the sense that they are morally complex. Typically such situations would encompass extenuating circumstances like duress, conflicting loyalties, decisions made without time to consider, a particular individual's proclivity to procrastinate and the like. It is precisely in such situations that the tension generated by the presence of both enormity and complexity can make certain sorts of judgement more difficult to defend.

One way of establishing how it is that complexity affects judgement is by shifting the focus of the discussion to the relationship between judgement and responsibility. There is some value in placing the discussion on judgement within a

---

7   Ibid., p. 71.

more nuanced understanding of responsibility. It is in the above context that I again question Lawrence Langer when he disputes an important conclusion of Christopher Browning's groundbreaking study[8] that most of us are capable of becoming killers under certain circumstances. Langer seems distinctly uncomfortable with Browning's position when he writes quite defensively that:

> The fact is that when ordinary men agree to mass murder, for *whatever* reasons, they cease to be ordinary men like the rest of us and assume the role of killers.[9]

Here I think he misses a crucial point. It is also arguable that 'the rest of us' possess the capacity, if circumstances are such, to commit terrible transgressions. That is what Browning's study so disturbingly demonstrates. My point here is that a discussion of responsibility in cases such as those described by Browning is crucial not only for what it can tell us about why individuals do wrong but also because it is core to the case for moral complexity and our understanding of the form of the tension. Accounting for why people do wrong requires that we unpack the complex moral byways that individuals travel. However, it also means that we need to move away from the traditional retributive understandings of the function of judgement and responsibility. Thus, my account of responsibility de-emphasizes ideas of responsibility as accountability in favour of understandings that foreground responsibility as part of our engagement with others with a view to developing our moral competencies.

There are benefits of a shift away from an understanding of responsibility as entailing too much of an emphasis on ideas of guilt, blame and punishment. Rather than necessarily focusing on some perceived imperative to mete out punishment or the idea that we treat individuals solely as responsible agents that must be held accountable, more nuanced ways of understanding the variety of dimensions of responsibility can be explored. In my account this also means maintaining a sense of the very centrality of responsibility in an understanding of the tension engendered by the combination of complexity and enormity. Let me also point out here that re-assessing how we might understand responsibility does not mean that the tension conveniently dissolves. On the one hand, the enormity of Holocaust experiences and such experiences as those that confronted Michael in *The Reader* remain intact. In some instances condemnatory statements, whilst they may not take the discussion very far forward, may sometimes still be appropriate. Failing to condemn the horror characterized by Holocaust experiences risks diminishing their moral significance in our eyes. Moreover, understanding the complexities of a situation, for example factoring in what individuals take to be their responsibilities or being able to account for the vulnerabilities that move people to act in reprehensible ways, complex and important though these issues may be, does not arguably lessen the requirement to also hold them accountable. However, understanding such moral complexities does

---

8   Christopher R. Browning, *Ordinary Men: Reserve Police Battalion and the Final Solution in Poland*, New York: HarperCollins, 1993.

9   Langer, *op. cit.*, p. xiv.

lend substance to the case for moral complexity and may convince us to modify our judgements.

A Weave of Ways of Understanding Responsibility

On my account, responsibility, though it may entail ascriptions of praise or blame, is not exhausted by them. I want to move the focus of the discussion to develop a more encompassing account of responsibility and how this account, in turn, lends substance to the claim for a tension between complexity and enormity.

I contend that the key to understanding life as morally complex lies, in turn, with understanding various different but related conceptualizations of responsibility. To help to visualize what I am proposing I suggest that the various nuances of responsibility be understood as analogous to a 'weave' comprised of differing threads. Taken together these threads represent a rich though complex moral fabric in contrast to the simple but powerful conceptual strand of moral enormity.

Following this analogy there are a number of different strands that can be identified as belonging to an understanding of responsibility. Among those that I shall discuss I find Primo Levi's notion of responsibility as somehow linked to a concept of goodness, Margaret Walker's 'practices of responsibility'[10] and Christopher Gowans' 'responsibilities to persons'[11] particularly interesting threads. As ways of understanding responsibility they do not of course exhaust how we may fruitfully understand the concept yet they are core to my account of moral complexity.

The first thread that I want to consider comes from a story by Primo Levi. On my understanding of this story Levi foregrounds the issue of responsibility in his view of how the Holocaust might be adequately understood. In this story and in reference to his friend Lorenzo, Levi evokes a strong sense of how responsibility can manifest itself even in the most life diminishing of circumstances. In an account of the way camp life emptied people of their humanity Levi surmises:

> I believe that it was really due to Lorenzo that I am alive today...for his having constantly reminded me by his presence, by his natural and plain manner of being good, that there still existed...a remote possibility of good...[and]...for which it was worth surviving.[12]

This quotation suggests that even amidst a systematic attempt to degrade human values, a moral perspective, in the form of accepting responsibility for other persons, can prevail. In Levi's account I interpret Lorenzo as having demonstrated the extreme importance of a belief in respect for self in the context of relations with the other. In the midst of this relationship, albeit only briefly discussed by Levi, it

---

10 See Margaret Walker, *Moral Understandings: A Feminist Study in Ethics*, London: Routledge, 1998, pp. 200–205.

11 See Christopher W. Gowans, *Innocence Lost: An Examination of Inescapable Moral Wrongdoing*, New York: Oxford University Press, 1994, pp. 16–25.

12 Primo Levi, *If this is a Man and The Truce*, London: Abacus, 1987, p. 127.

seems that two senses of responsibility are being played out. In the first instance, Levi claims that Lorenzo is in some measure, although perhaps even unknowingly, *responsible* for his survival. It also seems evident that Lorenzo helped to enable Levi to *take responsibility for himself* and so endure. Examples like that of Levi's account of Lorenzo goes to the heart of what I seek to convey in the understanding of responsibility I am presently defending as that which serves as the framework of our moral understandings of ourselves. I mention the case of Levi and Lorenzo in order to illustrate the view that taking responsibility for one's own situation is always to take responsibility within the context of our relations with others. It is within the context of our relations with others that we are able to grasp the dimensions of responsibility. In another context, in an interview with Giovanna Borradori, Jacques Derrida said that:

> Responsibility for a decision, if there is any and if one must answer for it, amounts each time…to a transaction between the imperative for autonomy and the imperative for heteronomy….[13]

If I understand Derrida correctly his point is that to be responsible is to understand, in some sense, the plight of the other. Lorenzo's responsibility for Levi is a paradigmatic case. My wider point here is that the way in which we take responsibility, in our relations with others, is how we come to map the complex byways of our moral relations.

In conjunction with the view that moral life is interpersonal, that is, that it is given meaning by virtue of our interactions with others, I want to introduce, as another aspect of responsibility, the idea that moral life is culturally situated and sustained by what Margaret Walker refers to as 'practices of responsibility'.[14] Elaborating on what she means Walker writes:

> …morality consists in a family of practices that show what is valued by making people accountable to each other for it. Practices of making morally evaluative judgements are prominent among moral practices, but they do not exhaust them. There are also habits and practices of paying attention, imputing states of affairs to people's agency, interpreting and describing human actions, visiting blame, offering excuses, inflicting punishment, making amends, refining and inhibiting the experience or expression of feelings, and responding in thought, act, and feeling to any of the foregoing. In all of these ways we express our senses of responsibility.[15]

I think that Walker has captured a very important aspect of responsibility. By linking responsibility to a variety of social practices, and indeed to morality itself, Walker raises the prospect that it is these ideas themselves that play an important part in

---

13 Giovanna Borradorri, *Philosophy in a Time of Terror: Dialogues with Jürgen Habermas and Jacques Derrida*, Chicago: University of Chicago Press, 2003, p. 132.

14 Margaret Walker, *Moral Understandings: A Feminist Study in Ethics*, London: Routledge, 1998, p. 201.

15 Walker, *op. cit.*, p. 10.

the expression of our sense of responsibility. And even more to the point, moral competency of the sort demanded by the sort of experiences that have become a trademark of the Holocaust requires that we pull together and attempt to render morally intelligible this complex composite of practices. The sort of practices identified above by Walker offer a sense of the intricacies entailed in living our lives as moral beings. In their own right they reflect something of the complexity that I contend is central to the moral lives of human beings. If, on the one hand, the sorts of moral practices described by Walker entail the ascription and/or the taking of responsibility they also strongly suggest that such analyses are going to be complex.

Another important idea connecting moral complexity with responsibility is Christopher Gowans' understanding of 'inescapable wrongdoing'.[16] I suggest that Gowans' idea of 'inescapable wrongdoing' supports the view that moral evaluations are complex. In his book *Innocence Lost* Gowans explores moral experience from the perspective of moral conflict and the claim that sometimes moral wrongdoing is inescapable. Gowans writes:

> Many philosophers maintain that in every moral conflict some course of action that is wholly free from wrongdoing is available to the agent (though it may be difficult, and perhaps in some cases virtually impossible, to know what this action is). In my view these philosophers are mistaken. We may find ourselves in moral conflicts in which, through no fault of our own we will do something morally wrong no matter what we do. In these situations we may choose the lesser of two evils and hence act for the best. But in acting for the best we still choose an evil, and in this sense we still do something wrong.[17]

By challenging the idea that it is always possible to avoid moral wrongdoing Gowans is contributing to an old debate in Western philosophy over the status of moral dilemmas. He argues that although a person may decide after careful deliberation that one of two conflicting responsibilities is more compelling than the other, the less compelling responsibility does not simply disappear. Instead the secondary responsibility is at best subordinated in the process of prioritizing. I agree with Gowans and hold that his argument holds even in the case of the Holocaust. The perpetrators, for example, though they knew they were doing something wrong could still be conflicted over what they take to be their responsibilities.

A key factor in this grading of responsibilities is the idea that in situations that would typically constitute serious moral conflict the agent experiences, as a matter of course, strong emotional responses. Such emotions seem to be, at least for Gowans, prima facie litmus tests for the presence of moral dilemmas. In other words, feelings such as anguish at the time of the decision and guilt after the decision result from the recognition that the situation cannot be resolved in a way that avoids the feeling and knowledge of moral transgression. Perhaps not surprisingly, such outcomes, emotionally painful though they may be, have the potential to enrich our

---

16 See Gowans, *op. cit.*, pp. 3–10.
17 Ibid., p. 3.

moral lives. Consistent with this, Gowans writes that it is important to recognize that '…our affective moral responses [to certain situations] can be a source of moral understanding'.[18] This takes me back to my earlier point about perpetrators. The fact that perpetrators typically felt serious emotional conflict over their behaviour, something that is well supported by such research as Browning's,[19] implies some sense of a deeper moral understanding of their own behaviour even if such understanding does not result in changes to the way they behave in the future.

As a means of tapping this potential for moral understanding in what he calls a 'logically consistent and systematic way' Gowans, following Rawls' conceptualization of 'reflective equilibrium' coins the term 'reflective intuitionism'. He argues that moral understanding or 'moral judgements' as he calls them result in large part from processes that are more than mere gut reactions. On Gowans' somewhat Aristotelian account, moral understanding comes about largely as the result of the acquisition and development of our experiences over time and handed down through successive generations. As for moral dilemmas, he is not saying that in every situation where conflicted feelings are present moral distress is appropriate. Rather he is stating that there are some situations where such feelings are appropriate and are felt intuitively.

I believe that Gowans' account of the factors at play in situations of moral conflict resonates strongly with the sort of understanding of responsibility that I am seeking to convey. I think that this is best demonstrated by considering the way in which he pulls his idea of inescapable conflict together with his understanding of responsibility. He says that our intuitions concerning feelings of moral anguish are best explained by the more fundamental proposition that in some situations moral wrongdoing is inescapable. He then proceeds to show that it is on the basis of responsibilities to specific persons that unavoidable feelings of moral distress are grounded. It is this connection between responsibilities to particular people and the feelings generated by such commitments that are of interest for my discussion on moral complexity. In regard to this important claim Gowans writes:

> …an agent's moral responsibilities are based on a recognition of the intrinsic and unique value of the particular persons (or social entities) with whom the agent has, in various ways, established some connection. Hence, an agent's responsibilities are ultimately responsibilities to specific persons. The nature of these responsibilities is defined primarily by the agent's relationship with those persons to whom he or she is responsible and is not simply a function of the outcome of the agent's moral deliberations about what ought to be done in a given situation. For this reason responsibilities to specific persons may conflict. When they do, the fact that deliberation of necessity directs the agent to fulfil his or her responsibility to at most one person does not mean that the responsibility to the other person has in this situation been eliminated. There will thus be occasions of conflicting moral responsibilities when, whatever the agent does, he or she will fail to fulfil at least one of these responsibilities. It is with respect to moral wrongdoing in the

---

18 Ibid., p. 19.
19 See Browning's evidence of conflicted feelings in *Ordinary Men*.

case of not fulfilling a moral responsibility so defined that I believe that moral wrongdoing is sometimes inescapable.[20]

It's worth emphasizing that the notion of responsibility, as Gowans understands it, cannot simply mean that one has duties and obligations towards others. I think, and if I understand Gowans, responsibility, and this means moral responsibility, is bound with the nature of our relations with specific others. Somewhat similarly to Walker, this in turn means that understanding moral life more generally needs to account for the complexities surrounding discussions about responsibility. Gowans' own example of Herman Melville's disturbing but compelling story of Billy Budd[21] is a good illustration of the sort of discussion I am referring to.

I believe that whilst our responsibilities might, and likely do, entail duties and obligations of one sort or another such ways of understanding responsibility are, on their own, insufficient as explanations as to how we arrive at the place where we are able to decide between one responsibility and another. The reason that duties and obligations, by themselves, are insufficient with respect to how we understand our responsibilities, is because of other significant factors that complicate our understanding of our responsibilities. In addition to Walker's practices of responsibility and Gowans' responsibilities to specific persons such factors as the role of individual disposition, luck regarding one's circumstances and others are pivotal to understanding how it is that we arrive at our perceptions of our responsibilities.

It is because there are a number of significant conceptual and practical factors that should be considered when discussing what it is that enables us to understand our responsibilities that I also believe that the analogy of a weave of ways of understanding responsibility has merit. This is perhaps nowhere more evident than in respect to the attempt to understand the moral dimensions of the Holocaust. In the course of a person arriving at a moral decision, a whole host of factors that relate to the ways that person understands their responsibilities 'weave' their way into the decision making process. The case of Hanna, the former camp guard in Schlink's *The Reader* typifies this point. In the course of the trial during which Hanna is charged with crimes relating to selections in Auschwitz and the death of several hundred women who burned to death in a church, she speaks about her responsibilities, both to herself and others. The narrator writes that in the course of the trial 'Hanna wanted to do the right thing…she took on a responsibility to admit what she could not deny'.[22] And elsewhere we can see how Hanna recalled her responsibilities as a camp guard. The narrator claims that:

Hanna described how the guards had agreed among themselves to tally the same number of prisoners [for selection and death in the gas chamber] from their six equal areas of responsibility.[23]

---

20 Gowans, *op. cit.*, pp. 19–20.
21 Gowans, *op. cit.*, pp. 3–24.
22 Schlink, *op. cit.*, pp. 108–9.
23 Ibid., p. 109.

And in the case of the women who burned to death, Hanna, responding to the judge's question regarding why she didn't unlock the doors to the church claims that, 'We couldn't just let them escape! We were responsible for them…'.[24] As a result of a complex combination of factors, amongst them the interplay of her perceptions of her responsibilities, her personal fears and the circumstances she found herself in, Hanna committed wrongs for which she would be held accountable.

If, as I have indicated, a discussion of responsibility is to underpin an account of moral complexity, it is also the case that a proper understanding of moral complexity contributes to understanding the extent to which the tension between judging and understanding is a central dimension of our moral lives. On a sympathetic reading of the story of Hanna we can claim to understand her account of her responsibilities yet still require judgement in the sense that she be held accountable for her actions. However, this requirement to both understand the complexities of moral life and yet hold a person accountable for what they do generates a tension that is unavoidable. Michael says as much when the narrator writes:

> I wanted simultaneously to understand Hanna's crime and to condemn it. But it was too terrible for that. When I tried to understand it, I had the feeling I was failing to condemn it as it must be condemned. When I condemned it as it must be condemned, there was no room for understanding.[25]

Returning to Gowans, a large measure of the success of his account of responsibility rests on the nature of the claim of specific relationships between persons. For Gowans, relationships, and in turn the responsibilities that derive from these relationships stem from differing sorts of associations, primary and otherwise, between individuals. In other words, moral responsibilities derive from particular concrete relationships such as those typified by relations of kinship, friendship and love.[26] The example of Michael in Schlink's *The Reader* is relevant here. Because of his past relationship with Hanna, as lovers, and because of his belief that a miscarriage of justice had occurred, Michael felt he had to act in her defence. His understanding of his responsibility towards Hanna was also based on the knowledge that he alone had regarding her illiteracy. Even in the presence of this deep understanding, but because of all the layers of complexity that it entailed, he was conflicted by the need to judge her for what she had done.

Gowans' account of responsibilities to specific persons as substantively informed by the nature of relationships between intimates represents an important insight into the way responsibilities are formed more generally. Moreover, I think the value of Gowans' account lies in its ability to unravel aspects of the practical operations of our moral relations.

---

24 Ibid., p. 126.

25 Ibid., p. 156.

26 In a similar vein to Christopher Gowans, Margaret Walker in her book *Moral Understandings*, develops the idea of a 'geography of responsibility' to explain how moral responsibilities evolve. See especially pp. 107–9.

One of the examples that Gowans uses is that based on the sort of intimate relationship between a parent and child.[27] In this example he describes the responsibility of a parent to nurture his or her child. Such responsibility, it is argued, comes from a number of sources not least of which is the accepted knowledge that the infant in question is his or her child and as such would usually be regarded as intrinsically and uniquely valuable. Gowans' intent is to establish a connection between this primary relationship and the way we perceive the morality of our relations more generally. He is suggesting that the way people with whom we do not share a close relation or even a distant relation may still be regarded as intrinsically valuable on the basis of the way we understand ideas of value and responsibility towards those with whom we are close. In this way Gowans builds an account of morality extrapolating from relations with intimates.

The Case for Moral Complexity

The discussion of responsibility to date, from Levi to Walker to Gowans is intended to show how the various ways of understanding responsibility contributes to an account of moral life, characterized by a tension between moral complexity and moral enormity. Gowans identifies how inescapable wrongdoing and moral conflict stem in turn from understandings of responsibility built up from among other things our ties with intimates. I am arguing that these concerns, moral conflict and responsibilities to persons, together with ideas of taking responsibility for one's self, other practices of responsibility and such accompanying issues as individual disposition, circumstances, luck and the like comprise the elements of the complexity of moral life. In short, these elements of moral life ensure that moral life is morally complex. In turn it is these same elements of moral life that enable us to understand why it is as difficult as it is compelling to judge perpetrators of crimes and indeed how it is that people commit such crimes in the first instance.

There is a key moment in *The Reader* that captures this tension poignantly. When questioned about her role and personal culpability in the selection of prisoners to be sent to the gas chambers Hanna answers with a question for the judge that goes to the heart of the claim for the moral complexity of moral life. She asks, or perhaps pleads, 'I…I mean…so what would you have done?'[28] The answer that the judge provides is starkly abstract and stripped of any real appreciation of what Hanna was asking, rendering it most unsatisfactory to all who heard it. What Hanna deserved to hear by way of an answer was what she should have actually done taking into account all facets of the complexity of moral life. The very tension at issue is what characterizes the question and what makes it impossible to answer satisfactorily. The answer that she received was a statement of the obvious. What she received was a statement of what she shouldn't have done. Yes her situation had been morally perilous but it had been made so by the moral complexity of her predicament.

---

27 See Gowans, pp. 122–3.
28 Schlink, *op. cit.*, p. 110.

By engaging directly with the judge Hanna is engaging with us all. This is a question for all who would seek to judge the Hannas of this world. It is a question that exposes the moral vulnerabilities in us all. It is a question that puts us all in her shoes and confronts all of us with the stark possibility that as fellow human beings we cannot guarantee that we would have behaved any differently faced with same set of moral complexities.

Following Gowans, an important part of our moral response to a particular situation should be based around an understanding of the well-being of the other, whomever that other may be. In the process of deliberating about the nature of our responsibilities to a specific person in a specific situation one vital concern ought to be maintenance of the well-being of the other. Of course, because of the wide variety of factors operating at the interface of deliberation and decision many different moral outcomes are possible. This is also why in concrete and often complex situations, the ways in which we understand our responsibilities can, and do, emerge in ways that generate conflict. The case of Hanna is a prime example.

Of related importance to the case for moral complexity, is the claim that moral life generally is characterized by complexity analyses. Among the most powerful representations of this claim, in my view, are accounts of Holocaust experiences. Though this discussion has dwelt on the story of Hanna, the tension between complexity and enormity that such stories generate is not restricted to the perpetrators of crimes. In an interview with Claude Lanzmann, Auschwitz survivor Abraham Bomba tells a story that conveys a powerful sense of the tension between complexity and enormity in its combination of ways of understanding responsibilities, individual dispositions, massively impoverished circumstances and the gamut of conflicted emotions that you might expect to accompany such a story. Recounting Bomba's story the narrator writes:

> I want to tell you something that happened. At the gas chamber, when I was chosen to work there as a barber, some of the women that came in on a transport from my town of Czestochowa, I knew a lot of them. I knew them; I lived with them in my town. I lived with them in my street, and some of them were my close friends. And when they saw me, they started asking me, Abe this and Abe that – 'What's going to happen to us?' What could you tell them? What could you tell? A friend of mine worked as a barber – he was a good barber from my home town – when his wife and his sister came into the gas chamber…. I can't. It's too horrible. Please.
>
> *We have to do it. You know it.*
>
> I won't be able to do it.
>
> *You have to do it. I know it's very hard. I know and I apologise.*
>
> Don't make me go on please.
>
> *Please. We must go on.*
>
> I told you today it's going to be very hard. They were taking that in bags and transporting it to Germany.
>
> *Okay, go ahead. What was his answer when his wife and sister came?*
>
> They tried to talk to him and the husband of his sister. They could not tell them this was the last time they stay alive, because behind them was the German Nazis, SS men, and they knew that if they said a word, not only the wife and the woman, who were dead

already, but also they would share the same thing with them. In a way, they tried to do the best for them, with a second longer, just to hug them and kiss them, because they knew they would never see them again.[29]

It should be borne in mind that the use of this example is not to serve as a point of reference to the story of Hanna. The two stories are clearly on a different moral footing and the distinction between victim and perpetrator is important. Nevertheless, both stories convey the strength of the tension between both the enormity and the complexity of the events portrayed. Albeit from very different perspectives both stories convey the sense of moral failure felt by those involved.

Towards an Understanding of Moral Life

Both moral complexity and moral enormity are present in Holocaust experiences and with respect to such experiences they are manifest in the deliberations that take place around our understandings of our responsibilities to self and others. My claim is that such deliberations with all that this implies, including the tension between judging and understanding, are what constitutes the moral complexity of our lives.

In the context of Michael's moral dilemma in *The Reader*, the discussion on moral complexity delivered a stark conclusion. Like Michael, if I the reader err too much on the side of judging the character of Hanna I run the risk of failing to understand her place in the course of events. Indeed I may fail to understand period. If, on the other hand, I factor in the moral complexity of her situation I arrive at the conclusion that, in her shoes, I cannot guarantee I would have behaved differently. Such a conclusion has the potential to compromise judgement. Yet judgement remains important. It is this predicament that underpins the tension between judging and understanding. Hanna made some poor decisions that led to terrible outcomes. Yet our deeper understanding of the moral complexity of her situation ought to acknowledge the need for a more reflective and compassionate appraisal of her. Such is moral life.

---

29 Claude Lanzmann, *Shoah* (NY: Pantheon Books, 1985), pp. 115–17.

PART II
Free Will, Determinism and Moral Responsibility: Challenging Retributive Judgement

Chapter 6

Moved Movers: Transfiguring Judgement Practices

Pedro Alexis Tabensky

Editor's Introduction

Starting by drawing on the insights and alleged problems with Martha Nussbaum's argument, embodied in her contribution to this collection, which reaches strikingly similar conclusions to those expressed in a literary form in *The Reader*, Pedro Tabensky argues for the wholesale elimination of our retributive practices; practices which require that at least in some instances individuals deserve to be punished for their misdeeds. Our best accounts of free will, which flow from a proper understanding of the narrative organization of life, but not only from there, are compatibilist, if by compatibilism one means the view that we can account for free will within a deterministic framework; if one does not, by contrast, also believe, as compatibilists often do, that moral responsibility, entailing the rightness of standardly admissible retributive practices, is required for free will. Tabensky believes that we do not need this variety of moral responsibility in order to have a will that is free. These views fly in the face of standard compatibilism famously exemplified by thinkers such as Peter Strawson and Harry Frankfurt who think that compatibilism is perfectly compatible with the sort of moral responsibility required for our standard retributive practices to be warranted. In fact, Tabensky argues that the balancing act where perpetrators receive their dues in equal proportion to the harm done and the levels of agent control, is ultimately incoherent and unjust, given that people are not the *causa sui* – the first movers – of their actions. This is something that both Kai Nielsen and Jonathan Mckeown-Green defend in their contributions and something that Thaddeus Metz sternly denies. According to Tabensky, a revaluation of our moral understandings and practices, contrary to Strawson's account of the reactive attitudes and most contributors to this collection, is both desirable and possible. He gives some indications as to how this revaluation may occur.

* * *

The *causa sui* is the best self-contradiction hitherto imagined, a kind of logical rape and unnaturalness: but mankind's extravagant pride has managed to get itself deeply and frightfully entangled with precisely this piece of nonsense. For the desire for 'freedom of the will' in that metaphysical superlative sense which is unfortunately still dominant in the minds of the half-educated, the desire to bear the whole and sole responsibility for one's actions and to absolve god, world, ancestors, chance, society from responsibility for them, is nothing less that the desire to be precisely that *causa sui* and, with more than Münchhausen's temerity, to pull oneself into existence out of the swamp of nothingness by one's own hair.

F. Nietzsche, *Beyond Good and Evil*,
trans. R.J. Hollingdale (London: Penguin, 1990), § 21.[1]

Judging and Understanding

There is, it seems, a tension between judging people for their actions and understanding them, particularly if the judging in question involves condemning in word and deed. The more one understands individuals, the more one understands the storyline of their lives, the more one comes to realize the extent to which individuals are constrained by their circumstances, the more one realizes the limits of agency and culpability. In 'Equity and Mercy' Martha Nussbaum explores this tension and argues in favour of merciful judgement and against standard retributive and deterrence models of judgement and punishment (although she does not argue against retribution and deterrence as such).[2] In working out the relationship between *dike* – impartial or symmetrical justice – and *epieikeia* – 'a gentle art of particular perception, a temper of mind that refuses to demand retribution without knowing the whole story'[3] – Nussbaum reaches striking conclusions regarding the aims of judicial practices, and of practices of judgement in general. Following Aristotle and particularly Seneca she concludes that one must be merciful in judging – one must seriously, caringly and systematically consider mitigating circumstances – insofar as understanding the narrative structure of life reveals that perpetrators of crimes are, to a great extent, yet not necessarily completely, victims of circumstances. In acknowledging this she defends a merciful approach to judgement and punishment over across-the-board impartiality.

Mercy is the opposite of revenge proper and retribution proper lies in between. Some might be tempted to characterize retribution as fair revenge, but this form of revenge, if indeed it is properly characterized as a form of revenge, must be

---

1   This passage was brought to my attention by Galen Strawson. See G. Strawson, 'Free Will', in E. Craig (ed.), *Routledge Encyclopedia of Philosophy,* London: Routledge, 2004, http://www.rep.routledge.com/article/V014SECT3.

2   M. Nussbaum, 'Equity and Mercy', in *Sex and Social Justice*, NY: Oxford University Press, 1999, (Chapter 1, this volume, pp. 3–42. pp. 154–83.

3   M. Nussbaum, 'Equity and Mercy', in *Sex and Social Justice*, NY: Oxford University Press, 1999), this volume, p. 10. p. 159.

distinguished from revenge proper, unjust revenge. However, and this is an important point, this last distinction depends on the idea that there is such a thing as just retribution (Nussbaum believes that there is). If there is no such thing, as I believe, then what we normally call 'retribution' just is a variety of revenge proper for it can never be just; it is always excessive.

Mercy is the opposite excess. It is excessively soft, so it too is, if one holds a purely retributive conception of justice, unjust, but only if retribution is warranted. The idea of mercy depends on the idea of retribution, for one can only be excessively soft if there is something to measure softness against. I must know that someone deserves to be punished thus and so, and then I must punish more leniently or not punish at all.[4] Nussbaum's position is that, although full retributive punishment is indeed warranted at times, retribution should not be the sole concern of those seeking to punish. Just punishment cannot be reduced to retribution. Justice should also aim at being excessively kind, circumstances permitting (the problem lies in cashing out the criteria for distinguishing mitigating from non-mitigating circumstances, as we shall see). A judge should not merely seek to rectify the retributive balance of justice, but she should also be benevolent – merciful. Mercy involves going beyond desert, beyond the urge to rectify the balance of justice, but the idea of 'beyond' can only be made sense of if we can make sense of the retributive idea of balance.

As I said, Nussbaum does not go as far as to argue that, in principle, retributive judgement and punishment are never warranted, but I think she is logically committed to arguing against these practices across the board. She never seems to doubt that retributive punishment is deserved in some instances. However, as I intend to show, there are no grounds for distinguishing mitigating from non-mitigating circumstances, and Nussbaum's explicit views on mercy commit her to advocating this distinction, for making sense of when mercy is warranted hangs on being able to determine when circumstances are mitigating. All relevant circumstances, circumstances that play a role in determining a given course of events, are mitigating, and this is really just to admit that, ultimately, there are no mitigating circumstances.

It is interesting to note that Nussbaum never considers non-mitigating circumstances in her study, nor does she give us an explicit account of the criteria for distinguishing mitigating from non-mitigating circumstances. Instead, she limits herself to arguing that a proper understanding of the narrative intricacies of specific human lives will, if we are properly disposed, as we should be, to paying attention to narratives that define human lives, invite us to practise the art of mercy. But, if this is so, then it seems that she must also be committed to the idea that all judgement ought to be merciful for all actions are constrained and determined by narratives

---

4   Contrary to first appearances, I agree with Kai Nielsen's position, expressed in his contribution to this collection, that one can speak of mercy on pragmatic grounds, but this is a different understanding of mercy – certainly not the typical sense (the sense that I am concerned to target). This sense of mercy is coupled with the pragmatic understanding of moral responsibility – a sense divested of the idea that people are genuinely culpable in a way that would warrant our standard retributive practices. See note 33 of his contribution.

that define human lives. However, if all judgements ought to be merciful, then, on final analysis, it is more precise to claim that the very idea of mercy loses its *raison d'être* for, as I have already shown, its *raison d'être* is related to the very possibility of retribution. Nussbaum is logically committed, by the force of her own arguments regarding narrative, to claim that in actual fact there are no grounds for mitigation or for mercy. What she is logically committed to is a more thorough revision of our judgement practices than the one presented in 'Equity and Mercy' and the present inquiry is an attempt to run all the way to the logical finish line of Nussbaum's views on the narrative organization of the lives of feeble creatures like you and I.

There is another problem, it seems, with Nussbaum's characterization of mercy. Mercy can be understood quite independently of mitigation. In fact, courts of law typically decide what the just thing to do is, from the purely retributive point of view, by considering mitigating circumstances when deciding on the sentence and one can be merciful quite independently of the idea that a given perpetrator *deserves* our mercy. In fact, mercy, by definition, ought never to be deserved from the purely retributive point of view. Mercy, if you will, is a violation of the principle of just retribution. But, Nussbaum is not claiming that mercy is at times deserved and at others not, depending on whether or not mitigation is warranted. What she is claiming is something slightly subtler. She is claiming that we should not typically aim at rectifying the retributive balance of justice. Rather, the more we realize the extent to which people are victims of circumstances, the extent to which they are pushed down the path of darkness by forces beyond their control, the less we will be inclined to aim at punishing with the full force of the law, the force that strives to maintain a 'perfect' balance. Her views surely depend on being able to distinguish mitigating from non-mitigating circumstances, but the way she thinks a merciful judge should deliberate, once the relevant circumstances are found, is different from the way the purely retributive judge thinks she should deliberate. She should aim at being excessively lenient rather than merely fair because she realizes that, to a large extent and in a crucial sense, people are not fully in control of their lives.

Nussbaum invites us to think about the narrative structure of life and the constraining role this structure plays in our existential moves. She is critical of Andrea Dworkin's 'anti-novel' *Mercy* on the grounds that there is no mercy in it and this lack of mercy stems from a kind of deliberate blindness, expressed in the novel itself, towards the narratives that define the lives of the men who abuse of Andrea, the protagonist.[5] The novel

> ... refuses to perceive any of the male offenders – or any other male – as a particular individual, and it refuses to invite the reader into the story of their lives. Like Andrea, it can't tell him from him from him ... her males have no history, no psychology, no concrete reason for action. They are just knives that cut, arms that beat, penises that maim by the very act of penetration.[6]

---

5 A. Dworkin, *Mercy*, NY: Four Walls, Eight Windows, 1991.

6 M. Nussbaum, 'Equity and Mercy', in *Sex and Social Justice*, NY: Oxford University Press, 1999, this volume, pp. 4–5. p. 155.

This blindness to particulars, to specific stories that define individual lives and, I might add, to the general lessons that can be learned from these specific stories (Nussbaum is also partly blind in this respect and this partial blindness plays a role in blinding her to the problems with the notion of mercy), is exemplified in Dworkin's 'anti-novel' insofar as, minimally, novels aimed at expressing the moral dimension of human lives are at their best when they effectively describe the unfolding of the lives of the protagonists in a way that clearly exhibits the constraints, internal and external, within which the lives of protagonists are played out. The lack of male particularity in Dworkin's novel is deliberate, but this in no way diminishes what is problematic about the novel. Men, in Dworkin's novel, become tools, means rather than ends, for female liberation. And one of the central requirements for being able to see a fellow human being as a thing rather than as a genuine person is a blindness to the narrative complexity characteristic of human lives, a narrative complexity that is replaced with a stereotype: men are sadistic rapists who see women as things to be used and abused, humiliated and destroyed – 'Penises that maim'. But my central concern here, as is Nussbaum's, is not specifically with Dworkin's militant feminism as with a certain sort of failure that comes with writing a novel aimed at dealing with the lives of individuals qua moral actors that ignores the narrative intricacies, the narrative law, that determines the unfolding of human lives. It is only this blindness, and Dworkin implicitly acknowledges this, that allows Andrea to come to the conclusion, after a life of systematic abuse by men, that she must go out of her way to kill men, any men, just because they are men. Dworkin's implicit admission is that revengefulness requires blindness to the stories of those who abuse, but that women should become selectively blind for the sake of overcoming male domination. Dworkin is demanding that justice be blind, not in the sense of being impartial but in the sense of being ignorant, and this is a truly strange and disturbing demand. But perhaps battles cannot be fought and won, not even just battles, unless one somehow manages to perceive some people as somehow less than fully human, as instruments for a greater cause. So, maybe Andrea has a case, grounded on plausible utilitarian grounds, for wanting to go on a killing rampage. I do not think she ultimately does, but this is a question that need not be settled here. What is important for our purposes is that, if one appreciates what follows from a narrative understanding of personhood, as Andrea seems to appreciate, at least to some extent, then, if one is committed to justice, one must grasp the choice of going on a killing rampage or, more generally, of hurting others for the sake of justice, as involving a sacrifice to justice for the sake of the greater good, of greater justice. But if one appreciates that lives have the form of a narrative, then, as I shall show, one can plausibly punish for utilitarian reasons in some instances, as Andrea does, but never because individuals deserve to be harmed for what they have done; a central requirement for getting standard retribution off the ground.

Let me illustrate Nussbaum's position with a novel written as if it were to a large extent a literary defence of views such as hers: Bernhard Schlink's *The Reader*[7], written, perhaps inadvertently, in the spirit of Seneca's thought.

The Reader

Hanna Schmitz, one of the two main characters, has committed terrible transgressions while performing the duties of an SS guard. The novel focuses particularly on Hanna's involvement in the deaths of hundreds of women who conceivably could have been saved by her from a fire that engulfed them in their journey away from a women-only camp near Krakow – a satellite camp feeding Auschwitz – in the last days of the war. The women could conceivably have been saved if, among other things, Hanna were less confused and bewildered at the time, less committed to following orders and more capable of making quick decisions in a moment of acute crisis. All in all, she could conceivably have acted otherwise if, and only if, she did not have the weaknesses that actually pushed her to act in the way that she did. Many of us might wish that she did not have these weaknesses, but in actual fact she did have them at the time, and these weaknesses played a role in determining a certain unfolding of events.

In addition to her involvement in the deaths mentioned above, which I shall discuss further shortly, Hanna was among those in charge of selecting sixty of the weakest prisoners every month for execution in Auschwitz. Given that the camp was overcrowded already and given that new prisoners were being transported in on a regular basis, it was inevitable that some prisoners had to be selected, unless one acted in ways that very few of us would dare act were we confronted with tremendous adversities. Hanna could conceivably have abandoned her terrible job (even if this meant her death), or have organized an insurrection (or something of this sort), but she did not. Instead, she diligently executed orders almost as if her primary responsibility was towards the orders. Again, one can explain her actions in terms of the manner in which her weaknesses moved her all the way to action; weaknesses that could not simply have been willed away at the time.

In the weeks before their final journey to Auschwitz, Hanna would select some of the frailest prisoners and make them read to her. Hanna is illiterate and keeps this, perhaps foolishly, as her darkest secret. Indeed, the circumstances that led her to become a camp guard are intimately related to her fear of being exposed as illiterate, or so we are invited to think. Before becoming a camp guard she worked in Berlin, but when she was offered a promotion, which would have forced her to expose her illiteracy, she fled and took the first job that she could that would allow her to keep her secret. That is why she joined the SS, or so we are invited to speculate.

Towards the end of the war the camp was abandoned and the prisoners were forced to march west under sub-human conditions. Hanna was with the prisoners at

---

7   B. Schlink, *The Reader*, London: Phoenix, 1997.

the time, forcing them to march, following orders diligently, insensitively, almost as if she did not understand that those marching were human beings, or as if she did not really care. Almost half the prisoners died while marching but most died in a fire, caused by a bombing raid, which consumed the church in which they had been housed. The female guards, including Hanna, could conceivably have saved them, but they did not. There were only two survivors. Many years later Hanna was tried, found guilty and sentenced to life.

After the war and before the trial, being in her mid-thirties, she had an affair with a teenager. The teenager – Michael Berg – is the narrator of the novel. They develop a deep love for one another, despite the age gap. Hanna, one could speculate, for one reason or another, possibly related to her illiteracy, was uncomfortable with relationships between equals and hence sought relationships in which she had the upper hand, and that is one of the things that motivated her to become a camp guard, and to have an affair with a teenager. Hanna never tells him about her past nor does Michael find out that she was illiterate until the trial, years after their affair abruptly ends with Hanna's unexpected disappearance. Later we discover that, yet again, she fled, it seems, in order to conceal her illiteracy from her employers, but perhaps also, in part, because of Michael's lack of commitment in the last days of their affair. Despite this, their affair had a profound effect on their lives. Michael got very close to her despite the fact that she never revealed her deepest secrets to him. Hanna, in this episode of her life, is portrayed as loving, enigmatic, sensitive and sensual. At times she behaves violently, but perhaps more out of fear and vulnerability, caused by her illiteracy, than anything else.

Their lives converge again, years later, during the trial. At this time Michael is a student of law and attends the trial, initially, as part of his studies but, later, because he finds Hanna on the stand. Like many of his fellow students who are all too young to have participated in the war efforts, he was initially consumed with a desire to condemn those who were old enough to have participated in the war efforts. But once he discovers that Hanna is being tried his attitude changes accordingly. He is forced to reconcile the image of the loving Hanna with the image of the camp guard. He discovers that she is illiterate and he is able, to some extent, to make sense of why she becomes a camp guard, and why she unexpectedly abandoned him. He is able, to some extent, to unpack Hanna's story, and hence to deeply understand where she is coming from. We are led to think that no one else but he is able to do this, because only he knows the intimate details of what moved Hanna to act, and it is in light of this understanding that the courtroom set-up seems so radically ill-equipped to judge her in any meaningful way. It is in the light of this understanding that Michael makes claims such as:

> Prosecution seemed to me as grotesque a simplification as defence, and judging was the most grotesque oversimplification of all.[8]

---

8   Schlink, *The Reader*, London: Phoenix, 1997, pp. 177–8.

Michael's deep understanding of Hanna makes it impossible for him to judge her in a way that warrants condemnation, although he repeatedly tries to do this, but fails. There is no denying that Hanna did act in deeply reprehensible ways, but the reader is invited to wonder, as Hanna at one point invites the judge to wonder, about what he would have done in analogous circumstances.[9] It must be pointed out that Hanna does not ask this question with the aim of being absolved. She was, it appears, genuinely curious to know how he would act. The judge skirts around the question for properly answering this question would, one is led to believe, make him come down from the high moral ground on which judges typically stand. Attempting seriously to address this question would, one is led to believe, seriously compromise the normal running of the courtroom. The judge qua judge simply could not afford to offer a satisfactory answer to this question. Too complex a story would have to be spun, too much detail would have to be included, and in the end this would make the kind of condemnation usually expected in a courtroom impossible.

Although it seems that the sort of strictly retributive judgement exemplified in a courtroom is to a large extent portrayed in the novel as undesirable, the novel also seems to leave some space for it. For instance, when briefly describing the other female guards being tried with Hanna, Schlink invites us to compare their fundamentally perverse and cowardly attitude with Hanna's apparently sincere attitude. Also, one does not find suggestions in the novel to the effect that, for instance, Hanna did not deserve to be punished for her crimes. It seems as if the novel invites us to accept that she deserves to be punished even with an understanding that, given her weaknesses and the adverse circumstances presented to her, she could not have done otherwise, or would have found it very difficult to do otherwise, at the time of the events that marked her life.

Arguably, one could punish someone even if that individual does not deserve to be punished. One could punish for instrumental reasons or perhaps for expressive reasons, but that is not, at least not primarily, the sort of punishment that is meted out and, to a limited extent, defended in the novel. The novel invites us seriously to consider the possibility that Hanna should have been punished mercifully and that the other guards should have been punished in a less merciful manner due to their fundamentally base behaviour. Interestingly, the portrayal of the other guards as perverse, and unambiguously deserving of condemnation, is intimately related to the fact that the novel does not explore the intricacies defining their lives. They are portrayed as simple, one-dimensional and fundamentally base creatures. The ease with which we find ourselves condemning them is intimately related to the fact that the narratives of the characters we are condemning have not been explored, like the narratives of the men in Dworkin's novel.

According to Nussbaum and, it seems, Schlink, the ideal judge is kind and merciful, open to understanding the specific narratives of the accused, but also able to judge harshly when necessary. But, when is this sort of judgement necessary? Never, I contend, especially if one is committed to thoroughgoing ethical naturalism which

---

9　See p. 110.

flows from our best – compatibilist as opposed to libertarian – accounts of agency. And, if I am right, we do not really need to know particular circumstances leading to villainous behaviour for, in principle, harsh retribution is never warranted insofar as we are part of the natural order of things. The views I will defend, moreover, build upon Nussbaum's and Schlink's literal and literary arguments, but I believe my views are those that both Nussbaum and Schlink should and probably would advocate were they to follow their arguments, based on their deep insights regarding the narrative structure of life, to their final resting point. I might of course be wrong, but I leave it up to the reader to decide. First, let me show how a proper understanding of the narrative structure of life, in fact, implies our best compatibilist accounts of agency.

Lived Stories

A human life has the shape of a story, and this is attested to by the simple fact that understanding a person primarily involves telling a story about the person's life.[10] Biographies provide the format for understanding our lives (be they written, oral, multifaceted and multidimensional, complex, partial or relatively complete). To be sure, we can get a good idea of who a given individual is by enumerating features of that individual's character at a carefully selected moment in time – from his or her adult life, typically – and features of his or her immediate surroundings, but this list of features always presupposes a story which has led to the present, and also presupposes a possible future which is determined by changing circumstances. We assume that an individual has come from somewhere and is going somewhere, and it is within this framework that we can make sense of a given segment of a life (we make sense of a given segment as a segment – as part of an unfolding unity). And indeed, if perchance we have reasons to suspect that little changes have and will occur in a given life, then we might think of the life in question as being stuck, which goes to show to what extent making sense of a life carries with it an expectation of unfolding. And, not just any old unfolding but, rather, an unfolding that has a coherence that can be expressed in the form of a story.

It must be stressed that the reason why a life has the shape of a story is not merely that it has a present and a past. The identity of a given segment of a life – its very character – is parasitical upon its location within a given lived story. Past, present and future feed off each other for meaning. We might, say, initially be rather annoyed that a given individual has a gloomy disposition but, once we understand where that individual is coming from, we discover the true meaning of that gloominess (and our attitude towards that individual should change accordingly). If, say, she

---

10 Alasdair MacIntyre deals effectively with arguments against a narrative understanding of life in 'The Virtues, The Unity of a Life and the Concept of a Tradition', *After Virtue: A Study in Moral Theory*, Notre Dame, Indiana: University of Notre Dame Press, 1984, pp. 204–25. Jeff Malpas also provides an enlightening defence of the view that our lives have a narrative structure. See J. Malpas, 'Holism, Content and Self', in *Place and Experience: A Philosophical Topography*, Cambridge: Cambridge University Press, 1999, pp. 72–91.

was brought up in a war zone and has suffered immense personal losses, we might consider the fact that she is merely gloomy, as opposed to being shattered, to be a sign of great moral strength. To use another example, circumstances toy capriciously with us throughout the course of our lives and, as it often happens, what might have appeared to be very important at a given moment in time fades into the background in light of the location of that happening within the overall narrative structure of a given life.

We have determined a fundamental compositional principle of life, namely, that the significance – the very identity – of a given segment of a human life is parasitical upon the unfolding dynamic narrative totality of a life. Life, one could say, is a holistic structure, which is to say that segments of behaviour have no meaning outside the context of a human life and, I might add, their significances are never stable insofar as the context of significance is permanently shifting as life moves on. To be sure, typically we can make (partial) sense of specific segments of behaviour without knowing the specific history of the author of the behaviour, but this is only because we are, hesitantly, able to conceive of a given segment of behaviour as forming part of some lived story. All actions, one could say, are understood in relation to a past, possible or actual, and a future, which is just another way of saying that actions are always and already understood as forming part of a lived story.

But, and this is a point that must be emphasized, the significance of a segment of a human life is not merely derived from the position in space-time that it occupies within an unfolding lived story. Rather, a segment of a life has significance because it plays a *role* in a life. To play a role is to play an active part in the life's narrative unfolding, and to play such a part is, minimally, to play a causal part. Indeed, it is because of this that a lived story can be understood a causal history. Minimally, an action is individuated by the role it plays in a causal history. Other non-causal relations may exist between different segments of lives, but this in no way detracts from the minimal characterization that segments of a life are just that insofar as they play a causal role in the narrative unfolding of a life.

So, lived stories are, minimally, causal chains. Indeed, a relatively exhaustive biography is one that explains how circumstances, weaknesses, strengths, goals, and so on and so forth *move* individuals in particular directions. To be sure, the life stories of concrete individuals can only be told retrospectively, but this does not challenge the understanding that what accounts for the agency of the subject of a biography is, at the very least, a positive account of how internal and external circumstances determine the overall direction that a life has taken – the overall character and identity of an unfolding life. What accounts for an action is what can be told in a narrative description. This last claim might seem to contradict the obvious, namely, that narratives that properly describe human lives, including the stories one tells oneself about one's own life, involve a large degree of indeterminacy and open-endedness. And, it is because of the indeterminacy and open-endedness that, in principle, narratives of concrete human lives can only be told retrospectively. However, adding complexity to our descriptions of what is involved does not take away from the basic fact that what explains a life must be intimately related to what moves a life qua the life of an agent, and what moves an agent qua agent, as opposed to, say, raw flesh displacing itself through space-time, is what can be explained positively in a comprehensive story. One could only be held accountable if at all, in a sense implying a retributive ethic, for what can be described in a comprehensive story. But, since a story is, minimally, a causal history, one cannot, on final analysis, be held accountable in a sense implying a retributive ethic, unless one thinks, as philosophers like Peter F. Strawson and Harry Frankfurt think, that our theoretical preferences regarding the nature of free will do not imply that we ought to change our practices of judgement. I shall tackle their arguments below.

Indeed, we would not be agents at all if the conclusions of our practical deliberations did not, for the most part, or to a large extent, lead us all the way to action. Our minds would, so to speak, be insulated from the world and our bodies would move quite independently of our hopes, dreams or obsessions. What allow us to explain the fact that we are responsible for what we do are the causal relationships between our actions and our mental states. And, crucially, our mental states have a causal history which plays a core role in rendering our mental state intelligible. If what moved us was some kind of uncaused will, or perhaps some partially uncaused will, then one would have to admit that one's moves are quite random, which means that the very idea of a totally or partially uncaused will is incoherent. One could not even make sense of one's behaviour insofar as claiming that I willed something for no reason explains very little indeed. What one must do instead of positing a kind of pure will outside of the stream of circumstances that make up the natural world is to place a subject in a given setting and to explain how circumstances and capacities determine a certain unfolding of events. This is what comprehensive stories do.

Against a Retributive Ethic

Contrary to Nussbaum and to Schlink, I believe that judging people, in a manner implying harsh retributive practices, always gets in the way of understanding them. The retributive practices I have in mind are those that express a retributive ethic. By 'retributive ethic' I mean:

> An ethic informed by the metaphor of the balance of justice where justice is reached by rectifying the balance lost by punishing the perpetrator in accordance with certain standards of due proportion. This ethic can be applied both at the institutional or non-institutional level, or, at a personal or interpersonal level, where punishing someone, including punishing oneself, is seen as warranted, not primarily because of the benefits it might bring to the future of that individual, the victims or the community at large, and not because of what could be described as the expressive or even symbolic value of punishment (advocated by those who believe that the criterion for understanding a misdemeanour qua misdemeanour depends on an understanding of appropriate

punishment), but simply because that individual deserves to be punished, deserves to suffer for his or her transgressions.[11]

When discussing Peter Strawson's views below, I will explain and endorse his critique of the consequentialists' proposed solution to the problem of determinism. Scolding a child might be warranted on consequentialist grounds, but some consequentialist solutions are clearly unjust. Think of arguments attempting to justify the death sentence on consequentialist grounds. If an ethic of retribution is not warranted, then sentencing to death on consequentialist grounds becomes problematic, at least in most cases. When one kills in order to set an example, one is violating the basic Kantian principle that people ought to be treated as ends in themselves and never purely as means; a very important principle, even if we hold, contra Kant, that this principle is not categorical insofar as other principles, such as the principle of diminishing harm, might, on some occasions, trump it. Andrea's decision to go on a killing rampage could be seen as an (imperfect) illustration of how the principle of diminishing harm (to woman), by instilling fear in men via exemplary executions, could trump the Kantian principle.

I might also briefly point out that standard expressive or symbolic accounts of punishment also seem to rely on the view that people deserve to be punished in a way that is not warranted by our best deterministic accounts of agency. There might be scope for expressive or symbolic considerations in our judgement practices within the framework I am proposing, but the framework will place constraints on which judgement and punishment practices are warranted on expressive or symbolic grounds. For instance, harshly punishing someone for a heinous crime cannot, it seems to me, typically be constitutive of our proper understandings of the crime in question if an ethic of retribution is not warranted. In fact, harsh punishment would typically amount to an expression of ignorance regarding the nature of crime. Besides, there are alternative means of expressing one's understanding of the seriousness of a given transgression (typically, doing nothing will not do). One way is to acknowledge in deed and belief that the perpetrator is, in some sense, sick, and to try as hard as

---

11 Although my primary concern here is with practices of condemnation I will briefly discuss the practices of approval below, expressive of an ethic of praise. By 'ethic of praise' I mean:

An ethic of approval, institutional or non-institutional, personal or interpersonal, where approving of someone, including approving of oneself, is seen as warranted, not primarily because of the benefits it might bring to the future of that individual, those who have benefited from the approval-warranting behaviour, and not because of what could be described as the expressive or even symbolic value of approval, but simply because that individual deserves approval, deserves rewards for good behaviour. Needless to say, once it is clear why an ethic of retribution ought to be banished from moral discourse it will also be clear why an ethic of praise should suffer the same fate for the criteria for determining when praise of the relevant variety is warranted is the same as the criteria for determining when retribution of the relevant variety is warranted.

we can to cure him or her, or to change the circumstances leading to recalcitrant forms of criminal behaviour. Changing the inequitable economic arrangements in South Africa, and the racist structures that helped bring these arrangements about in addition to perpetuating them, to take one example, will, in all likelihood, extinguish the causes leading to the endemic crime problem in that country. Admittedly, bringing these changes about would be no easy task, but engaging in the arduous task of transforming the causal conditions leading to crime would indeed be a sign of a deep understanding of the seriousness of the crime problem. In fact, a standard retributive approach, where the specific perpetrators are the sole targets of justice, seems clearly to express deep ignorance regarding the significance of crime, regarding what it means to be a victim and a perpetrator of crimes of the sorts that plague South Africa. I see no reason why expressing one's understanding of the seriousness of a given transgression necessarily requires that one aims one's actions exclusively or primarily, if at all, at the individual who committed the crime. On other occasions, one may very well be warranted in expressing one's dismay at a crime by punishing the perpetrator, but for good utilitarian reasons and not because the perpetrator deserves to be punished.

A retributive ethic is typically, but not exclusively, accompanied by a libertarian account of free will where ruffians are conceived of as capable, in actuality, of having done otherwise at a given moment in time, but who choose the crooked path of evil instead. Circumstances are understood as playing a constraining role in the existential moves of individuals but, ultimately, moves flow from a pure – quasi-divine – will, unaffected, at some mysterious level, by the natural order of things. I happen to think that most people hold an ethic of retribution and most of its defenders are implicit or explicit libertarians, but the best available account of free will is compatibilism and this account entails that, if someone is to blame, in a manner involving a retributive ethic, then retribution of this sort is warranted, even if one could not genuinely have done otherwise at a given moment in time. But how can one be held to blame in a manner implying a retributive ethic if one had no genuine alternatives at the moment of committing a given misdemeanour? How could one be held to blame in this way for what could not be avoided? And, if one cannot be held to blame in this manner, how can we justify those practices of punishment that involve a retributive ethic?

Free Will, Determinism, Accountability

In order to judge someone in a non-gratuitous way, one must understand the author of the act to some extent, but as soon as one judges someone in a way that presupposes a retributive ethic, one is stopping oneself from more fully understanding the nature of that individual's behaviour for, given our best accounts of agency, supported by a proper understanding of the narrative shape of life, people cannot be responsible for what they do in a way that warrants retribution. For this reason, judging people for what they do, in a manner implying a retributive ethic, will always hinder understanding (although some degree of understanding might be required for judging). But one must differentiate three varieties of judgement: the first involves retribution, the second involves judging individuals for who they are – for the quality of their character – and the third involves judging an action. What I am arguing here, to repeat, is that judging individuals in a way that involves deploying a retributive ethic hinders understanding them, but one can certainly judge in a way that involves determining the moral status of an individual or of her actions. Jack the Ripper's character is, trivially, reprehensible, but that does not mean that he is morally responsible, in a sense involving a retributive ethic, for the quality of his character, or for the horrendous nature of his deeds. His character would be reprehensible even if all we were warranted in doing is trying to cure him of his ailment and separate him from society for the sake of the greater good. And, a heinous action is just that independently of whether or not a retributive ethic is warranted. In short, we could judge individuals and their actions without holding them to account, in a manner involving a retributive ethic.

What informs the views I am currently defending is the basic idea that human action is made intelligible in relation to the relevant motivations and circumstances that *cause* people to act. In other words, one succeeds in explaining human behaviour qua human behaviour when one succeeds in specifying the *relevant* causes leading to action (explaining human action in the language of molecular biology will not do). The insight that human action is explained in causal terms is the central insight that informs the compatibilist understanding of agency. The compatibilism I have in mind, and which I endorse, is what could be characterized as mild compatibilism. This is the thesis that free will is compatible with determinism, but it is agnostic with regard to any specific version of determinism. I am happy to accept the possibility that two lives which are identical in every way – external circumstances included – until a certain point in time, could diverge at that moment, but, contra indeterminism, not for reasons that could be cashed out in folk-psychological terms, in terms that are relevant to the task of apportioning blame. This version of compatibilism contrasts with what could be characterized as strong compatibilism – compatibilism involving strong metaphysical commitments regarding the specific nature of causation. All that is needed for our present purposes is to hold that a successful explanation of human action qua human action is one where one succeeds in explaining the relevant causes of a given action. More specifically, what picks out the agency of an agent is a narrative descriptions of how propositional attitudes, and the circumstances that determine these attitudes, move people all the way to action, but these explanations could be rough and, I might add, endlessly revisable. The best causal descriptions of a given subject's behaviour might not, in principle, rule out why that subject chose one option over some other possible option(s), but all that one could be held to account for, in a way that implies a retributive ethic, if we were in fact justified in holding people to account in this way, is what could be explained positively in a causal description of psychological mechanisms, for only these descriptions pick out what is relevant for the purposes of retribution.

It seems curious that although most philosophers within the analytic tradition interested in human action are compatibilists (strong or mild), very few think that this account of free will is incompatible with a retributive ethic. If compatibilism is correct, then people must be understood as being determined by circumstances to go on as they do, and if they are so determined, then it is hard to see how they could be held accountable in a way that implies a retributive ethic. Perhaps the reason why what seems to be a relatively straightforward conclusion has not been endorsed by more philosophers is that it is perceived that the consequences of acknowledging that there are no grounds for retribution would be unbearable.

Two of the most influential attempts to fit accountability, involving retribution, within a compatibilist framework have been carried out by Peter F. Strawson (following Hume's lead) and Frankfurt.[12] Those on Strawson's side hold that we have commonplace reactive attitudes which we cannot theorize away and, hence, it is argued, we cannot theorize our standard practices of judgement away. They must remain largely intact. The advocates of the Frankfurt position, on the other hand, think that we need not theorize our standard practices of judgement away for the locus of responsibility, standardly conceived, is the two-tier structure of mind which is constitutive of the levels of control required for being responsible, in the sense implying a retributive ethic. I will deal with both of these camps, through their most influential representatives, in turn.

Commonplace reactive attitudes: the Strawson camp

Although I agree with the advocates of the Strawson Camp, largely inspired by Hume, that we do have commonplace reactive attitudes, I disagree that these attitudes admit solely of the sorts of descriptions that directly or indirectly allude to an ethic of retribution. In the first instance, I wonder whether there are good empirical grounds for assuming that all normal relatively mature specimens of the species human act in ways that entail a retributive ethic. Take the following example:

> 'Westerners', recently remarked Marcos Sandoval of the Triqui people of Oaxaca, 'represent justice with a blindfolded woman. We want her with her eyes well open, to fully appreciate what is happening. Instead of neutrality or impartiality, we want compassion. The person committing a crime needs to be understood, rather than submitted to trial.'
>
> These open eyes of their justice do not, for example, look for punishment when a person violates a shared custom. He or she is perceived as someone in trouble, who needs understanding and help; including the opportunity to offer compensation to the victim

---

12 My discussion on Strawson is based primarily on P.F. Strawson, 'Freedom and Resentment', in *Proceedings of the British Academy*, 48, 1962, pp. 187–211. For a book length defence of the Humean approach see P. Russel, *Freedom and Moral Sentiment: Hume's Way of Naturalizing Responsibility*, Oxford: Oxford University Press, 1995. My discussion on Frankfurt is primarily based on H. Frankfurt, 'Alternate Possibilities and Moral Responsibility', in *The Importance of What We Care About: Philosophical Essays*, Cambridge: Cambridge University Press, 1988, pp. 1-10; and H. Frankfurt, 'Freedom of the Will and the Concept of a Person', in *The Importance of What We Care About: Philosophical Essays*, Cambridge: Cambridge University Press, 1988, pp. 11–25.

of his or her misdemeanour ... Rather than confine wrongdoers in jail, many of these communities tie them to trees or confine them to places for a few hours or days with the express hope of allowing their passions to calm down; or for the safe return from their delirious condition. These practices are not conceived as forms of punishment. Instead, they offer communal support: according opportunities for the soul to heed the wisdom and advice of elders, when they come to converse and reflect with those who have wronged others.[13]

This is a clear case, assuming the field-worker has got it right, where the practices of judgement of a specific people do not seem to imply an ethic of retribution. I think we can safely grant that basic reactive attitudes of the Triqui people are much the same as those had by peoples who are more infatuated with the idea of retribution. Commonality of attitudes, including reactive attitudes, as Donald Davidson has argued throughout much of his corpus, is a necessary condition for interpretation, for making sense of the furthest peoples.[14] Humans qua humans, we can safely assume, react with rage and frustration when someone close to them is hurt, praise people for their accomplishments, feel bad about having done something wrong and so on, but these trivial observations do not entail commitment to a specific narrowly-defined set of practices of judgement. Some people, for instance, are far less revengeful than others. Arguably, some even completely lack the attitude of revengefulness and this should not surprise us for, contra Strawson, the attitude of revengefulness is laden with robust theoretical commitments which are not commonplace. Typically, one will seek revenge if one believes that a villain could genuinely have done otherwise, but chose, out of pure malice, whatever that might mean, to take a stroll down the path of darkness.

Examples abound of people who choose not to seek revenge for crimes committed against them or against those closest to them. Some family members of victims have even gone so far as to try to help the perpetrators regain their lost dignity. Moreover, our practices of judgement have varied enormously across the span of time. It would be the height of absurdity to claim that our reactive attitudes have never changed in the light of the flux of history, and Strawson acknowledges this plurality, but only to a limited extent. Reactive attitudes do change but, at the same time, given that we are able to make sense of the furthest peoples, there must be a lot between us that is shared, including our emotional responses to things.

There are seemingly good reasons for thinking, as Strawson would think, that what is left once we rid ourselves of a retributive ethic is insufficient for making sense of the basic. What I must show now is why I think an ethic without retribution is more promising than the one currently informing our practices. The terrain of the psychological is vast so I can at best show, via a few examples, how the threat of total psychological collapse, brought about by a rejection of retribution, is spurious.

---

13 G. Esteva and M.S. Prakash, *Grassroots Post-Modernism: Rethinking the Soil of Culture*, London: Zed Books, 1998, pp. 111-12.

14 See, for instance, D. Davidson, 'Radical Interpretation', *Inquiries into Truth and Interpretation*, Oxford: Oxford University Press, 1986, pp. 125–39.

I will discuss guilt, pride, reward and punishment and how basic adjustments to these attitudes are possible and indeed desirable.

Guilt and pride At one time or another, most of us suffer from these emotions and at times it might seem that these emotions play a crucial role in character building and in regulating human behaviour. Guilt, or what we might characterize as positive guilt, that is, guilt that plays a positive moral role, allows us to fully embrace the seriousness of a given transgression committed by us, and we might think that no alternative reactive attitude could play this important role. If we are not emotional nincompoops, and if our actions are not informed by the account of agency developed above, we typically feel guilt when we have done something wrong, and this feeling could trigger a moral transformation. The problem is that guilt, in the most basic cases, is expressive of a self-imposed retributive judgement. Arguably, when we are guilt ridden, we not only think that we have done something wrong, but we also think that we should have avoided doing whatever it is that we did and we believe that we in fact could have avoided doing that (as opposed to believing that we could have avoided doing that if circumstances were relevantly different). To be sure, we might feel guilt for having done something that we could not avoid, but this would seem to be a case of irrationality. We should certainly not be indifferent to the suffering inevitably brought upon others, but not guilt, or at least not guilt in the most basic sense. So, it appears that guilt involves a retributive ethic and retribution plays a pivotal role in our psychological lives. Hence, it seems, we have a dilemma.

The case of pride, the converse of guilt, presents similar problems. Pride, at least in many basic instances, seems to be a core constructive emotion. We are proud of ourselves, typically, when we feel that we deserve accolades. Pride helps us grasp the importance of the good things that we have achieved. We typically feel proud when we think that we have done something against all odds, that is, that we have done something despite adverse circumstances and that the very same circumstances could have undermined our prospects of success, but that personal strength and fortitude stopped that from happening. So, it seems that the mirror-image ethic of a retributive ethic – an ethic of praise – is as problematic as a retributive ethic and it is a condition for pride, at least typically. We have, it appears, another closely related dilemma.

But there is another sense of pride which we have not considered. We can be proud in the sense of having respect for ourselves and self-respect is not logically incompatible with our best accounts of what it is to be a subject. We can be proud in this sense insofar as we like the way that we are. So, we can push this sense of pride aside.

If indeed it is the case that guilt and pride are, at least in some basic instances, expressive of an ethic of praise and retribution, and I think this claim is hard to refute, then it seems that we are not warranted in having these emotions (in the relevant instances), that is, if I am right to think that the relevant notions of praise and retribution should be banned from moral discourse. But, are we not giving up too much here? I think not, for there are alternative emotions that play analogous moral roles and which are compatible with our best available accounts of agency. Rather than feeling guilt, involving a retributive ethic, for mistakes that could not be avoided, namely all mistakes, we ought to feel disappointed, even disappointment involving deep grief and sorrow, for having done a wrong, and we should, out of disappointment, wish that circumstances were different and work towards effecting change.

We realize that things could not have been different, but we wish that they could have, and we commit ourselves to trying to do all in our power to ensure that similar circumstances do not recur. This would preserve what is constructive about guilt, namely, the fact that guilt calls us to change our ways or calls us to do things to right our wrongs, without buying into a retributive ethic. Note also that this sense of disappointment does not come with the typical destructive attitudes that accompany guilt, for the disappointment I am speaking of is accompanied by a clear sense that we could not have done any better, thus encouraging us to reflect on what we have done, attempt to change things inside of ourselves to avoid repeating our misdemeanours and, finally, to move on when and if this is possible.

Pride involving a retributive ethic, on the other hand, could be replaced by a sense of joy for having accomplished worthwhile things. This emotion, I suggest, would do much the same positive moral work as productive pride, but without implicating an ethic of praise. We are not justified in feeling the relevant sort of pride for a good deed, for we do not deserve praise, in the sense involving an ethic of praise, from ourselves or from anyone else for that matter. But, we can feel joy for who we are and for what we have accomplished. We could feel that we are lucky that destiny has been so generous to us. This could trigger in us the right sorts of dispositions for continuing to do what is good. You will note that this alternative emotion has the added advantage of warranting a more humble attitude than the attitude that readily accompanies pride.

We have resolved the dilemmas, or so it seems. There is plenty of what is good about guilt and pride that can be preserved with the sort of account of agency presently being defended. The moral roles of our standard conceptions of guilt and pride could, where warranted, be replaced by the moral roles of a kind of productive frustration, perhaps involving what could be described as reflective grief, and a kind of joy. With the examples of guilt and pride I have shown how relatively minor adjustments in our lives can preserve, and perhaps even improve on, what is positive about aspects of our psychological lives that are no longer warranted by our best accounts of agency.

Reward and punishment. Typically, we are given promotions at work if we are perceived to be performing adequately and we are penalized if not. Under one interpretation, reward and punishment for our doings entails the sort of ethical outlooks I am proposing we should banish, but this is not the only interpretation. Under another a reward could be understood as an incentive and punishment as a disincentive. So, reward and punishment can be understood as playing a causal role in directing action, and this interpretation is not incompatible with our best accounts of agency. We need not receive an incentive because we deserve an incentive nor must we get disincentives because we deserve to be penalized (desert implying the ethics of praise and retribution). However, I am not suggesting that our best accounts of agency entail that we must go on as usual, not at all. If we understand incentives and disincentives in the way I am suggesting, then changes in our conceptions and attitudes will inevitably ensue. Offering a disincentive cannot amount to a form of condemnation (implying a retributive ethic) nor can offering an incentive amount to a form of glorification (or something like this, but less extreme). Instead incentives and disincentives could be understood as ways of motivating us to work on improving.

Advocating the elimination of the relevant varieties of guilt (which might, in the end, be all varieties), and of other reactive attitudes, infected with an ethic of retribution, does not entail commitment to the psychologically unsound view that we do not have a complex set of commonplace reactive attitudes. So, I am happy to go halfway with the Humeans in holding that there are commonplace reactive attitudes, but I do not think we need to be committed to the sort of reactive-attitude-conservativism that stunts the commitments we ought to have to live our lives in accordance with our best understandings of the human situation. To live in this manner, I might add, is not, contrary to what Strawson believes, to embrace what he refers to as the 'objective attitude' of detachment – on the contrary. It is, rather, to live in ways that accord most properly with our nature as creatures that find incoherences that we are aware of, particularly important ones, difficult to live with. The objective attitude I propose, as an alternative to Strawson's, is not of a detached observer looking down upon people from a third-person perspective (as judges are typically expected to look down on the judged). Instead, it is the attitude of someone who acknowledges that human beings are, crucially, creatures at the mercy of circumstances that form part of the natural order of things. It is commonplace to feel bad for what we have done and to feel bad when others harm those we love, but feelings of guilt or revenge do not necessarily follow from feeling bad in these manners. It is commonplace to dislike people who have done things that we find morally tasteless, and, for that matter, to like people who have done things that we respect, but it is quite another to dislike people in a manner that involves condemnation (implying retribution) and to like them in a manner that implies the opposite of condemnation; praise involving the converse of a retributive ethic. At times we choose our friends because we like the way that they are and we avoid the company of those we dislike, but these unremarkable everyday practices need not imply an ethic of praise and retribution. Welcoming and shunning practices could merely involve appreciation and dislike for the characters of our friends and foes.

One of Strawson's central strategies is to invite us to consider how our reactive attitudes form part of a system which is constitutive of our embodied understandings of what sorts of creatures we are, so having them is not an optional extra. This is a persuasive strategy which I think is largely correct, but his particular implementation of this strategy is not. He is rightly critical of those who are optimistic that our practices of judgement are not threatened by the genuine possibility of determinism. The optimists in question are those who advocate the standard consequentialist response to the problem of determinism and Strawson is right to think that their views cannot be right on the grounds that punishment must be just, and it cannot be just in the relevant way if people are not to blame (in the relevant manner). However, his attempt to beef-up the optimists' position fails, for all he ends up claiming is that people are to blame in the relevant way simply because we cannot avoid blaming in this way. Strawson's views commit him to believing that compatibilism conflicts with the system of reactive attitudes that define us, but to expect this contradiction to go away is psychologically untenable. The best we can do might be unsatisfactory but that is the best we can do and hence it is, paradoxically, *just* to go on as we normally do with our practices of judgement. So, Strawson provides us with a 'justification' for why it is just to be unjust. This, clearly, cannot be right.

The structure of the will and retribution: the Frankfurt camp

Let us now see why someone with views such as Frankfurt's might want to defend the view that a retributive ethic must be preserved. We could be tempted, *à la* Frankfurt, to hold the view that, if we have free will, if, as Frankfurt understands free will, we take responsibility for what we will and, in addition, if we are able to act in ways expressive of our will, then we are morally responsible for our deeds – accountable, in the sense implying a retributive ethic. Frankfurt seems implicitly to hold the view that all we need in order to provide an account of moral responsibility is to provide an account of responsible action. Indeed, Frankfurt does not seem to be aware of the possibility that one could be responsible for our doings and yet not be morally responsible. Needless to say, I do not think responsibility for our actions entails moral responsibility. We could be agents proper, responsible in the sense of being the locus of action in the robust sense of having power over our will and actions, without being morally responsible. I think it is true that, if we are able to act in accordance with the will that we have chosen, then we are more responsible, more in control, say, than a wanton (in Frankfurt's technical sense of the term), but I do not think this means that we are morally responsible, at least not in a way implying a retributive ethic. Frankfurt's slip between two distinct understandings of responsibility, I suggest, is one of his central mistakes, and it is a mistake that allows him to (wrongly) conclude, at least implicitly, that retribution is compatible with compatibilism.

Frankfurt explicitly argues that the principle of alternate possibilities is false, and he takes this conclusion, which for the purposes of this argument I am assuming is correct, to be a defence of the compatibility between accountability involving a retributive ethic and determinism. But, contra Frankfurt, it merely ends up being an argument against one possible argument against the view that determinism and accountability involving a retributive ethic are incompatible. The principle of alternate possibilities states that 'a person is morally responsible for what he has done only if he could have done otherwise'.[15] Frankfurt's rejection of this principle follows from

---

15 Frankfurt, 'Alternate Possibilities and Moral Responsibility', in *The Importance of What We Care About: Philosophical Essays*, Cambridge: Cambridge University Press, 1988, p. 1.

his account of agency. Agents proper are those that take responsibility for what they will and are ideally able to act in ways that are expressive of what they will. At times we act without considering alternatives, and the fact that at times we do this need not make us less responsible. A ruffian, arguably, could make the desire to commit some illicit deed his will, and commit that deed, without giving the matter second thoughts, which indeed seems to imply that the principle of alternate possibilities is false, for in a scenario such as this one it would not matter whether, for purposes of apportioning blame, the ruffian could have done otherwise. A person could, Frankfurt concludes, be held morally responsible even if she had no alternatives, even if no alternatives existed, *even if his or her behaviour were fully determined.* According to Frankfurt, what matters, for the purposes of apportioning blame, is, to repeat, whether one's actions flow from a will that has taken responsibility for itself. So, Frankfurt thinks, what seemed all along to make determinism incompatible with moral responsibility does not hold. Moral responsibility, it appears, is not incompatible with our best theories of agency. Indeed, if Frankfurt were right then the issue of moral responsibility can be settled independently of the determinism/ indeterminism debate.

The problem with this argument, or one of the problems at any rate, is its starting point. The reason why determinism is incompatible with moral responsibility, implying retribution, is not because, or at least not primarily because, a person could not have done otherwise. Rather, in order to be morally responsible in the relevant way one would have to be responsible for the first causes – the *causa sui* – of one's moves and that would involve situating the will, or a component of the will at any rate, outside of the causal chain of events that constitutes a human life. Such a will, or such a component of the will, is incompatible with our best accounts of agency. Indeed, such an account of the will is incoherent. For starters, in order to be the first cause unmoved in a way that made actions intelligible qua actions, an agent would have to have reasons for acting, but to have reasons for acting is to have a causal history that motivates us to move on in one way rather than another. If a will were the first cause of action it would be a will that willed for no particular reason at all. It would be a blind will and hence, on final analysis, no will at all. So, Frankfurt might very well be right to believe that the reason some determinists who are sceptical about strong accountability elicit in order to justify their views are wrong, yet this is only an argument against one of the reasons it is thought that one cannot consistently be a determinist about free will yet hold an ethic of retribution.

I do not think Frankfurt has done enough to set the determinism/indeterminism debate aside. Frankfurt's characterization of why we are responsible provides us with some of the conditions required for being responsible, but I disagree that he has given us a convincing account of full-blown moral responsibility. What he has not shown us, and what he ought to have shown us, if he wanted to defend moral responsibility, involving a retributive ethic, are not only some conditions that move us qua responsible agents, but also the conditions that move us to become responsible agents in the first instance. A proper account of moral responsibility, involving a retributive ethic, requires an account of these second conditions. People may act in accordance with the desires that they choose to be theirs yet not be morally responsible in the full-blown sense.

It might very well be that a willing addict's 'will is not free, for his desire to take the drug will be effective regardless of whether or not he wants this desire to constitute his will. But when he takes the drug, he takes it freely of his own free will'.[16] That, after all, is what makes him a willing addict. And, hence, according to Frankfurt, the willing addict is morally responsible for the addiction. What I have shown entails that, for the willing addict to be morally responsible in the full-blown sense, in addition to the conditions for merely being responsible, he or she would have to be free to choose what he or she wants to will in a manner implying indeterminism, and for the will to be free in this manner it would have to be a *causa sui* rather than a will that was able to will otherwise, but this is an incoherent position.

But there is more. In order to be responsible our volitions must flow from reason – they must have a rationale. They cannot just be random occurrences. If they were random it is hard to see how they could be volitions in the first place. So, if I am morally responsible I would have to have second-order volitions in addition to having reasons for having chosen these volitions. However, an account of how we are motivated to act, of the rationale for action, is a causal account and with this move the determinism/indeterminism debate is dragged back into the epicentre of the debate on the conditions for moral responsibility. I am not responsible for what I do simply because my action flows from a chosen will. I am also responsible insofar as I am responsible for the reasons for my willing in the first place. But, if I am responsible in this manner then I cannot be morally responsible insofar as my reasons form part of the natural order to things. Note that my rejection of Frankfurt's views end up being much the same as the reasons I provided, and many have provided before me, regarding the randomness that libertarians are committed to by virtue of their obstinate insistence that free will can only be explained within an indeterminist framework. The morally responsible agent, following Frankfurt's argument to its absurd end, is one that selects which desire to make his will for no reason at all for, once reasons are elicited, so too is determinism and the conclusions about the nature of agency which most seem to find disturbing and I fully embrace.[17]

---

16 Frankfurt, 'Freedom of the Will and the Concept of a Person', in *The Importance of What We Care About: Philosophical Essays*, Cambridge: Cambridge University Press, 1988, pp. 24–5.

17 Although I have been targeting Frankfurt here, I hope it is clear that, in criticizing his position, I am also implicitly criticizing all views that attempt to locate the source of moral responsibility (entailing a retributive ethic, it goes without saying) in some structural feature of the will. I could equally have argued against the idea that moral responsibility is tied up with the idea that people can be more or less rational (or more or less receptive to reasons). The more rational our actions, the idea goes, the more culpable we are. No amount of subtle analysis aimed at finding the source of moral responsibility in features internal to the will warrant our retributive practices. The last views that I am targeting are famously defended by Gary Watson. See his 'Free Agency', *Journal of Philosophy*, (72)8, 1975, pp. 205–20. For

Conclusion

Ignorance must necessarily be involved in the act of holding individuals accountable for their actions, in a manner implying a retributive ethic, given that the account of agency upon which this form of judging is founded is mortally flawed. Attempts to preserve our standard judgement practices, in the light of our best accounts of agency, fail. It follows that properly understanding people is incompatible with holding them accountable in the relevant sense. But this understanding does not follow from an understanding of the narrative intricacies of specific lives. Rather, it follows from a proper understanding of the general principles informing the unfolding of narratively-formed lives in general. We do not need to know the details of Hanna's life to know that she did not deserve to be punished in a manner implying a retributive ethic. All we need to know is that her life, like any other human life, has the shape of a story. In a crucial sense, Hanna, or any other perpetrator of crimes, could not avoid being taken down the path of darkness, and this entails, contra Strawson and Frankfurt, that she does not deserve to be punished in a manner expressive of a retributive ethic.

---

an effective critique of views such as Watson's see Jonathan McKeown-Green's piece in this collection.

Chapter 7

Philosophy, Determinism and Moral Responsibility in Times of Atrocity

Chandra Kumar

Editor's Introduction

Taking his lead from Richard Rorty's pragmatism and Kai Nielsen's, Chandra Kumar is suspicious of what he characterizes as 'metaphysics' and, in particular, he is suspicious that a particular theory of free will can help us solve basic moral problems relating to moral responsibility, desert and retribution. Kumar argues that novels such as *The Reader* can do a better job than metaphysics and so he is critical of Tabensky's claim that the *logical conclusion* of views expressed in *The Reader* is across-the-board scepticism about our current practices of judgement and punishment (although he does shed some, not across-the-board, sceptical doubt on current practices, but not for reasons relating to the metaphysics of free will). In his words: 'It seems to me that all these notions [moral responsibility, desert and retribution], if we reflect on our actual deployment of them, can be seen to float free of the determinism/indeterminism question'. Kumar argues that the idea that Hanna did not deserve to be punished, assuming she did not deserve this, presupposes the idea that at times people do deserve to be punished so, the very idea, attributed to Tabensky among others, that no one ever deserves to be punished is problematic and he goes on to suggest in what sorts of contexts talk of moral responsibility can be appropriate. Kumar proposes what could be characterized as a context sensitive account of the tension between judging and understanding. In some cases, depending on context, understanding does exculpate, but in others it does not, and he uses examples, relating particularly to the US invasion of Iraq, to illustrate his point. Moral responsibility and desert come in degrees. At times, understanding, understanding the actions of the Bush administration for instance, will lead us to condemn in the harshest possible way, but the story of the naïve foot soldier (someone relevantly like Hanna) could be quite different. Not all causes leading to action exculpate, but some do, and which ones do or do not will depend on many considerations which 'float free of the determinism/indeterminism question'. In a more egalitarian world, a world very distant from ours, Kumar suggests, talk of moral responsibility would be far less problematic than it is now.

* * *

I. Introduction

After a few discussions with the editor of this volume, Pedro Tabensky, I was invited to write about the tension between judging people and understanding them, a tension provocatively and sensitively depicted in Bernhard Schlink's *The Reader*. My discussions with Tabensky were primarily philosophical arguments about free will, determinism, moral responsibility, desert and retribution. On most things, including important things, we agreed (and do agree). Our main point of disagreement, as I see it, centred on the implications (or lack thereof) of certain philosophical debates for our actual moral and political lives, our actual practices. Tabensky seemed to think that one's metaphysical views matter in these areas in ways that I do not think they do. He claimed that one's general views on determinism and on something called 'the nature of agency' have deep implications for our practices. I maintained, and still maintain, that if anything such views function as barriers to the sort of insight and understanding that may be gained from, among other things, novels.[1]

Thus I found myself *partially* disagreeing with Tabensky's position as he formulated it in an earlier paper (earlier than the one he has written for this volume). Reflecting on Schlink's novel, Tabensky reasoned as follows:

> Schlink argues, in a literary fashion, that the more one understands someone the more difficult it is to pass judgement on them. However, the novel stops short of reaching what I think is the logical conclusion…that attributions of blame *necessarily* depend on ignorance regarding the causes of action….[and that] there is no space in moral discourse for an ethic of desert. Reaching this rather radical conclusion will involve going beyond the phenomenological inquiry embodied in the novel and dealing with core metaphysical issues regarding the nature of free will [emphasis added].[2]

In his contribution to this volume Tabensky modifies his stance, now targeting what he calls an 'ethic of retribution' which holds punishment justifiable on the grounds that wrongdoers deserve to be punished for their transgressions *regardless* of the consequences of punishing. Though I wonder if there *are* any reflective 'retributivists' *so* unconcerned with consequences, I think Tabensky's argument is now more subtle and plausible than in his earlier formulation, and no less provocative. I largely share

---

1   My general views here have been shaped in large part by the meta-philosophical writings of Kai Nielsen and Richard Rorty. On the general irrelevance of traditional *moral* philosophy (including meta-ethics) to actual moral life and moral decision-making, it is worth reading Nielsen's *On Transforming Philosophy: A Metaphilosophical Inquiry*, Boulder, CO: Westview Press, 1995, pp. 143–270; and Rorty's 'Trapped Between Kant and Dewey: The Current Situation of Moral Philosophy', in Natalie Brender and Larry Krasnoff (eds), *New Essays in the History of Autonomy*, Cambridge: Cambridge University Press, 2004, pp. 195–214. I have written about the lack of normative and explanatory significance of certain theories of human *nature* (not human 'agency') in C. Kumar, 'Progress, Freedom, Human Nature and Critical Theory', *Imprints*, 7(2), 2003, pp. 106-30.

2   P.A. Tabensky, 'Judging and Understanding', *Law and Literature*, 16(2), 2004, pp. 207–8.

Tabensky's critical sentiments about retribution and the practices of holding people morally responsible, punishing, blaming and praising. These practices, we agree, merit careful critical reflection. Even with the modifications, however, it seems to me that Tabensky remains, perhaps despite himself, within the rather non-radical philosophical tradition initiated by Plato inasmuch as he believes that metaphysics has great normative significance; that if we adopted certain metaphysical views, contrary to the ones he thinks are culturally dominant, we would be much better off and we would radically alter our practices. Here I want to question the assumption that our general views on the determinism/indeterminism debate and on 'the nature of agency' have any such radical implications for our moral/political practices (such as the practice of legal punishment).

Although I will refer to Tabensky's articles as a springboard for discussion, this view of the importance of philosophy-as-metaphysics certainly is not unique to Tabensky. It can be traced at least as far back as Ancient Greece and it continues to be an important part of contemporary intellectual culture, though Plato's particular doctrines now have few adherents. Ted Honderich, Robert Kane and Thomas W. Clark, to mention only a few, also write about the free will/determinism question and, like Tabensky, they maintain that there are crucial senses of 'moral responsibility' that would be undermined with an acceptance and a taking-to-heart of determinism, that is, the view that every event or action is caused, an effect of something preceding it, something (or set of things or events or actions) sufficient to bring it about.[3] Is determinism compatible with free will – in some non-arbitrary sense of 'free will'? 'Compatibilism' is the name of the doctrine that the two things *are* compatible. Tabensky calls himself a compatibilist whereas Honderich refuses both labels (compatibilist or incompatibilist). Whatever the label, both believe (as do Kane and Clark) that one's position in the determinism/indeterminism debate has important consequences for our practices of holding people (including ourselves) responsible, praising, blaming and punishing.

My view, to put it bluntly, is that we philosophers should stop being so presumptuous; we needlessly muddy the waters when we try to make the 'core metaphysical issues' relevant to morality. We should appreciate Peter Strawson's important essay 'Freedom and Resentment' in which Strawson argues that in these areas moral discourse can get on just fine without such metaphysical backing or

---

3   And as the excellent quote from Nietzsche at the beginning of Tabensky's contribution to the present volume shows, Nietzsche also seemed to hold this view of the importance of general, metaphysical conceptions. But for more contemporary versions, see T. Honderich, *A Theory of Determinism: The Mind, Neuroscience, and Life-Hopes*, Oxford: Oxford University Press, 1988; and 'Determinism as True, Compatibilism and Incompatibilism as both False, and the Real Problem', *www.ucl.ac.uk/~uctytho/dfwVariousHonderichKanebook. htm*; R. Kane, *The Significance of Free Will*, NY: Oxford University Press, 1996, 'Freedom, Responsibility, and Will-Setting', *Philosophical Topics*, 24(2), 1996, pp. 67–90, and 'On Free Will, Responsibility and Indeterminism: Responses to Clarke, Haji, and Mele', *Philosophical Explorations*, 2, 1999, pp. 105–21; and T.W. Clark, 'Crime and Causality. Do Killers *Deserve* to Die?', *Free Inquiry*, 25(2), 2005, pp. 34–7.

theorizing, in this case theorizing about free will and determinism.[4] It probably is true that, more often than not, 'the more one understands someone the more difficult it is to pass judgement on them' – as Michael, the narrator in Schlink's novel, realizes as he reflects on his conflicting attitudes towards Hanna. But there is no interesting 'logical conclusion' to be drawn from this insight, an insight often rooted in reflection on tragic experience. In particular, contrary to Tabensky (and Nietzsche), there is no basis in determinism for dropping (or retaining, for that matter) *any of our important, working notions* of moral responsibility or even of desert and retribution. It seems to me that all these notions, if we reflect on our actual deployment of them, can be seen to float free of the determinism/indeterminism question.[5]

That is, we can make sense of these notions, see something of their rationale, without tying them to a position such as determinism or indeterminism. This is not to say that general views such as determinism and indeterminism cannot play an ideological role in sanctifying current practices (or in challenging them). But such general views, again, are not really the bedrock on which our talk of moral

---

4   Tabensky does critically discuss Strawson's article in his contribution to this volume. Again, I am largely in agreement with Tabensky's views on Strawson's paper, particularly his point that Strawson too easily takes as universal certain practices of blaming and judging people responsible that are not in fact universal. Nevertheless, I think what is more significant in 'Freedom and Resentment' is Strawson's main thesis, namely, that moral life, linked as it is to the 'reactive attitudes', does not require metaphysical grounding, and that our views on determinism (a doctrine he regarded as being rather unclear) do not dictate that we retain or abandon such 'reactive attitudes' and the judgements associated with them. These attitudes and judgements are more basic than any general philosophical theory about ubiquitous causation or the lack of it; which is not to say that we cannot question them and modify them but that general views such as determinism or indeterminism are not going to do the trick. See P. Strawson, 'Freedom and Resentment', *Proceedings of the British Academy*, 48, 1962, pp. 1–25.

5   None of the writers I mentioned (Tabensky, Honderich, Kane, Clark) take Wittgenstein sufficiently seriously. This allows them to go on as if there is an essence of moral responsibility, of desert, of retribution. They ignore Wittgenstein's point that a concept is just the use of a word in particular socio-cultural contexts. If they took this to heart, perhaps they would be less inclined to think, for example, that 'moral responsibility' essentially involves an appeal to a notion of an uncaused will. Paying attention to the use of the words 'moral responsibility' in live contexts may lead us to see its functioning independently of such philosophical assumptions about the 'will'. It may lead us to adopt Rorty's 'relaxed, pragmatical, Humean attitude – the attitude which says that there is no deep truth about Freedom of the Will, and that people are morally responsible for whatever their peers tend to hold them morally responsible for.' See R. Rorty, *Consequences of Pragmatism*, Minneapolis: University of Minnesota Press, 1983, p. xxii. While I would not speak so much of 'peers' as of relevant 'communities' or 'cultures', this is not a substantial departure from Rorty's main point that there is no culture-transcendent perspective on, or ahistorical essence of, moral responsibility. To see how very *modern* certain conceptions of individual responsibility are, consider Iris Murdoch's *The Sovereignty of Good*, NY: Routledge, 2001, pp. 1-44; and Rorty's discussion of this in the 'Introduction' to *Consequences of Pragmatism*, pp. xxii-xxiii.

responsibility rests. If a reflective retributivist came to believe that his talk of retribution (and responsibility) was bound up with a problematic denial of determinism, then he could drop the problematic denial without dropping the commitment to retribution; he could rely on other ways of justifying the practices he holds dear – he could even appeal to the good social consequences of an 'ethic of retribution'. One could (and in my view should) accept that in the world as it currently is – hierarchically structured, class-dominated, racist, patriarchal, replete with atrocities commanded from on high – talk of moral responsibility, desert and retribution is often cruelly ideological, even morally obscene; but this need not imply commitment to a position in the determinism/indeterminism debate that has raged among philosophers (particularly analytic philosophers). Being *politically* or *morally* radical does not require being *philosophically* conservative. We need not be Platonists in order to call into question, for example, our practices of punishment.[6]

So in my view we should attune ourselves to the morally sensitive, humane themes of *The Reader* while happily accepting its metaphysically non-committal character. Again, novels can be more enlightening here than Philosophy.[7]

II. Compatibilism and Moral Monsters

A few words are in order about the doctrine known as compatibilism. This can be seen as a kind of deflationary doctrine, one that deflates the apparent significance of determinism. Many philosophers have defended a version of this doctrine: for example, Hobbes, Spinoza, Hume, J.S. Mill, and in the twentieth century, Moritz Schlick, A.J. Ayer, Ernest Nagel, Sydney Hook, R.E. Hobart, Peter Strawson, Kai Nielsen, Richard Rorty and many others.[8] These philosophers say that determinism, if true, is, perhaps contrary to appearances, entirely compatible with human freedom of choice and conduct. They hold that the distinctions made in moral and legal discourse, in which we acknowledge degrees of culpability, responsibility and freedom of choice, are not inconsistent with determinism. Tabensky, like Honderich, contends that some important ways in which we talk about moral responsibility,

---

6   By 'Platonist' here I mean one who thinks that our moral practices rest on, or need, an ahistorical, metaphysical base. Michel Foucault is a good example of a non-Platonist critic of modern practices of punishment. See his *Discipline and Punish*, New York: Pantheon Books, 1978.

7   By 'Philosophy' I mean the tradition going back to Plato that seeks to uncover the essence of Knowledge, Reality, and Morality, or to provide foundations for our moral/political, scientific, religious and artistic practices. I do not mean philosophy as the attempt to see 'how things hang together' (or how they ought to do so); in this latter sense of 'philosophy' the novel can plainly be more philosophical than some of what gets studied in Philosophy departments. For more on this distinction between Philosophy and philosophy see R. Rorty, *Consequences of Pragmatism, op .cit.*, pp. xiv-xvii, and K. Nielsen, *Naturalism Without Foundations*, Amherst, NY: Prometheus Books, 1996, pp. 200–201, n.1.

8   See, for example, the collection, edited by B. Berofsky, *Free Will and Determinism*, NY: Harper and Row, 1966.

people getting or not getting what they deserve, and retribution, are inescapably tied to indeterminism and he thinks that by reflecting on the 'core metaphysical issues' involved here we may come to see that such conceptions are irrational. As I have indicated, I think this probably gives metaphysical views more credit (or blame) than is warranted; or, even if determinism is construed as a broadly empirical rather than metaphysical conception, as John Mackie and Ernest Nagel have construed it, still the choice between it and indeterminism (a version of which is sometimes called 'libertarianism') probably does not, in itself, have the sorts of consequences for our practices that have often been attributed to it – and not only by professional philosophers.[9]

Another compatibilist, John Hospers, in an essay first published in the 1930s, expressed a view similar to the one that Tabensky attributes to Schlink. Hospers wrote:

---

9   See E. Nagel, 'Determinism in History', in William H. Dray (ed.), *Philosophical Analysis and History*, NY: Harper and Row, 1966, pp. 347–82. An acceptance of determinism may, however, as Nagel stressed, make us more inclined to seek causal explanations (from both the natural and social sciences) where we hitherto refrained from doing so, or to seek broader, more comprehensive explanations than the ones currently accepted. So perhaps we can predict that a culture in which determinism was widely accepted would be more cautious in blaming and punishing than one in which it was rejected, since members of this culture would be more inclined to seek causes for why people behave as they do that are broader than explanations that merely appeal to their intentions and reasons – these latter types of explanation being more amenable to judgements of individual responsibility and blame. These connections between determinism, the search for broader explanations, and being more cautious about blaming and punishing people are not, however, necessary. Conceivably, a culture could accept determinism and, without contradicting that position, discourage curiosity – discourage the seeking of better explanations for why people do what they do; and it could accept determinism, encourage this sort of curiosity but could go on blaming people and punishing them as before, particularly if the curiosity encouraged by the culture is not informed by egalitarian moral convictions – or at least by a sense of our mutual, human vulnerability and finitude, a sense that in *some* basic ways we are all in the same lot and that no one's life matters more than anyone else's. Without such sympathetic or compassionate humanistic attitudes our ability (and willingness) to give more comprehensive explanations of ourselves and others may not lead us to opt for less punitive practices or to be less inclined to find people blameworthy. Thus in my view what does most of the work when we soften our judgements towards those who have done terrible things, is a certain understanding of our human situation that stresses our mutual vulnerability, our finitude, the contingency of our lot, a sense of the arbitrariness and luck involved in our being who we are and in the circumstances in which we find ourselves, a sense of compassion, a sense that everyone's life matters and matters equally, and an understanding of their *specific* history and circumstances. But these connections, again, do not seem to be matters of logical or metaphysical necessity (whatever that could be). Take, for example, the connection between understanding someone and judging them less harshly than we would without such understanding. Michael's intimate understanding of Hanna made him judge her less harshly than he otherwise would. But is it not sometimes the case that the more intimate understanding that comes from personal relationships has the opposite effect?

Let us note that the more thoroughly and in detail we know the causal factors leading a person to behave as he does, the more we *tend* to exempt him from responsibility [emphasis added].[10]

Hospers went on to question certain conventional assumptions about when criminals should be held morally responsible for their actions. He argued that there are all sorts of factors often dating from childhood, that, if adequately taken into account should lead us to consider much criminal behaviour as a kind of compulsive behaviour – or, if not compulsive, far less free and autonomous than is generally believed. In his essay Hospers focused on psycho-analytical explanations of criminal behaviour but this is not the relevant point in this context; of greater significance here is that, like Schlink, Hospers did not infer (indeed he carefully avoided inferring) from the fact that we often *mistakenly* and *hastily* hold people morally responsible, judge them harshly and speak of their deserving punishment for their crimes, that given the truth of determinism we should *never* do so. Like Schlink, Hospers did not draw the 'logical conclusion' that such notions should be put aside because they rest on a false or incoherent view of the nature of reality and of human agency.

As I have noted, determinism is the view that every event has a cause, that there are no uncaused events or actions. What is a cause? While there may be no single definition giving us necessary and sufficient conditions for something to be a cause, it is possible given our usage of the term to say some general, minimal things about it. For example, a fairly standard, Humean characterization of cause is that A causes B if and only if, whenever A occurs, B follows. This is a conception of cause as 'constant conjunction'. There have been criticisms of this conception, to be sure, but it does I think capture a good bit of our ordinary usage and something slightly different will suffice for our discussion: we can say that 'Every event or action is caused' means 'For every event or action, there are/were antecedent conditions, events and/or actions that are/were sufficient (though perhaps not necessary) to bring it about.'

Most philosophers nowadays who are determinists view such ubiquitous cause-effect relations within a general, naturalistic framework. They assume that we can only observe or intelligibly posit causes and their effects (which are also causes) as existing in the spatio-temporal universe; and that humans are metaphysically on a par, so to speak, with other species. Naturalists reject claims about a transcendent God, or a transcendent self or ego, causing this or that to happen. Certainly it is problematic to speak of something existing 'outside' or 'beyond' space and/or time somehow causing spatio-temporal events. With such talk, it seems, our typical, working conceptions of cause are being misused or abused, for we do not have any clear idea how causal transactions may, even in principle, span the natural and (allegedly) supernatural or 'transcendental' worlds. Our talk of cause and effect is bound up with our empirical knowledge and it seems clearly intelligible and applicable only within that broadly empirical (not empiricist) framework. It is, perhaps, largely for

---

10 J. Hospers, 'What Means This Freedom?', in B. Berofsky (ed.), *op. cit.*, p. 35.

this reason that the idea of an 'uncaused action' or a 'contra-causal' will has seemed barely intelligible to many (modern) determinists. Such notions suggest a realm of reality inaccessible through more or less empirical means, inviting the question, 'How can we know that something from the transcendental or non-empirical world was sufficient to bring about something in the empirical world – the only world we seem to have any coherent idea about?'

Neither Tabensky nor Honderich (or Nietzsche for that matter) believes in a form of supernatural or 'transcendental' causation. They are all, in some sense, naturalists. In this important way they are as non-Platonist or anti-Platonist (or anti-Kantian) as anyone. Yet in their reasoning about responsibility both Tabensky and Honderich seem to rely (as did, apparently, Nietzsche) on the idea that there is some necessary connection, or at least a very tight connection, between the 'libertarian' idea of an 'uncaused action' (or 'acausal' or 'contra-causal' will) and our talk of moral responsibility, desert and retribution. Honderich, however, unlike Tabensky, believes that the libertarian idea is not incoherent or unintelligible.[11] Though I think Tabensky is probably right about libertarianism being incoherent, I also think that this should make him more suspicious than he is of the idea that it is inseparable from the language of retribution and moral responsibility. Honderich, by claiming that the libertarian idea is not actually incoherent, creates more leeway for himself for making these connections. But I will come back to this point.

Tabensky rightly maintains that Hanna, in *The Reader*, should not be deemed a 'moral monster' though she knowingly participated in the atrocities of the Nazi regime. Hanna is a tragic figure; one can, with Michael, sympathize with her and see that if one were placed in her circumstances, had her weaknesses, faced with the choices she faced, one may well have done what she did. The novel makes us see Hanna's life in a different light than we (anti-Nazis) would see it if all we knew was that she knowingly participated in mass atrocities carried out by the Nazis. So

---

11 Honderich's argument for this opinion seems to me a bad one. He rests his case on an analogy between believing in 'originative', uncaused actions on the one hand, and believing that petunias need sun on the other. I leave it to the reader to judge whether it is a good analogy. He wants us to regard the former claim as being on a par with the latter, plainly intelligible claim. Here is what he says about the latter:

Suppose I have no idea of why the petunias on the balcony *need sun*, but am persuaded they do, no doubt by good evidence. [Can we be persuaded 'by good evidence' that there are uncaused 'originative' actions? What sort of evidence could do so?] Despite the evidence, I have no acquaintance at all with photosynthesis, not even any boy's own science of the matter. It does not follow, presumably, that I lack [a coherent] idea that the petunias *need sun*. I could have the idea, too, in a pre-scientific society where news of the science of the thing would for a long time make no sense. Could I not also have [a coherent, intelligible] idea [of petunias needing sun], in a later society, if all of many attempts to explicate the need had broken down in obscurity and indeed contradiction? [Is an affirmative answer to that question as obviously correct as Honderich implies?] (T. Honderich, 'Determinism as True, Compatibilism and Incompatibilism as both False, and the Real Problem', *www.ucl.ac.uk/~uctytho/dfwVariousHonderichKanebook.htm*).

far, this squares with the attitude that Tabensky attributes to Schlink and that was expressed by Hospers: that the more we come to know about a person's circumstances and history the less inclined we are to judge them harshly. Hanna, we see, is not quite the moral monster we would have thought her to be prior to acquiring a richer understanding of her circumstances and capacities.

What makes that a meaningful thing to say, however, is that if Hanna had a *different* history and/or *different* character and capacities, then it would have been more appropriate to deem her a moral monster. Suppose, for example, she came from a privileged background, was quite literate and well-educated, came to love causing pain and humiliation, felt sexually aroused by such things, cared not a whit for the victims of the Nazi regime even after having engaged in non-evasive reflection about them and their treatment by the Nazis, was mainly interested in pleasing the Führer and had plenty of opportunity to start a meaningful life outside Germany. The *specifics* of the causal history matter, not the mere fact that there *is* always a causal history. That Hanna is not a moral monster makes sense insofar as we can conceive of circumstances in which she (or someone who did what she did, but with different motives, different abilities, and different knowledge) would be one. If participation in carrying out atrocities could never be morally monstrous there would be little point in saying that Hanna was not a moral monster.

Analogously, consider for a moment one of the official narratives of the fateful events of 11 September 2001. According to this narrative, those who struck the US did so primarily because they 'hate freedom'. If that were so and if we had little or no additional understanding of the attackers except that they were in favor of a harshly patriarchal and theocratic rule, then we (anti-fundamentalist humanists) would, with good reason, regard them as being moral monsters. But if there is a more plausible, more complex narrative that adequately considers the long history of atrocities and injustices inflicted by the US government on Muslims (and others) throughout the Middle East and elsewhere, then, although we may still regard the act as an atrocity, a crime against humanity and inexcusable, the moral simplicity of the official narrative would have to be rejected. At the very least we would recognize that the perpetrators (assuming they are who they are said to be) were themselves responding to moral monstrosities from the other side.[12]

III. Clint Eastwood and the Idea of Desert

Nevertheless, I need to say something more specific about the ideas of desert, moral responsibility, and retribution. Let me start with the idea of people deserving (or not deserving) things.

---

12 For a cogent critique of the US 'war on terror' that takes these atrocities and injustices into account, see S. Meckled-Garcia, 'International Justice, Human Rights and Security After 11th September', *Imprints*, (6)2, 2002, available online at *http://eis.bris.ac.uk/~plcdib/ imprints/meckled-garcia.*html.

Tabensky insinuates that *The Reader* is insufficiently hostile to ideas of desert and retribution because '[o]ne does not find suggestions to the effect that…Hanna did not deserve to be punished as she was.' He continues:

> It seems as if the novel invites us to accept that she should be punished even in light of a full understanding that, given her weaknesses and the adverse circumstances presented to her, she could not have done otherwise at the time of the events that marked her life.[13]

Before discussing the crucial idea that Hanna 'could not have done otherwise' – a phrase about which much ink has been spilled in the determinism debates – I want to comment on the suggestion that Hanna did not deserve her punishment.

There are at least two ways of understanding this claim, one metaphysical and the other not. One way, the non-metaphysical way, is to understand it in the spirit of Clint Eastwood in his film *The Unforgiven*. In that film, the character played by Eastwood has a friend, a decent man, who is savagely murdered by a sheriff, a not-so-decent man played by Gene Hackman. Towards the end of the film, Eastwood's character, to avenge the murder of his friend, shoots the sheriff. The sheriff's last words are 'I don't deserve this.' Before pulling the trigger, Eastwood says, in characteristically terse style, 'Deserve's got nothin' to do with it.' In the context of the film, taken as Eastwood's commentary on Hollywood Westerns (the film is a kind of anti-Western) it is possible to interpret Eastwood's message as follows. In the world of the Wild West, good guys don't always win and bad guys don't always (or even usually) lose; people tend *not* to get what they deserve, contrary to the moralism of most Hollywood Westerns. This, I suggest, implies a non-metaphysical idea of desert; it implies that in some other, empirically possible circumstances, a world very different from the Wild West (to say nothing of the real world of class domination, patriarchy, racism and so on) perhaps it *would* be meaningful, or more meaningful, to speak of desert, to speak of it without a bad conscience. On this way of speaking of people getting or not getting what they deserve, there is a non-vacuous contrast to 'He did not deserve X'; we can well imagine circumstances in which he (or someone) did deserve it.

But we may, feeling the force of determinism, want to say that since every action is caused, every desire and human trait an effect of something else, leading back to causes and circumstances over which one had no control, we should never say that anyone ever deserves anything. Reflection on determinism, not on anyone's specific history and circumstances, seems to render talk of desert senseless or at least problematic. But then, not only did Hanna not deserve her punishment, nobody ever deserves anything and the novel's context-sensitivity is irrelevant to that; we need no narrative about Hanna to see that she did or did not deserve to be punished for her actions. We need only to understand that every action is caused and that the causal chains will always lead back to antecedent conditions over which one had no control.

Is this a convincing way to dispense with all claims about people deserving or not deserving something? Is the language of desert inseparable from what amounts to a

---

13 P. Tabensky, *op. cit.*, p. 211.

denial of determinism in the name of some mysterious 'contra-causal' Free Will? If so, then even to say 'Hanna did *not* deserve to be punished' would be problematic; for if the very idea of desert depends upon an assumption of a contra-causal will, then 'She did not deserve it' seems no less problematic than 'She did deserve it'. But why assume that the 'very idea' of desert (putting aside questions about the dubious, un-Wittgensteinian notion of 'the very idea') rests on a general thesis in an esoteric philosophical debate? Clint Eastwood, at least, could be interpreted in a less problematic way.

Generally, we need to ask: Why make ideas that at least seem to make sense in everyday language make little or no sense by linking them to more or less unintelligible philosophical views, in this case the view that the self or will can stand 'outside' the natural order of causes? Though it is not always unreasonable to maintain a sceptical attitude towards what passes for 'common sense', perhaps we should not so easily dismiss the language of the folk; we should try to give it a charitable interpretation before we judge it wanting in light of our favourite general theories about the structure of reality or the 'nature of agency'.

IV. 'Could not have done otherwise' and Moral Responsibility

Similar things can be said of the phrase 'could have (or could not have) done otherwise'. The claim that Hanna 'could not have done otherwise', like the claim that she did not deserve the punishment meted out to her, can be understood in more or less metaphysical ways. For philosophers, it is tempting to link the meaning of 'could not have done otherwise' to the debate about determinism. One strategy is to note that moral responsibility requires that agents could have done otherwise, then to argue that since no one ever could have done otherwise in a deterministic world, talk of moral responsibility rests on illusion.

However, everything here depends on how we understand 'could not have done otherwise'. As compatibilists have repeatedly stressed, typically when we say 'I could have done otherwise' we do not commit ourselves to a denial of determinism. If anything, we commit ourselves to an assertion that takes the form of a conditional such as 'I would have done otherwise if I had wanted to or if I had tried.'[14] Or

---

14 J.L. Austin, in his famous 'Ifs and Cans' paper, raised doubts about whether we even (or always) commit ourselves to such conditional claims when we say 'I could have (or could not have) done otherwise'. See J.L. Austin, 'Ifs and Cans', *Philosophical Papers*, Oxford: Oxford University Press, 1961, pp. 153–80. One might well ask whether we need any *analysis* of such 'can' claims at all. If someone actually doubts whether we can at least sometimes do other than what we in fact do, perhaps the one doubting should reconsider the theory that makes him doubt what we never really doubt in practice. Perhaps the problem is with the theory rather than with our common sense. Kai Nielsen has made me aware of this Moorean line of argument on more than one topic, but especially on the topic of epistemological scepticism. It is not always the case that common sense must, if we are to be reasonable, give way to a theory. Sometimes it is the other way round.

we mean something like 'I had the ability and opportunity to do otherwise but I chose not to.'[15] There does not seem to be anything deeply problematic, in everyday speech, about 'I could (or could not) have done otherwise.' None of these senses implies that there is such a thing as a 'contra-causal' freedom or will. Moreover, sometimes when we say 'I could not have done otherwise' we are not denying but affirming our moral responsibility. Daniel Dennett points out that when Luther said 'Here I stand; I can do no other' he was not 'ducking responsibility' but affirming it; he was saying that his own rational and moral capacities were such that he could do no other; to do otherwise would be to contravene his own better self and he, as a matter of conviction, would not do that. That is an example where 'I could not do otherwise' is an *affirmation* of moral responsibility.[16]

In other instances, Dennett notes, when we ask, 'Could he have done otherwise?' we mean something like 'Given his character and capacities, would he have done the same thing in roughly similar or even very different circumstances?' If the answer is no, then his action might be explained by some unanticipated event that led him to do something he would not in most circumstances do; it was 'out of character' and we are satisfied that he could have done otherwise; if yes, then we might say that he could not have done otherwise, meaning that his basic character and capacities had a kind of stability over many different circumstances, that he is likely to perform the same type of action even under constraining or adverse or unanticipated conditions. But, as Dennett rightly stresses, none of this implies or entails a denial of moral responsibility for at least some of the things we do or refrain from doing. So what sense of 'could not have done otherwise' does commit one to in some sense denying moral responsibility?

Consider Tabensky's claim about Hanna that, 'given her weaknesses and the adverse circumstances presented to her, she could not have done otherwise at the time of the events that marked her life.' One way of reading this is to take it as the claim that, given *all* the causal antecedents of Hanna's (or indeed anyone's) actions, all the events, circumstances, desires and beliefs that actually caused her behavior, she could not have done other than what in fact she did when she did it. It should be noted that this reading comes close to being a tautology: If all the things that caused a person to do X were to occur in exactly the same way they did occur, where the causes include the characteristics, beliefs, desires, and so on that 'constitute' that person, then X would occur. To put it another way, 'If exactly the same things happened in exactly the same way in exactly the same circumstances, the same thing would happen.' It is this sort of thought that led Dennett to say, in exasperation, 'So what?'

---

15 See P.H. Nowell-Smith, 'Ifs and Cans', and 'Freedom and Responsibility', both in B. Berofsky (ed.), *op. cit.*, 322–38 and 364–72 respectively.

16 D. Dennett, 'I Could Not Have Done Otherwise – So What?', in Robert Kane (ed.), *Free Will*, Oxford: Blackwell Publishers, 2002, pp. 83–94. For Dennett's more developed views on these topics, see his *Freedom Evolves*, NY: Penguin Books, 2003.

P.H. Nowell-Smith, another compatibilist philosopher, observed that sometimes it helps to see 'She could not have done otherwise' as an answer to the question 'Why did she do it?' When we so answer, 'She could not have done otherwise' means something like 'She had neither the ability nor the opportunity to do otherwise' or 'She had no opportunity to do otherwise even if she had the ability' or 'She could not have done otherwise no matter how hard she tried or what her attitude was.' These are *exculpatory* or *excusing* uses of the phrase 'She could not have done otherwise' and, in everyday moral and legal discourse, they do have non-vacuous contrasts. Thus if 'Why did she do it?' was answered by 'She accepted a bribe' or 'She didn't give a hoot about the innocent people that would be adversely affected' or 'She was just interested in acquiring lots of money and power', we tend to find these answers less exculpatory or excusing and to find her more blameworthy than with the former sorts of answers. Here 'She could not have done otherwise' does have contrasts and in these cases the phrase functions as a way of indicating the presence of what Dennett calls 'local fatalism' – the idea that she could not have done otherwise given the circumstances no matter how hard she tried or how much she wanted to. But fatalism is not determinism and to assert the presence of small 'pockets of fatalism', as Dennett puts it, is not to commit oneself in the determinism/indeterminism debate. And in moral and legal discourse we routinely distinguish between more or less mitigating circumstances, implying that praise and blame can be more or less appropriate, regardless of our position (if we have one) in that debate. These distinctions are routinely made without anyone pausing to figure out whether, for example, the apparent indeterminism that has been claimed for quantum-level phenomena has implications for our talk of responsibility, punishment and so on (nor is it clear why anyone *should* pause to figure that out).

But now what if it is said that even when we distinguish more or less mitigating circumstances, find people more or less blameworthy, everyone is in the same lot since everyone's actions are equally determined? Rich and poor alike are subject to the universal law of causation;[17] neither had or have 'ultimate control' (whatever that is) over the genetic and environmental circumstances that made them who they are. That was a matter of luck (good or bad). So in fact, and contrary to appearances, no one really could have done anything but what they in fact did; everyone is equally determined by a chain or web of causal relations 'ultimately' beyond their control. Thus, to speak of people being morally responsible is, as Tabensky puts it, a 'seductive illusion'. No one could have done other than what they in fact did when they did it.

But notice that in *this* (what I would call metaphysical, unverifiable and unfalsifiable) sense of 'could not have done otherwise' there seems again to be no clear contrast case that would make the expression meaningful. On this understanding of determinism and of the phrase 'could not have done otherwise' there are *no* circumstances in which it would be correct to say that a person *could* have done other than what she in fact did when she did it; but then it is not clear that

---

17 I believe that was Moritz Schlick's way of putting it.

'She could not have done otherwise' is a meaningful expression in this context – let alone a false one. If we have no grip on when someone could have done otherwise, we have no grip on when they could not have done otherwise. And if 'She could have done otherwise' is so apparently meaningless, then so is 'She could not have done otherwise.' At this level, we should say neither that people are or are not responsible or worthy of praise or blame. We should say, instead, that it is something like a 'category mistake' even to use these terms.[18] But for 'could not have done otherwise' to play such an important role in an argument for dropping ideas of moral responsibility, would we not need a more meaningful, less technical reading of the phrase? Should we not say, as Rorty does, that 'concepts like "right", "ought" and "responsible" are not technical concepts, and [that] it is not clear what special training could enable you to grasp the uses of these words better than the laity' – the laity in this case being those who freely use these words without linking them to the thesis that *everything* is (or *not* everything is) caused or capable of being 'brought under a causal law'.[19] Whatever the verdict on this, enough has been said, I think, to cast doubt on the suggestion that Schlink's novel is 'logically committed' to the idea that moral responsibility, in any sense that matters, rests on an illusion. There is nothing incoherent or even incomplete in the non-metaphysical views that Tabensky finds inscribed in 'the phenomenological inquiry embodied in [*The Reader*]'.

V. Four Tempting Fallacies

One is not, just in virtue of noting a tension between judging and understanding, committed to any views on the free will/determinism debate. Moreover, a *tension* is not the same as a *contradiction*. Suppose one wants an explanation for the recent US bombing, invasion and occupation of Iraq. One possible answer is that the dominant policymakers wanted to acquire control over the second largest energy reserves in the world, the better to maintain leverage on its main competitors (such as Germany, France, Russia and China) and to establish a stronger military presence in a strategically important part of the world – a presence that would not have been possible prior to the collapse of the Soviet Union; and perhaps also to begin to reverse the trend of the oil business being conducted with Euros rather than US dollars. Probably most people, or at least anyone who thinks Iraqi lives are not worth less than Western lives, when given such an explanation and when sufficiently, vividly informed of the mass atrocities that have been necessary to achieve these goals, and the amount of taxpayers' money that has been siphoned off to fund the continuing destruction and humiliation, would find the members of the Bush Administration and their corporate backers blameworthy and would hold them morally responsible. Where is the contradiction here between understanding and judging? It might be said that the understanding (the causal explanation of the bombing, invasion

---

18 Hospers, in 'What Means This Freedom?', put forth a similar argument.
19 Rorty, 'Trapped Between Kant and Dewey: The Current Situation of Moral Philosophy', *op. cit.*, p. 196.

and occupation) is not sufficiently detailed and that were we to acquire a thicker description of causes that made the members of the Bush Administration the sorts of people they are, then we would judge them less harshly; we would see that their being the sorts of persons they are resulted from many circumstances and antecedent events that were 'ultimately beyond their control'. I think this sort of response (which I do not attribute to Tabensky) would be fallacious in at least four ways, though there is one way in which we might find judgements of moral responsibility, even in this context, wanting. Let me explain.

1. First, the force of such a response depends on our not noticing that in fact the *subject has been changed*. The initial explanation was an answer to the question 'Why did the dominant policymakers in the US order the bombing, invasion and occupation of Iraq?' In order to find answers to this question, perhaps we should look to the work of those (Noam Chomsky, William Blum and David Harvey, for example) who have, in a critical spirit, meticulously researched and analysed US foreign policy and US interventions generally. If we look to these sorts of works we find that they do not provide lurid details about the personal lives of Bush, Cheney, Rumsfeld and the rest. What they do is identify patterns in US foreign policy, statements made by relevant policy institutes, think-tanks, agencies (such as the Project for a New American Century or statements made in the National Security Strategy Documents), and other relevant, usually publicly available information. Their explanations almost never go back to, say, Bush's childhood to unearth repressed memories, to the night Bush Senior and Barbara conceived their future son, or to anything like that. A detailed account of Bush's early socialization may indeed be interesting but it would rightly be judged irrelevant to the question we want answered about the invasion of Iraq. Usually, when asking such a question we would not be asking for an account of early childhood history – or something of the like – or of such factors that are, of course, 'ultimately beyond the control' of the current policymakers. And if we judge them morally responsible for what they have done in their capacity as policymakers we are not implying that they actually do have control over what happened to them in early childhood or over where they were born or who their parents are, and so on. To bring these factors in and to appeal to them as a way of saying they were not morally responsible for their current actions in their capacity as policymakers is, among other things, simply to change the subject.

2. I think one reason it may be tempting for determinists to perform this trick is that they do not sufficiently appreciate the *context-dependence of explanations*. This gives them a false idea of what a 'complete' explanation would be. All explanations have a stopping point, a point beyond which we do not seek further antecedent causes of the thing we want explained. Where this point lies depends on context, on the nature of the question we are asking and the purposes we have in asking it. Our purpose is never (or almost never) to find the cause of something as far back as the Big Bang. We don't need to know about Bush's childhood to answer the question about Iraq because our purpose is to understand what effectively motivates people in their capacity as

policymakers in the dominant state in today's world. Perhaps we want to know what things politically, economically, socially would have to be otherwise to bring about a world in which such aggression and atrocities will not occur; often, when we want to explain something, what we really want to know is what things would have to be otherwise for something to be prevented or significantly diminished. Facts about the mating habits of Bush the elder, for example, are irrelevant here, whereas facts about the Bush family's close ties with the oil and arms industries may well be relevant; but there is no algorithm or global rule or formula for telling us in advance of inquiry which factors will be relevant.[20]

3. Another temptation, one to which Tabensky occasionally succumbs, is to argue as follows:

> Determinism is incompatible with moral responsibility not because, or at least not primarily because...a person could not have done otherwise. Rather, to be morally responsible one would have to be responsible for the first causes of one's moves, and that would involve situating the will (or a component of the will at any rate) outside of the causal chain of events that constitutes a human life.[21]

This is the key claim. *Does* 'moral responsibility' presuppose such a metaphysical notion of Free Will? *Do* people, when holding others or themselves morally accountable or responsible, commit themselves to such a view? Elaborating on this metaphysical conception, Tabensky continues:

> If a will were the first cause of action, it would be a will that willed for no particular reason [presumably because acting on reasons, deciding to do this or that for this or that reason, is only possible *inside* 'the causal chain of events that constitutes a human life']. It would be a blind will and hence, on final analysis, no will at all.[22]

In other words, the idea of a 'contra-causal' will is, if not incoherent, deeply problematic. So Tabensky's claim seems to be that the idea of moral responsibility presupposes, 'in the final analysis', an apparently incoherent view of the self as unmoved mover somehow transcending causal relations. This is surely debatable. First, there is no 'final analysis'. As mentioned above, all explanations are context-dependent (and purpose-relative) and we almost never, in seeking a causal explanation, try to go back to the Big Bang or to whatever we think the origins of the universe are – assuming 'origins of the universe' is meaningful; there is no 'final analysis' or 'complete explanation' in that sense or in any other context-free sense. Thus, the idea that the notion of moral responsibility depends 'in the final analysis' on an unintelligible notion of the self or will as first cause or unmoved mover is

---

20 For an excellent book on the context-dependence of explanations, see A. Garfinkel, *Forms of Explanation: Rethinking the Questions in Social Theory*, New Haven, CT: Yale University Press, 1981.

21 Tabensky, *op .cit.*, p. 215.

22 *Ibid.*, pp. 215–16.

rather obscure; it is, in any case, not obviously true. Since we can and do make distinctions in actual moral and legal discourse between degrees of responsibility without, it seems, contradicting determinism and independently of any claims about a 'contra-causal' will or 'unmoved movers', it would seem that Tabensky's argument depends upon *importing* a philosophical account of the self as acausal, or partially acausal, into everyday language. But why should we do this when we can perfectly well make the following *sorts* of distinctions (if not precisely in these ways) made long ago by Sydney Hook:

> If we make a list of the circumstances behind actions for which we hold individuals responsible and those for which we do not, we shall find that as a rule the first class consists of those in which evidence exists that praise and reward, blame and punishment, tend to influence the future conduct of those involved and/or those tempted....in addition to susceptibility to reward and punishment, we attribute responsibility where there is a tendency to respond to valid reasons, to behave rationally, to respond to human emotions in a human way. [Here perhaps Hook should have said 'respond in a *reasonable* way' and he should have stressed that our conceptions of reasonability are normative, not purely descriptive.] Perhaps a third element involved in the attribution of moral responsibility to voluntary action is *approved* action. A man is morally responsible for an action he commits to the extent that he *approves* of it. If he sincerely disapproves of his action, regards it as wrong and condemns it as wrong but still commits it we tend to regard him as ill, as acting under 'compulsion'...[23]

There is another argument, voiced by both Hook and Hobart, against the view that notions of moral responsibility, desert and retribution depend on some version of indeterminism or libertarianism.[24] The argument is that these moral notions actually have nothing to do with indeterminism and in fact they might even be *less* meaningful or plausible were something like indeterminism true. Against the thesis that notions of retribution, desert and moral responsibility depend upon a version of libertarianism, Hook and Hobart maintain that this gets things backwards. For if libertarianism were true and the self or 'will' somehow able, 'outside the natural order of causal relations', to make decisions to act in one way or another, perhaps the will would be, as Tabensky puts it himself, a 'blind will' and why should we hold a blind, in principle unpredictable will responsible for anything? Moreover, let us ask, as Hook does, why it is that we find retributive punishment wrong – those of us that do. Hook suggests that actually we find it wrong,

> ...[n]ot because the wrongdoer 'ultimately did not shape his own character' [or was not the 'first cause' of his character] – whatever that may mean – but simply because the pain inflicted on him gratuitously adds to the sum total of suffering in the world without any compensating alleviation of anybody else's suffering. Even if an individual were

---

23 S. Hook, 'Necessity, Indeterminism, and Sentimentalism', in Berofsky (ed.), *op. cit.*, p. 48.

24 R.E. See Hobart, 'Free Will as Involving Determination and as Inconceivable Without It', in Berofsky (ed.), *ibid.*, pp. 63–94.

considered able 'ultimately to shape his own character' and were held morally responsible for an evil act, punishment that would be purely retributive and that did not contribute to deterring him or others from evil doing, or did nothing toward rehabilitating him, would still be morally wrong.[25]

Whether or not one *agrees* with Hook here (as I do), his reasoning is sufficiently lucid to show, contrary to appearances, that there is no *logical* connection between indeterminism or libertarianism, on the one hand, and punishment as retribution on the other. Moreover, there is not always a *psychological* connection between attributions of moral responsibility and retribution either. As Hook points out, many Christians, for example, have held both that some people should suffer eternal purgatory *and* that they were not responsible for the sorts of people they were or even the evil actions they committed – perhaps the devil made them do it.

4. Finally, there is another common confusion, noted by compatibilists such as Schlick, Ayer, and Nielsen, between the idea of 'cause' and the idea of 'constraint' or 'compulsion'. To say that A caused B is to say, roughly, that whenever an event of type A occurs, an event of type B follows. To say that A *forced* or *compelled* B to occur is simply metaphorical, an anthropomorphism that results from conflating human legal laws with causal laws. Only the former prescribe, compel and coerce, and 'it is because of the metaphor, and not because of the fact, that we come to think that there is an antithesis between causality and freedom'.[26] Causes can be more or less constraining *or* enabling, more or less freedom-diminishing *or* freedom-enhancing. The relevant contrast to freedom is not determinism but compulsion, coercion, manipulation, and the like. *This* is the sort of contrast that allows us to make distinctions, fully compatible with determinism, between freedom-enhancing (and hence responsibility-increasing) causal contexts and freedom-diminishing (and hence more exculpatory and excusing) causal contexts. It allows us to say, for example, that the members of the Bush administration and their corporate backers (or masters) bear a greater degree of moral responsibility for the murder and impoverishment of Iraqis than the poverty-stricken teenagers who join the army and end up killing Iraqis or being killed; that the members of the preceding, Clinton administration bear a greater degree of responsibility for the premature death of well over one million Iraqi civilians than those who were on the ground enforcing the US-UK sanctions from which this suffering and death (predictably) resulted;[27]

---

25 S. Hook, *op. cit.*, p. 50.

26 K. Nielsen, 'The Compatibility of Freedom and Determinism', in R. Kane (ed.), *op. cit.*, p. 42.

27 Lesley Stahl, on the CBS news program *60 Minutes* (5/12/96), addressed this question to US Secretary of State Madeleine Albright in 1996 (after the first five years of a decade of sanctions imposed on Iraq):
We have heard that a half million children have died [as a result of the sanctions]. I mean, that's more children than died in Hiroshima. And, you know, is the price worth it?

and it allows us morally to distinguish (in terms of degrees of responsibility for evil) between the industrialists and bankers who encouraged and materially supported the Nazi regime and the relatively powerless Hannas of the world with far less freedom or autonomy. Responsibility, like freedom, comes in degrees, and so even if we hold Hanna responsible, her responsibility, on this understanding, pales in comparison to that of the high officials and wealthy individuals who made the crucial policy decisions.[28]

VI. Systemic Causes and Moral Responsibility

Even if all my reasoning so far is accepted, still it may plausibly be argued that even in the contexts of the Nazi regime or the current authoritarian neoliberal world order managed and policed by the US, talk of individual moral responsibility, even in reference to the most inhumane thugs wielding power, is, in an important way, inadequate. In a paper on 'Retribution and Reconciliation', David Crocker rightly suggests that '[i]t is morally repugnant to punish the reluctant foot soldier as severely as the architects, chief implementers, or "middle management" of atrocities.'[29] Indeed, but why? Because the architects have more say in the matter, they are privileged, they have more freedom and they can do more as individuals to prevent the atrocities; this is why we (should) say their responsibility is greater. We should tailor our conceptions of responsibility, in this way, to our egalitarian convictions,

---

Albright's revealing, infamous reply is recorded for all who wish to see:
I think this is a very hard choice, but the price – we think the price is worth it.

Albright's comment, Rahul Mahajan notes, 'calmly asserting that US policy objectives were worth the sacrifice of half a million Arab children, has been much quoted in the Arabic press [and has] also been cited in the United States in alternative commentary on the September 11 attacks (e.g., Alexander Cockburn, *New York Press*, 9/26/01)'. But, Mahajan laments, it hardly ever appears in mainstream commentary, particularly in the US. See R. Mahajan, '"We Think the Price is Worth it": Media Uncurious About Iraq Policy's Effects – Here or There', *Extra!*, November/December 2001, *www.fair.org/index.php?page=1084*. Mahajan (and several other informed commentators) also puts to rest the State Department's claim, when too many people were criticizing the 'genocidal' nature of the sanctions, that the deaths from the sanctions were really the responsibility of Saddam Hussein. Even the UN officials who were on the ground and in charge of the so-called oil-for-food program deny this claim; it is hard to believe that the top people in the State Department actually believed it themselves. The relevant part of the interview with Albright is all over the internet and can be found simply by typing 'we think the price is worth it' at the 'google' prompt.

28 A fact worth remembering in this context: It is always, or almost always, *leaders* and *elites* who declare war, not the general public. People tend not to want to be involved in wars and the atrocities that almost always accompany them; typically they need to be *manipulated* into participating in or otherwise supporting these endeavours.

29 D. Crocker, 'Retribution and Reconciliation', Institute for Philosophy and Public Policy, *www.puaf.umd.edu/IPPP/Winter-Spring00/retribution_and_reconciliation.htm*.

if we have them, without the assistance (or crutch) of some general metaphysical theory to back up these convictions and conceptions.

But what if the 'architects' are themselves driven by the imperatives of a system not of their own making? Perhaps a predatory capitalist would not behave as he does, for instance, if he were not living in a world dominated by capitalist social relations, if he did not have to exploit people and to use the force of the state to ensure future profits and 'market share' (particularly when the system of power and privilege is threatened or in crisis).[30] Is he not just doing what that system requires him to do if he is to remain a capitalist? Perhaps he is, but these 'architects' still have more option to step down (even though someone else is likely to take their place) than the 'foot soldiers' who tend to be poor and otherwise uneducated and unemployed; and the 'architects' are not forced to participate in the system in the ways they do, they would not starve or become destitute (or anything remotely close to that) because of their decision not to so participate.

Crocker claims that Nuremburg 'vindicated the notion of individual responsibility for crimes against humanity and defeated the excuse that one was "merely" following orders'. But what if one was following orders on pain of death, or unemployment, or if there was such effective, pervasive propaganda that one didn't really know what *we* may know with the benefit of hindsight? There is a consequentialist argument here: we want in future to deter people from simply following orders to carry out atrocities. Thus it makes sense to punish such things and it makes sense to hold such people morally responsible, again not nearly to the degree that we should hold the 'architects' of policy responsible. Note how our conception of responsibility here is not just 'read off' the facts or the nature of agency but is being shaped by our goal of deterring future atrocities. This, I submit, is nothing to worry about; again, tailoring our conceptions of responsibility to our politics is what we in effect do anyway, so let us be honest about it. We can still argue, in a reasonable way, about our politics.

Still, if all we ever do is to hold wealthy and powerful individuals morally responsible, albeit far more than ordinary people (the 'foot soldiers'), this seems rather self-defeating if there are good systemic reasons for the selection of such morally reprobate personalities. If a socio-economic order is structured in such a way as to select for such depraved individuals, to ensure that those willing to command the worst atrocities will be the ones who, when the system of power and privilege requires, obtain key commanding positions, then it is an inadequate moral response simply to focus on the individual moral shortcomings of these 'architects'. If we really want to change things so that such systematic atrocious behavior is significantly diminished, we should take to heart Kant's maxim that to will the end is to will the necessary means; what is needed, it would seem, is a collective movement

---

30 See D. Harvey, *The New Imperialism*, Oxford: Oxford University Press, 2003, for a lucid account of the 'war on terror' and of the resurgence of imperialism cast in these systemic terms. See also Harvey's masterful 'Neoliberalism and the Restoration of Class Power', *www.sum.uio.no/research/changing_attitudes/humanism/harvey080604.pdf.*

to transform the structures, the institutions, the system and the culture that breeds such 'moral monsters', and this is far more difficult, but also far more important, than efforts to hold powerful, morally depraved elites (such as Pinochet, Goering, Kissinger or Bush) accountable for their actions.

VII. Concluding Remarks

To make myself clear, I do not deny that there is an apparent tension between determinism and ideas of moral responsibility. When we honestly and carefully reflect on the causes of action and character-formation, we cannot avoid thinking that we are products of our environments (our genes and our social and physical environments). What we should keep in mind is that we use the language of responsibility for different purposes than those for which we use a more scientific, 'objectifying' language of cause and effect; this latter type of language, as Rorty likes to point out, is mainly for purposes of prediction and control, and prediction and control is not always a bad thing, even when we are talking about people. It would be a good thing, for example, if we came to know about the structural causes (if there are any) of war and terrorism, the better to change our environments significantly to diminish these things. And there are good moral/political reasons, as I have tried to bring out, for retaining talk of responsibility, though I think Tabensky is dead right in stressing that this language is over-used, that it is often insensitive to the causal circumstances and capacities that make people the sorts of people they are, and that it is often a smokescreen for ignoble instincts of revenge. (I would add that it is also often shot through with racist, sexist and classist ideology.) Nevertheless, when faced with the suggestion (which I do not attribute to Tabensky) that we should abandon such language altogether and treat wealthy and powerful fascists and their ilk as objects merely of pity, in my view we should not be so Christian-minded (if that is an apt expression) as to erase all vestiges of militant rage against individuals who preside over and formulate policies that predictably lead to mass suffering and death. If it makes sense to say that they too are victims of a badly structured socio-economic system, it makes no less sense to stress that they are 'victimized' in very different, less onerous ways, and to a far lesser extent, than most of the rest of us. We should hold these people (the Kissingers of the world) responsible, morally responsible, even if they too can be described as being products of, and constrained by, a particular socio-economic system.

Finally, one good thing about novels, as opposed to general philosophical views such as determinism or indeterminism or libertarianism or even compatibilism, is their context-sensitivity. One of the things that Schlink does in *The Reader*, is to remind us, through a context-sensitive portrayal of a life under the Nazis, just how capable we are, each of us, of participating in the worst atrocities. This should at least temper our judgements towards those unlucky people who have done terrible things. (We are lucky not have been in Hanna's shoes, let alone the shoes of the Nazi's more obvious victims.) Good novels can do this sort of thing, provide this sort of humane, sympathetic (or even empathetic) understanding and evoke compassion far better than general views about the nature of reality or 'agency'.

Chapter 8

Is to Understand to Forgive or at Least not to Blame?

Kai Nielsen

Editor's Introduction

Kai Nielsen argues that '[w]e make our own history, as Marx said, but not under conditions of our own choosing'. He sides with the compatibilists in the Free will/determinism debate – arguing that we are the products of a 'genetic and social roulette'. However, whereas most compatibilists believe that no revision is required regarding our understandings of moral responsibility and desert, he believes that we should revise these understandings. However, contra Peter Strawson and some contributors to this collection, he thinks that this revision would neither altogether threaten our moral understandings nor our capacity to act in the face of heinous wrongdoings. Analogously, the abandonment of other influential moral concepts such as original sin, heresy and apostasy has not, as we know, brought about a moral collapse. We can be free in the Rawlsian sense of freedom and autonomy without having to worry about the sort of moral responsibility required by retributivism.

The grounds for condemning 'moral monsters' such as Hitler are pragmatic (or consequentialist). Hitler's life, like everyone else's, was a product of 'genetic and social roulette', but we should still have aimed to punish him for what he did (were he to have lived), although we should aim at inflicting the minimal amount of suffering necessary for reasons of deterrence, incapacitation and rehabilitation (forward-looking reasons). In Nielsen's words, '[t]he thing is to use blaming, holding responsible and punishment to stop the men with the machetes from butchering innocent Tutsis and the philandering husband who has all kinds of unprotected sex and then passes his acquired HIV on to his wife.' In this regard he seems to be in broad agreement, as he himself claims, with Chandra Kumar's contribution to this collection, although he stresses that, in a deep sense, no one is ultimately responsible for what they do, something that both Jonathan Mckeown-Green and Pedro Tabensky also stress in their contributions.

* * *

I

Arguably the dominant and most persuasive method for both explaining and justifying moral and normative political beliefs, commitments and whole accounts of morality is the method of wide reflective equilibrium. It attempts to get our various considered judgments or convictions, uncontroversially accepted empirical beliefs and uncontroversial theoretical scientific theories plus beliefs of critical and reflective common sense into a coherent pattern of consistently held beliefs and judgments. This is a coherentist method but not a *purely* coherentist method for it takes our considered judgments, uncontroversial empirical, scientific and common sense beliefs to have some *initial* credibility. It seeks to forge these varied beliefs into a consistent and coherent pattern, perspicuously displayed, showing how they are not just a jumble, and in the processes, winnowing some of them out. In this way it is a self-correcting method. To achieve this is to achieve for a time a wide reflective equilibrium. It will only be for a time for as inquiry and reflection go on any reflective equilibrium will be upset and hopefully and reasonably expected to be replaced by another and more adequate reflective equilibrium. (Perhaps this is too Whiggish?)

This method has, of course, been widely criticized. John Rawls,[1] Normal Daniels,[2] T.M. Scanlon[3] and in effect Brian Barry[4] have defended it and with attentiveness and sophistication have further explained and extended this account. And I have tried to do the same thing.[5]

I mention this not to enter into that thicket again, but to give notice that I presuppose this method in what follows and importantly and critically so. Central to what I will say are four intuitions (four considered convictions) which, on the surface at least, fit badly with each other but each of which I think *in some form* is vital to retain and that, appearances to the contrary, they can be shown, or so I shall argue, to be in wide reflective equilibrium. They are (1) every macro-event (including every human action) has a cause (a set of sufficient conditions which causally necessitate it); (2) that sometimes some people, though causally determined in doing what they do, still in a perfectly normal sense act freely; (3) that not infrequently people are humanly speaking (practically speaking) responsible for what they do and that it is often practically speaking essential to hold them to that; and (4) that, (3) to the contrary

---

1   John Rawls, 'The Independence of Moral Theory', *Proceedings and Addresses of the American Philosophical Association*, 48, 1974, pp. 5–22.

2   Norman Daniels, *Justice and Justification*, Cambridge: Cambridge University Press, 1996.

3   T.M. Scanlon, 'Rawls on Justification', in Samuel Freeman (ed.), *The Cambridge Companion to Rawls*. Cambridge: Cambridge University Press, 2003, pp. 139–67.

4   Brian Barry, *A Treatise on Social Justice*, vol. II: *Justice as Impartiality*. Oxford: Clarendon Press, 1995.

5   Kai Nielsen, 'Philosophy as Wide Reflective Equilibrium', *Iyyun*, 43, 1994, pp. 3–41; and *Naturalism Without Foundations*, Amherst, New York: Prometheus Books, 1996, pp. 14–15, 169–205, and 219–20.

notwithstanding, no one should be made to suffer just for what they did because the very idea of *moral* desert is so deeply flawed that, if we reflect carefully in a cool hour, we will come to see that no one morally speaking deserves to suffer even if they did something vile, horrible or gruesome. But it is hard, perhaps impossible, to get these four beliefs into wide reflective equilibrium. The fourth proposition is the most obviously the odd one out. Many people, including many philosophers, will think that (4) is not only incompatible with (2) and (3) but is plainly false.[6] I shall be concerned, going against the current, to defend a properly understood (4) as both having at least initial credibility and to its being, again properly understood, in reflective equilibrium with the other three beliefs. I shall try to show how we can, initial appearances to the contrary notwithstanding, forge these views into wide reflective equilibrium thus showing (at the very least *prima facie*) that we have here a justified pattern of beliefs.

---

6   It will be asked whether you will ever be willing to forgive Hitler? That certainly is a hard pill to swallow. Vis-à-vis Hitler and his likes, I am not saying 'to forgive' but not 'to blame'. Hitler was a twisted monster who caused unspeakable misery. (He was indeed a heinous moral monster. Whatever he may have been at the end, he was for the bulk of his political life an evil man and not a mad man utterly out of control. He knew what he was doing when he did the evil things he did and could in some compatibilist sense have done otherwise. Hence the phrase 'moral *monster*' not 'moral *madman*'. If he had really been mad there would not have even been a presumptive case for blaming him. But why 'not to blame'? Not to blame him, it is tempting to say, is an absurdity and (to understate it) a morally untoward one at that. If anyone is ever to blame, he is. But that is just it. When (or so will be the burden of my argument) we see clearly, and take this matter to heart, the contingency and arbitrariness of our (all of us) social and genetic (and more generally biological) inheritance and how we cannot but be a function of that, we will also see (if we can hold on to our brains) that we cannot really have it in our hearts to blame *anyone* (though doing something like that will often be pragmatically necessary). After all, we should have stopped the Hitlers of this world from doing the things they did and now stop present aspirants for such a role. But 'moral blame', 'moral desert', 'retributive punishment' will drop out of our moral vocabulary as part of the barbarity of the spirit of revenge. Does this mean 'to forgive'? Well, it means 'to not blame'. Perhaps to ask to forgive is to ask too much. Yet if Hitler had not committed suicide and had been captured, put on trial, and sentenced to life imprisonment and after years of increasingly tortured thought had come to realize fully the evil that he did and to take that matter to heart and to have genuinely undergone a radical 'transformation of soul' should we not, under those circumstances, forgive him? Many of us still could not, but is it so obvious that we should not if we can? And for 'Hitler' read any of the other moral monsters and as well as us 'normals' for the wrongs we do. But forgiveness goes a bit beyond understanding and not blaming. It is crucial to be clear that 'not to blame' does not entail 'forgiving'. It is possible not to blame Hitler without welcoming him back into the moral fold. But if the change had taken place as in the counterfactual situation I have just described, should we not (if we can) even do that?

II

However, we need first to take a few steps backward and to start with something less controversial. Take compatibilism for the view that (1) and (2) – determinism and freedom – are compatible. It is a view which has historically and paradigmatically been held by Thomas Hobbes, David Hume and John Stuart Mill and less paradigmatically but still without qualification by Baruch Spinoza and Karl Marx. Among contemporary philosophers it has been widely held by many philosophers including G.E. Moore, Moritz Schlick and A.J. Ayer, but it has as well been firmly opposed by many able contemporary philosophers including notably J.L. Austin, Anthony Kenny, Keith Leher and Roderick Chisholm.

In the 1950s through 1960s, I taught introduction to philosophy to large classes at NYU and I always started the course by discussing 'Freedom and Determinism' for I thought (rightly) it captured the students' interest and that it provided what at least had the appearance of an intractable philosophical problem not easily (or even readily, if at all) up for Wittgensteinian dissolution or readily shown to be what logical positivists used to call a pseudo-problem. I then *ambivalently* argued for a compatibilism (sometimes more ambiguously called 'soft-determinism'),[7] namely a view that held that determinism and freedom are compatible *and* that determinism (at least for macro-objects and macro-beings, e.g. human beings) is true.[8] But, perhaps neurotically and confusedly, I remain intermittently haunted by hard-determinism, namely the belief that though determinism is true, that free actions – genuinely free actions – are non-existent for to be in the deepest sense 'free' they cannot be deterministically caused (to be redundant). Moreover, indeterminism or some form of 'contra-causal' freedom, it seemed to me and still seems, are absurd and illusory views. That something could be uncaused always seemed to me to be patently false and that so-called agent-causation (something somehow distinct from causation by events and somehow out of our causal networks) while a little better is still in effect non-explanatory if not obscurantist. The whole problem, I ambivalently felt, was up for a Wittgensteinian dissolution; it was more metaphysical rubble to be cleared away. (Again this is still something I feel.) Some form of compatibilism, I felt and also still feel, must be true just as some form of physicalism (perhaps anomalous monism) must be true though, not unsurprisingly, it was in both cases hard to say which form. So I, not being metaphysically inclined, to put it mildly, set both issues aside for greener pastures and remained content, over these issues, to live with what are perhaps my dogmatic slumbers.

---

7   Kai Nielsen, *Reason and Practice*, New York: Harper and Row, 1971, 13–24.

8   Soft-determinists need not claim that it is easy to show how it is true or even that it is true. 'Every event has a cause' is after all not like the grammatical remark (analyticity?) 'Every effect has a cause'. The former's logical status is puzzling. It should also be noted that a compatibilist need not accept determinism. She is only committed to saying that determinism and freedom are compatible.

III

A lot of water, however, has flowed under the bridge since I first wrote about freedom and determinism in the 1960s. I continue to think some form of compatibilism as well as physicalism must be so. Not all our actions are compelled, constrained, coerced or forced. We do not always act compulsively or under compulsion. I can (normally) go for a walk because I just want to but sometimes I am compelled to move my car whether I want to move it or not and I am required to stop at a red light. There are at least for some people psychological compulsions as well. We plainly and unproblematically have these non-vacuous contrasts exemplifying the difference between acts which are free and acts which are not. The proper contrast, it is tempting to think, is not between freedom and determinism but between freedom and constraint. The first action is done by me because I want to do it and is in that way free; the last two are not. In such a way differences remain so no matter what causal story we tell. This is so even in a completely deterministic world. To try to characterize such free acts in terms of indeterminism, contra-causal freedom or as being uncaused or in terms of self-caused agent causation (something like an uncaused cause) are all complete non-starters.

IV

However, if we take something roughly like Harry Frankfurt's path about freedom of the will, we can make some sense of freedom beyond just a non-controversial freedom of action, a freedom, that is, that consists in being able to sometimes (indeed for many of us frequently) to do things we want to do and that in an unconstrained way even in a world in which every event has a cause. For, to repeat, there being a cause why we do something is not the same thing as our being compelled or constrained to do something. This is the familiar compatibilist stuff of Philosophy 101 (Nielsen 1971, 17-94).

However, beyond classical compatibilism, but while still remaining compatibilist, Frankfurt gives us a plausible conception of the will (something Gilbert Ryle thought impossible) and of the freedom of the will that advances matters while remaining firmly compatibilist. We do not get an adequate conception of freedom just by recognizing that we have certain wants, desires, motives, motivations and, in accordance with them, we can and do make choices and in such unproblematic ways are free. It is distinctive of us, and only of us, that we human animals want to have (or not to have) certain desires and preferences. We (or at least most of us) are also capable of wanting to be different in our preferences and purposes from the way we actually are. Other animals 'appear [at least] to have the capacity for what we call "first-order desires" which are simply desires to do or not to do one thing or another. No animal, other than the human animal, has as well the capacity for reflective self-evaluation, that is manifest in the formation of *second-order* desires (desires about or for desires)'.[9]

To get a handle on this we must get clear about what it is for a person to *will* something and what freedom of the will is. When someone states that A wants to X and means to convey that it is this desire that is motivating or moving A to X, do what he is actually doing or that A will in fact be moved by this desire (unless he changes his mind) when he acts, we are then talking about his will. This what identifies A's will. 'To identify an agent's will is either to identify the desire (or desires) by which he is motivated in some action he performs or to identify the desire (or desires) by which he will or would be motivated when or if he acts, (Frankfurt 1988, 14).[10]

However, that (*pace* Frankfurt) will not yield a conception of freedom that is strong enough to support retributivism or the ethics of moral desert. Because of this (if it is so) – or so I shall argue – the intuitions we tend to have about moral responsibility and some of us have about moral desert will have to be radically revised. Here proposition (4) hoves into sight.

To begin to see this note the following. To identify a person's will we identify the notion 'of an *effective* desire – one that moves (or will or would move) a person *all the way to action*'[11] (italics mine). Where she has a desire that her will be different than it is, then 'She wants to X' does pertain to what she wants her will to be. As Frankfurt well puts it, 'In such cases the statement means that A wants the desire to X to be the desire that moves him effectively to act'.[12] Frankfurt goes on to observe, 'Now when the statement that A wants to want to X is used in this way, it does entail that A already has a desire to X. It could not be true both that A wants the desire to X to move him into action and that he does not want to X. It is only if he does want to X that he can coherently want to desire to X to "not merely be one of his desires, but more decisively to be his will"'.[13] Where, as here, he wants a desire of his to be his will, his *second-order* desires are also his *second-order volitions*. This Frankfurt takes to be essential to be a person.

Part of what it means to be free is to be able to act freely and this is fundamentally a matter of doing what one wants to do. This, as we have observed, relatively unproblematic notion captures 'at least part of what is implicit in the idea of an agent who *acts* freely'.[14] But it 'misses entirely', Frankfurt goes on to say, 'the peculiar content of the quite different idea of an agent whose *will* is free'.[15] Non-human animals do not have freedom of the will, but they may be free to run in whatever direction they want to go. 'Thus having the freedom to do what one wants to do is not a sufficient condition of having a free will. It is not a necessary condition either.

---

9   Harry G. Frankfurt, *The Importance of What We Care About*, Cambridge: Cambridge University Press, 1988, p. 14.

10 Ibid.

11 Ibid.

12 Ibid., p. 15.

13 Ibid.

14 Ibid., p. 20.

15 Ibid.

For to deprive someone of his freedom of action is not necessarily to undermine the freedom of his will.'[16] A person may be deprived of his freedom of action – say, locked in a small cell – so that he is not able to translate his desires into actions or to act according to the determinations of his will, but he may 'still form those desires and make those determinations as freely as if his freedom of action had not been impaired'.[17] *The question of the freedom of the will of a person concerns his desires themselves. Whether a person has freedom of the will means roughly whether she is free to want what she wants to want.* This comes to its being the case that she is free to will what it is that she wants to will – to, that is, have the will she wants. 'It is in securing the conformity of his will to his *second-order* volitions...that a person exercises freedom of the will'.[18] Where there is an awareness of a clash between his will and his *second-order* volitions, we have a situation where a person comes to realize that he does not have freedom of the will. His will is not the will he wants. When we have the *second-order* volitions we want to have and when our desires are such that they are desires to have and to want to be as our will wills we have freedom of the will. Where we can't have the will that we want, be the sort of person we aspire to be, we lack freedom of the will.[19] But sometimes we can at least be the sort of person we want to be – or approximately so; we can sometimes have, that is, the will we want and then we have – determinism or not – freedom of the will. (Though [see note 19] this is not the only situation in which we have freedom of the will, it arguably is the situation where our freedom of the will is the fullest.)

V

However, are these various kinds of freedom, plainly forms of freedom that human beings can and some do have, sufficient to yield when, of course, certain other quite different things also obtain (e.g. moderate scarcity, limited egoism and freedom from debilitating wars), an account of morality that will fit with our reflective and informed moral expectations and fit into wide reflective equilibrium?

One reason to think that it might not is reflection on the contingency and the arbitrariness of the facts of genetic and social roulette or inheritance. Is it not the case that whatever we can do, whatever choices we make, whatever images of ourselves we have, whether we can be even approximately the sort of person we want to be is itself a function of whatever genetic makeup we just happen to have *and* the sort of social enculturation that just happened to have been ours? Are the

---

16 Ibid.

17 Ibid.

18 Ibid.

19 It can be argued that I am giving the wrong spin on Frankfurt's claims here. It might be thought that from the above I am giving to understand that only those who can be who they want to be are morally responsible. This is not Frankfurt's view and it is not mine. We have freedom of the will in good compatibilist fashion if our actions are guided by *second order* volitions.

effective desires that 'moves (or will or would move) a person to action'[20] not a function of a combination of our genetic inheritance and our acculturation?[21] We, whether we like it or not, are the subjects of the forces of our genetic and social roulette (our specific biological nature and our enculturation). What we are and what we have the strength of will to be are the result, to put it metaphorically, of the luck of the draw. Indeed it is something that is a brute luck. What our social and genetic makeup is determines what we are and what we can be: even of what we can want to want to be. None of Frankfurt's adroit maneuvers concerning the freedom of the will gainsay that. One cannot want a certain desire to be one's will and still not want to want it. But one can want a certain desire to be one's will and it might still not be an effective desire enabling one to do as one's will enjoins. What that *effective* desire (if we have one) is is something *given to us* not something we can choose. Whether we can choose what *motivates* that choice or whether we can choose at all is something we cannot choose. *Perhaps*, to put it more cautiously, we can choose at least some of our effective desires. But what we cannot choose are the background conditions that enable us to choose. We cannot, that is, be the *causa sui* of our actions.

To see what is at issue here consider four different addiction cases. In all four they are all addicted to the same drug.

> *Case One:* The person is in a physiological condition so that try as he will he will inevitably succumb to his periodic desires for the drug to which he is addicted. He will always end up taking the drug. He hates his addiction and always struggles desperately but still to no avail against the thrust of his desire to take the drug. We could call him the *unwilling drug addict*.

> *Case Two:* He is in the same physiological condition as the person in *Case One*. He also will always in the end take the drug but he has no desire to have the will of someone who will not take the drug or struggle against the taking of it. He does not hate his addiction. He is not an unwilling drug addict, but a willing one in the sense that he is indifferent to what desire constitutes his will. He does not hate being a drug addict; he does not want to want to be the person who is a drug addict or not to want to want to be such a person. He is *indifferent* to such matters. We could call him the *willing drug addict*.

> *Case Three:* Again we have someone who is in the same physiological condition as obtains for *Case One* and *Case Two*. In the end he too will always take the drug. But he *loves taking it* and *loves being a drug addict*. He is altogether delighted with his condition. *He is a willing drug addict who would not have things any other way*.

---

20 Frankfurt, *op. cit.*, p. 14.

21 Note this could be maintained and have the force I maintain for it independently of any theses about determinism.

Case Four: Here we have someone who is in a slightly different physiological condition than the above three. He is also strongly addicted but not quite so strongly as the other three so that if he intelligently tries hard he can resist his strong desire for the drug and, like the *Case One* addict, he hates his addiction. Being an addict is not the person he wants to be. And he struggles mightily and overcomes it to become the person he wants to be.

All four cases can be instantiated by people in our world.[22] But whether an individual is exemplified by one case or the other (or still some other case) is determined (caused) by his genetic and social makeup. He cannot be one or the other (or anything else) independently of that makeup no matter what we correctly say about the freedom sometimes to do what we like (and with that freedom of action) or of freedom of the will (freedom of want to want that a certain desire be one's effective desire). I suppose most of us, if it were the case of any of the above four cases being so for us, would – being normals – want to be a person of *Case Four* type. But though people of the *Case Four* type are more in control of their lives than the others and in that way are freer and can more clearly be said to have what Frankfurt perspicuously characterizes as freedom of the will, still whether they have the strength of will or can summon up the strength of resolution to overcome their addiction is beyond their control. No one is in a position to determine *fundamentally* what kind of person or non-person (Frankfurt's wanton) he or she is or will come to be. We always work with something given: something that is always beyond our control and is set by 'the brute luck of the draw' of genetic and social roulette. We cannot will our genetic makeup or our initial social condition. We cannot just determine what will be our *effective* desire or whether we will have an *effective* desire to be the person we want to be or the person we are.[23] (Put otherwise: all option luck is rooted in brute luck; whether you can or cannot have option luck is determined [caused] by brute luck.)

VI

What I am most concerned with is the consequences of this. I believe and claim that if we take to heart what having the consequences of our genetic and social roulette entails then we will have something disturbing for ourselves concerning our conception of being an autonomous agent.[24] Here in speaking of 'genetic and

---

22 I make no claims about how realistic any of these examples are. 'Can be instantiated' is to be taken in a weak logical sense.

23 This is what we see powerfully displayed in Eugene O'Neill's *Long Day's Journey into Night* and in Malcolm Lowry's *Under the Volcano*.

24 I do not want to say that anything I say here cuts against the way John Rawls talks about autonomy or justice or even (as a practical measure) about responsibility. They all continue to have their role to play in practical discourse and in practical life and Rawls characterizes brilliantly how this is so. But note that neither Rawls nor for that matter Robert Nozick or Fredrich Hayek has any time of day for the notion of 'moral desert'. For Rawls on this see the

social roulette' I am referring to the fact that what we are and can be, no matter how much Frankfurtian free will we have, is a function of some combination of our social and genetic (biological) inheritance. Just carefully think through the implications of this and you will abandon an ethics of moral desert and the related doctrines of retribution, punishment and a fixation on determining people's moral responsibility and irresponsibility. If we take to heart the above view, we should get out, as much as we can, of the blaming and punishing business except where something like it is practically speaking needed to deter or reform people inclined to do or being prepared to do the terrible things which unfortunately are so much a part of our world. But coming down hard on them to keep them or others from doing or allowing (where something can be done about it) the horrible, even gruesome, things that have been done and continue to occur (including some in the *name* of justice) is something required of us only where it can be an effective deterrent or have an educative function and then bearing down on them should be no more than is absolutely necessary to keep them from doing, encouraging or allowing the horrible things they do, encourage, allow or turn a blind eye to. Where coming down hard on them (and we know this) will not stop them or deter others from doing similar things, coming down hard on them is just cruel and vengeful or a matter of our own anxieties and fears. We become, if we so act, too much like those whom we would deter.

Of course, there are moral monsters (including morally deluded self-righteous ones) and moral madmen; we must not let either of them run loose where we can do anything about it, including perhaps most dangerously the righteous ones who firmly believe that in doing, abetting or aiding in the doing of the vile things they do, abet or aid, that they are doing what is absolutely right and required of them. (Think, for example, of Goebbels going to the Nazi concentration camps and urging the 'administrative staff' to overcome their scruples and feelings of guilt and do their duty knowing, so he said, that it was right. They were producing, he thought, 'the utopia' of a *Juden-frei* world. Moreover, things like that are not just things that happened in the past.) Of course we must not let them proceed and do their will if we can stop them; moreover, we must utilize all our energies to the fullest to stop them. So we must, to try to keep life from being nasty, brutish and short, do everything we can to rein them in. That is obvious and not at issue here.

However, we should learn to do whatever of this preventive sort of thing that we must do to achieve this with a different mindset and with that we will sometimes do things in a somewhat different way. We must – reining in our vindictiveness and our urge for revenge – not cause these moral monsters or anyone else any more pain

---

succinct, accurate and powerful account given by Norman Daniels in his 'Democratic Equality: Rawls's Complex Egalitarianism' in Samuel Freeman (ed.), *The Cambridge Companion to Rawls*, Cambridge University Press, 2003, pp. 241–76. For an account of autonomy that is insightful and crucial in our moral and political thinking see Chandra Kumar, 'Progress, Freedom and Human Nature', *Imprints*, 7(2), 2003, pp. 106–30. Nothing I say above gainsays that as a bit of practical reasoning.

or suffering than we absolutely need to in order to keep them from harming others and to serve as a deterrent to others from doing likewise and (if this can be done) to change people into being different kinds of persons who will not do such things and who will clearly see why they must not. And even here we must be uneasy about a *purely* deterrent function. It has the smell of treating people as means only. We are there not making them suffer because we believe they *deserve* to suffer for the suffering they have caused or because we believe it will make them better persons. We may make them suffer because we believe that by inflicting pain or suffering on *them* we will deter *others* from doing those horrible things. But, it may seem, that is to treat the agents of these vile things as means *only*. If we say 'So be it' we are caught up in the spirit of simply instrumentalizing people.[25] But if we think clearly we can come to see that we are not treating them as a means *only* for we make them suffer to deter *others* and we would not make these vile doers suffer if we did not think that is so or that it would help change the vile doers into being decent human beings. We can, of course, be self-deceived here but that is another matter.[26]

When we come to clearly see that a person who did some wrong thing could not have done otherwise, no matter how hard he tried or because he was not capable of even trying or that he was so unteachably blinded that he could not see the wrongness of what he did, we, if we are reasonable, rational, reflective and have some of the milk of human kindness in ourselves, will withhold *retributive* blame.[27] We will not think that he should be made to suffer for what he did because he just deserved to suffer and we will realize (if we are religious) that there but by the grace of God go we or (if we are not) that there but for the luck of our genetic and social inheritance go we. Even if it is not simply straightforwardly evident that he could not have done otherwise but that he *wanted* as well to do it, believing grotesquely that it is right, but that his doing it was actually made the case by someone else he still should not be subject to retributive judgments and punishment. For his very wanting to do it

---

25 It is important to keep in mind Kant's qualifier that we should never treat human beings as means *only*. We certainly treat people as means (and rightly) when we go to the barbershop, the checkout counter in the supermarket or to the doctor, but we do not, if we are being decent, treat them as means *only*. But there are terrible situations where we *may* be justified or perhaps even morally required to treat people as means only, but we should never feel good about it or do it lightly. Moreover, we must never do it where it is *not* inescapably the lesser evil. The film *The Battle of Algiers* is instructive here. Here issues of terrorism and torture come to the fore. See my 'On the Moral Justifiability of Terrorism (State and Otherwise)', *Osgoode Hall Law Journal*, 41(3) and (4), Summer/Fall 2003, pp. 427–44.

26 Again I am not saying as a practical or pragmatic matter we never rightly hold anyone responsible for what they do. Is this a matter, on my part, of the philosopher's penchant for first saying it and then taking it all back? I hope not!

27 Some might say that that is a very religious attitude and that Nielsen, an old hard bitter atheist, is becoming religiose in his old age. Not at all! That something in our culture has its *origins* in religion does not mean that it is presently religious or even religiose. Moreover, atheists needn't, and shouldn't, think that everything in religion or that comes from religion is bad. That is false.

and thinking that it is right itself rests on his genetic constitution and acculturation. And for that he could not have been responsible. He can't be his own parents or the controller of his *initial* situation. It is finally something which is out of his control.

We will and should, as a practical, pragmatic matter, have it be the case (seek to make it the case) that people are to be stopped from doing what they do or threaten to do when these things are vile. But, *except for such pragmatic reasons*, we will get out of the judging, blaming, punishing business for we will see that in one way or another it is often to cause harm to someone for something that he could not help doing and sometimes cannot be reformed or deterred into not doing. We may do something *like* punishing him(call it telishment if you will) where it will help him to come to see that this thing was wrong – it caused harm to others and perhaps to himself – but we will drop notions of moral desert seeing such judgments as irrational and we will come to see retribution as closely akin to vengeance rather than to seeing that justice is being done. 'Retributive justice' will drop out as one of our critical moral tools. And, while we keep desert as a kind of entitlement, e.g. 'He wrote the prize essay and thus deserves to get the prize', we will stop thinking in terms of an ethics of *moral* desert. We will give up condemning *people* though we will continue to condemn the deeply destructive *things* they do, and, where we can, take steps to prevent their occurrence or repetition. Is the spirit of revenge so strong in us that we cannot accept that? Where the spirit of retribution is operative in us it is a human failure in us, though it may be for most of us an unavoidable one.[28]

It isn't that we come to abandon morality, not at all, or come to have an error theory of morality: all moral beliefs rest on error or illusion. But we will jettison *a part of what has historically and culturally been taken to be an integral part of morality*, something that we will have come to see is not only irrational but harmful to human beings. After all moral language-games as other language-games do change and sometimes for the better. People used to speak of sin, damnation, heaven, hell, apostasy, heresy and the like and take this to be a part of their moral vision of things. Now many of us no longer so conceive of things. It is not a part of the conceptual framework of our morality. It is not the way we talk and think. Moreover,

---

28 We should like to *reduce* cruelty rather than to *add* to it by engaging in retributive punishment. Our moral monsters have produced enough suffering in the world. It is bad enough that it is there without adding to the suffering by making them suffer themselves. Pinochet (for example) should (as it is now coming to be the case) be tried and if found guilty, should be publicly disgraced, stripped of his ill gotten gains and it should be clearly marked what he has done to the Chilean people and it should be something that every Chilean school child should be vividly made aware of down the corridors of Chilean history. His acts should be clearly specified and condemned. But he should not be made to suffer any more than his public disgrace (which is for the public) may make him unavoidably suffer. No unnecessary suffering for him should be intended. Making him suffer just because of what he did should not be what is moving us to act. What should be moving us to act is the desire to get the Chilean state to publicly and plainly acknowledge that Pinochet's acts were deeply immoral. But Chileans should not be moved by a need to seek revenge. It is completely understandable that such feelings may obtain, but they should be resisted.

though this is the case for many of us, morality has not collapsed. It is not this change that has brought about the swinish world with which we are so familiar. Our reconceptualization is more likely to have helped a little bit to make the world a little less ubiquitously swinish than it otherwise would be. Similarly we could drop, as part of our conceptual framework of morality: moral desert, guilt, guilty, retribution, the condemnation of wrong doers, punishment and blame.[29] If we did so perhaps morality would not collapse anymore than it collapsed when the morality of some became more secularized. In fact, quite to the contrary, I conjecture that it would improve our morality. Without a morality of moral desert and retribution we would have a kinder, gentler, more tolerant world that would not at all be a world of moral indifference but one that would eschew all forms of vengeance and retribution: an eye for an eye and a tooth for a tooth. Where practices of retribution stood practices of reciprocity would be in their place.[30]

Some might say I have completely forgotten my pragmatism. My punishment-like, blaming-like practices come in practice to be so like the old practices of punishment and blame that the old and new functionally come to the same thing. And a difference that makes no difference is no difference. Well, there should, as Peirce insisted on, be no *conceivable* difference for the alleged difference in the sense relevant to pragmatism to make no difference. But that aside, I am claiming that there would be an actual difference between the 'old morality' and the 'new morality'. The latter, to repeat, would make for a gentler, kinder, more tolerant world with a greater understanding and sympathy between persons.

Is the slogan 'To understand is to forgive' a good one?[31] Well, turned into an indicative sentence it would be a hyperbole. I still think, however, it is a good *slogan* if we de-link it from the notion that anything goes and that no acts or practices are to be rejected and prevented. But it is so de-linked in what has been said here. The people who do these terrible things are not to be taken, except in the pragmatic sense specified, to be blameworthy, punishable, made to suffer for their evil deeds, or be someone upon whom to take revenge. We see that in the deepest sense they cannot be responsible for what they do. Being what they are they could not freely have done otherwise. And, given their genetic and cultural makeup, they could not have been people who could be otherwise than they are. But the same thing obtains for all of us. Some have the capacity *and* the strength to change. Some do not. Some have the ability to develop the strength to do so and some do not. But this is just

---

29 It has been put to me: 'Do you really want to say anything so strong? Should we not, for good pragmatic reasons' scold children, hold under normal circumstances people to their promises, still condemn certain actions and deeds, still say of someone that she deserved the promotion?' There are good pragmatic reasons for doing these things and I have gone out of my way to acknowledge that. But we should do this with a *different mindset* and not in the spirit of revenge and retribution.

30 Here in our conception of morality we would move in the direction of the way Rawls and Scanlon see things.

31 Except as a slogan, 'To understand is not to blame' would be better for the reasons alluded to in Note 1.

something *given* by people's genes and acculturation (taken in its broadest sense). It is something that they and we just come to have. Some people can come to try and sometimes to succeed in changing themselves but whether or not they can even try is not in their control. It is not something over which they (or we) have control and deserve to suffer for because they (or we) do not have such an ability. If we recognize this (are able to recognize this) and take it to heart, we will understand that to understand is to forgive or at least not to blame; if we are lucky enough to have an extensive understanding and are able to forgive or to withhold blame (except for pragmatic purposes) we will so orient ourselves. Finally, to put it metaphorically again, it is all a matter of the luck of the draw in genetic and social roulette. We cannot transcend or non-evasively avoid this roulette.

VII

Let me end with a kind of coda. I began this essay with a brief articulation and defense of the method of wide reflective equilibrium. My claim is that it is the most adequate method we have for justifying our various clusters of beliefs including our moral and politically normative beliefs. Risking *hubris* and exaggeration, I am even inclined to believe that it is the only adequate way of justifying belief in a holistic and non-balkanized manner which indeed itself is the only way of thoroughly justifying beliefs. I have sought to use this method – presupposing its soundness – in giving an account of judgment and understanding embedded in a compatibilist account of freedom and determinism. But it might well be thought that on my own account here I have failed in this endeavor. I listed four propositions I wished to defend. I have perhaps got the first three into wide reflective equilibrium and I perhaps have shown that taken together they are amenable to a compatibilist account of freedom and responsibility. But the fourth one, it may be thought, is the odd one out. In effect, it is plausible to believe, it commits me to the *incompatibilism of hard-determinism and to the denial that anyone can be responsible – really responsible – and blameworthy for anything.* This is so because when one looks closely at what I have called genetic and social roulette one will see that it is plainly true and that if this judgment of mine is so – if it really is plainly true – then no one can be really and truly free or responsible and that this, aside from at best being paradoxical, clashes with my compatibilism and this shows I have not got my belief-set into wide reflective equilibrium.

I have tried to dispel the paradoxical air of my fourth claim in the body of this essay and to defend its intelligibility and truth. Now I want to try to show that this belief does not invoke a commitment to hard-determinism. A belief in hard-determinism would indeed be out of sync with my other beliefs. But what I am saying in proposition four is not a commitment to hard determinism and, properly understood, it fits with the others into a wide reflective equilibrium. But this, of course, needs to be shown and not just asserted.

Note that I am not saying to be 'really free' we must refute hard-determinism and to show how we could, in some non-metaphorical sense, be creators of our own selves: choose our own lives. That, at best, is utterly mythical, as bad as the myth of Er. But while we cannot swing free from the causal network resulting from, among other things, our genetic and social inheritance, we can (if we are lucky enough as in this respect many of us are) be free in all the ways compatibilists speak of, including (importantly including) freedom of the will *à la* Frankfurt. My claims about genetic and social roulette do not clash with that; instead they are quite compatible with that. I am not saying absurdly something like we would have to be free of the determination of our genetic inheritance and acculturation to be 'really free'. That, beyond absurdity, is incoherent. It, as I have remarked, is like trying to say we would have to be our own parents, to initially choose our own lives, to be 'really free'. I am not saying to be 'really free' there would have to be some purely agent causation free of any causal network. These notions are too incoherent even to be false or coherently mythical. But this leaves compatibilist freedom standing.

What I have tried to show is that we, or at least many of us, have a deep but confused penchant to *try* to posit some such 'real freedom' when we are faced with the realization that what we are and can be is determined (caused) by what I have called genetic and social roulette. But, if we can think non-evasively and if we have our emotions in order, we will see this 'real freedom' that we try to posit in response is an illusion. It is not something that could be so. Moreover, there are various adequate ways that, genetic and social roulette or not, we can be compatibilist free and that we can come to realize that an ethic moral desert and *retributive* punishment are things that are irrational given that what we are and can become is a function of some combination of our genetic and social inheritance and of nothing else.[32] We can live well and, in a Rawlsian sense, autonomously without such conceptions and without a belief in 'real freedom'. We can so live and still make sense of our lives.[33]

---

32 How, it might be asked, can we be sure of the 'and of nothing else'? The answer is that we can't, but there is little, if anything, we can be *sure* of. Fallibilism is inescapable. But we need to ask ourselves what else could there be? And it looks like we come back with a stutter.

33 I want to thank Pedro Tabensky for his insightful and instructive comments. Without them this essay would be weaker than it is. Our views (as can be seen from his essay, Chapter 6, this volume) clearly have a family resemblance. However, he thinks that forgiveness (at least in its paradigmatic forms) falls with the fall of the idea of *moral* desert. I would not make such a strong claim. We can, he has it, if we realize what they are, neither forgive nor not blame a Hitler, Stalin or Pinochet. If they are just a part of the natural order of things, like the natural disasters that sometimes strike us, the very idea of moral responsibility (even pragmatically taken) does not take hold so there is no room for talk of forgiveness. It is as silly here as it is to talk of forgiving Hurricane Katrina for the suffering it caused. But Hitler *et al.* are not like a natural disaster and this is why I distinguish between moral monsters and moral madmen. The historical Hitler was too plainly evil to welcome back into the moral fold. But I have described (Note 1) *counterfactual* circumstances in which he could and should be welcomed back if it is possible for us. But if he really was deeply insane – as perhaps he was at the end – there would be no more sense in blaming him than it would be for us to blame an infant for kicking over a lantern and starting a fire or for Hurricane Katrina for causing suffering. But, if as I believe, Hitler (at least for most of his life) was a moral monster rather than a moral

Addendum I

In his contribution to this collection, Thaddeus Metz defends a form of retributivism and interestingly argues against both me and Pedro Tabensky that we make the common error 'of thinking that...to be responsible, we must be responsible for the conditions that make us responsible' (Metz, Chapter 10, this volume). For retributive punishment to be acceptable, that is, we must specify the conditions that now enable us to act responsibly but not the conditions which initially enabled us to act as we do now. For that, he echoes me (and many others) in saying we would have to be our own parents or the controller of our initial situation to really be responsible and that we plainly cannot be. Indeed he agrees that it makes no sense to talk in this manner. In that very fundamental but for him irrelevant sense none of us could have done otherwise than what we did. Things *finally* are not in our control. We make our own history, as Marx said, but not under conditions of our own choosing.

However, Metz says that that consideration is irrelevant and unnecessary *for to be responsible, one need not be responsible for being responsible.* For, as he alternatively puts it, 'to have control over one's behaviour one need not have been in control of the fact that one has control over one's behaviour'. That is correct and important to keep in mind, and to take to heart. We can (if we are lucky) be in control of our behavior now even if that results from and depends on things over which we have and had no control. That is what we compatibilists have repeatedly insisted on. But it doesn't take us to the vindication of retributive punishment, to claims about 'moral desert' or the lack thereof or to any form of blaming other than what is pragmatically necessary for reforming and deterring. The thing is to use blaming, holding responsible and punishment to stop the men with the machetes out to butcher innocent Tutsis and the philandering husband who has all kinds of unprotected sex and then passes his acquired HIV on to his wife. We should use such censuring devices where they stand a reasonable chance of being effective to prevent such behavior. We do not, in doing so, have to decide whether 'they really deserved punishment' or whether 'they were ultimately responsible'. The thing is that such behavior must be stopped and (if possible) its reoccurrence prevented. It is plain (if we have a sense of our own moral discourse and use an appeal to considered judgments in wide reflective equilibrium) that such behavior is evil and must be stopped and that, where the language of censure can be effective to this end and is necessary to achieve it, that it should be used. But what Metz (or as far as I know anyone else) has not shown is that this requires (or justifies) an appeal to

---

madman, his behavior, under favorable circumstances, could be affected by blame or at least by plausible threats. He had some control over his life so rational considerations could have influenced his behavior. So it makes *pragmatic sense* to blame him. And if he, while living in prison, had radically changed himself in certain crucial ways, he should be forgiven. But does it make it right (gross pragmatic considerations aside) to blame him or anyone else in a deeper sense given genetic and social roulette? Here I am more skeptical than most people. Understanding, really deeply understanding, carries with it a reluctance to blame. Is this really religiose?

retributive justice: to making people suffer just because they deserve it (really deep down deserve it) and that this is the way to order things whether it is effective in reforming or deterring or not.

To have a Kantian or Rawlsian autonomy is a very wonderful and precious thing indeed deserving of our deepest respect and hope for its widest occurrence. But when we also see that whether we have or even can have this autonomy is contingent on genetic and social roulette – what I call metaphorically the brute luck of the draw – we will recognize the relevance of keeping firmly in mind the very contingent and fragile conditions that enable us to be responsible. When we see that they are massively determining and that for most of them one cannot be responsible, we (if we are clear-headed) will realize (for some of us whose situation in life and genetic inheritance is favorable) both that we are fortunately capable of Kantian-Rawlsian autonomy and that that is a very desirable condition of life. But we will also realize that for some others it is not achievable. Moreover, we will recognize that which group we belong to is largely a matter of brute luck or *perhaps* we should say ultimately a matter of brute luck. We will also recognize that such autonomy is precious for us to have if we can have it. We will, as I have repeatedly said, realize that a practical discourse (a pragmatically justified discourse) is necessary to protect that autonomy, make it as extensive as possible, and as well to make evident its deep importance (something that Rawls, Scanlon and Charles Larmore effectively do). But this does not require or even encourage retributive justice with its harsh use of the language of vengeance and of making the really evil suffer just for its own sake (or as it is sometimes obscurely put 'just to balance the scales of justice') whether it deters or reforms or not.

To translate this into the concrete: consider Bigger Thomas – a fictitious black man from the slums of Chicago in the 1930s – depicted unforgettably and realistically by Richard Wright in his novel *Native Son* (Wright 1998). Bigger did terrible things and for them he was tried, found guilty and executed. Perhaps some other person in Bigger's circumstance would not have panicked and as a result killed as he did. But panic or not panic are things that have causes and for some but not for others – again a matter of brute luck – certain causes trigger uncontrollable panic. Whether you are the first sort or not is finally something that is not up to you. And there are some people who live in circumstances that will not trigger that action, say a young white man affluent and well-educated living in security in northwest Chicago. For the latter (at least in such respects) it is easier to be responsible. But he, no more than Bigger, chooses his own conditions in any fundamental sense and it is these conditions which largely determine whether people can act responsibly or not. Reflecting on such considerations – or so I claim – we will (if we can be clearheaded) get out of the retributive blaming business. We won't worry about who is most to blame, to a lesser degree to blame or not to blame at all except where it is useful for reforming or deterrent purposes. We will recognize that we need some form of blaming and punishing discourse, and the practices that go with it, but we will come at it with a different mindset and not with the vindictive and brutalizing talk of just making people pay for their evil deeds no matter whether the punishing would have any deterrent or reforming effects or not. People with this new mindset will stop clamoring for that kind of 'justice'. *Pace* Metz, if this came to obtain, we would have a kinder, gentler, more tolerant and everything said better world.

I want very briefly as a kind of addition to note the following: I have, as I think is proper, been considering things from the third-person perspective. When we turn to a first-person perspective things (at least initially) look rather different. Put otherwise, to hold *others* responsible or not is one thing; to hold *ourselves* responsible or blame ourselves is another. Though I hold that no one is (pragmatic matters aside) really to blame for what they do, I will not say the same things for myself. But isn't that an irrationalistic exceptionalism? It is not for it is the perspective that matters here, and this holds for anyone, thus giving us the proper universalizability here.

When we are reflective and non-evasive about ourselves we will not automatically and indeed not normally say 'I could not have done otherwise'. In many circumstances we will hold ourselves responsible. I think this is often not an irrational thing to do. Not to do so is in effect to acknowledge that one lacks control over one's life and perhaps even bitterly to acquiesce in it as well. It is in effect to undermine one's self-respect. Penetratingly, and in a morally exhausting way, in Eugene O'Neill's *Long Day's Journey Into Night* some of the central characters come to the debilitating realization that they are not in control of their own lives: that they cannot be at all what they want to be or do what they want to do. They come to see with unbearable clarity that they are destructive to others and to themselves and the only cessation of this, notwithstanding their repeated resolutions, is death. And they also see clearly that it is them and not all or even most others who are in that boat. This is not how all human beings must be, but how they, all their struggling to the contrary notwithstanding, must be. This drives them to despair and to utter desolation.

It is hard to view ourselves – taking the third-person perspective – as I say we should view humanity. Hard or not, shouldn't we, if we can be non-evasive and utterly tough-minded, so view ourselves? From both the first- and the third-person perspectives we can see that some persons can control their lives to some significant extent and some cannot and many (perhaps most of us) are somewhere in between. Probably in some crucial respects where people want to control their lives they cannot. But there are all kinds of degrees here yielding degrees of freedom. Yet it is always the case that it is our social and biological inheritance in some complex way working together which determines where we are on this spectrum. It is not up to us. Even where we are lucky enough to be able to move upward on this spectrum – as sometimes we can – it is not in any deep sense up to us. It is easier to see and tolerate this for others than ourselves. And perhaps so unblinking a seeing of ourselves may dull the edge of native resolution to struggle to be autonomous persons. But where we can be utterly tough-minded we will come to see that we are all in the same boat. In that respect there is no significant difference between the first-person and the third-person perspectives.

Addendum II

Chandra Kumar has written a splendid essay that I hope will be carefully studied (Kumar, Chapter 7, this volume). For what it is worth, I agree with the 'big things' in it as well as with most of the 'small things', including his insightful political asides. I suppose (like every other philosophical article I have ever read) if I read it several times, rather than just twice, and with a careful studying of it, I would find things to disagree with – probably only small things – but on two readings I did not. My concern here is neither to praise his essay nor to critically examine it but to say that I very much wish that I had seen it before writing my own essay for there are things in mine that may seem to conflict with it and indeed *may* actually conflict with it and, if that is so, I believe I may have got off on the wrong foot because I do find myself in substantial agreement with Kumar.

We both, along with Richard Rorty, have almost identical, if not identical, metaphilosophical views; we both have no time of day for metaphysics; we both stress the importance of context and perspective and the importance of literature in thinking about life and society and share a common view about the poverty of moral philosophy as usually practiced. What I worry about is whether in the light of what he has said I have been contextual enough in my present essay and whether, with my talk of compatibilism, genetic and social roulette and with what I said about blaming I have been *unwittingly* metaphysical. (I would not be the first or no doubt the last to have unwittingly succumbed to that.)

I shall examine some of these matters. At the very end of his essay Kumar remarks on something that presses repeatedly on my thought (and I expect as well on Tabensky's), namely that when 'we honestly and carefully reflect on the causes of action and character-formation, we cannot avoid thinking that we are products of our environments (our genes and our social and physical environments)'. But then immediately after that passage Kumar goes on to talk of something else that is very important, which my (in effect) just gesturing at it, with talk of a pragmatic justification of our talk and our practices of moral responsibility, blame and praise and of punishment, I tend, in effect, to discount and to treat as of lesser importance, than that *P*hilosophical talk (i.e. epistemological, metaethical, perhaps even unwittingly metaphysical talk) in which I engage here. But it should be the other way around. When we non-evasively push matters as far as we can (or believe that is what we are doing), if what I say about people never being ultimately to blame for what they do or ultimately responsible for what they do is taken to undermine what Kumar says just after the remarks from him I have quoted above, then I am mistaken and have to go back to the drawing board.

The remarks I have in mind are the following:

What we should keep in mind is that we use the language of responsibility for different purposes than those for which we use a more scientific, 'objectifying' language of cause and effect; this latter type of language, as Rorty likes to point out, is mainly for purposes of prediction and control, and prediction and control is not always a bad thing, even when we are talking about people. It would be a good thing, for example, if we came to know about the structural causes (if there are any) of war and terrorism, the better to change our environments significantly to diminish these things. And there are good moral/political reasons, as I have tried to bring out, for retaining talk of responsibility, though I think Tabensky is dead right in stressing that this language is over-used, that it is often insensitive to the causal circumstances and capacities that make people the sorts of people they are, and that it is often a smokescreen for ignoble instincts of revenge. (I would add that it is also often shot through with racist, sexist and classist ideology.) Nevertheless, when faced with the suggestion (which I do not attribute to Tabensky) that we should abandon such language altogether and treat wealthy and powerful fascists and their ilk as objects merely of pity, in my view we should not be *so* Christian-minded (if that is an apt expression) as to erase all vestiges of militant rage against [such] indidividuals…. We should hold these people (the Kissingers of the world) responsible, morally responsible, even if they too can be described as being products of, and constrained by, a particular socio-economic system. (Kumar,Chapter 7, this volume).

We should attend to the context-dependence and purpose-relativity of explanations. In doing so we will become aware that there are always issues that are irrelevant to any explanation and that explanations are of different types given for distinctive and often very different purposes and that we have no idea of what a context-independent, all purpose, complete explanation would be. What Bush's or Cheney's toilet training regime was *may* be interesting and relevant for certain purposes. But not in explaining and assessing the Bush administration's policy in Iraq. It is what they are doing there and the rationale for it that is relevant. It is for such policies – for such specific actions – for which they should be held responsible and here our ordinary language of praise and blame and attributions of moral responsibility are quite in place.

My point in this essay was not to jettison or even downgrade such practices – practically something that we clearly need – but to take out the retributive, vengeful parts of them and to use them for deterrent and, to a lesser extent, for reforming purposes. And here we should be sparing in our use. We should not abandon such practices, but reform them and use them with a different mindset. And I do not speak here of becoming Christian-minded.

Still, all these practicalities aside, when we think of genetic and social roulette – when we non-evasively reflect on the causes of action and character-formation – must we not acknowledge that we are the products of our environments (our genes and our social and physical environments)? Some of us sometimes can successfully resist certain aspects of them, but isn't that always because of other things in our genes or social and physical environment? There is – or so at least it seems to me – no escaping that. No one, ultimately, really, deeply could do other than what they do. In the last analysis no one is really responsible for what he or she does. But beware of this; beware of the use of such words as 'ultimately', 'deeply', 'really', 'in the last analysis'. Do we really understand what we are talking about when we employ them in such contexts? I.A. Richards and Charles Stevenson should have taught us to beware of them. Implicit *persuasive* definitions may be at work here. How does 'ultimately not responsible' differ from 'not responsible'? What is it for something to be 'in the last analysis'? I do not say that nothing can be made of these uses or that they are never useful or in place. But they certainly do not wear their meanings on their sleeve.

Still, we have our genetic and other biological inheritances and we have our social inheritances – these are matters that we do not choose or determine but matters that condition, perhaps determine, us.[34] All of our actions have causes though many as well have reasons (which also may be causes). What it is we did or do, think or believe, is caused, and causal chains will always lead back to antecedent conditions over which we have no control.

Yet where 'could have done otherwise' or 'could not have done otherwise' clearly make sense, they should have a non-vacuous contrast. And they at least often do in the language-games we characteristically play with them. But this does not gainsay the truth of what I have just said and it does not show I have implicitly appealed to some mysterious and metaphysical sense of 'contra-causal freedom' in a desperate attempt to make human freedom really possible. That indeed, on the contrary, would make freedom an illusion. But there is no need or sense in engaging in such 'contra-causal' talk.

I am here making no untestable claims. 'Every effect has a cause' is a grammatical remark. 'Every event has cause' is not. But its denial: 'There are causeless events' is problematic to put it mildly. But unlike 'There are causeless effects', it does not appear to be a contradiction in terms. Yet its status (even for macro-objects) is problematic. We do not understand what it would be like for something to be 'a causeless event'; 'caused event' seems at least to be pleonastic. Considerations like these might make us skeptical about the coherence of determinism or for that matter indeterminism. Compare 'Every event has some cause' with 'Every substance has some solvent'. The latter is neither decisively confirmable nor decisively disconfirmable or falsifiable. But it is weakly testable (confirmable or infirmable). If all the substances that we know of have a solvent then we have *some* reason to think every substance has a solvent and if we come across a substance that we have now no known solvent for, we have some reason to think that if we look carefully enough and long enough we will find one. But a long and systematic search that comes up with no solvent would give us some reason to doubt that for every substance there is some solvent. Nothing can be decisive here. Fallibilism is the name of the game. But

---

34 There may be trouble for my account here. 'Determines' is one thing; 'conditions' is another. 'Our genetic-social inheritance *determines* our behaviour' is my usual formulation. But *perhaps* all we are justified in claiming is the truism 'Our genetic-social inheritance *conditions* our behaviour'? The latter gives us little that would warrant claiming that as a result of our genetic and social inheritance we are locked into a certain behavior – that we must act in a certain way. This talk of 'conditions' is much more plainly compatible with our practical talk of moral responsibility and perhaps empirically speaking it is all we are entitled to. But 'determines' seems more accurately to capture what is involved and, if that is so, I have given an account, and Kumar has more fully, of how our practical discourses are compatible with it. Still we have something here that needs further examination. Yet I fear the tides of metaphysics may be running high here.

'Every substance has some solvent' has empirical meaning. It is weakly testable and does not make a metaphysical or transcendental claim.

It would seem that 'Every event has some cause' is in the same boat and again is not a metaphysical or utterly untestable claim. But is it? We have some reasonably clear idea of what it would be to find a substance for which it would be plausible to say that it has no solvent. But it is less clear (to put it minimally) as to what it would be like for there to be an event for which it would be plausible or perhaps even intelligible to say it had no cause. This is too much like trying to say non-metaphorically of some lost object that it just disappeared into thin air. But need it be? If after a very scrupulous and systematic search no cause turned up for an event would it be so implausible to say that it was causeless? If we continue to say that can't be doesn't it become clear that we are treating 'every event has some cause' metaphysically? But are there any rational considerations driving us to do so? Why not treat 'Every event has some cause' as being very like 'Every substance has some solvent'?

Yet for many of us 'Every event has some cause' continues to be anomalous and with that determinism (as well as indeterminism) is anomalous. To set aside such considerations (to not commit myself to determinism my inclinations not withstanding) I stuck with genetic and social roulette. It is – or so it seems – independent of the determinism controversy. Someone – say an Austin or Strawson – could regard 'determinism' as a name for nothing sufficiently clear to be reasonably affirmably or deniable and still say, in an utterly non-metaphysical manner, what I said about genetic and social roulette.

What I am claiming is that what we are, can be and can do is determined by (is a function of) our genes (more generally our biology) *and* our social inheritance and acculturation. That A acts one way and B another is determined by determinate differences here. What makes us act one way rather than another is determined by (is a result of) some combination of these factors *and nothing else.* But this 'nothing else' does not indicate an implicit metaphysical turning. We may not have the foggiest idea of what this 'and nothing else' would be but we do not rule out the *possibility* that there could be something else. But the burden here is on someone who thinks there is something else to specify – at least through a glass darkly – what this is. And that would be an empirical matter. But no one has been able to and this justifies us in saying what I and others (Stuart Hampshire, for example) say about genetic and social roulette. But no metaphysics looms into sight here.

Still, when we reflect on this and take it to heart, we find it difficult to understand how we or anyone else can be deeply responsible for what we are and do. And this is unsettling. We can say that it is 'deeply' like 'ultimately' that causes the trouble here. We perhaps have here what the positivists used to call 'verbal magic'. But doesn't what I have specified, in specifying what I have called genetic and social roulette, show what talk of 'deeply' comes to here?

We can agree with all the contextual, pragmatic, political-sense-making and moral-sense-making reasons that Kumar has adroitly given us and still think that in a 'deep' sense we can't be responsible. It is unavoidable that there are things antecedent to us which make us what we are.[35] But does this mean we are *all* in Hanna's shoes? This seems very implausible for the reasons that Kumar, and Metz as well, give us. Sometimes the more we know about a person the less inclined we are to judge him. But sometimes it is the reverse: the more we know about a person the more we are inclined to judge him. (Is this just or at all our anxieties showing?) Think of Shakespeare's Richard III or of Goebbels or Kissinger. We have no necessities here. When I started to write this essay (and indeed for much of my life) I thought to understand – to really understand – was to forgive or at least not to blame. I no longer think that. What is left over from my initial attitude is a reluctance in a great range of circumstances to judge or condemn and a rejecting of the ethics of moral desert and retributivism.[36]

---

35 It might be thought that I am forgetting Metz's point which I agree with, namely that to be responsible we need not be responsible for the conditions that make us responsible or, put otherwise, that to be responsible one need not be responsible for being responsible. That is a good compatibilist point (I do not suggest that Metz is a compatibilist). There is an ordinary way of speaking of responsibility that has a point, but it does not – or so I say – push matters far enough in speaking of responsibility. The genetic-social roulette considerations bring out that that way of understanding responsibility does not push matters far enough. When we see that physical-social conditions determine how we must act in determinate situations our sense of responsibility is unsettled. We could not act otherwise than those conditions make possible. (But here reflect on the previous note.)

36 Am I evincing here the philosopher's penchant to first say it and then take it all back? And on another matter, my argument here should not be taken to one bit lessen the need to resist, to struggle against and to fight the forces that in one way or another work to make the world the swinish place that it is.

Chapter 9

The Real Me

Jonathan McKeown-Green

Editor's Introduction

Jonathan McKeown-Green does not focus primarily on the tension between judging and understanding, but his views have important repercussions that are directly relevant to the concerns that have motivated this collection. He is a sceptic about our standard understandings of moral responsibility. McKeown-Green refers to contemporary accounts attempting to render the culpable/excusable distinction intelligible, Frankfurt's and Watson's included, as *executive control* theories. I have executive control over my actions if 'the acts and omissions for whose consequences I am responsible are those which are truly mine, or those which occur because I will them, or those over which I exercise sufficient control, or those which I perform autonomously, or those which are motivated by reasons with which I identify.' His central aim is to show us that no account of *executive control* allows us properly to account for the culpable/excusable distinction, which is core to our standard understandings of moral responsibility. We are all part of the natural order of things and explanations locating responsibility for actions on specific individuals has all to do with our pragmatic concerns for explanatory salience and nothing to do with special causal mechanisms, like agent causation, elicited in order to explain the levels of control agents may have when they go about the business of being agents. When attributing responsibility to a given agent we do so because we wish to locate the primary cause determined as primary in relation to our goal of preventing or promoting a given state of affairs. These pragmatic concerns are no different in essence from those we have when attributing responsibility to inanimate objects such as thermostats. In his words, we 'routinely hold artefacts and natural processes "responsible" for their conduct in much the same way that we hold persons responsible for theirs'. The sense of responsibility relevant for properly accounting for human responsibility is not one that alludes to the culpable/excusable distinction. Ultimately, this category belongs to an old psychology that is incompatible with naturalism. So, if Mckeown-Green is right, then to correctly understand agents entails that we are just as responsible as thermostats are. Praise, blame and desert, standardly conceived, go out of the window. This is a conclusion endorsed by other contributors, particularly by Pedro Tabensky and, in a qualified way, by Chandra Kumar and Kai Nielsen.

* * *

Our world teems with acts and omissions that invite moral commentary: shop-lifting, sleeping in till eleven, letting the tomatoes go to seed and helping retired stock-brokers across the street. All are intentional: they are effects of deliberation or of failure to deliberate; they are outcomes of attempts to satisfy the doer's desires in the light of the doer's beliefs. We assess intentional conduct for its moral worth – for its rightness, goodness or acceptability. Only sometimes, though, does moral assessment of an act or omission cleave to the doer as well as the deed. Only sometimes do we say that *she* was good or that *he* was right to do or refrain as he did. Other times, the shoplifter is a kleptomaniac, the sleeper-in is clinically depressed, the negligent gardener is in mourning and the stockbroker's escort is hypnotized. In those cases, however good or bad the act or omission, we do not hold the actor morally responsible. We excuse on grounds of severe constraint, compulsion, accident or reasonable ignorance.

The challenge is to tell a story about why I am morally responsible for some only of my morally evaluable intentional conduct – a story that is more revealing and explanatory than a checklist of excuses. Perhaps it should also not be a story which says that a thoroughly rational agent with sufficient understanding of what makes us all tick would excuse everybody for everything. This challenge is usually met nowadays with the idea that to hold me morally responsible for some item of conduct or its legacy is, in a robust sense, to attribute something to *me* – some aspect of behaviour, some state of mind or body which constitutes or is a principal cause of the conduct. The thought is that the thoughts, acts and omissions for whose upshots I am responsible are those which are truly mine, or those which occur because I freely will them, or those over which I exercise sufficient control, or those which I perform autonomously, or those which are motivated by reasons with which I identify. Let's say that they are the deeds over which I have *executive control*. And the deeds I cause or perform for which I am not responsible are those which are more tangentially connected with me: factors external or extrinsic to me limit my options, attenuate the degree of control I can exercise over my desires and behaviour, or wrest a significant proportion of that control from me. Confounding external factors might include the sources of information on which I draw and agents or aspects of nature which can circumscribe or override my decisions. You ought not to hold me responsible for conduct so confounded, though you can attribute it to me, in some much weaker sense.

Maybe this *executive control* idea delivers only a partial demystification of the contrast between culpable and excusable conduct: maybe an agent with executive control over her act is morally responsible for it only if she *also* engages appropriately (whatever that means) with the morals of her community. But maybe, after all, executive control suffices for moral responsibility: maybe my failure to recognize the community's moral demands on me is a kind of ignorance and a story about my executive control might count reasonable ignorance as a disqualifier.

Theories which develop the executive control idea are variously billed as theories of moral agency, free agency, personal autonomy, full-blooded action, personhood, the nature of the Will, or self-determination. At any rate, they are routinely read, with or without authorial endorsement, as germane to the difference in causal history between culpable and excusable conduct. That's how I will read them. First I survey the textbook problems faced by such theories, so construed, and then I add a worry of my own. I regard the executive control idea – the idea that I *identify* more with some of my intentional doings than I do with others – as confused. I doubt that any precisification of it illuminates the debate about moral responsibility. I argue at length that we can analyse moral responsibility for thoughts, acts, omissions and their outcomes without invoking this idea. The trick is to realize that we attribute something like responsibility to all sorts of things: weather patterns, great novels and thermostats, as well as moral agents. Certain ways of highlighting persons in explanations are described by us as cases where they are autonomous, or where their Wills operate, but the same highlighting, without the same terminology, is equally apt for objects which cannot desire, value or intend. The analogy between attributions of responsibility to persons and corresponding attributions to non-persons is very tight. Much can be said about the pragmatic considerations that influence when we can and when we cannot make the relevant attributions. Once we realize this, we can develop a story about responsibility which applies relatively smoothly to inanimate objects as well as persons and has no need for any appeal to executive control.

This has implications for any theory of the conditions under which we can assess moral agents. The more we understand an agent, her environment and her predicament, the more tempted we might be to deny that she is free or has executive control. Even so, if the story I will tell is right, we can ascribe moral responsibility to her, no matter how well we understand her. Such ascriptions are not deep or metaphysical, however. They are just explanatory heuristics which serve us well as things stand. You may judge that I am morally responsible for something, but you must not take that judgement any more seriously than you would if I were a thermostat.

1. Executive Control Theories of Responsibility

Any account of human agency which contrasts conduct over which I have executive control, via domestic causal factors, with conduct over which my executive control is diminished, thanks to exotic causal factors, confronts what I will call the *Uniformist Hypothesis*. This says that all my intentional conduct, excusable or not, results from deliberative, psychological events *within me* and that motivational reasons are the principal causes of *all* intentional behaviour. If we buy this assumption, it's initially unclear how the culpable can be attributed to me unless the excusable is too. A theory of executive control should also pay due respect to the *Naturalistic Suspicion* that I am continuous with physical reality – that all my doings can be explained, insofar as they are explicable at all, by physical processes together with whichever deterministic or probabilistic laws govern them. If this suspicion is confirmed, the worry is that I am not a locus of control over my intentional conduct so much as another venue where the forces of nature slug it out. That would make it hard to see why I should be held morally responsible for anything, if moral responsibility requires executive control.

Some writers, so-called *libertarians*, most conspicuously, are sceptical about either the Uniformist Hypothesis, the Naturalistic Suspicion or both. Agent-causationists explicitly reject Uniformism.[1] They say that when I have executive control over the performance of an act, as opposed to merely participating in mental events which cause it, the act is at least partially caused by a substance, a *true me* which gets in on the causing of only some acts. This means that sometimes substances can cause events, but since substances are never effects, the actions caused by me really do originate with me. One challenge for agent-causationism is reconciling it with explanations of behaviour that invoke mental states. 'I bought the wool because I wanted to knit an umbrella cosy and believed that buying wool would supply me with the requisite resources for knitting one', suggests that my desire and my belief together cause my act, even though I might be morally responsible for performing it. Can motivational states figure in the causal aetiology of the act without rendering agent causation redundant? If not, how do intentional states come to feature in explanations? Another challenge for agent-causationists is to explain what sort of substance can cause and how it can cause other than by contributing to the network of physical events. Can we make sense of Timothy O'Connor's view that agent-causation is an ontologically basic, emergent process which owes its being to, but is not constituted by, physical events?[2] Or must we go dualist and abandon attempts to square agent causation with a purely scientific world-view? (If so, then we deny the Naturalistic Suspicion as well as the Uniformist Hypothesis.)

Even a coherent account of substance causation and its role in human agency is unlikely to supply a sufficient condition for culpable behaviour. If I open the safe because you hold a gun to my head, no doubt I exercise control over the safe opening just as I do if there is no rational compulsion. So if there is agent causation, no doubt I cause the safe to be opened, but a third party should excuse me.

As noted, avowed agent-causationists explicitly deny uniformism: there is, they insist, a crucial difference in causal history between acts which are truly mine and the rest. For many promoters of executive control, however, the starting-point is instead rejection of the Naturalistic Suspicion. Whether or not they finish up as agent-causationists, their guiding thought is that a human being truly exercises control only when her acts are something other than the mere application of physical laws to her current circumstances. Thanks to the right kind of slack in the laws of nature, I truly do exercise a kind of control over some actions which is different from, not merely

---

1 Prominent contemporary agent causationists include Randolph Clarke (see, for instance, Randolph Clarke, 'Toward a Credible Agent-Causal Account of Free Will', *Nous*, 27, 1993, pp. 191–203; Randolph Clarke, 'Agent Causation and Event Causation in the Production of Free Action', *Philosophical Topics*, (24)2, 1996, pp. 19–48) and Timothy O'Connor (see especially his *Persons and Causes: the Metaphysics of Free Will*, NY: Oxford University Press, 2000).

2 Ibid., pp. 108–12.

an upshot of, any control that the past and the laws exert. But what kind of control is this? Merely saying that my autonomous actions are not fully explicable in terms of the (deterministic or probabilistic) laws of nature is not yet to say that they are under my control. Agent causation is sometimes invoked at this point and we have already noted the issues this raises. But other paths have been explored, including the speculation that the events over which I have control result from a special strain of event-causation which is not explicable in terms of the laws.[3]

Meanwhile, plenty of other writers on human agency are straightforwardly uniformistic and naturalistic: they locate my executive control in events whose only causes are physical events. They defend stories about the structure of my motivation and use some analysis of my capacity for reflective judgement to argue that only some of my beliefs, desires, motives, intentions, judgements or decisions are *truly* mine. An item of my conduct is *truly mine* just if I identify with some crucial motivating state or mechanism in accordance with which it is produced. But with what sorts of internal, purely physical, states or processes can I identify? And what is it for me to identify with them?

These theorists treat my intentional behaviour as the output of a system which comprises my propositional attitudes together with mechanisms for acquiring, sustaining and prioritizing them. They posit some feature or pattern that is manifest in the structure of this system when and only when I exercise executive control and they maintain that this pattern or feature indicates which motivational states are the ones with which I identify.

For example, Harry Frankfurt[4] highlighted what he took to be a unique feature of the motivational systems of persons: only persons entertain desires about desires. To see why this feature of our deliberation could point the way towards the mental states or processes with which I identify when I exercise control, note first that thinking about thinking is surely a defining characteristic of introspection and rational reflection, activities which seem to be necessary for moral reasoning. The motives with which I identify must survive reflective scrutiny and that suggests that those motives are mandated by a higher-order or counterfactual desire or something similarly characteristic of reflective deliberation. And note also that although an intentional act which I perform only under duress is arguably one that I want to perform, it is never one that I *really* want to perform; it is one which I would not perform had I my druthers. Putting these ideas together, why not characterize 'what I really want' in terms of 'what I *want* to want'?

According to Frankfurt's first pass at a theory, an act that I (intend to) perform is truly mine just if I identify with my desire that I perform that act, where this means that I want my desire that I perform it to lead me all the way to acting. The smoking

---

3   Robert Kane, *The Significance of Free Will*, New York: Oxford University Press, 1996.

4   Harry G. Frankfurt, 'Freedom of the Will and the Concept of a Person', *Journal of Philosophy*, 68(1), 1971, pp. 5–20. Reprinted in Gary Watson (ed.), *Free Will*, Oxford: Oxford University Press, 2003, pp. 322–36.

of an unwilling addict is not an act that is truly hers because she does not desire that her desire that she smoke lead her all the way to smoking. Similar behaviour from a willing addict can be truly his, though, since he does desire that his desire that he smoke lead him to smoke.

There are counter-examples: second-order desires, like the desire that my desire to smoke leads me to smoke, can be formed in reasonable ignorance or compelled, just like first-order desires can. The willing smoker might not have desired that he desire that he smoke if the tobacco companies had warned him about the hazards, or if the hypnotist had not given him a desire that he desire that he smoke. So what I want to want is not after all a perfect indicator of what I really want. Ascending to third-order desires or higher in search of the feature that determines the conduct with which we identify will not rescue the theory. Name any desire of arbitrarily high order! Let no desire of higher order than it be a desire that the named desire not be satisfied. It remains possible that a hypnotist implanted the named desire.

This illustrates a more general worry. According to Frankfurt's theory of executive control, I identify with a desire to act only if it bears the right sort of relationship to a higher-order desire, a desire whose *content* is a proposition about desires. The general worry undermines any theory of executive control according to which I identify with a mental state only if that state bears the right sort of relationship to a mental state with a special sort of content. How can ensuring that a mental state has a special sort of *content* guarantee that state a role in determining my Will or the conduct that is truly mine? Surely any desire, belief or intention, no matter what it is about, could be one which I hold in reasonable ignorance or am compelled to hold or constantly struggle to overcome. Isn't it more likely that the mental states which determine the conduct that is truly mine are distinguished by their causal history, rather than their content?

Some theorists deflect this general worry by claiming that there are indeed desires, distinguished by their content, which every normal human agent holds and endorses. David Velleman, for example, has argued that I identify with any envisaged course of action which I take to be the most reasonable in the circumstances; I have

> … a desire to act in accordance with reasons, a desire that produces behaviour, in [my] name, by adding its motivational force to that of whatever motives appear to provide the strongest reasons for acting, just as [I am] said to throw [my] weight behind them.[5]

Let's suppose for now that the desire to act in accordance with reasons, or something like it, really does allay my general worry. Still, if the mental states privileged by one of these motivational structure theories are meant to play a causal role in the production of behaviour, as Velleman's privileged desire clearly is, then the theory

---

5   J. David Velleman, 'What Happens When Someone Acts?' *Mind*, 101, 1992, pp. 461–81, 479. In this piece Velleman says that the *de dicto* content of this privileged desire need not be that I act in accordance with reasons; the *de dicto* content might be that *p*, where *p* is true only when I act in accordance with reasons.

courts a circularity objection. Velleman's proposal is an immediate casualty. When my 'desire to act in accordance with reasons' is causally active – as it must be sometimes if any act is truly mine – then on those occasions, it combines with some means-end belief to produce its outcome. Will that outcome be an act that is truly mine? That depends on whether I take it to be the outcome that I have reason to produce in the circumstances because, given the theory, the acts which are truly mine are those which are motivated in part by the desire to act in accordance with reasons. So in asking whether the outcome is truly mine, I am asking whether the desire to act in accordance with reasons is the desire I have reasons to act in accordance with. Velleman's account of what happens when someone acts is, in effect, the theory that an act which is truly mine is an act which is truly mine. (Theories other than Velleman's which require a class of privileged desires might skirt vicious circularity if the class is suitably large and diverse or if executive control over my conduct is not taken to be a causal notion.)

Given this concern about circularity, moves like Velleman's arguably don't quell the worry that a mental state's role in determining which conduct is truly mine is settled by its causal history, not its content. But what sorts of mental states are guaranteed an aetiology that excludes reasonable ignorance and compulsion? Well, all the foregoing theories develop the idea that if an act is truly mine, the reasons that recommend it can survive sustained reflection. Gary Watson[6] argued that this assumption seems credible only because the Acts with which I identify are those which accord with my values and I access my values via reflection. Unfortunately, it's unclear that retreating to values is progress. First, values talk had better be something more or other than talk of a class of desires with a certain sort of content, or we are back where we were. Second, what, short of stipulation, ensures that our values are never formed in reasonable ignorance or under compulsion? Finally, it seems that I can *truly perform* and be held morally responsible for acts (like stealing your umbrella) which I know conflict with my values. So underwriting an act of mine with a value of mine is not a necessary condition for my culpable executive control over it.

All of this illustrates the hard graft involved in characterizing executive control if you cling to the Uniformist Hypothesis, that is, if you deny your theory the luxury of a special intervention embodying my agency. My preferred option at this stage is scepticism about the very idea of executive control. More cautiously, I doubt that any such idea grounds the distinction between the culpable and the excusable.

2. Three Kinds of Identification

Although one sometimes speaks and thinks as though one has more of a stake in some of one's intentional acts than in others, this device performs different functions

---

6   Gary Watson, 'Free Agency', *Journal of Philosophy*, 72(8), 1975, pp. 205–20. Reprinted in Gary Watson (ed.), *Free Will*, Oxford: Oxford University Press, 2003, pp. 337–51.

in different contexts. There are various axes along which one can plot perceived psychic distance between oneself and an intentional act. I consider three and argue that none of them contributes informatively to an account of the culpable/excusable contrast. I suspect that if there are significant disambiguations of identification talk besides these three, the same goes for them.

2.1 The axis of ownership

I am not saying that identification phenomena are always irrelevant to responsibility attributions. Sometimes when I *identify myself* with a class of acts, this means that I claim ownership of them. Just as I can say, 'That's my umbrella you're about to take home', so I can say, 'Those were my words.' Here the assumption of ownership seems to be an acceptance of responsibility for an action or its outcomes.

This kind of identifying links identification talk with moral responsibility, but from the fact that my identifying myself with an act can mean that I accept responsibility for it, nothing follows about the nature of responsibility judgements themselves. Plausibly such identification behaviour is a way of reporting that one is responsible rather than something which explains why one is responsible. Besides, my identifying myself with an act sometimes means something quite different.

2.2 The axis of authenticity

Sometimes when I identify myself more strongly with some acts than with others, this means that I have a view about the kind of bloke I am, want to be, or should be, according to which acts of the first kind are genuine expressions of my personality while the others are uncharacteristic. I might say, 'I am the kind of bloke who knits!', and this declaration may be useful as I allot my time, plan my future and buy wool. In deciding or, as it might seem to me, discovering what being Me is all about, I need not endorse what I find. Perhaps I wish I could be the kind of person who blows up buildings for a just cause. But, sadly, I'm more the kind that knits. So one's 'fundamental values' need not constrain, reflect, or be reflected in one's conception of oneself.

This could be the sense of 'identifying' in which an Unwilling Addict

> ... identifies himself [...] with one rather than with the other of his conflicting first-order desires. He makes one of them [his desire not to take the drug] more truly his own and, in so doing, he withdraws himself from the other [his desire to take the drug]. It is in virtue of this identification and withdrawal [...] that the unwilling addict may meaningfully make the analytically puzzling statement that the force moving him to take the drug is a force other than his own [...].[7]

Surely, however, no one thinks that whether I am responsible for an act depends on how consistent it is with my, or their, take on the kind of person I am, want to be, or should be. I can be responsible for *inauthentic* acts: for driving under the influence

---

7   Frankfurt, *op. cit.*, p. 329.

on just one, heady, uncharacteristic occasion. 'That's not like you!' seldom signals that I am excused from responsibility for my conduct.[8] Conversely, I can *fail* to be responsible for *authentic* acts: If I am a kleptomaniac who regards himself as incurable and grounds his momentous decisions in this conviction, I cannot be held responsible for my compulsive, authentic thieving (though I may be responsible for my defeatist self-conception). So the axis of authenticity does not line up with moral responsibility.

2.3 The axis of participation

Sometimes I feel a special affinity with an item of my conduct because I am aware of myself producing it. When I move or make a decision or churn through a problem in recursion theory, I have the impression that there is a *me* directing the process – forming the intention to act and moving his limbs in accordance with the intention, making the decision, drawing the inferences – a *me* whose presence and intervention in my/his doings is not obviously explained by a psychology of mental events which conspire, unsupervised, to bring it about that I act as I do.

Not always, however. Sometimes it seems that I move, decide or infer without *my* intervention. As I walk to the office, churning through a problem in recursion theory, I identify with the churning and withdraw from the walking.

The idea that I *participate* in some only of my intentional behaviour is roughly the idea that this phenomenology echoes a real-life contrast between my intervention and my displacement.

Velleman,[9] who takes himself to be contributing to the Frankfurt project and adopts Frankfurt's unwilling addict, characterizes an act *par excellence* as one in which the agent participates.

> In a full-blooded action, an intention is formed by the agent himself, not by his reasons for acting. Reasons affect his intention by influencing him to form it, but they thus affect his intention by affecting him first. And the agent then moves his limbs in execution of his intention; his intention doesn't move his limbs by itself. The agent thus has at least two roles to play: he forms an intention under the influence of reasons for acting, and he produces behaviour pursuant to that intention.[10]

---

8 'It's the bottle talking!' sometimes does, but only because we are excusing *compelled* rather than *inauthentic* behaviour.

9 Velleman, 'What Happens When Someone Acts?'.

10 Frankfurt, *op. cit.*, p. 463. Frankfurt says that he is analysing the structure of the Will and the conditions under which it is free. Velleman ('What Happens When Someone Acts?') says that he is engaged in the Frankfurt project but denies that it is the project of understanding Free Will because ('Freedom of the Will and the Concept of a Person') Free Will requires indeterminism. He describes the project as one of explaining what it is for an agent to be causally involved in the performance of one of his intentional acts.

Participation too fails to delineate the culpable/excusable contrast. I can rightly be held responsible for an act in which I don't participate, such as my walking over your knitting. And when I am insane, I fail to be responsible for an act in which I participate, like my decision to blow up a building, even if I am aware of myself making it.

Maybe the conduct in which I participate coincides with my consciously-motivated conduct. Velleman's principal example of non-full-blooded action suggests this.

> Suppose that I have a long-anticipated meeting with an old friend for the purpose of resolving some minor difference; but that as we talk, his offhand comments provoke me to raise my voice in progressively sharper replies, until we part in anger. Later reflection leads me to realize that accumulated grievances had crystallized in my mind, during the weeks before our meeting, into a resolution to sever our friendship over the matter at hand, and that this resolution is what gave the hurtful edge to my remarks. In short, I may conclude that desires of mine caused a decision, which in turn caused the corresponding behaviour; and I may acknowledge that these mental states were thereby exerting their normal motivational force, unabated by any strange perturbation or compulsion. But do I necessarily think that I made the decision or that I executed it? Surely, I can believe that the decision, though genuinely motivated by my desires, was thereby induced in me but not formed by me; and I can believe that it was genuinely executed in my behaviour but executed, again, without my help.[11]

If the distinction between participatory and non-participatory conduct tracks the distinction between conscious and unconscious motivation, we can see why there is no correspondence between *participatory* conduct and conduct for which the agent is responsible: We have already noted that I am responsible for my unconsciously-motivated walking. Attenuated consciousness typically exonerates only when it signals mental illness or, as in somnambulance, undermines the attribution of intentionality.

So is there any more to participation than fully-conscious deliberation? You might think so if you think that either of the following scenarios is possible.[12]

(a) An unconsciously motivated act can be performed with my participation

Example: I knit a scarf while watching CNN. Every manoeuvre I execute with the needles has a predominantly unconscious aetiology and yet there is some fact about the structure of my motivation in virtue of which, although I am knitting on automatic pilot, *I* am the knitter. I have withdrawn from the microstructure of the enterprise but I still exercise as much control over the outcome as I would had my eyes and thoughts remained on the wool – a fact that becomes evident when I immediately notice the selvedge unravelling. Velleman's quarrelsome subject lacked this kind of control.

---

11 Velleman, *op. cit.*, p. 464.
12 These scenarios develop ideas put forward in discussion by Gideon Rosen.

(b) I can be fully conscious of performing an act and of the motivating reasons I have for performing it and yet fail to 'sign off' on it

Example: I watch CNN while I'm really knitting a scarf. Although that description of my conduct is accurate enough, it doesn't capture my detachment from the news. I am aware of it, but I am not *really* watching – as I would tell you if you wanted to change channels.

I am not convinced that these examples disentangle participation from conscious motivation. We can make sense of any features they have which are not mopped up by the conscious/unconscious distinction if we utilize the other two axes of identification: perhaps I *am prepared to accept responsibility* for the consequences of my knitting but not for what's on television; perhaps I *see myself* as a bloke who knits, not a news junkie. Even if there is a robust notion of participation which differs from conscious motivation, it remains an aspect merely of how things seem. We need a reason to think that experiential data betrays the relevant causal processes before we can take this issue any further.

In sum, the Executive Control idea at work in much autonomy, free agency and responsibility literature conflates at least three ideas: ownership, authenticity and participation. Maybe no individual authors conflate them, but I doubt that any precisification of *executive control* plays a role in a satisfactory account of moral responsibility for acts. Identifying and distancing locutions sometimes express responsibility judgements, but there is no reason to think that the right theory about the nature of moral responsibility need say any more about such locutions than that.

3. Responsibility: the Very General Case

I now sketch an executive-control-free approach to the culpable/excusable contrast.

As we know, only some of the acts resulting from my intentions are explained in a way which highlights my contribution. Compare: 'This dress arrived because I went out and bought it' with 'this dress arrived because the Devil made me buy it'. We find the same explanatory contrast in cases where inanimate objects are the only explainers. Only some of the circumstances which come about because of the dispositions of a thermostat are explained in a way which highlights the thermostat's contribution. Compare: 'The ship flooded because a thermostat failed' with 'the ship flooded because a crucial circuit was defective and impeded a thermostat's performance'.

In this section, I argue that we routinely hold artifacts and natural processes 'responsible' for their conduct in much the same way that we hold persons responsible for theirs. Responsibility, or some *generalization* of it, can be attributed to any item which figures centrally in causal explanations. Moral responsibility is just a special case. Clearly we cannot found the general notion on executive control or motivational structure, because these are not applicable when the 'culpable' object is inanimate.

Nor, as I will argue in section 4, are they required to explain what is special about the moral case.

3.1 The causal agent

When an event E^* figures in the causal history of an event E, we often say that there is some thing A such that E^* is constituted by A's having (or lacking) some property at a time or by A's behaving (or failing to behave) in a particular way at that time. This seems like a good thing to say so long as the salient property or potential to behave is *intrinsic* to A. It seems like a good thing to say even when the relevant causally-efficacious facts about A are made true by other causal facts about processes internal to A or about components of A.

We shall say that any thing A which helps to constitute some event with causal powers is a *causal agent*. A could be a novel, a screwdriver or a bus driver.

It does not follow from my being a causal agent which helps to cause some event that some explanation would mention me as one of *the* causes of that event. I would be a causal agent if you picked me up and threw me onto the sofa so that my landing thereon caused the cushions to fly everywhere. In the simplest version of the case (not the one where I ask you to throw me onto the sofa) I am *a* cause, but an explanation of the flying cushions need not highlight my role. (I am not even an intentional agent because the cushions did not become airborne as a result of some act of mine that was caused *in the right way* by a belief-desire complex of mine.)

3.2 The evaluatively-implicated agent

Much of the activity of (causal) agents, animate and otherwise, is subject to the institution and enforcement of criteria for success. The community evaluates the conduct of agents on particular occasions by appealing to these criteria because conformity with norms is crucial for the achievement of whatever purpose the evaluated activity is supposed to serve.

A particular item of an agent's conduct might be assessable in accordance with many different *criteria of evaluation*. One would standardly assess A's belief that p for its verisimilitude, its evidential support and its consistency with other beliefs that A has not revised. However, if p is a proposition about the future and A is at a motivational conference, her belief will be assessed for its optimism. A sudden bodily movement might be assessed in one context for its social aptness, in a second for its effectiveness in achieving some end and in a third for its gracefulness.

The criteria employed when evaluating items of conduct for their conformity to some standard are also used to evaluate the *agents* whose conduct it is. If the community judges that an item of conduct falls short of some standard, the community might also judge that the agent whose behaviour it is falls similarly short. This does not always happen, though, so we can distinguish a *non-implicating* from an *agent-implicating* evaluation of conduct. Associated with any set of criteria for evaluating some feature of conduct is a set of *preconditions for* (agent-implicating) *evaluation*. A particular evaluation of an item of conduct is an *agent-implicating evaluation* when and only when an agent whose conduct it is satisfies the associated *preconditions for evaluation*.

Suppose I say that A's beliefs are not well-supported. This evaluation primarily concerns a collection of propositional attitudes. Now if A has been brainwashed and if this is why A believes as A does, mine isn't a fair evaluation of A; construed as A-*implicating*, it is an unjustified assertion because the criteria to which we appeal when assessing A's own conduct *qua* believer are applicable to A herself only if A satisfies the associated *preconditions for evaluation* and not being brainwashed is one of those preconditions. You ask me why the ballet was a scream and I tell you that the principal dancer was not exactly graceful. You are entitled to think that this is an indictment of both dancing and dancer unless I cancel that implicature, which I can do by explaining that the principal dancer was recovering from a hip operation and was taking this opportunity to display her courage and good humour. You will then appreciate that my evaluation applied to dancing but not to dancer: the evaluation was *non-Principal-Dancer-implicating* because the criteria to which we appeal when assessing this dancer's conduct *qua* graceful conduct cleave to *her* only if her *normal* capacity for gracefulness is unimpaired. If it is impaired, the principal dancer fails to satisfy the preconditions for evaluation associated with these criteria.

In these cases and, I think, in general, to say that an agent meets the preconditions for (agent-implicating) evaluation is roughly to say that the agent conducts itself *normally*. When an agent's situation is abnormal with respect to some such criteria, ordinary evaluative practice suggests that we think it unjust, uninformative or irrelevant to consider how that agent *herself* measures up to the usual standards if we think the abnormality of the circumstances has influenced the conduct.

In many, though perhaps not all, cases, this aspect of our practice expresses itself in the idea that an agent's failure to satisfy the preconditions for evaluation indicates that an *external* or *extrinsic* influence 'beyond the agent's control' (a brainwashing, a hip complaint) renders the agent's circumstances abnormal. This idea persists even when we all agree that the 'internal/intrinsic capacities' of the agent under scrutiny (and hence that agent's doings in normal circumstances) are completely determined by external influences.

To see this, imagine a thermostat which fails to operate when its threshold temperature is reached. Investigation reveals that the thermostat was faulty when installed. In such circumstances, we typically report not only that the thermostat did not operate, but also that the thermostat (itself!) was *defective*. We know that the thermostat has this disposition because of events external to it – a manufacturing or handling error, perhaps – just as we know that A holds unjustified beliefs because A was brainwashed and that the principal dancer moved ungracefully because of a hip operation. However, the case of the thermostat is different from the two earlier cases. We didn't want to describe A herself as irrational or the dancer herself as ungraceful because the conditions were deemed abnormal: brainwashing and hip complaints are not standard fare for A and the dancer. By contrast, the conditions in the new case were such that a thermostat would have operated normally absent some permanent defect in it. So if we want to evaluate this thermostat *qua* thermostat – to evaluate it on how well it performs its function – we are not prevented from doing so by any failure on its part to satisfy the *preconditions* for *evaluation*. Our evaluation of its performance is *this – thermostat-implicating*. (Our evaluation of the thermostat by no means forecloses on the possibilities that (a) the thermostat-maker or installer is also implicated in an unfavourable evaluation and (b) some associated hardware is also defective.)

Let's change the story so that the thermostat failed *only because*, microseconds before the threshold temperature was reached, it was punctured by shards of hot aluminium. Now we are likely to think that, at the time when the thermostat failed to perform, the conditions were abnormal and that this abnormality explains the failure; the normal conditions under which we evaluate thermostats *qua* thermostat exclude the scenario in which they have recently undergone that treatment. So if we want to evaluate this thermostat on how well it performs its function, we are prevented from doing so because it fails to satisfy the relevant preconditions for evaluation. Our evaluation of its performance is non-implicating.

Let's change the story again. The thermostat was defective when installed *and* punctured by hot shards. The failure of the thermostat is causally overdetermined. The conditions at the time of the failure were not normal – thanks to the hot shards – but even if they had been normal, the thermostat would have failed. So we cannot claim that abnormal conditions prevented the thermostat from operating as it should. The evaluation of its conduct is thermostat-implicating. (This is the thermostat analogue of Frankfurt's 'willing addict' case.)

One final version. A mock thermostat was installed by mistake. Under normal conditions for mock thermostats, we would not expect them to behave like real ones so an evaluation of the mock thermostat is not mock-thermostat-implicating.

This distinction between defective and thwarted agents might seem arbitrary: a thermostat which is hit by hot metal is as defective after the impact as one that was mishandled before installation. How many microseconds before the failure must the damage occur before we rule that the thermostat satisfies the preconditions for evaluation and is deemed defective? A seasoned dancer with a hip problem is as graceless thereafter as one whose mother should never have put her on the stage. Would the first dancer have satisfied the preconditions for evaluation and been deemed graceless had she been born with a hip problem?

The answers depend on which conditions are taken to be normal for the agent *qua* locus of conduct. Which conditions these are depends on community concerns because it is in the pursuit of these that we evaluate agents. We evaluate agents because whether or not an agent achieves the benchmark set by the community impacts on our lives. Just when and how it does is reflected in our choices of preconditions for evaluation. If a thermostat fails in conditions for which it was not designed, most of us find that quite boring. So if we are interested in evaluating thermostats for their reliability *qua* thermostat, we will deem such conditions abnormal. Of course, motor-racers may evaluate thermostats for their robustness and may not always take conditions for which they were not designed to be abnormal. And of course, we should expect grey area conditions which aren't quite normal and aren't quite abnormal.

3.3 The obligated agent

The community often rules, demands or expects that an agent *B* behave in a certain way or undergo some process in response to an evaluation of some item of conduct. The conduct might be *B*'s own: *B* is a thermostat which breaks down; *B* thereby fails to meet the relevant standard of performance; the community demands or reasonably expects that *B* be repaired or replaced. Or *B* is a vandal who damages your property; such conduct is inappropriate; the community may demand that *B* make suitable reparations.

The conduct might be that of a distinct agent *A*: *A* lies injured by the road; this behaviour falls short of the standard for flourishing; the community urges *B*, a passerby, to be neighbourly and not to walk by on the other side. Or *A* damages your property; the community may rule that *B*, *A*'s guardian, compensate you.

In these cases, the conduct at issue fails to meet the appropriate standard, but in other cases the community demands that *B* reward an action that is judged good or acknowledge that a standard has been met.

Given any community and (not necessarily distinct) agents *A* and *B*, we shall say that:

> *B* is *obligated* by an evaluation of an item *i* of *A*'s conduct with respect to a feature *f* just if the content of the evaluation, the nature of *i* and the conventions maintained in the community for evaluations with respect to *f* together prescribe or strongly suggest that *B* respond in a particular way.

Among the examples of being obligated just considered are some in which an agent is obligated by an *agent-implicating* evaluation. If I damage your property and I satisfy the preconditions for evaluation of such conduct in my community, I (as well as my action) am judged reprehensible; I have failed to measure up. My guardian and I are obligated by this evaluation and should therefore recompense you, feel shame, resolve to avoid similar situations henceforth and so on. Conditions are normal, so the preconditions for agent-implicating evaluation are met and the community typically prescribes that we respond by attending to the state of the implicated agent if we wish to prevent or promote similar future circumstances. In such cases, the implicated agent often stars in the explanation of the evaluated conduct. If we explain an event by saying that it was the thermostat that failed, we suggest that it needs repairing or replacing if we want to avoid similar disasters. If we say it was I who (wilfully) bought the dress, we suggest that I am exhibit *A* if we care about whether events of this sort should happen again. By contrast, when an explanation legitimately passes the buck (to another circuit or the Devil) because preconditions for agent-implicating evaluation are not met, something other than the object, some feature of its history or environment, becomes the legitimate focus of concern.

3.4 Responsibility

I think the above considerations about explanations and our responses to them provide a framework for understanding responsibility judgements.

Somebody from a given community who holds that an agent A is *responsible* (in a very general sense) for some item i of conduct insofar as i has feature f holds that,

(1) There are facts, some of which involve A, and there are causal relationships among those facts in terms of which i can be (causally) explained;

(2) In virtue of those facts and causal relationships, A satisfies the preconditions for agent-implicating evaluation which inform evaluations with respect to feature f; and usually also

(3) Some agent B is *obligated* by the A-implicating evaluation of i.

A is responsible (in the general sense) just if the claim that A is responsible is true.

On my picture, an agent, any agent, is responsible for an item of its conduct (insofar as that item has a given feature) only if the preconditions for evaluation of conduct of its kind (*qua* conduct with that feature) are satisfied. What then are the preconditions for evaluation of acts, decisions, desires and intentions *qua* morally evaluable states?

4. The Special Case: Moral Responsibility

A promising suggestion about the preconditions for moral evaluation – and hence about how to draw the culpable/excusable distinction – develops work by Philip Pettit and Michael Smith.[13] The suggestion is that evaluations of morally significant and perhaps other sorts of conduct are agent-implicating just if, due to its internal dispositions, the agent can:

(1) Recognize which norms govern this conduct, and

(2) Make adjustments of conduct in order to conform with those norms.

This bipartite standard is not appropriate as a precondition for agent-implicating evaluations generally. With respect to its normal operations, a thermostat cannot *recognize* when something is a standard to which its conduct is answerable; it is not a device for recognizing what thermostats are supposed to do. It is, of course, able to *do* what the norm requires – switch on at the threshold temperature – if it is in good working order, but the recognition failure disqualifies it from meeting the proposed standard.[14] Even so, there is a bunch of normal conditions, determined in some other

---

13 Phillip Pettit and Michael Smith, 'Freedom in Belief and Desire' *The Journal of Philosophy*, 93(9), 1996, pp. 429–49.

14 Objection: No, the response happens automatically and not because the device is responding to norms. My answer: true, but I allow that this suffices for satisfaction of condition (2), in order to keep the two conditions logically independent. If we insist that, in order to

way, such that if a thermostat meets those, it is responsible for its conduct, in my general sense. A disappointed police recruit who misses out by 4 cm can recognize the height restrictions, but he cannot *do* what they require: he can grow no taller. Even so, the rejected recruit is responsible (again in my general sense) for his height; it's *his* height.

However, in the special case where we assess intentional conduct for its moral rightness, the *ability to recognize* and the *ability to do* conditions seem appropriate. I am not morally responsible for my intentional actions if I just flew in from somewhere where that kind of conduct is acceptable and thus fail the *ability to recognize* condition, or if I performed them under the influence of my medication and thus fail the *ability to do* condition. Whether meeting the conditions suffices for moral responsibility is more controversial. What if I meet them but am ignorant of some fact such that, if I knew it, I would question my competence with the moral code? And what if I grasp that code only because the hypnotist ensured that I do? I suspect (but am not certain) that an agent which internalizes the relevant moral system in all its nuance and can select conduct which conforms to it rather than conduct which does not is morally responsible if anything is. Dodgy causal history may undermine attributions of free agency, autonomy, or executive control, if such things there be, but I argued that these might not be reliable indicators of moral responsibility; we do better by exploring the analogous roles played in explanations by moral agents and other causal agents.[15]

---

meet condition (2), the thermostat must respond to its threshold temperature in order to satisfy a normative principle, it could not do so unless it recognized that there was this normative principle and then the thermostat would satisfy condition (1) also. Against my version, one might urge that people who we do not call responsible might still meet both conditions, given my story: they might know full well what the norms are and accidentally behave in such a way as to conform with them. I respond: My condition (2) cannot be met by an agent unless that agent adjusts its conduct in response to the norm. It is not enough that its conduct just happens to coincide with the prescribed conduct. A mock thermostat that suddenly caused a circuit to close when its mock threshold temperature was reached would not thereby meet condition (2). The real thermostat meets that condition because it reliably responds to the norm because of what the norm is. What I am denying in my version is that it must also respond to the norm because the norm is a norm.

One more objection to my version: The thermostat may be customized to respond to what is in fact a norm, but we do not have the kind of counterfactual resilience we want of something that reliably responds to a norm. If the norm were slightly different, the thermostat would be unable to adjust its behaviour to conform with the change; it cannot track norms. My response: According to the analysis of moral responsibility under construction, a person is morally responsible for her act if, given her circumstances, she could have done the right thing. Nothing follows from this about what would happen if the norms were (even slightly) different: Suppose that I know what's actually right and can do what's actually right. Then I meet the two conditions and hence am morally responsible. Still, there is a sceptical world in which what these capacities amount to is the tracking of a set of almost-norms.

15 Pettit and Smith argue that this standard applies not only to the evaluation of desires (and, by extension, of intentional action) for their moral features but also to the evaluation

There is more evidence that the ability to recognize and conform to norms of desire constitutes, in the view of the moral community, the normal conditions for desiring. It comes from the assumptions people make – unless they have reasons not to – about what one is able or likely to think or do and about how the desire sets of themselves and of others evolve.[16] The community's default assumption is not that people approximate perfect intentional systems – *loci* of intentional states which evolve in accordance with principles of theoretical and practical rationality in the pursuit of a specified goal. For one thing, although we expect ordinary desirers to be more or less rational, we also expect them to be subject, to a normal extent, to pride, prejudice, conflicting loyalties, natural caution, inertia, fatigue and other obstacles to rational thought. We expect them to muster whatever resources are at their disposal and overcome these handicaps rather than to be deterred from their task and the resources at their disposal may be nonrational. For another thing, rather than doing whatever serves their own ends, we expect ordinary desirers to aim at what is right. This requires an ability, whether rationally underwritten or not, to distinguish the right from the rest and to orient one's goals rightwards. The default assumption, it seems, is that one can choose to do a good or right thing from among options and then do it.

Pettit and Smith call the agent who meets the *ability to recognize* and *ability to do* conditions an *orthonomous* agent.

> Responsible [...] desirers are orthonomous subjects, in the sense that they recognize certain yardsticks of [...] right desire and can respond to the demands of the right in their own case. They may vary among themselves in how far they actually conform their [...] desires to those yardsticks; they may be more or less thoroughly ruled by the right. But outside the domain of disabling obstacles, they are all equally orthonomous in at least this sense: they are all able to answer the call that the right makes upon them.[17]

The suggestion that morally culpable conduct is conduct with respect to which an agent is orthonomous is compatible with scepticism about moral responsibility. Perhaps we are not orthonomous with respect to some or all morally evaluable conduct because we are ignorant of crucial facts about moral norms or unable reliably to adjust our conduct so that it accords with significant moral norms. Perhaps there are no moral norms.

---

of beliefs for their truth, evidentiary warrant, consistency and so on (see 433-6). *A* is not responsible for the beliefs she acquired during her brainwashing because, even if she is capable of recognizing that her beliefs should be true, updated in the light of new evidence and consistent with one another, she cannot reliably adjust her beliefs in accordance with these norms: she fails the *ability to do* condition. I will not engage with issues about responsible belief, except to note that this unified treatment of belief and desire chimes nicely with the underlying theme of the previous section: that there is a notion of responsibility far broader than the moral variety and that we should sometimes expect similarities among the varieties.

16 Pettit and Smith, *op. cit.*, pp. 441–3.

17 Ibid., p. 442.

By imbedding the Pettit-Smith account in the very general framework developed in the previous section, I motivate a remark that Pettit and Smith make in passing.

[I]t may be useful to give up on the ideal of autonomy or self-rule in favour of the ideal of "orthonomy" or right rule.[18]

My story says that I have no special psychological causal relationship with the acts for which I am responsible that I do not have with the remainder of my intentional conduct, except insofar as the former are most usefully explained as effects of my own intentional efforts while the latter attract an explanation to which my contribution is less central. That's why we should 'give up on' autonomy – at least insofar as it informs a theory about the nature of moral responsibility for acts. (Discussion of the impact this move has on debates about free will and agency in general must be postponed.)

If, as I suggest, we are right to supplement my very general story with the Pettit-Smith account, my intentional effort is of central explanatory significance with respect to the morally evaluable features of my conduct only when I am capable of recognizing and doing what is morally required of me. However, this is only a *suggestion*. Maybe there are superior accounts of the preconditions for moral evaluation. My commitment here is to the general framework of the previous section. I invoked Pettit and Smith to indicate one way in which that framework might be filled out in the case of central interest to us.

Fleshing out my very general story about responsibility along these lines goes much of the way towards a story about the nature of moral responsibility. It certainly gives us a story about the culpable/excusable contrast. But we might also want to know what, if anything, the moral community demands or expects by way of a response to culpable conduct. After all, if the moral responsibility of an agent for an act implies the explanatory salience of that agent with respect to that act, a community which cares about the act probably cares about how the responsible agent is treated subsequently. That, I have argued, is part of the baggage that comes with explanatory salience.

I take it that the community-sanctioned responses to agent-implicating moral evaluations are to be found among what Peter Strawson called the *reactive* attitudes and behaviours,[19] shame (for one's own wrong act), resentment (for another's wrong act), pride (in one's own exemplary act), esteem (for another's exemplary act) and so on, along with punishment, reward and other downstream responses. Strawson maintained that these attitudes and behaviours come for free with participation in ordinary interpersonal relationships.[20] They might indeed be intractable features of human interaction, but we can usefully regard them also as measures or expressions

---

18 Ibid.

19 Peter Strawson, 'Freedom and Resentment', *Proceedings of the British Academy*, 48, 1962, pp. 1–25. Reproduced in Gary Watson (ed.), *Free Will*, Oxford: Oxford University Press, 2003, pp. 72–93, 76–7.

20 Ibid., pp. 81–3.

of feeling which are deemed appropriate, given the impact on the community of the act and the fact of culpability. We can ask whether they really are appropriate responses: should we resent? Should we punish? Here be breeding-grounds for another kind of scepticism about moral responsibility.

5. In Conclusion

I have posited a significant similarity between the way that people, on the one hand, and mere things, on the other, feature in explanations and evaluations of their behaviour. Sometimes we explain a phenomenon by slating a certain gadget, process or event as the item that made things the way they are. Other times, although the same gadget, process or event is in the mix, we don't regard it as the item that made the difference. The same goes for moral agents. My view is that explanatory salience, when it occurs, and not any exercise of executive control, underwrites our moral responsibility attributions and our practice of praising and blaming.

Three final observations. First, the explanatory salience of an object, whether it be me or my thermostat, persists no matter how well you understand that object in its context. Hence, there is no reason to think that we would stop attributing responsibility if we sufficiently understood that object's situation. The apparent tension between judging moral doings and understanding the doer plausibly stems from the worry that a rich understanding of the doer's predicament is incompatible with attributing executive control. That worry does not arise on my account and responsibility judgements are accordingly less momentous than they are standardly taken to be.

Second, my account finds a place for accountability in a naturalistic world, but not for hatred or adulation of those held accountable. For all that I have said, intense emotional responses to doers are indeed ruled out by an adequate understanding of them *in situ* and are as irrational as disgust with a faulty thermostat is.

Lastly, the parallels between judgements about artifacts and judgements about people do not show up systematically in the use we make of words like 'responsible', 'fault' and 'deserving'. Yes, we sometimes say, 'El Nino is the culprit', but if this is evidence for my view, it is equally good evidence of our anthropomorphizing propensities. Those who deny that workers can blame their tools are surely right to think either that these words apply literally to moral agents and only figuratively to stuff, or else that a worker can blame his tools felicitously, but only unjustly. Which is the safer conclusion probably depends on whether ships have windows.[21]

21 Thanks to John Bishop, David Braddon-Mitchell, Matthew Dentith, Aness Kim, Justine Kingsbury, Vanya Kovach, Fred Kroon, Phillippa McKeown-Green, Siong Ngor Ng, Michael Smith, Pedro Tabensky and Myles Webster. Thanks also to audiences at the University of Auckland, Waikato University, Victoria University and the Australian National University.

PART III
The Ethical Function
of Condemnation

Chapter 10

Judging Because Understanding:
A Defence of Retributive Censure

Thaddeus Metz

Editor's Introduction

Thaddeus Metz defends the retributive theory of punishment against challenges mounted by some of the contributors to this collection (Kai Nielsen, Brian Penrose, Samantha Vice, Pedro Tabensky and Marc Fellman). People, he thinks, ought to be censured in a way that is proportional to what they have done and for which they are responsible. Understanding does not conflict with judging. On the contrary, according to him, the more we understand, the better we are able to censure appropriately. Metz's argument is Kantian insofar as he argues that 'respect for persons [victims, responsible wrongdoers and the community at large] requires condemning people proportionately to their responsible wrongdoing and hence that understanding a person merely indicates what would be proportionate, not that proportionality is unjustified'. His reason for thinking that Kantian respect requires retribution is that, as in non-retributive cases such as economic justice, compensatory justice, and justice in healthcare rationing, it requires imposing burdens on persons because of their responsible choices. Finally, Metz argues that *The Reader* supports his thesis rather than the thesis that understanding must temper judgement and punishment. He interprets *The Reader* to be a plea for appropriate retributive judgement. To use his slogan, 'judging is apt because of understanding'.

* * *

I. Introduction

Several contributors to this volume maintain that there is a tension between understanding another person and her wrongful actions, on the one hand, and judging her on retributive grounds, on the other. By 'retributive' reasons for judgement, I mean any consideration that could be invoked to justify censuring a person for, and in proportion to, wrongdoing for which he was responsible. For example, one (but not the only) retributive reason to condemn someone might appeal to the bare fact that he deserves condemnation because of, and to the same degree as, his having voluntarily done wrong in the past, which rationale appeals to no expected consequences of the condemning such as the prevention of wrongdoing. A number of authors believe that the more one understands someone who has done wrong, the less reason one finds to blame the person merely on the basis of, and strictly proportionate to, the wrong he has done.[1] Now, these authors all find blaming for wrongdoing permissible; none even advocates abolishing punishment *in toto*. But what they have in common is the view that understanding another person shows that it is unreasonable to impose the sort of censure that a retributive theory would ideally require.

In my contribution to this volume, I maintain that there is no tension between retributive judging and understanding. I argue that, upon understanding another agent and his actions, one never thereby finds reason not to judge him retributively; instead, coming to understand another invariably helps a judge to ascertain precisely what is retributively warranted.

I begin the chapter by specifying with care what I mean by 'understanding' and 'retributive judgement' (II). I also clarify the principled tension between them that others see as one that is epistemic in nature: invariably, the more one understands another person (in a certain sense), the more evidence one has that a full-blown retributive judgement of her is morally unjustified. Then, I present an argument for thinking that there is no such tension between judging and understanding (III). My argument is Kantian in nature; it says, very roughly, that respect for persons requires condemning people proportionately to their responsible wrongdoing and hence that understanding a person merely indicates what would be proportionate, not that proportionality is unjustified. Next, I consider arguments for thinking otherwise, which come from the contributions of others to this volume (IV). I first address the claims that understanding another person reveals that retributive judgement is altogether disrespectful or otherwise impermissible because we learn that he is not an unmoved mover (Pedro Tabensky), he could not have done otherwise (Kai Nielsen), or we would have done the same thing in his position (Brian Penrose and perhaps Marc Fellman). I then address the claim that understanding another person shows that retributive judgement, while not altogether disrespectful or impermissible, must be tempered by mercy because we learn that this person, like everyone else, is frail (Samantha Vice and Marc Fellman). I conclude the paper by discussing respects in which, contra others' assessment, *The Reader* coheres with my thesis that judging is apt because of understanding (V).

---

1   Note that this normative thesis about what one has reason to believe or do upon understanding differs from an empirical thesis about what happens to one upon understanding. In particular, Ward Jones, Brian Penrose and Samantha Vice discuss the claim that the more one understands another person, the less one will in fact be inclined to blame her on retributive grounds. I am not interested in any descriptive claim about how our psychology operates, focusing exclusively on the prescriptive claim about what our behaviour ought to be.

II. The Terms of the Debate

In this section I aim to articulate the sort of conflict that one might suspect exists between judging a person retributively and understanding her and her behaviour. I first analyse the two major concepts, and then discuss the kind of conflict that others see between them and that I deny exists.

I believe that there is no conflict between retributive judging and understanding however 'understanding' another person or his deeds is construed, and I therefore construe 'understanding' in a very broad sense to mean any kind of empirical knowledge. Some authors in this volume focus on 'understanding' in a much narrower sense, e.g., some use it to denote merely an awareness of the agent's reasons for acting, an apprehension of the other's first-person point of view. Others use it to refer to knowledge that would accompany a more third-person point of view, e.g., an appeal to unconscious motives, psychological laws or social causes. When I speak of 'understanding' a person or her actions, I refer to any of the myriad ways of explaining why a person is the way she is or why she has done what she has done.

I also construe 'retributive judgement' of a person or her acts in a very broad sense, again more inclusively than some other contributors to this book. For me, the phrase denotes the following sort of cluster of cognition, conation and volition. First off, 'retributive judgement' includes a *belief* that if a person has done wrong and is responsible for the wrong, then he warrants a proportionate negative sanction at bottom for having done it. It also includes the belief that many times these conditions are fulfilled, i.e., that people often do wrongs for which they are responsible. These beliefs imply the claims that there are degrees of wrongful behaviour (from forgetting to return a borrowed book to engaging in crimes against humanity), degrees of responsibility (from being an insane child who accidentally pulled the trigger to being a clear-thinking adult who intentionally did so), and degrees of negative sanction (from wagging a finger to physical punishment). The worse the immorality and the greater the responsibility for it, the harsher the burden that ought to be imposed because of it. 'Retributive judgement' here also means a *desire* that the proportionate negative sanction be imposed on a wrongdoer for the reason that he has responsibly done wrong; it refers to an inclination to see an offender burdened in like degree to, and because of, his immorality. In addition, the phrase denotes an *action* proximately caused by this belief and desire, namely, the actual imposition of the proportionate negative sanction, or at least support for its imposition by someone else.

Retributive judgement, in short, is to censure a person to the same degree as, and basically because of, wrongful behaviour for which he is responsible. This definition of 'retributive judgement' is broad for referring to censure or blame as such, as opposed to a specific sort such as punishment. Since I am particularly keen to show that retributive punishment of a person by the state is consistent with understanding him, in the rest of this chapter I often focus on it, as opposed to censure in general.

The definition of 'retributive judgement' is also broad for including a variety of policies that are 'backward-looking' in the sense of basing the rationale for, and amount of, legal punitive censure solely on facts about the past. There are three different reasons why the historical fact of having responsibly done wrong might be thought to warrant a proportionate negative sanction such as state punishment. First, there is the desert theory, which says that a person should be burdened for his wrongful behaviour because he deserves to be.[2] The worse the wrong and the more control he had over it, the harsher a penalty is deserved and hence should be imposed. Second, there is the fairness theory, the view that, by having broken a just law, a person undergoes fewer burdens than those who obeyed the law and yet benefits from the order produced by their obedience, and that he therefore should receive a burden so as to make his share of burdens equal to those of law-abiding citizens.[3] The worse the crime, the greater the liberty the wrongdoer has voluntarily taken at the expense of others, and hence the harsher the punitive burden must be to rectify the exploitation. Third, there is the (intrinsic) expressive theory, which claims that the point of punishment should be to treat the offender as responsible for his behaviour, to affirm the value of his victim, or to disavow wrongful actions.[4] The worse the offence and the more responsible the offender is for it, the stronger the expression of disapproval must be and hence the harsher the punishment should be.

Each of these three theories is on occasion called 'retributivism' in the literature, but I here use the word to denote the general backward-looking perspective that encompasses all three particular instances. Such a perspective differs from any sort of 'forward-looking' view that would fundamentally base the rationale for, and amount of, legal punitive blame on facts about the future. Three influential forward-looking theories are that state punishment is justified because it will: scare people from committing crime (deterrence theory), physically prevent people from committing crime (incapacitation theory), or reform people's values or their psychological abilities to act in accordance with them (moral education theory). Benthamite utilitarianism and Aristotelian *eudaimonism* are often invoked as theories of morality that would fundamentally ground a forward-looking theory of legal punishment, but one could hold a Lockean rights-based moral theory instead, claiming that the ultimate justification for state punishment is that it promises to protect citizens'

---

2   E.g., Andrew von Hirsch, *Past or Future Crimes: Deservedness and Dangerousness in the Sentencing of Criminals*, New Brunswick: Rutgers University Press, 1987; Robert Nozick, *Philosophical Explanations*, Cambridge: Harvard University Press, 1981, pp. 363-97; and Michael Moore, *Placing Blame: A General Theory of Criminal Law*, New York: Oxford University Press, 1997.

3   E.g., Jeffrie Murphy, *Justice, Retribution and Therapy*, Boston: D. Reidel Publishing Co., 1979; Wojciech Sadurski, *Giving Desert Its Due*, Boston: D. Reidel Publishing Co., 1985; and Michael Davis, *To Make the Punishment Fit the Crime*, Boulder: Westview Press, 1992.

4   E.g., Jean Hampton, 'An Expressive Theory of Retribution', in Wesley Cragg (ed.), *Retributivism and Its Critics*, Stuttgart: F. Steiner Verlag, 1992, pp. 1-25; Andrew von Hirsch, *Censure and Sanctions*, Oxford: Oxford University Press, 1993; Thaddeus Metz, 'Censure Theory and Intuitions about Punishment', *Law and Philosophy*, 19, 2000, pp. 491-512; and 'Realism and the Censure Theory of Punishment', *Archives for Philosophy of Law and Social Philosophy*, 85, 2002, pp. 117-29.

rights of self-ownership. The key point is that retributive judgement contrasts with any forward-looking theory of punishment by the government; it denies that the point of legal punitive blame is to achieve any state of affairs such as crime control that will obtain after the blaming. Instead, retributivism here is the view that punitive blame serves a morally sound function because it is in itself an appropriate response to what has happened in the past.

Having analysed understanding and retributive judging, I can now articulate the claim – which I aim to refute – that there is a tension between them. There are two different kinds of tension one might see between understanding and retributive judging, only one of which is really advocated by other contributors to this volume and is prima facie plausible. I mention both kinds simply in order to highlight my target.

The implausible sort of tension that other contributors do not advocate is this: the more one understands a person or his actions, the less *moral* reason there is to judge him or his actions retributively. According to this view, if one did not understand a person, then one could have strong moral reason to judge retributively. But none of those who sees a conflict between judging and understanding maintains this; all instead argue that, when one comes to understand a person, one *discovers* (instead of *creates*) a moral reason not to judge in the way a retributivist ideally would. In other words, these authors maintain that, if one failed to understand a person and judged her in a full-blown retributive fashion, one would be doing something immoral.

The proper way to articulate the putative tension, then, is to say this: the more one understands another person, the more *epistemic* reason one has to think that a perfectly retributive judgement of her is morally unjustified. This sort of tension implies that retributivism is a false theory of punishment, or at least should not be the sole factor informing one's decisions of whether to punish and how much to punish. Understanding a wrongdoer and his deeds provides evidence that retributivism should not guide one's behaviour solely, if at all. For instance, some contributors claim that, upon understanding another, one always becomes aware of the causes that necessitated her behaviour and that therefore make retributive punishment impermissible.

In the next section, I provide an argument for thinking that there is no epistemic tension between understanding and retributive judging. Upon understanding another person and his deeds, one never thereby finds evidence that retribution would be unjustified; instead, understanding invariably helps one to determine precisely what retribution requires in a given case. Afterward, I rebut arguments for thinking otherwise.

III. Dignity, Respect and Tracking

I present a Kantian reason for thinking that the belief that one ought to retributively judge another person epistemically coheres with understanding him. The basic idea is that the principle of respect for the dignity of persons justifies punishing a person because of, and in proportion to, his wrongdoing, so long as the person is in a certain, naturalist sense responsible for the wrongdoing.[5] Coming to understand a person and his deeds, one thereby discovers natural facts about whether and to what degree a person has been responsible for a wrongful act. Given the principle of respect, understanding him will reveal evidence of how much punishment, if any, is warranted from a retributive standpoint.

I appeal to a Kantian account of responsibility, one that differs from Kant's own.[6] Kant's non-natural account of retributivism is notoriously controversial, even implausible, and the account I offer avoids the more problematic features of his theory such as atemporal causation and noumenal freedom. Even though I offer a thoroughly naturalist argument, which comports with the worldview of my interlocutors in this volume, I should explain why an appeal to a Kantian perspective is dialectically appropriate. First, the principle of respect is an intuitively plausible moral foundation, one that survives the questionable metaphysics and epistemology of Kant. Second, it, or at least its corollary of not treating people merely as a means, is explicitly accepted by most of those I argue against (Tabensky, Nielsen and Vice), and otherwise does a good job of explaining the prima facie force of other objections (Penrose and Fellman). I of course do not have the space to argue for a Kantian outlook relative to, say, a utilitarian one. I instead take such a perspective as reasonable and as constituting some common ground between those who differ on whether there is a tension between retributive judging and understanding.

The principle of respect for the dignity of persons, as I understand it, instructs agents to treat other agents as having the highest intrinsic value in the world. An agent, or person, is a being that has the ability to act on the basis of ends it has adopted upon principled deliberation. It contrasts with a being who acts merely on instinct or by conditioning, a being that lacks the capacity to judge whether its desires are worth fulfilling and to act in light of such judgement. Call this capacity 'autonomy.'

---

5 My account of respect and its implications for punishment are partially drawn from Thaddeus Metz, 'The Reasonable and the Moral', *Social Theory and Practice*, 28, 2002, pp. 277–301.

6 Immanuel Kant, *Critique of Pure Reason* B560-86. Kant distinguishes between a theoretical standpoint from which we describe events and a practical standpoint from which we make a decision to act, and he argues that, from a practical standpoint, we must think that we have the ability to act independently of natural causes, which ability is, by the principle of respect for persons, necessary and sufficient for retributive judgement. I differ from Kant in that I: draw no distinction between viewpoints; do not entertain the possibility of non-natural free will or responsibility; and reject the idea that such a non-natural capacity is necessary for retributive judgement. I hold a naturalized metaphysics and epistemology, which still counts as 'Kantian' for maintaining that the fundamental moral principle is to respect the dignity of persons, where such dignity is a function of a certain capacity for autonomy.

If you were driving a bus and had to choose between running over a squirrel or a person, you must, morally speaking, run over the squirrel.[7] At least part of the best explanation of that moral requirement is that the person is worth more than the squirrel,[8] and, moreover, that the person is worth more than the squirrel in virtue of her personhood, that is, because she has autonomy.[9] This superlative intrinsic value, or dignity, warrants respect, which respect forbids sacrificing it for something worth less than it and, more generally, forbids treating it merely as a means to an end. Respect also requires treating persons as equals (since they by definition have the capacity for autonomy to the requisite degree) as well as helping them on occasion to develop their capacity to choose goals or to attain the goals they have chosen.

Furthermore, and of central concern to retributive judgement, respect requires at least institutions (if not individuals) to track the responsible actualization of the capacity for autonomy, even at substantial cost to the general welfare.[10] By 'responsible' choice I (roughly) mean the exercise of autonomy that has been undermined to a large degree neither by external factors such as duress, brainwashing and trickery, nor by internal factors such as psychosis, sleepwalking and being a minor. A choice for which one is responsible is not one independent of all natural laws, as in Kant's view; it is rather a choice that is within one's control or is a product of one's deliberation, which conditions are, for all we know, causally determined. By 'tracking' such choice I mean not merely reacting to a person in light of the decisions she has made, but also responding in kind, i.e., imposing burdens in reaction to wrong choices and not doing so (and perhaps offering benefits) in reaction to right ones. Finally, by such tracking coming at 'substantial cost to the general welfare', I mean that it would forgo a large aggregate of improved quality of life, whether that gets cashed out in terms of pleasure, desire satisfaction, happiness, *eudaimonia*, excellence or meaning.[11] In sum, when I say that institutions should track the exercise of autonomy even at the expense of the general welfare, I am claiming this: respect

---

7   Some people might run over the person if the person threatens other persons. However, I am not considering such a case. And even if I were, a good explanation of why protecting persons is worth doing is that they have a dignity that demands respect (cf. the Other-Defence case discussed below). Others might be inclined to hit the person if he is guilty of having harmed others in the past (but poses no threat in the present). However, the best explanation of that inclination is a belief in the aptness of retributive judgement, which of course supports the thesis I aim to defend in this essay.

8   Neither that the person or his relatives would suffer more, nor that you would get punished, be sued, or feel guilty. Imagine you are a heartless bastard in the middle of nowhere striking an orphan who will die instantly. It would still be wrong of you to do so.

9   Not because she is a human being or part of our community. Imagine you are striking an intelligent Vulcan from afar or a 'swamp human', one who has spontaneously arisen from a mixture of chemicals in a bog. It would still be wrong of you to do so.

10   Here I draw on material from Thaddeus Metz, 'Arbitrariness, Justice, and Respect,' *Social Theory and Practice*, 26, 2000, pp. 25–45.

11   Quality of life here does not include the capacity for autonomy that is developed or provided resources. I believe that the strong reason to track responsible choice can be

requires placing burdens upon those who have done wrong as opposed to those who have not, if the wrongful deed was substantially within the agent's control and even if society would be less well off as a result. What follow are four non-retributive examples to illustrate and support this claim.

First, respect pro tanto mandates a court to make a tortfeasor pay compensation to his victims, if he can. Suppose that you, disliking my ugly sweater, intentionally spill yellow mustard and red wine on it to express your disgust. A judge has strong reason to make you bear the cost of buying me a new sweater, even if overall utility would be higher if I did so instead. Call this the 'Tort' case.

Second, respect in the normal case requires a soldier to harm aggressors when necessary to protect their potential, innocent victims. Suppose you are a United Nations peacekeeper in Rwanda and see five armed Hutus targeting a defenceless Tutsi merely because she is a Tutsi. Uncontroversially, you must shoot the assassins if required to protect the woman from getting hacked to death with machetes. Indeed, if it is necessary to defend the innocent women, you must kill all five assassins, and that is true even if we suppose that more intrinsic value of whatever sort would obtain in the long run if you were to let them kill her. For instance, imagine that the five assassins, who have lots of friends and family, would be happier in the long run than the woman, who is a loner, if they lived. Assuming for the sake of argument that letting the five aggressors kill one innocent person would eventually produce a better world than killing the five and saving the one, respect for persons still demands killing the five aggressors. This is the 'Other-Defence' case.

Third, ceteris paribus, respect obliges a hospital to distribute scarce medical treatment to those who have not brought about their need for the treatment by virtue of having made wrong choices. Suppose that a husband cheats on his wife, having unprotected sex with dozens of casual partners. Imagine that he acquires HIV, that he passes it on to his wife, and that a hospital has enough antiretroviral treatment for only one of the parties. It would be moral madness to suppose that a physician ought to give the treatment to the husband (or that she should flip a coin to decide who gets it). Instead, the physician has the most principled reason to give the wife the treatment, even supposing the husband would have a higher quality of life in whatever sense if he were the one to survive. For example, imagine that, upon being given the treatment, the husband would morally reform and add somewhat more excellence to the world than would be produced if the wife were to live. Even if that would be the outcome and were somehow known to the physician, she must save the wife instead of the husband. Let this be known as the 'Rationing' case.

Fourth, respect provides strong moral reason for a business to base wages on how long and hard a person qualified for the job has worked at it. Suppose that Abe works many hours and works diligently during them, while Brenda breaks her contract by rarely showing up for work and slacking off when on the job. All things being equal, it would be disrespectful of a boss to give more money to Brenda, even if she would

---

overridden when autonomy would be reduced in substantial ways. For discussion, see Metz, 'Arbitrariness, Justice, and Respect'.

live a more meaningful life with the money than Abe would with it and even if productivity would not increase if Abe were provided with more money (imagine he and his other colleagues have a strong work ethic, perhaps because of their religion). Let's make this the 'Wages' case.

In all four cases, what respect for persons requires is clear.[12] Furthermore, even many of those who might reject respect as a moral foundation will find their moral common sense inclined to think that burdens ought to be allocated in the way respect would require. The principle operative in the four scenarios is this: an institution has strong moral reason to place burdens upon those who have acted wrongly in a way for which they are responsible, even supposing for the sake of argument that so placing the burdens would fail to produce the most available well-being or other intrinsic value. Respect for the capacity to make decisions for good reasons requires distributing burdens in accordance with the way this capacity has been actualized, as opposed to some non-agency criterion such as the amount of welfare at stake. Compensatory, military, healthcare and economic justice are all a function of tracking responsible choice, at least from a Kantian standpoint.

Now, by analogy, so is criminal justice. I claim that the four non-retributive tracking cases above are analogous to instances of retributive judgement. Here, a judge imposes burdens on people in proportion to, and because of, wrongdoing for which they are responsible, even if doing so comes at substantial cost to the aggregate of improved quality of life available. Specifically, the desert theory says that the state should punish an offender in a fitting way because he deserves it for having done wrong over which he had control, even if such punishment would increase the overall amount of suffering in the world. Fairness theory says that the state should punish a criminal proportionately to his crime because in doing the crime he has voluntarily taken a free ride at the expense of law-abiding citizens; an offender gets the benefit of others' obedience without undergoing his fair share of the burden of obedience, with a punitive burden required to remove the unfair advantage he has obtained, regardless of whether society would be happier without that punishment being imposed. Finally, censure theory says that the state should punish a lawbreaker in proportion to his injustice for which he was responsible in order to stand up for the worth of his victims or to treat the lawbreaker as an agent with autonomy as opposed to an animal or automaton, again, even if the consequences for the general welfare would be better without such punishment.

Of course, these three kinds of retributive tracking are not identical to the relatively uncontroversial cases of non-retributive tracking considered above. The most striking difference is that the non-retributive tracking cases are ones in which burdens are unavoidable. Someone must suffer the monetary cost of a sweater, death, a lack of medical treatment, or a reduced amount of money, and the question is whether it should be the innocent or the guilty who undergo the burden. Retributive tracking differs from these cases in that it demands a burden be imposed even if such

---

12 Barring extreme amendments to the cases, particularly in which the autonomy of third parties would be gravely compromised by tracking responsible choice.

burden is entirely avoidable. Retributivists do not demand the state to negatively sanction the guilty only when necessary to protect the innocent from crime; their defining point is prescribing harm to the guilty regardless of whether it will prevent harm to the innocent.

While this is a difference between the cases, it is not an unwelcome one. After all, an analogy works by comparing two different but relevantly similar sorts of cases, one of which is less controversial than the other. I cannot invoke a case that is too similar to retributivism, lest I beg the question by proffering one that is just as controversial as retributivism. So, I have suggested non-retributive cases that I presume those who reject retributive judgement would accept (at least if – but not only if – they also accept the principle of respect of persons), and I now point out that they are relevantly similar to retributive judgement; for they all involve tracking responsible choice at the expense of the general welfare.

It remains for me to point out how this argument undercuts any claim to a tension between understanding another person and her deeds, on the one hand, and having epistemic reason to believe that retributive judgement is morally appropriate, on the other. Suppose I am correct that respect for persons requires retributive judgement in response to responsible wrongdoing (strong evidence for which is that respect for persons requires analogous non-retributive tracking of responsible choice at substantial cost to the general welfare). If respect requires retributive judgement, and if respect for persons is sound, then one is justified in believing that retributive judgement is justified any time one comes to understand another agent and her actions. Understanding another person and her behaviour simply serves the function of indicating the degree of blame she warrants, if any, from a retributive perspective.

For instance, suppose that an agent has murdered his spouse for the insurance money, that one comes to learn this of the agent, and that one discovers in this agent's background no external or internal factors that substantially mitigate. That is, imagine one comes to understand the agent, in whatever sense one prefers, and learns that the agent made a choice to hire a hit man to kill his wife for the purpose of obtaining money, where such a choice was largely within his control in the sense that he was, say, neither brainwashed into doing so, nor had an abusive upbringing that irreparably damaged his capacity for empathy. One learns that he wanted some excitement in his life and calculated that the easiest way to obtain it would be by means of murder of someone whom he no longer loved. In such a case, respect for persons entails that, upon coming to understand the man, one will discover plenty of epistemic reason to judge retributively and therefore impose harsh punishment.

One might suspect that the thought experiment is incoherent, in the sense that trauma simply must underlie the man's caring about being able to afford to take a cruise in the Bahamas with a hooker more than his spouse's life. But such immoral behaviour is not invariably the product of trauma. In my ethics classes I routinely ask how many of my students would be willing to press a Button of Death™ if such existed and if they could get away with doing so. Pressing this hypothetical button would put a million dollars into a Swiss bank account in the button-presser's name but would cause an innocent stranger to die a painful and protracted death. In almost every class I have taught, about 10 per cent to 15 per cent of the students are willing to raise their hands and publicly announce that they would commit murder for money if they would not get caught. Surely, not all of these students have been traumatized. Understanding the history of those who have not been traumatized would reveal no reason to refrain from harsh retributive censure if they pressed an actual Button of Death™.

In fact, my argument entails that understanding *never* undermines retributive judgement of persons. To see why not, consider those cases in which one might be tempted to think otherwise. Suppose that upon understanding another person, one discovers factors that have substantially reduced the control he had over his criminal action. For example, poverty, addiction, abuse, passion, neurosis, ideology and duress might cause a person to commit crime, and such causes can greatly reduce a person's control over the crime. Reduction of control over an action is a reduction of an agent's responsibility for it, where reduction of responsibility means reduced reason for the agent to bear a burden for having performed the action. When one comes to understand a person and thereby learns that control over a wrongful deed was weak, then one will obtain evidence that punishment is either out of place entirely or must be reduced.

Now, notice that it is *precisely retributive judgement* that most likely underwrites that evidence. Retributive judgement is the practice of imposing negative sanctions on people fundamentally because of, and invariably in proportion to, their responsible wrongdoing, where degree of responsibility is a function of degree of control.[13] If an agent did a wrong that he could not control at all and hence was not responsible for (or if he did no wrong), then retributive judgement would forbid any punishment of him. And if the agent did wrong over which he had less than full control, and hence was less than fully responsible for it, then retributive judgement would require less punishment of him than would have been required for a fully responsible act. To maintain that no or less punishment is justified because of uncontrollable factors that fully or partially excuse wrongful behaviour is best construed as a matter of judging retributively.[14]

---

13 This identification of proportionate control with proportionate responsibility and warranted proportionate burden in retributive judgement is also found in the non-retributive tracking cases discussed above. In Tort, for example, if you have ruined my sweater simply because you wanted to express your disgust, then you were in control of your action and hence were responsible for it so as to warrant the burden of replacing the sweater. But if you dumped wine and mustard on my sweater because you were intentionally tripped, or because someone threatened your child if you did not, then the control over, and hence responsibility for, your action would be greatly reduced and you would not be liable to pay for the sweater (the tripper and kidnapper would be liable).

14 Utilitarians can of course accept the concept of a mitigating factor, but they cannot conceive of the mitigating factor fundamentally in terms of facts about the past. Instead, any basic reason to lighten a penalty for a utilitarian must appeal to facts about the future, namely, the consequences of a light penalty.

In sum, it is of course true that understanding another person and his deed *sometimes* reveals mitigating factors requiring one not to punish him or not to punish harshly. However, that is quite different from the claim that understanding is ever evidence that one ought not *judge retributively*. And, in fact, it is retributivism that best entails and explains the claim that understanding sometimes reveals mitigating factors – those related to reduced control over the action – requiring one not to punish or not to punish harshly.

IV. Causality and Commonality in the Opposing View

I have argued that since respect for persons requires tracking responsible choice even at the expense of the general welfare, which includes retributive judgement, coming to understand a person will never provide evidence against retributivism, but instead will invariably provide evidence of what retributivism exactly requires in a given case. In this section, I consider four defences of the contrary view that understanding reveals the disrespectfulness or otherwise impermissibility of retributive judging, which defences are made by other contributors to this volume. My basic strategy against all four arguments is to advance this *reductio*: if understanding another person were to reveal full-blown retributive judging of him to be unjustified, then understanding would also reveal non-retributive tracking to be unjustified, which is absurd.

Liberty of spontaneity: no unmoved mover

Pedro Tabensky argues that retributive censure, particularly in its desert version, is justifiable only if people have libertarian free will. To be able to deserve blame, one must not only be free from antecedent natural causes, but also be an originating source of causes in nature. '(I)n order to be morally responsible one would have to be responsible for the first causes – the *causa sui* – of one's moves and that would involve situating the will, or a component of the will at any rate, outside of the causal chain of events that constitutes a human life.' When we understand people, we discover they are not unmoved movers; instead we become aware of the particular causes that have determined them to act. Hence, understanding people invariably reveals they are not responsible for their behaviour of the sort that could ground retributive censure.

The logic of Tabensky's argument oddly entails a rejection of the non-retributive tracking cases discussed above. Take, for instance, Tort, in which you have ruined my sweater merely out of aesthetic distaste for it. Surely the burden should be on you to replace my sweater, because you are the one responsible for having ruined it – and that is so even if we assume that more well-being would be produced if I paid for it. But Tabensky cannot say this, for you are not an unmoved mover. Since you did not start a causal chain, but were merely a cog in a causal chain that had already begun, you are not, in his view, responsible for your action in such a way as to warrant the imposition of a burden. By Tabensky's reasoning, to decide who ought to pay for the sweater, we cannot appeal to something about the past action of the person who ruined it, but instead must appeal to something about the future such as utility, which, I submit, is patently unjust.

Similarly, Tabensky is forced to say that the wife is not clearly entitled to the scarce medical treatment in Rationing. Recall here that her husband has deceptively broken his vows by having lots of unprotected sex with other women, and has infected himself and his wife with HIV as a result. Common sense says not merely that, if only one party can receive antiretroviral treatment, it must be the wife since she is not responsible for her condition and her husband is, but also that the wife must be offered the treatment even if more *eudaimonia* or welfare would be produced in the future by giving it to the husband. But, again, Tabensky cannot make this judgement, since the husband's actions were not the product of a will that operates independently of antecedent natural causes.

In order to sensibly account for the non-retributive tracking cases, one must cash out responsibility of the sort warranting imposition of a burden in terms of an agent who is, in some naturalistic sense, in control of his behaviour. Control is, roughly, a matter of one's actions being determined by one's reflection, where one's reflection is of course determined in turn by antecedent natural causes. If control is sufficient for responsibility in non-retributive tracking cases, then it is also sufficient for responsibility in retributive tracking cases; being an unmoved mover is not necessary. With regard to people who have control over their behaviour, institutions ought to place burdens on those who have chosen wrongly, even at substantial cost to the general welfare.

I think the deep mistake that leads Tabensky astray is the common one of thinking that, for us to be responsible for having performed an act in such a way as to warrant the imposition of a burden, we must have been in control of the conditions that have put us in control of our behaviour.[15] Tabensky says that, to show that a retributive ethic is justified, one must specify 'not only some conditions that move us qua responsible agents, but also the conditions that move us to become responsible agents in the first instance'. I claim the second conditions are unnecessary for being responsible for a wrongful action of the sort that warrants a proportionate burden for having performed it. For one to be responsible in that sense, one need not have been in control of the fact that one has control over one's behaviour. This point is illustrated by the four non-retributive tracking cases. And it is fundamentally explained by the principle of respect for persons: since the ability to control one's choices has a dignity, it makes sense to honour it, and hence to track its exercise, wherever it happens to exist and however it was brought about, even if it was brought about (as it always is) by factors over which one lacks control.

---

15 See my 'Arbitrariness, Justice, and Respect', for discussion of this claim in the context of economic justice.

Liberty of indifference: no causal indeterminism

Kai Nielsen's account of what is necessary for retributive censure to be permissible is somewhat weaker than Tabensky's. Unlike Tabensky, Nielsen does not say that one must be an unmoved mover; instead, Nielsen claims that one must have the ability to do otherwise than one does. And since the fact of determinism means that we lack this ability, retributive censure is disrespectful, or at least impermissible. Nielsen says,

> When we come to clearly see that a person could not have done otherwise, no matter how hard he tried or because he was not capable of even trying or that he was so unteachably blinded that he could not see the wrongness of what he did, we, if we are reasonable, rational, reflective and have some of the milk of human kindness in ourselves, will withhold retributive blame. [quoted from Nielsen's piece in this collection. (Ch. 8, this volume, p.***.)]

In sum, when one comes to understand a person, one always learns that he lacked the ability to otherwise than he did and hence discovers epistemic reason not to judge retributively.

Nielsen believes that a morality without retributive judging would still be attractive; we would have 'a kinder, gentler, more tolerant world'. Perhaps, but one would also have a morally upside-down world in which non-retributive tracking is out of place, since all choices are ones that have been necessitated. That is, one would live in a world in which, in the Other-Defence case, the peacekeeper lets the aggressors take machetes to the innocent Tutsi woman. Recall that I assumed in this case that protecting the innocent Tutsi would require killing all five aggressors and, further, that more intrinsic value (of whatever sort) would be produced if the five aggressors lived and she did not. I claim that killing the aggressors under these conditions is obviously the right act, but Nielsen cannot account for that claim since the aggressors cannot help themselves. Because the assassins cannot do otherwise, in his eyes, they are not responsible of a sort warranting imposition of a burden because of their aggression. I hesitate to call this a 'kinder', 'gentler' and 'more tolerant' world than a retributive one, but, if it is, it is also disrespectful, unjust and, to me, horrifying.

Nielsen's rationale for thinking that retributive tracking requires the ability to do otherwise than one does stems from the same mistaken reasoning I have suggested moves Tabensky. Both believe that, to be responsible, one must have been in control of the fact that one is now in control of one's behaviour. Nielsen says of someone who wants to do a wrong act,

> (H)is very wanting to do it and thinking that it is right itself rests on his genetic constitution and acculturation. And for that he could not have been responsible. He can't be his own parents or the controller of his initial situation. It is finally something which is out of his control. (Ch. 8, this volume, p. ***.)

As I have said above, with a Kantian ethic, one is at bottom required to express respect for an autonomous will because it has a superlative intrinsic value. How the capacity for autonomy came to be in existence is irrelevant. One may not have had control over the fact that one now has control over one's actions, but merely having such dignified control is sufficient to make it morally correct to track it as a way to express respect for it.

There but for the grace of god go I

Brian Penrose and Marc Fellman suggest a third distinct reason for thinking that understanding a person reveals the inappropriateness of imposing a negative sanction on her fundamentally because of, and in proportion to, wrongdoing for which she is responsible. Although Penrose and Fellman seem more interested in explaining what is happening when our censorious judgement in fact changes upon understanding another person, their discussion occasions awareness of an argument for thinking that our censorious judgement ought to change upon understanding. When we become aware of a person's nature and nurture, then, Penrose says,[16] we recognize that 'despite our initial impulse to judge in a condemnatory way, our own moral capacity to have done otherwise than the person being judged is often tenuous at best'. I take this remark to mean that, because we would have done the same wrong deed had we been in the wrongdoer's shoes (which we discover upon understanding him), we lack moral reason to censure him as retributive judgement would require.[17]

Now, what is it about the fact that we would have done the same thing had we been in the wrongdoer's situation that makes it inappropriate to impose a penalty on him because of, and proportionate to, an immoral act over which he had control? Neither Penrose nor Fellman answers this question. One possible answer might be this: the fact that we could not have avoided performing the same act as the wrongdoer indicates that causal determinism is true. However, since I have already critically discussed that issue in the context of Tabensky and Nielsen, I here look for other plausible explanations.

I can think of two that merit discussion. They at bottom make the common point that we are objectionably being arrogant in some way, if we both would have done the same thing as the wrongdoer and censure him retributively for his wrongdoing. Here is one reason for thinking that arrogance is present here: to punish another person because of his wrongdoing, when you also would have done wrong, is to treat the other person as though he is worse than you, which he is not. If you would

---

16 In his presentation at a conference devoted to Bernhard Schlink's *The Reader* that was held at the Johannesburg Goethe Institute in November 2004.

17 Penrose and Fellman might hold the weaker view that Vice does, that retributive judgement is not altogether out of place but must be tempered by mercy. Even if that is their view, the best argument I can develop on their behalf entails the stronger view that retributive judgement is entirely inappropriate.

have done wrong in the wrongdoer's situation, then you are just as bad a person as he is, even if you haven't performed as wrong an action. And if you are just as bad a person as he is, then to punish him for wrongdoing is to disrespectfully (or otherwise objectionably) act as though he is a worse person than you.

This argument is unconvincing. For one, retributive censure is in reaction to actions, not agents, and so does not express the attitude that the person being censured is a worse person. To punish retributively, as construed here, is not to base punishment on how bad a person is, but rather on how wrong her behaviour was. Now, one might still suspect that retributive censure can indirectly express something about the worth of persons even if it is directed in the first instance towards their acts. Consider, therefore, that censure could easily avoid expressing the attitude that the person censured is worse than the person censuring, if the person censuring were to allow the other to censure him in return. (I whip your back, you whip mine.) Hence, there is nothing inherent to retributive censure that makes it arrogant in the manner this argument maintains.

Let us consider a second argument for the claim that retributive judgement is arrogant in some way. The previous argument maintains that, in censuring retributively, you are putting another lower than you are, which he is not. We might instead try the line that, in censuring retributively, you are raising yourself higher than you are. A Christian reason for thinking that retributive censure is arrogant is that we are not qualified to censure retributively if we, too, would have done wrong. 'Let he who is without sin cast the first stone', where sin is mainly a function of character (perhaps that one is born with), not primarily of actions one has willed. In order to have the authority to punish on retributive grounds, an agent must have a very good – perhaps perfect – character, which character we always rediscover that we lack upon understanding another person and seeing that we would have also done the wrong that he did.

This Christian rationale clearly sets too high a standard for having the authority to retributively judge another person's actions, for it absurdly entails that non-retributive tracking is impermissible. In fact, the previous rationale for finding arrogance in retributivism also faces this *reductio*. The principle operative in both arrogance rationales is this: it objectionably treats yourself as superior to impose a burden on another person for having made a wrongful choice that you yourself would have also made (either because you are deeming yourself to have a certain authority that you lack, or because you are wrongly treating the other as worse than you). That principle deeply conflicts with our firm considered judgements in Tort, Other-Defence, Rationing and Wages, where we believe that it is permissible for an agent to impose burdens on the guilty instead of the innocent (at substantial expense to the general welfare), regardless of whether the agent would have also been guilty in a proximate possible world.

Take Other-Defence, for instance. Suppose that, after pleading with and warning the five machete-wielding aggressors, the UN peacekeeper shoots them in order to protect the innocent Tutsi woman (thereby reducing the aggregate of long-term well-being). Suppose further that he, too, would have been an aggressor had he been exposed to the xenophobic influences they had. It does not strike me as arrogant for the solider to use force in such a case, or, at the very least, not impermissibly arrogant, but the principle of the arrogance rationales entails that it is. From that perspective, the soldier is either impermissibly assuming that he has the purity of heart required to impose burdens in reaction to wrongdoing or impermissibly treating the aggressors as worse than himself. Neither is inherently true of harming the guilty to protect others from becoming victims, and hence I submit that neither is necessarily true of harming the guilty, say, to affirm the worth of victims (censure theory), to remove the unfair advantage the guilty have taken at the expense of law-abiding citizens (fairness theory), or even to give the guilty the penalty they deserve as a matter of respect for their capacity for autonomous choice (desert theory).

Frailty and fallibility

Unlike the previous arguments that reject retributive censure in its entirety, Samantha Vice (following Martha Nussbaum[18]) accepts retributivism but argues that it invariably must be tempered by mercy. To act on mercy is to impose a disproportionately light sanction. So, Vice is clearly not merely making the *retributive* claim that there can be mitigating factors that reduce the punishment a person should receive. Instead, merciful judgement by definition involves reducing punishment below whatever would be proportionate to the agent's degree of responsibility or control. Being merciful does not abjure retributivism in general, for it is to punish in light of a proportionate benchmark, though not strictly in accordance with it.

Vice claims that we always find evidence that mercy is warranted when we understand another person, but, interestingly, never (or very rarely) when we understand ourselves. Consider the other-regarding case first, where a party understands the general human condition and how it has led a particular offender to commit his offence. 'Placing himself in the position of another, he realizes that his own, similar frailties could easily have led him to do the same in those circumstances, and he will therefore be inclined towards gentleness. This identification itself depends upon thinking of humans as prone to making such mistakes, and of the world as encouraging them.'

I detect two distinct claims in this quotation. One is the idea of the party thinking that he, too, would have done the crime had he been in a like situation. I set this rationale aside, having addressed it above in the context of Penrose and Fellman. The other idea is that, even if the party does not think that he would have done the crime had he been in a like situation, the party does come to see that human beings are imperfect. Upon learning about human nature, one realizes that persons are commonly fallible and hence finds reason to punish somewhat less than is proportionate to how wrong the offence was and to how responsible the offender was

---

18 Martha Nussbaum, 'Equity and Mercy', *Philosophy and Public Affairs*, 1993, pp. 83–125 (Ch. 1, this volume, p. ***.) Marc Fellman's contribution, also in this volume, (Ch. 5) can also be read along these lines.

for it. '(I)f the human condition really is to be so frail, the circumstances of the world really so harsh, and people in general banal rather than extraordinary in their crimes, then imaginative engagement and mercy are indeed ideals for which to strive.'

Now, in the self-regarding case, Vice claims that mercy is not an ideal to pursue. Upon coming to understand oneself and one's wrongful actions in light of the human condition, according to Vice, one does not find reason to think one ought to temper one's guilt or to receive a disproportionately light penalty. Why not? It is important to quote Vice's two-part answer at length:

> To think that my background could mitigate responsibility and guilt would be to renounce agency and authority over myself: I am no longer answerable to others for who I am and what I do. To be in this position is no longer to be a moral agent among others; it is to forgo citizenship of the moral kingdom. And second, when I am able to consider my weaknesses as those merely typical of humanity, this cannot be used as mitigation if it leads one to terrible acts. To be morally mature is precisely not to be overwhelmed by ordinary weaknesses to commit extraordinary (or ordinary) crimes. (Ch. 4, this volume, p. 103.)

In short, Vice is claiming that, since one must treat oneself as a responsible agent, one must not be merciful to oneself in light of the frail and fallible human condition.

I claim, in response, that what is good for the goose is good for the gander. One has a moral obligation not merely to treat oneself as a responsible agent, but to treat any responsible agent as such. If treating oneself as a responsible agent forbids disproportionately light guilt and punishment despite typically weak human nature, then, by analogy, treating others as responsible agents forbids disproportionately light censure despite typically weak human nature. Since we must treat others as citizens of the moral kingdom and acknowledge that others can be morally mature, we must judge them retributively in the same way Vice maintains we must judge ourselves. I can see no reason for thinking that respect for others does not require the same thing that respect for oneself does.

Now, someone other than Vice and myself might suggest that a parity does obtain between self and other, but not the one I have suggested. I have proposed that, just as one should not be merciful to oneself in light of the banality of evil, so one should not be merciful to others in light of it. However, a critic might instead think that, just as one should be merciful to others in light of the banality of evil, so one should be merciful to oneself in light of it. I need to offer a reason to reject this merciful parity in favour of the retributive one.

The reason to favour a retributive parity between treatment of oneself and others is that the merciful parity has counterintuitive implications about non-retributive tracking. For instance, if the generally frail and fallible human condition were sufficient reason to impose a disproportionately light punitive burden for a crime, then it would be sufficient reason to impose a disproportionately light compensatory burden for a tort. Concretely, because people are typically bad at restraining their impulses, a judge should reason that, in the Tort case, you need not pay for the entire cost of the sweater you have ruined. However, that is absurd. Surely, you must pay for the total cost of the sweater, for you are solely and fully responsible for having ruined it.

The kernel of truth in Vice's discussion, I believe, is that, from a retributive standpoint, the scale of penalties for human beings should perhaps be less than that for other, possible agents who would not face so many temptations, pressures and obstacles. If intelligent creatures from Alpha Centauri had weaker ids and stronger empathy with strangers, then, generally speaking, the censure they receive for committing a given wrongdoing should be stronger than what we receive. Compared to these agents, humans are generally less responsible for their wrongdoing because we have less control over it. However, it remains the case that, with respect to the human scale of penalties, any one of us ought to receive the full penalty that is proportionate to his wrongdoing and degree of responsibility for it.

V. Conclusion

I conclude this essay by quoting from *The Reader*.[19] Many contributors to this volume take *The Reader* to express a tension between understanding and retributive judging, but I claim (as Peta Bowden and Emma Rooksby do in their contribution) that there are strong themes and clear passages illustrating the thesis that understanding serves the function of helping one to retributively judge more accurately.

The Reader is about a relationship between Michael and Hanna. After their romantic relationships ends, Michael learns that Hanna had been a guard at a concentration camp in Nazi Germany during the Second World War. At the camp she selected which prisoners would be killed, and, in the process of moving prisoners from the camp, she allowed a group of them kept in a church to burn to death. Eventually, Hanna is put on trial for her crimes, and Michael observes the prosecution, the guilty verdict, and the sentence of life in prison handed down.

Michael often objects to the nature of the trial, but those passages from *The Reader* that might be deemed critical of retributive judging as such are, I think, better construed as critical of legalistic judging. In fact, Michael's central objection to the trial is one that a retributivist would make. Specifically, Michael complains of 'oversimplification' (p. 179). To make a well grounded retributive judgement, one should have an intimate knowledge of the complex character of the wrongdoing, the wrongdoer, and the extent to which the wrongdoer had control over the wrongdoing. Michael laments the fact that the court sometimes is not aware of mitigating factors such as Hanna's illiteracy (pp. 132-37), sometimes hurries things along and does not pay sufficient attention (pp. 136-37), and sometimes is aware of mitigating factors but refuses to treat them as such (pp. 128-29). All these are criticisms of a trial that is *insufficiently* retributive for not accurately appraising the true, intricate nature of the crime and the criminal.

---

19 Bernhard Schlink, *The Reader*, Carol Brown Janeway (trans.), New York: Vintage Books, 1997.

Other cases where one might initially see tension between judging and understanding can also be fairly read otherwise. For instance, at one point in the text, Michael finds it hard to reconcile understanding and judging (p. 157). However, eventually Michael does judge Hanna. He believes it was right for her to be proportionately punished in light of what she had done in the past (not because of what punishment would bring about in the future), and he believes so in light of a fuller understanding of her and her background than the court had (pp. 137, 201).

For another example, at two points in the trial Hanna asks the judge what he would have done if he had been in her shoes (pp. 111, 128), which might be taken to suggest that he should seek to understand her rather than judge her. However, it is instead reasonable to see Hanna as requesting the judge to become better informed of her and the situation she faced before presuming to judge her. Consider that, toward the end of the story, when Hanna has completed her prison term, she says to Michael:

> I always had the feeling that no one understood me anyway, that no one knew who I was and what made me do this or that. And you know, when no one understands you, then no one can call you to account. Not even the court could call me to account. But the dead can. They understand. They don't even have to have been there, but if they were, they understand even better (p. 198).

Setting aside the empirical assertion that no living person is capable of understanding – which Michael fairly questions (p. 201) – the normative principles expressed are that calling to account is appropriate and that it is facilitated by empirical information about a person and her deeds. Understanding Hanna would have involved apprehending, at bottom, poor judgement on her part. Becoming a guard to cover her illiteracy, she valued avoiding the embarrassment that would come from others learning of her illiteracy more than she valued avoiding participation in a sinister injustice. And she ranked maintaining order and being a good worker over a need to save the innocent lives of those trapped in the church. Here there are, from a retributive standpoint, factors warranting punishment as well as factors warranting mitigation in its imposition, which factors one discovers upon coming to understand the offender and her offence.

It is striking that it is the wrongdoer herself who expresses this viewpoint. Hanna does not say that to understand all is to forgive all; rather, her claim is that to understand all is to be in a position to call to account. If calling to account means retributively censuring, then she is saying that to understand is to be able to censure retributively. In short, judging is apt because of understanding.[20]

---

20 For helpful comments on an earlier draft of this essay, I thank Ward Jones and Pedro Tabensky.

Chapter 11

Understanding Condemnation: A Plea for Appropriate Judgement

Peta Bowden and Emma Rooksby

Editor's Introduction

Following Marion Smiley's pragmatic approach to moral responsibility and using *The Reader* as a case study, Peta Bowden and Emma Rooksby argue for the view that Michael's experiences, particularly regarding the tension between judging and understanding, are '*internal* to social practices of condemning'. They choose to 'sidestep' issues relating to the metaphysics of free will for they do not believe that such an approach will truly capture the complex context-sensitive roles of our condemnatory practices; roles which are constitutive of 'socio-ethical' arrangements. Their pragmatic methodology aims at showing how it is that moral-responsibility-entailing practices are constitutive of our self understandings and define our 'socio-ethical' roles; roles which are 'the basis of social life'. Following Hannah Arendt, they believe that 'withdrawal from practices of condemnation, imperfect though they may be, is a betrayal both of our own responsiveness to the social relations in which we participate and of the potential responsiveness of those whom we would blame'. In light of this, they think that the tension between judging and understanding is part and parcel of our morally complex lives and does not diminish our need to condemn (when appropriate). Proper understanding of the full complexity and specificity of moral lives will lead to proper judging, including proper condemning. Not to condemn, when appropriate, would amount to taking a step outside of the moral space that defines human 'socio-ethical' life. Following a very different trajectory, Bowden and Rooksby reach relevantly similar conclusions to Thad Metz and to Andrew Gleeson as expressed in their contributions.

* * *

'I wanted to pose myself both tasks – understanding and condemnation. But it was impossible to do both.' (Bernhard Schlink, *The Reader*, p. 156)

Introduction

Michael, the protagonist in Bernhard Schlink's novel *The Reader*, discovers that his former lover, Hanna, is on trial for crimes committed while working as a Nazi prison guard. Shocked, Michael struggles to condemn Hanna's crime as it deserves, while also understanding how she could have acted as she did. He concludes that the attempt to understand Hanna's actions undermines the force of his condemnation, while condemnation without understanding is a betrayal of her as a person.

On one interpretation Michael's dilemma illustrates the incompatibility of determinism with the contra-causal freedom necessary for moral responsibility: to both understand Hanna and to blame her is to work on two inconsistent presumptions that she both does, and does not, possess contra-causal freedom (or metaphysical 'free will'). On this interpretation, Michael's dilemma can be resolved by accepting determinism, and moving beyond the reactive attitudes of blame and condemnation.[1]

But other, less radical interpretations of the tension Michael experiences in trying to both judge Hanna and understand her are also available.[2] In this chapter we argue that the tension Michael experiences does not result from an apprehension of metaphysical – or epistemological – inconsistencies, but from other sources. First, Michael starts out with an incomplete understanding of the complexity and significance of social practices of condemnation (i.e. social practices of moral understanding and responsibility); second, he assumes, too hastily, that the truth of determinism – or the epistemological demands of understanding – require the renunciation of the practice of making moral judgements. On this alternative interpretation, the tension

---

1   Two clarifications concerning our use of this interpretation are necessary here. First, the stark terms of this interpretation allude to textbook discussions of the free will/determinism dilemma. Most philosophers who are cognizant of the problem have, of course, developed more sophisticated accounts of metaphysical free will and/or determinism in order to soften the dilemma. We highlight this interpretation, however, because philosophical discussions of moral responsibility are almost exclusively devoted to the fine-tuning of accounts of contra-causal freedom. Second, we do not want to claim that this interpretation is the grounding position for *The Reader* (or for any of the characters in *The Reader*). Indeed, discussion with Bernhard Schlink suggests that the incompatibility that is his concern is epistemological rather than ontological. Although our target in this paper is the metaphysical incompatibility thesis, our arguments are also relevant to versions of epistemological incompatibility that lead to a rejection of condemnation.

2   For example, understandings and ascriptions of causal responsibility can be seen to be mutually implicative: notions of intention and of knowing what a person is doing that are central to understanding that person dissolve without allied notions of what is or is not under her self-control. As the character Hanna observes, 'when no one understands you, no one can call you to account', Bernhard Schlink, *The Reader*, London: Phoenix, p. 196. All subsequent references to this work are given in the text by page number in parentheses.

Michael experiences can be read as *internal* to social practices of condemning, in the sense that it is not related to the question of whether or not to have a practice of condemning, but to that of when condemnation is *appropriate*.

As we shall argue, pervasive features of the social practice of condemnation make such tensions commonplace and sometimes warranted. The practice is relational and multiple, or context-relative: what is appropriate is not solely in the hands of the condemner, and not simply a matter of applying necessary and sufficient conditions to a set of facts.[3]

The Role and Significance of Practices of Condemnation

Outside a certain stream of metaphysical debate, contra-causal freedom is not generally considered necessary for blameworthiness, or even relevant to ascriptions and assessments of moral responsibility.[4] Practices of condemnation, and of blame more generally, can still function so long as human beings can be said to have some, perhaps very weak, form of control over their behaviour. In this paper, however, we propose to sidestep metaphysical debates about free will, and to focus instead on explicating certain tensions internal to social practices of condemnation. Drawing on Marion Smiley's pragmatic account of moral responsibility, in *Moral Responsibility and the Boundaries of Community*,[5] we explore the important socio-ethical role played by practices of condemnation, and their inclusion of norm-infused empirical

---

3   This view is not, and should not be read as, culturally relativist. As we argue in what follows, we hold that practices of condemnation are not unitary, and that attributions of causal and moral responsibility are contestable. But, we do not agree with the relativist that condemnations (or other moral judgements) are right or wrong, appropriate or inappropriate, relative only to particular *cultural* frameworks. We do not accord cultural frameworks any particular priority in determining whether a particular condemnation is appropriate, or accept an 'anything goes' approach to condemnation. Also, unlike many relativists, we note that there is widespread agreement regarding the condemnability of certain actions and moral characters. Thanks to Kai Horsthemle for suggesting we clarify this point.

4   Several theories, both pragmatic (Peter Strawson, 'Freedom and Resentment', in *Freedom and Resentment and other Essays*. London: Methuen, 1974, pp. 1–25; Marion Smiley, *Moral Responsibility and the Boundaries of Community: Power and Accountability from a Pragmatic Point of View*, Chicago: Chicago University Press, 1992; Margaret Walker, *Moral Understandings: A Feminist Study in Ethics*, London and New York: Routledge, 1998; R. Jay Wallace, *Responsibility and the Moral Sentiments*, Cambridge, MA: Harvard University Press, 1994) and compatabilist (John Martin Fischer and Mark Ravizza, *Responsibility and Control: A Theory of Moral Responsibility*, Cambridge: Cambridge University Press, 1998; Harry Frankfurt, 1988. *The Importance of What We Care About*, Cambridge: Cambridge University Press, 1988; Ishtiyaque Haji, *Moral Appraisability: Puzzles, Proposals and Perplexities*, Oxford: Oxford University Press, 1998; Susan Wolf, 'Asymmetrical Freedom', in John Martin Fischer (ed.), *Moral Responsibility*, Ithaca, NY: Cornell University Press, 1986, pp. 225–40), are extant.

5   Smiley, *Moral Responsibility, op. cit.*

assessments. This exploration elucidates the moral value of condemnation, and helps us to defend our view that tensions inherent to the practice of condemnation can, to some extent, be dissolved by moral understanding.

We begin by describing, in general terms, the practice of moral condemnation, and its important socio-ethical role. Condemnation is one of many kinds of moral judgement that play related though distinct roles in social life.[6] Like moral judgements more generally, condemnation and blame are pervasive in social interactions as part of the 'rule-following' that structures any meaningful practical engagement; they map the dynamic and variegated boundaries of inclusion and exclusion, of accession and violation. From the micro-moralities of interpersonal intimacies, exemplified in *The Reader* by Michael and Hanna's fights, threats and surrenders (47), to larger contexts of social coherence and law (such as intergenerational shaming in contemporary Germany and the trials of Nazi collaborators like Hanna), judgements between the acceptable and unacceptable, excusable and inexcusable, conscionable and unconscionable,[7] are part of the enabling conditions of social relationships.

Among these judgements, condemnation is distinctive in that it is a very strong form of blame, typically (though not exclusively) applied only to extreme contexts of atrocity. Sometimes condemnation is also judged to warrant punishments in the form of exclusion from the community (such as shunning or incarceration). However, the intricacy of practices of condemnation far outruns the sharp lines associated with the extremes of these formally institutionalized versions. Along with assignments of blame and reproach, setting the terms of what has and hasn't been done, determining the limits on excuse-making and the measures of punishment and forgiveness, they also include resisting, deflecting and negotiating, limiting one's exposure to damage, showing shame, remorse and offering reparations. Adding to this complexity and variety of relational forms is the diversity of the objects of condemnation. We can condemn and be condemned for particular actions and goals, for roles we create or take up, for exercising or not exercising discretion in those roles, for outcomes from our actions and consequences that ensue from those outcomes, for attitudes, dispositions, habits and traits.[8] Additionally, every tiny move in these comings and

---

6   For reasons of space, we restrict our discussion largely to condemnatory judgements.

7   Determinist arguments, with their emphasis on the links between judgement, and chains of cause and effect, may seem to suggest that judgements are made solely in consequentialist terms. However, it is important to note that the social practices of judgement which we describe here are not necessarily based on consequentialist grounds but may include deontologically based ascriptions. For example, we may condemn the loss of innocent lives in war, regardless of longer term outcomes of the violence. Thanks to Thaddeus Metz for suggesting we clarify this point.

8   While philosophers and legal theorists may be concerned to distinguish condemnation of persons from condemnation of their acts, everyday talk does not usually take up this issue. In the passage in which Michael claims that it is impossible for him to satisfy the tasks of both understanding and condemnation, he seems to slip easily from saying 'I wanted simultaneously to understand Hanna's crime and to condemn it' to 'even as I wanted to understand Hanna, failing to understand her meant betraying her all over again.' (156)

goings of interpersonal exchanges is coloured by the imperfections and vulnerabilities that characterize all human affairs, the limits of capacities and personalities, and our understandings of situations and contexts.

Condemnation thus involves a complex of judgements, made by particular people of particular objects, framed by particular contexts, relationships, and social and ethical norms and expectations. And such judgements are never pure. They are perhaps even inevitably tragic as they struggle to connect the universal and the particular.[9]

Throughout these many-faceted and imperfect judgements are explicit and implicit ascriptions and expressions of agency and responsibility. It should be noted, though, that on our account of condemnation as a set of social practices, issues of agency and responsibility are negotiated in ways that differ markedly from orthodox (incompatibilist) understandings of moral responsibility, on which causal connection with harm and the possession of metaphysical free will are taken to be jointly sufficient for blameworthiness.[10] On our account, the practical relations of condemnation are internally linked with and shaped by other judgements that attribute certain outcomes and states of affairs to human agency, and that take ourselves and others to be to some extent answerable for these outcomes. Our position does not dismiss the relevance of causal chains of events so important to the incompatibilist position, but insists that they are only one of many elements drawn together in judgements of moral responsibility, including condemnations. Rather, as Marion Smiley puts it, people '*choose* within them a particular act or event to hold causally responsible for the harm in question, on the basis of both physical and social considerations'.[11] As we illustrate below, such choices, which might be called empirico-normative assessments, also come into play in ascriptions of blameworthiness to people judged to be causally responsible for harms.

At the same time, these ascriptions are also expressions of willingness to take up responsibility for one's judgements,[12] and to respect the potential responsibility of the condemned. To condemn is to affirm another's agency and responsibility, and one's own, to acknowledge both of us as participants in a shared project. To be an object of condemnation is to be judged capable of responding to and participating

---

9   Immanuel Kant, *The Critique of Judgement [1790]*, trans. James Creed Meredith, Oxford: Clarendon Press, 1952, claims that judging is the activity of subsuming particulars under relevant universals or finding the appropriate universal with which to grasp a given particular. See Ronald Beiner, *Political Judgment*, Chicago: University of Chicago Press, 1983, for a discussion of the fragility of political judgement.

10   Smiley, *Moral Responsibility*, *op. cit.*, pp. 7–9.

11   *Ibid.*, p. 205.

12   Expressions of willingness to take responsibility for judgements are, like other human actions, themselves amenable to moral judgement. An expression of willingness to take responsibility for one's judgements doesn't guarantee that one's judgements have actually been made 'responsibly', with care and reflection; they may have been made 'irresponsibly', unreflectively applying biased or individual social standards for condemnation. Either way, just as assertions can (ordinarily) be read as expressing the speaker's willingness to vouch for their truth, so condemnations can (ordinarily) be read as expressing the condemner's willingness to take responsibility for her judgement.

in the reciprocal relations that sustain communal life, even if the condemned, or one of her actions, is judged not to have lived up to that capacity. Withdrawal from practices of condemnation, imperfect though they may be, is a betrayal both of our own responsiveness to the social relations in which we participate and of the potential responsiveness of those whom we would blame.[13]

From this perspective, we can see that condemnation is not simply a matter of ascriptions and appraisals, but has a number of more specific functions. Condemnation, like other moral judgements, performs a guiding or regulative function: condemning indicates that we (as individuals and as members of a community) hold others to certain expectations, and that they have not lived up to (the most basic of) those expectations. Its carrots and sticks aim to persuade others and ourselves to accept those expectations as the grounds of participation in interpersonal and communal engagement. Condemnation is important to resisting the moral drift and excuse-making that undermine the relational expectations that it was meant to protect. Compassion rather than lack of moral responsibility may be the motivation for claims such as 'anyone would have done the same in this context' (for example, a context in which one's agency has been de-moralized by illiteracy). However, the empathy that links a wrongdoer's moral weakness with our fears that we too would not be able to stand up to our own moral principles in contexts of duress, readily becomes an excuse for resistance to seeing that there is anything wrong with what is being done. Failure to hold to the boundaries of moral expectations may be a failure to sustain the basis of social life. (See below: 'Some pressures against appropriate condemnation'.)

Condemnation also has an expressive function: our voicing of moral judgements expresses our expectations of what it is to be a self-in-relation, to go on 'indomitably expecting', as Simone Weil puts it 'that good and not evil will be done' to us.[14] Our (norms of) appraisal are part and parcel of our communicative expressions with each other concerning what others are doing; and our standards of individual responsibility and self-control express recognition of the relationship between blamer and blamed.[15] In the words of Barbara Houston, 'Our expectation of good will [. . .] reveals that we regard ourselves as persons of worth and dignity; as persons who are vulnerable, [. . .] who can be hurt by indifference or contempt [. . .] and as persons who are capable of reciprocity in these matters.'[16]

Condemnations express our view that the condemned has not met (the most basic of) these expectations and carries the burden of redressing this wrong (whether or not she is capable of doing so). In blaming others we express our feelings of disappointment, resentment and anger, and our practices of condemnation shape

---

13 Hannah Arendt, *Eichmann in Jerusalem*, New York: Viking, 1963, gives an insightful analysis of the significance of the link between judging and individual moral responsibility.

14 Simone Weil, 'Human Personality', in Sian Miles (ed.), *Simone Weil: An Anthology*, New York: Weidenfeld & Nicolson, 1986, p. 51.

15 Smiley, *Moral Responsibility*, *op. cit*, pp. 241–2.

16 Barbara Houston, 'In Praise of Blame', *Hypatia: A Journal of Feminist Philosophy* 7(4), 1992, p. 41.

the meaning of these feelings. When we are the objects of blame, we typically find that feelings of being somehow obliged or bound to respond, of reciprocal resentment or anger, of remorse, repentance or shame, or of being misunderstood or unjustly maligned are aroused. Accordingly, practices of condemnation are important expressions of our moral attitudes, not simply instruments for control and management of interpersonal relations.

Intricate in these expressive and guiding functions of condemnation is the shaping, defining and reproducing of shared understandings, of what it means to be a responsible agent, of what the moral purpose of particular relationships and communities might be. Practices of condemnation are not only responsive to established socio-ethical expectations, but also shape our understandings of who is accountable to whom for what, what values are protected, how injury to them might be redressed, and so on.

Together, these functions of condemnation are essential to the ethical give-and-take of social interaction. For instance, the expressive function of condemnation (either by or on behalf of victims) is, in some cases at least, vital for the psychological survival of victims. Victims of atrocity may blame themselves, if they have nobody else to blame.[17] They may be psychologically crippled, filled with fear and alienation, by the belief that what happened to them is sanctioned or tolerated by others. And for the condemned, condemnation can enable rehabilitation, a move from social exclusion to re-integration: subjected to condemnation, the condemned may come to feel, and to express, remorse and contrition for her actions. There may also be potential for reconciliation between the victim and the condemned; as noted above, the condemned may offer reparations and express remorse or willingness to reform, or engage in a process of purification through confession, and the victim may accept these gestures and even grant absolution.

So, to summarize, moral condemnation is important to the sustenance of the community, to the articulation of the socio-ethical expectations of its members and to victims' recovery from extreme violations of those expectations. From the perspective of the condemned, condemnation signals that they have violated social expectations; unless their crimes are judged to be of intolerable atrocity, condemnation also offers possibilities for rehabilitation and reconciliation.

While they sustain and protect moral conceptions and boundaries of interpersonal relationships, at least implicitly including the condemned in the realm of potentially responsible participants, practices of condemnation at the same time divide us into those who are worthy participants and those who are not, those who merit inclusion in communal practices and those who are unable (at least temporarily) to 'follow the rules'. In so doing they obstruct or withdraw good will, frequently inflicting harm and injury on those indicted. It is comforting to the condemner to argue, along with Strawson, that this breach of the general social demand that others should be spared suffering is 'the consequence of *continuing* to view [her or] him as a member of the

---

17 For example, the tragic breakdown of Sophie Zawistowska recounted in William Styron's novel *Sophie's Choice*, London: Corgi, 1983, is a poignant illustration of this dynamic.

moral community; only as one who has offended against its demands'.[18] However, this may be little comfort to the condemned who are excluded from social intercourse, and to condemners concerned about these divisive effects, the ruptures of attachments and the risks of mistakes. Consequently the conditions for, and associated difficulties with, exercising appropriate moral condemnation deserve close attention.

Assessments Involved in Exercising Appropriate Moral Condemnation

In this section we will unpack some of the empirico-normative assessments that form part of the practice of condemnation, illustrating that the identification of causal connections between individuals and harms is only one part of the practice. Using *The Reader* to illustrate, we show how empirico-normative assessments, which are often applied unselfconsciously by 'condemners', may create tensions between judging and understanding. We suggest that a deeper understanding of the circumstances of the condemned, one that grasps the impact of these factors, can help to diffuse the tensions, or at least make it possible to work through them. In *The Reader*, Michael's struggle to come to terms with Hanna's crime (at least partially) exemplifies this process; in this section we examine some of these factors, showing how and to what degree Michael comes to understand their roles in the practice of condemnation.

As we illustrated above in the section on the 'role and significance of practices of condemnation', condemnation expresses, regulates and shapes socio-ethical expectations, such as those applied to all community members, and those associated with various social roles. Normative and moral assumptions concerning social roles, community boundaries and values, expectations of competence, knowledge and levels of control over our actions are bound up in assessments of the facts of the situation. These assumptions and expectations are frequently complex and opaque. Judgements incorporate and take into account 'a variety of normative expectations that are themselves grounded not only in our configuration of social roles, but in the interests, power relations, and structures of community that support such roles in practice'.[19]

Some empirico-normative assessments are typically explicitly acknowledged as part of the practice of condemnation, and taken into account by both condemner and condemned (and by many standard theories of moral responsibility). One commonly recognized assessment is that of the causal connection between the condemned's action (or omission) and a harm. Such a connection might be judged to be direct (as when a person with the key to a burning church in which prisoners are trapped fails to unlock the door to release them). Alternatively, the connection may be judged to be indirect, with some degree of mediation between the action and the harm (as when a person withholds information about an accused that would likely render a legal judgment and subsequent punishment invalid). In *The Reader*, the connection

---

18 Strawson, 'Freedom and Resentment', *op. cit.*, p. 22.
19 Smiley, *Moral Responsibility, op. cit.*, p. 185.

between Hanna's actions and the death of her charges seems fairly direct,[20] and Michael appears well aware of the relevance of such connections.

Another assessment that is commonly recognized as relevant to condemnations is that of the significance of the harm in question. The intensity or severity of an injury or moral violation is a significant factor in considering whether or not condemnation is deserved. Of course, context matters here too: for example, in some indigenous Australian communities, 'pay-back' punishment is sometimes considered appropriate, but would count as severe harm for most non-indigenous Australians. In *The Reader*, there is little doubt on this score: the horrendous outcome of Hanna's act is clear, and clearly recognized as such by Michael.

Judgements of intention, too, are closely bound up with assessments of causal connection. Whether a harm is the result of a deliberate act or not usually figures overtly in ascriptions of blame: deliberately caused harms, and deliberate omissions that are certain to result in harm, are frequently seen to merit censure. But this is not always so, as in the case of harms perpetrated in an abnormal state of mind. Similarly, harms unintentionally brought about may or may not be condemned, as in the case of the unwitting results of acts performed in states of ignorance that may or may not be regarded as acceptable. Michael is very cautious here; his concern with the chains of cause and effect that impact on actions, appears to make him reluctant to use the language of intentionality. On several occasions he refers to actions occurring without decisions or intentions (2, 13) and to the course of his life as being somehow independent of his will: 'It was the path my life had taken' (214). However, he is still unwilling to dismiss the importance of deliberation altogether. As a preface to a remark on the way behaviour does not flow directly from decisions, he says: 'I don't mean to say that thinking and reaching decisions have no influence on behaviour' (18).

The relatively uncontroversial role played by assessments of causal connection and significance of harm, together with Michael's diffidence concerning intentionality in *The Reader,* work to throw into relief his attempts to grasp the relevance of a fourth kind of assessment, namely social understandings and expectations of (normal) moral competence. Generally, a judgement that someone lacks moral competence is understood within practices of condemnation as a reason not to condemn that person, or to do so less harshly; it mitigates or excuses rather than justifying harm. A judgement that someone lacks moral competence may appeal to many different factors: a person's maturity, their sanity,[21] their conditions of upbringing,[22] the influence of external forces such as coercion on a person's actions, and permissible ignorance concerning the harm in question, may all be judged to excuse, to mitigate,

---

20 However, the details of how Hanna's actions contributed to the deaths of prisoners emerge only through a trial process the reliability of which the reader is given reason to doubt.

21 Many varieties of insanity may be judged to excuse individuals, including pyschopathy, dementia and neurosis. There are also borderline cases, such as poor planning ability (Michael Bratman, 'Responsibility and Planning', *The Journal of Ethics*, 1, 1997, pp. 27–43).

22 For a powerful discussion of the relevance of conditions of upbringing, see Gary Watson, 'Moral Responsibility and the Limits of Evil', in Ferdinand David Schoeman (ed.), *Responsibility, Character and the Emotions*, Cambridge University Press, 1987, pp. 256–86.

or to exempt from moral responsibility altogether.[23] Such judgements are not discernments of objective matters of fact, but the normatively-permeated judgements of particular socially-embedded individuals. As such, they are suffused with social and political values, and may reflect special interests.[24]

The issue of normal moral competence is focal to Michael's struggle with condemnation and understanding in *The Reader*. Once aware of Hanna's illiteracy, he judges her to be morally underdeveloped, taking this as a reason to hesitate before condemning her. He sees her as having chosen a certain path (becoming a prison guard) in part because her terrible fear of having her illiteracy discovered made her (abnormally) insensitive to important moral reasons *not* to choose that path. His judgement of her moral (in)competence pulls strongly against his evaluations of the causal link between her actions and the horrific deaths of her charges, intensifying the difficulty for him of understanding her crime.

Other, less commonly acknowledged, empirico-normative assessments are also part of the complex of judgements associated with social practices of condemnation. These assessments often affect moral judgements, including condemnation, but are commonly applied unselfconsciously, by people who remain unaware of their (often significant) influence. Condemners and condemned alike may remain unaware that such assessments form part of, or are taken into account in, their moral judgements. Accordingly, it may be harder to resolve tensions or ambivalence that they produce. Condemnations that do not take these assessments consciously into account may be irresponsible, in that they make an incautious presumption of rectitude, and simply impose the condemner's will without reflection. (See below: 'Some pressures against appropriate condemnation'.)

One essential empirico-normative assessment relevant to condemnation is that of the relationship between those being condemned and those doing the condemning. Relationships take many forms, including peer-relationships (such as some friendships and voluntary group membership) and hierarchical relationships, such as relationships of dependency, relationships of domination and subordination, and asymmetrical relationships, marked by inequalities in education, economic resources or other goods. Hierarchical relationships support the 'normalization' of some individuals' or groups' socio-ethical expectations at the expense of others', and affirm who has authority and power to judge whom, to speak in the name of a communal standard.[25] Accordingly, condemnations across dependency, domination and asymmetry may unduly reflect the interests of the powerful, and be excessively demanding of the powerless. Alternatively, the powerless might not be blamed by the powerful, but instead treated paternalistically, as if they were incapable of responsible behaviour in some or all aspects of community life.

While these relationships (and individuals' assessments of them) routinely play significant roles in practices of condemnation, the very processes by which

---

23 Strawson, 'Freedom and Resentment', *op. cit.*, p. 8.
24 Smiley, *Moral Responsibility*, *op. cit.*, p. 231.
25 Ibid., p. 239.

they are taken into account often render their workings transparent or invisible, particularly to those who stand to benefit from them. For example, patterns of domination and subordination might be subtly reinforced by dominant groups' greater ability to influence public perceptions, and to employ others to promote their perspective. Equally, members of a subordinate group may internalize their own oppression, blaming themselves for harms with which they, as well as dominant groups, are causally associated. A critical awareness of the role of relationships in structuring practices of condemnation is essential for avoiding the reinforcement of hierarchies.

The relationship between Michael and Hanna appears to be an important consideration in *The Reader*, although it is not thematized. Michael does raise the issue of relationships, focusing on that between the post-holocaust generation and that of their parents (168). But he overlooks the possibility that the changing nature of his relationship with Hanna may be responsible for some of the tension he feels. Initially a child infatuated with and partially dependent on an older woman, by the time of Hanna's trial, Michael is a highly educated adult, fully independent of Hanna after having ended their relationship. Yet, because of their past relationship, he remains complicit in her guilt and inextricably associated with her plight. Perhaps he is suspicious of his desire to understand Hanna because he takes it to be partially engendered by their former intimacy, a partiality with no place in condemnation.

Another often overlooked set of assessments closely linked with these relationship factors concerns social roles, and the expectations associated with them. Within communities, a plethora of social roles associates individuals with particular privileges, freedoms and responsibilities. Roles range from relatively formal (such as those of doctor or judge) to informal roles established within chosen associations. Roles and associated responsibilities vary with context and evolve over time; individuals may have multiple roles (raising questions of adjudication between competing role-responsibilities), and may move in and out of roles; nor is there any objective 'fact of the matter' about how far role-responsibilities extend.[26] Nevertheless, we often unselfconsciously identify people with (one of) their roles, as, for instance, women have traditionally been identified exclusively with motherhood (and condemned for not taking up its practices and responsibilities).

Whether or not condemnation is judged appropriate often depends, then, on assessments of social roles and expectations associated with that role. For example, in the past, industrialists were not expected to provide for workers' occupational health and safety, and so were not condemned for ill-health, injury or even death experienced by those they employed. Today, however, it is generally considered appropriate to blame industrialists whose workplace arrangements lead to the (serious) ill-health or injury of workers. Of course, there is often disagreement over the appropriateness of the expectations associated with social roles. Today's unanimously high expectations of industrialists to protect workers' occupational

---

26 Ibid., pp. 144–5.

health and safety are often contested, especially in respect to activities in Third World countries.

Here expectations of social roles intersect with the dynamics of what Cheshire Calhoun has called moral context, or the configuration of moral attitudes towards a given type of action within a society. Calhoun uses the term 'abnormal moral contexts' to describe situations in which most members of a society accept a practice but a minority believes them to be mistaken and the practice unjustified. In abnormal moral contexts, the minority finds that both blaming (unwitting) participants in a harmful practice *and* refraining from blame may be problematic.[27] Yet blame may still be valuable in abnormal moral contexts for its ability to change attitudes and behaviour. Michael's reluctance to condemn Hanna may result in part from a belief that the responsibilities associated with her role as prison guard, horrible though they were, were expected of anyone occupying the role in question. However, assessing the situation as an abnormal moral context, that is, a context in which socially normalized role expectations merit change would support him reproaching her.[28] Of course, such an evaluation itself emerges from further complex empirico-normative assessments relating to contested and shifting (but sometimes shared) understandings of the roles and responsibilities through which social life is maintained.[29]

The social roles particular to practices of condemnation have their own set of expectations. Whether the roles are formalized (as in the legal system), or informal (as in a personal relationship), they are associated with particular (variable, context-relative and evolving) expectations. As we noted above, condemners may ask for an accounting, request explanations, express emotions such as shock, anger or outrage, pass judgement. The condemned may try to account for their behaviour, demonstrate contrition, make reparations.[30] Assorted takings-up of these complementary roles by individuals support the expressive, guiding and shaping functions of the social practice of condemnation, with all its flaws and virtues. Behaviour that belies these roles (such as the accused asking the judge how he would have behaved in her position (110), or the 'condemner' refusing to pass judgement) goes against the grain of the practice.

---

27 Cheshire Calhoun, 'Responsibility and Reproach', *Ethics* 99, 1989, p. 390.

28 Calhoun, 'Responsibility and Reproach', *op cit.*, argues that moral reproach for engaging in accepted but unacceptable practices is an effective tool for social change. Blame (or condemnation) is inappropriate where agents do not have access to relevant moral knowledge that would enable them to assess their practices appropriately.

29 This 'social practices' view of moral judgement does not provide the bedrock of moral certainty to which many anti-relativists aspire, instead tying condemnation to the complex of assessments characteristic of practical moral life. Whether particular judgements are rationally or morally justified (or justifiable) is a different question. What is practically possible for the reproduction of social life together with the accumulated history of success and failures in the myriad mutual accountings and evaluations of affirmation and condemnation shape its boundaries.

30 Smiley, *Moral Responsibility, op. cit.*, p. 239.

Michael appears to have some critical awareness of the roles of condemner and condemned, and of some differences between the more rigid expectations of legal trials and the more fluid ones at play in interpersonal relationships. His attitude to the trial shows disquiet with formal, legal condemnations, which strike him as clumsy and insensitive (177-8). However, he seems indifferent to the reciprocity that is built into interpersonal relations. Perhaps he confuses the role of personal condemnation with that of legal judgment in which the institutional framework exempts judge and jury from any moral accounting; perhaps he fears that his blame reflects badly on his (former) intimacy with Hanna. At any rate Michael appears not to recognize that he owes Hanna any explanation of his personal condemnation of her crime, or his ambivalent behaviour to her following her imprisonment. In all, he appears aware of the relevance of the conventional roles of condemner and condemned, though uncertain how to perform in his role of personal 'condemner' of Hanna.

An understanding of the workings of the empirico-normative assessments that form part of the social practice of condemnation is essential to overcoming the prejudices and special interests that such assessments introduce. But it may also make people reluctant to condemn others, sometimes with good reason: in some contexts, a condemnation may seem only to reinforce some interests at the expense of others and so to reduce to an irresponsible battle of wills; in others the complexity of the assessments involved is good cause for caution. We return to this point in the section entitled 'Some pressures against appropriate condemnation'.

The Compatibility of Condemnation and Understanding

We have illustrated how, in *The Reader*, Michael's condemnation of Hanna and her crime is influenced by various empirico-normative assessments. We would like now to emphasize that his condemnation is also *informed by*, and *is compatible with*, understanding. Michael's understanding of Hanna develops not through his discovery of new causal connections (that is, connections leading to a deterministic interpretation of her behaviour), but rather through his growing appreciation of the social practice of condemnation.[31]

Michael focuses particularly on how social expectations of normal moral competence affect judgements of Hanna's blameworthiness, and to some extent on the relationship between condemner and condemned. He reflects deeply on the circumstances of Hanna's life, how they influenced her actions and decisions, and on his own attitudes and responses to her, while trying to bring his increased understanding of the practice of condemnation to bear on these particulars.

Importantly, Michael's attempt to understand Hanna is not merely an intellectual exercise, but also an emotionally engaged and compassionate (if ambivalent) attempt to grasp the complexities of condemnation, and the situation of the person he is

---

31 For arguments for the importance of understanding to judgement, see Hannah Arendt, 'The Crisis in Culture', in *Between Past and Future: Six Exercises in Political Thought*, London: Faber, 1961.

condemning. He tries diligently to understand Hanna's character, behaviour and circumstances. He is emotionally engaged: proud of her success in learning to read and write, and aware of how difficult the task was for her (123).

While Michael does condemn Hanna for her actions, his growing understanding of her character and circumstances, and of the practice of condemnation itself, help him to do so more appropriately, and to avoid some of the insensitivity he so disliked in Hanna's legal trial. He develops an understanding of her as a person who lacks paradigmatic moral competence (132-3), while concluding that this lack is not a full excuse (136). He also gains some understanding of the relevance of his relationship with Hanna to his judgement of her (168-9). In all these ways Michael's journey in *The Reader* illustrates our claim that critical awareness of the complex of empirico-normative assessments interwoven in moral judgements can help people to engage more appropriately in practices of moral condemnation.

Some Pressures against Appropriate Condemnation

Before concluding we would like briefly to review some of the pressures that militate against appropriate judgement, including condemnation. We have suggested already that awareness of the influence of empirico-normative assessments on the practice of condemnation may make individuals reluctant to condemn others, and offenders unwilling to acquiesce. The complexity of the evaluations required, awareness that they inevitably take place in contexts of normative plurality, and that they have strong negative repercussions for the condemned may be powerful disincentives for judgements of blame. The work of moral reasoning is rarely simple,[32] and reflective and responsible members of the community may hesitate before the array of competing effects of interconnected but diverse, and diversely significant, considerations. In face of the seriousness of the obligations of mutual accounting and shaping of responsibilities that practices of condemnation fulfil, fear of misjudging due to ignorance of relevant empirical or normative factors, or of the sins of unconscious personal bias and ill-judged paternalistic impositions, may result in resistance to condemning. Alternatively, confusion, exhaustion, and apathy (a form of moral paralysis) may result from the often painful, and seemingly endless and bewildering work of moral attention and evaluation.

However, while significance and complexity may warrant caution, these responses, and the escape from judgement that follows them, are often born out of an idealistic hope for moral perfection (the notion that moral judgements can be transparently accurate) and the quest for an understanding and exercise of responsibility and judgement that is capable of reaching definitive, universal and enduring conclusions. Yet Michael is all too aware (177-8) of the constraints placed on judgments of legal

---

32 See Peta Bowden, 'Ethical Attention: Accumulating Understandings', *European Journal of Philosophy*, 6(1), 1998, pp. 59–77, for a discussion of the intricate labours of moral engagement.

responsibility by what Joel Feinberg refers to as 'ulterior practical purposes'.[33] Perhaps on the flip-side of his sense of the demands of understanding, Michael, like Feinberg, harbours an enduring hope that judgements in the moral terrain will be free of these worldly limitations, capable of reaching the pure essence of ideal liability. Such ambitions run against the picture of imperfect, messy and context-sensitive moral practices of judgement and responsibility we have described here, and may well be a source of bewilderment, trepidation and avoidance of condemnation. We suggest that this failure to engage in condemnation is simultaneously a failure to understand the important expressive, regulative and shaping roles of these practices in social life.

Sometimes resistance to condemnation comes, not from misunderstandings of the nature of the moral terrain, or misplaced reticence in light of its complexity, but from a sense of the negative repercussions for ourselves, our community or the potential condemned. We noted earlier that ill-judged compassion readily becomes an excuse for withdrawal from condemnation and disguised moral abnegation. Reflexive awareness of the stressful situations in which atrocities are committed by 'ordinary' individuals like ourselves, who seem somehow to be the unwitting victims of extraordinary circumstances, may generate fear that we, too, would not be sufficiently courageous in this situation.[34] It is distressing to be reminded that we are not very brave ourselves, that placed in a similar situation we would probably have acted in similarly offensive ways, that we, too, would be unlikely to be able to resist the pressure from external forces on our lives. Consciousness of our own weaknesses and their prospective blameworthiness, and empathy for the condemned's difficult, perhaps even tragic circumstances, can deflect us away from the crucial social functions of judgement. However, as Hannah Arendt explains, judging a wrong does not presuppose that we ourselves would be incapable of committing it.[35] Anna Funder, reflecting on the German reception to her book, *Stasiland*,[36] also reminds us that recognition of the power of this fear is precisely what awakens an obligation to judge, to delegitimize a regime that runs on fear.[37]

Misplaced empathy, compassion, pity and the personal biases of love, of unwillingness to deal with a possible rupture in a relationship, or to harm another, as we mentioned above, along with fear of retaliation, can also all take their toll on the resolve of responsible judgement. The severity of condemnation relative to other forms of moral accounting, with its slippage between condemning a crime and a

---

33 Joel Feinberg, 'Problematic Responsibility in Law and Morals', in *Doing and Deserving*, Princeton: Princeton University Press, 1970, p. 26.

34 See Christopher R. Browning, *Ordinary Men: Reserve Police Battalion 101 and the Final Solution in Poland*, New York: Harper Perennial, 1998, for a chastening reminder of the moral fates of ordinary men in extraordinary circumstances.

35 Hannah Arendt, 'Personal Responsibility Under Dictatorship', in Jerome Kohn (ed.), *Responsibility and Judgment*, New York: Schocken Books, 2003, p. 19.

36 Anna Funder, *Stasiland*, Melbourne: Text Publishing Company, 2002.

37 Anna Funder, 'State of Denial', *Australian Financial Review Magazine*, October 2004, p. 19.

person, reinforces their effects. In all these cases, where the potential of condemnation for (immediate) positive outcomes is dubious (or limited), incomplete understanding of its moral significance may lead individuals to betray the ethico-social role of the practice by failing to make or avoiding appropriate judgements.

In pointing to the reasons why individuals may be reluctant to condemn or blame others, however, we do not want to convey the impression that the importance of practices of condemnation necessarily or always justifies their judgements. Over-hasty condemnation, erroneous, ill-informed, self-righteous and irresponsible judgements, may misunderstand the role and significance of the practice in the same ways that failure and avoidance do. Where lack of judgement abets the moral drift and excuse-making that undermine the ethical fabric of society, judgements and accusations imposed without understanding, and without taking responsibility for their implications and outcomes (the complex web of normative and empirical evaluations they pre-suppose, and the social purposes and interests they support), also contribute to moral breakdown. Social divisions and conflicts are sharpened by inappropriate blame and the absence of warranted assessment renders retrieval of the inbuilt divisive and exclusionary effects of condemnation well nigh impossible. Neither refusal to condemn nor condemnation without understanding is morally appropriate.

Conclusion

In this light, the move to a determinist position looks suspiciously like a path a would-be-condemner might take so as to avoid performing the (often difficult) task of understanding the situation of the would-be-condemned, or the (often painful) task of condemning fellow-members of the moral community. As we have argued in this chapter, a concerned and compassionate understanding of the circumstances of both 'condemned' and 'condemner', and a critical grasp of the social practices of moral judgement within which both are situated are essential to appropriate moral judgement. On this interpretation of understanding, it facilitates, rather than undermines, condemnation. Without understanding, condemnation may be blindly conventional or personally biased; with it there is greater hope that condemnation will be appropriate: that it will sustain the integrity of the moral community, and that it will do justice to both condemner and condemned.[38]

---

38 Our thanks to Pedro Tabensky for encouraging us to write this paper and for organizing the Judging and Understanding Colloquium: Homage to the Ten Years of Democratic Rule in South Africa, Goethe-Institut, Johannesburg, November 2004 at which it was presented. Thanks also to Bernhard Schlink for writing the novel that inspired the paper and for his, and all the other Colloquium participants', insightful comments on it.

Chapter 12

Humanizing Evil-Doers

Andrew Gleeson

Editor's Introduction

Understanding appalling evil and its authors is a complex matter and Andrew Gleeson explores two extreme alternatives in a continuum of possibilities and settles for an intermediate position which avails itself of what is allegedly good in both and, following authors such as Raimond Gaita, rejects an assumption common to both, namely that basic or minimal respect is something to be earned. On one end stand the liberals with their emphasis on compassion, understanding and mercy, their desire to exonerate, to forgive, their a priori conviction that there will always be mitigating circumstances, their belief that no one truly is ultimately to blame, that everyone ultimately deserves, because they have earned it, basic respect. On the other side of the continuum stand the moralists who believe that one can lose one's right to basic respect if one's actions are evil enough. A basic problem with the liberal position is that universal respect comes at the cost of incapacity properly to judge and properly to differentiate victim from perpetrator. While discussing two novels, one of them being *The Reader* (the other is Helen Demidenko's controversial 'holocaust novel', *The Hand That Signed the Paper*), Gleeson claims that, 'I believe it is fair to say that *The Reader* to some extent fails fully to reveal Hanna's suffering and her victims' suffering in their distinctively different lights'. One of the problems with the moralist position, on the other hand, is that its representatives cruelly and insensitively believe that 'perpetrators [of extreme evil] are "sub-human" or "animals", deserving of extermination much as one would eradicate vermin'. Gleeson's position is that one can have basic respect for human beings without, so to speak, letting them off the moral hook. Reflection on our common vulnerability to evil can create a compassionate understanding that 'affords all human beings a protection (the "ring of immunity") against wholesale alienation from the human family'. So, for Gleeson, contrary to the liberal position, there is no tension between judging and understanding. Understanding does not necessarily make judging hard. Rather, with proper understanding one can judge adequately. In this regard, Gleeson's conclusions are similar in important respects to Thaddeus Metz's and to Peta Bowden's and Emma Rooksby's, although the paths they tread are significantly different.

* * *

Human beings do terrible things to one another. They commit atrocities so vile that we understand why some people would say the perpetrators are 'sub-human' or 'animals', deserving of extermination much as one would eradicate vermin.[1]

We are rightly disgusted at the attitudes and behaviour of people who take this attitude to evil-doers – at those who pelt the man in the stocks, or throng menacingly around the house of a child molester. But only liberal naiveté or condescension would refuse *all* sympathy to the impulse behind those behaviours. Sympathy for victims is unsustainable without at least the *temptation* to indignation at perpetrators. I do not have space to argue that point in detail. My argument will proceed on the assumption it is so. The moral for liberal opponents of vengefulness is that they cannot dismiss indignation towards evil-doers without undermining the compassion they claim as their inspiration.

The ideal of compassion even for the worst of evil-doers is a noble one. But it is unimaginably difficult. We are tempted to make evil-doers more palatable to us, by diluting the seriousness of their deeds, finding some redeeming feature of their characters, or some mitigating circumstance of their history. Sometimes we say no one can be 'all bad'. But why not? Even so perceptive a writer as Martha Nussbaum seems to me to underestimate the depths evil can plumb when she recommends a criminal jurisprudence which grounds mercy in the capacity to find mitigating circumstances. She seems completely confident that we always will, if only we can scrutinize the 'narrative' detail of a life closely enough.[2] But can we sure it is *always* so? Can there not be people whose actions are sickening beyond words, whose characters are without redeeming features, and whose personal history includes nothing that would induce sympathy? Perhaps not, but (at the least) who can be sure? If there are such people is mercy – and indeed, the recognition of them as human beings more generally, that is as beings not to be exterminated in the spirit of getting rid of vermin – to be denied them? Do we really want this recognition to hinge on the gamble there are no such people?

I want to suggest a more robust way in which we can – and do – recognize the humanity of people. The generous liberal impulse towards offenders is too feeble by itself. We need a more resilient spirit, one not sustained by a supposition that unqualified evil-doers do not exist, or fuelled by an unsustainable contempt for indignation and vengeance. But before describing that spirit, in the last section of the paper, first I want to say more about the attraction of the liberal ideal, and about the various pitfalls that surround it. I do that in the first two sections, using literary examples.

---

1   The image is from Raimond Gaita, *Good and Evil: An Absolute Conception*, 2nd edn, Abingdon: Routledge 2004, p. 7.

2   'Equity and Mercy', Ch. 1, this volume, p. 32. In saying this I do not mean to suggest that Nussbaum would be unmerciful towards anyone she became convinced had no redeeming features.

I

Whether for good or ill, the Nazi attempt to destroy the Jewish race is our foremost emblem of evil-doing. Whatever we think of that pre-eminence, a reaction against it was, arguably, inevitable. I am writing from Australia where this reaction surfaced in the 1990s, in the controversy over the novel *The Hand that Signed the Paper*.[3]

The Hand was published in 1994. In 1993, in manuscript form, it had won *The Australian*/Vogel award. After publication it won the 1995 Miles Franklin Prize, Australia's premier literary award. The author was a young Queensland woman who called herself Helen Demidenko, and who claimed Ukrainian ancestry. This was important because the novel concerns a young Queensland woman of Ukrainian descent, Fiona Kovalenko, whose father and uncle were Nazi collaborators, who participated enthusiastically in the murder of Ukrainian Jews during the German occupation. The Australian government wants to prosecute Uncle Vitaly. The novel depicts the Ukrainian complicity in the Nazi crimes as hate-filled retaliation against Jewish leadership in the Stalin-inspired Ukrainian collectivization and famine of the early thirties, and more generally as another wave in humanity's endless cycle of tit-for-tat vengefulness. Though avowedly a work of fiction in detail, the novel clearly offered its history of Ukrainian involvement in the Holocaust as true in general principle. Demidenko's own Ukrainian ancestry lent credibility to this. That, however, received a blow when it came out that Helen Demidenko was really Helen Darville, the daughter of English immigrants with no Ukrainian ancestry.

Darville's admirers saw *The Hand* as an inspiring plea against war, racism and hatred, a hatred still living in the determination to hunt down ageing war criminals. For a while, that view prevailed. But from mid-1995 on a river of criticism flooded over the book. The most important criticisms were:

1. Errors in the account of Ukrainian history. Jews were not prominent in the Soviet Communist Party by the early 1930s, or in the party's apparatus in the Ukraine. Ukrainian involvement in the 1940s' Holocaust was not revenge for the 1930s' famine, but another expression of centuries-old Ukrainian anti-Semitism.

2. In thus mis-describing Ukrainian history, Darville succumbed to *the* Nazi anti-Jewish slander: the stereotype of the 'Jewish Bolshevik'. Some went further, and noting the ugly depiction of most Jews in the novel, said squarely that the novel was anti-Semitic.

3. The novel's description of Holocaust atrocities is morally empty. There is no light of goodness present in the novel from which the evil can be seen *as* evil.

---

3 Helen Demidenko, *The Hand that Signed the Paper*, St Leonards: Allen and Unwin, 1994.

4. The novel rolls all human criminality together into an amorphous mass of evil, in which there are no distinctions and no responsibility. Victims and perpetrators of the Holocaust are treated as morally equivalent, and to pursue the latter for punishment is cruel and unjust.

Many who defended *The Hand* sympathized with its antipathy to the pre-eminence of the Holocaust as a symbol of evil. Others sympathized, understandably, but in my judgement with culpable naiveté, with its attempt to extend human sympathy and solidarity to evil-doers, to see the pain and humanity inside the darkest heart. They were especially receptive to the book's message that one evil begets another, and that we are all, in our frailty, caught up in cycles of violence and revenge, and that this should caution us against pointing the finger at others.

This sentiment was sometimes expressed by saying the book attempted to understand the Holocaust from the point of view of the perpetrators. But if 'understanding their point of view' is to help see their humanity – or *humanize* (un-demonize) them – then that point of view needs to show them in a light that will engage our sympathies. And it cannot do that unless it renders their emotions and actions 'understandable' or 'reasonable' in some way. And that means that their reasons for actions are ones that we can imagine ourselves (or at least the average person) acting on, were we (or they) in that situation. Our sympathy would not be engaged by a brute-causal explanation, say one in terms of neurophysiology. Nor by a reason-giving explanation which merely cited their hatred of Jews, or that made their actions reasonable only in the light of beliefs (like the Jewish Bolshevik myth) that are false, offensive, and palpably rationalizations of an independently existing hatred. That brings us to the whole problem with humanizing evil-doers by trying to 'see their point of view'. It will work only if there is, so to speak, 'something to be said' (something attractive) for their point of view. But there may be *nothing* to be said for their point of view. Their point of view may be as wicked as their actions. What then? Then, the less scrupulous are inclined to fabricate histories to license a lying point of view, such as the *Hand's* distortions of Ukrainian history according to the libel of the Jewish Bolshevik.

A second strategy for 'humanizing' evil-doers is to relativize their actions to the wrongs of which we are all guilty, or easily could have been guilty. This strategy is present in abundance in the *Hand*. The first half-dozen pages set this theme. In the very first sentence, the narrator, Fiona, announces a startling moral equivalence:

> As I drive down the Pacific Highway, the French are busy dropping bombs into the waters in which my nieces swim, the Americans and Iraqis are engaged in a bizarre competition to see who can destroy the world many times over most, and my uncle will soon be on trial for war crimes and crimes against humanity.

Page three declares that 'the Ukrainian famine bled into the Holocaust and one fed the other', establishing the theme that atrocities in general are at least typically a vengeful response to earlier crimes (and that the Holocaust in particular was). This is followed on the same page with:

The [TV] news was full of Somalia and Bosnia ... Two Serbs wipe their feet on the Croatian flag. A sad little village nestled between soft green hills burns. Two lean black men drag the naked, punctured body of a US marine down a dusty street.

Then on page five:

Vitaly did unspeakable things. I have known about these things for some time now. How poor and hungry Ukrainians shot Jews for bread and sausage and vodka. How my father and my uncle became part of the machinery of the Holocaust. How my aunt married a senior SS officer. How people slaughtered without compunction. My brother Bret went to Vietnam, and came back nearly mad from what he did, with dreams about little gook children pocked with bullets and Vietnamese girls raped by both Americans and Vietcong. My father is sane. So are Vitaly and aunt Kateryna. None of them mad. Not one.

The cumulative effect of juxtaposing these atrocities is so to mount one upon another that the reader is worn down with world-weariness. His or her moral faculties are blurred by the diet of evil, and a cynicism is born towards any attempt to introduce distinctions between crimes of different types and gravity. This cynicism then masquerades behind the thoughtless cliché 'War is a crime, of itself'. Darville puts those words into the mouth of one of her minor characters (page four), but it might stand as an epigram for the book as a whole. 'We are all guilty' would do similar service.

The problem, of course, is that we are *not* all guilty – not of the same crimes, or crimes of comparable gravity. Does that mean the full humanity of those who perpetrated the Holocaust is forever beyond our grasp? Moreover, by pressing us all into a porridge of moral equality, the perfect excuse is provided to let us all off the hook; where all are guilty, none are. The strategy buys humanization at the price of moral accountability. Distasteful as it sometimes is, unless all accountability is to be abandoned, we have to make detailed comparisons of different evils, not only to decide what punishment there should be, but also to understand and remember accurately and lucidly what some people have done and what others have had done to them.

The third humanizing strategy in *The Hand* is to present the perpetrators of the Ukrainian Holocaust as 'ordinary' people, fathers and uncles, aunties and lovers, enjoying all the domestic pleasures of any ordinary person: human beings, not demons. Darville even presents the notorious Ivan the Terrible relaxing at home with his Jazz records after a hard day's work in the camps. There is a deep irony in this, identified by Robert Manne who points out that '[i]n their own dull, suburban way, the Kovalenko brothers embody the kind of decency to which [Heinrich] Himmler referred'[4] in his infamous description of the men and women carrying out the Final Solution:

---

4 Robert Manne, *The Culture of Forgetting: Helen Demidenko and the Holocaust*, Melbourne: Text, 1996, p. 131.

Most of you know what it means when 100 bodies lie together, when 500 lie there, or if 1,000 lie there. To have gone through this, and at the same time, apart from exceptions caused by human weaknesses, to have remained decent, that has made us hard.

The point is not that these portraits of the killers may not have been right, at least about some of them. The point is that this unthinking normality – what Hannah Arendt called the 'banality' of evil – is, in its own perverse way, as terrifying as the savagery of the out-and-out sadists. There can be no normality, no 'decency', in people who staff the killing chambers then escape into a remorseless, undisturbed ordinariness the rest of the time.

We can say of all the strategies of humanization so far described that they try to humanize their subjects by overlooking or diminishing the evil of their deeds or characters. Is humanization possible without that extenuation? I believe it is. But first I want to look at another literary attempt at the humanization of evil-doers.

II

Bernhard Schlink's *Der Vorleser* was published in Germany in 1995 and translated into English in 1997 as *The Reader*. The novel is an attempt by a member of the post-war German generation to come to terms with his parents' era. The hero, Michael Berg, is seduced by Hanna, an older woman, when he is fifteen. Hanna is a tram conductor. After their love-making he reads to her from Homer and Tolstoy. Gradually, he becomes more interested in his peers, and finds himself 'betraying' Hanna by trying to hide the relationship from them. Then one day she disappears. Years later Michael is a law student at university. One of his classes follows a trial of minor Nazi war criminals in a nearby town. Michael attended every day of the trial. He discovers one of the defendants is Hanna. She had been a member of the SS and a guard in two death camps, where she also had prisoners read to her. The judge is harsh and impatient. Hanna's inept attempts to defend herself only make things worse for her. Michael realizes that she is illiterate and that she has been trying to hide this shame from the court, even making a damaging false confession to avoid exposure. She took the job in the SS as the only alternative to a factory position that required reading and writing. Hanna is sentenced to life in prison. After several years of neglect, and the collapse of his marriage, Michael starts to send her tapes of him reading. Shortly before her release on parole, he visits her in prison. She has learned to read and write. But on the eve of her release, she commits suicide.

The book provoked some controversy in Germany, and somewhat more in English-speaking nations, because of its attempt to humanize Hanna by making her a victim, and extending her at least as much sympathy as it extends to her victims.[5] In the light of her deeds, and the comparative unimportance of her own misfortune, this is offensive, complain the critics. Where are the real victims here?

---

5   For example, Cynthia Ozick, 'The Rights of History and the Rights of Imagination', *Commentary*, March 1999, pp. 22–7.

The only answer to that cry is that the sympathy must be matched with an unwavering sobriety, frankness and justice in judgement – and here that means condemnation – of her deeds and her character; one that steadily sees that her own sufferings are insignificant by comparison with the suffering she inflicted. *The Reader* seems to me to go at least some way to meeting this requirement – but, arguably, not far enough. For example, near the end, when she is nearing release from prison, Michael asks Hanna whether, right back when they were having their affair, she ever thought about her actions in the war. She answers:

> … I always had the feeling that no one understood me anyway, that no one knew who I was and what made me do this or that. And you know, when no one understands you, then no one can call you to account. Not even the court could call me to account. But the dead can. They understand. They don't even have to have been there, but if they were, they understand even better. Here in prison they were with me a lot. They came every night, whether I wanted them or not. Before the trial I could still chase them away when they wanted to come.[6]

The passage is suffused with self-pity. She is not without right to object to the rough treatment she received at the court's hands, but what she says here goes beyond that – the living cannot judge her at all. The dead can, but only because they 'understand' her, and indeed her victims 'understand' her best of all. While Hanna does apparently describe being haunted by the ghosts of her victims, that remorse is blunted by the victims' 'understanding' (deftly contrasted with the cold, asinine court) – nearly as if the victims' forgiveness were already bestowed, as though victim and perpetrator shared a common experience and solidarity.[7] By removing judgement wholly to the world of the dead, Hanna effectively exempts herself from accountability.

To his credit, Michael Berg sees most of this. Reacting against his own guilt at his various betrayals of her, he says he:

> … accused her, and found it both shabby and too easy, the way she had wriggled out of her guilt. Allowing no one but the dead to demand an accounting, reducing guilt and atonement to insomnia and bad feelings …

But then spoils this recognition (as he realizes) with his own self-pity:

> – where did that leave the living? But what I meant was not the living, it was me. Did I not have my own accounting to demand of her? What about me?[8]

---

6   Bernhard Schlink *The Reader*, Carol Brown Janeway (trans.), London: Phoenix, 1997, pp. 196-7.

7   Inga Clendinnen rather bizarrely interprets a story concerning Nazi death camp guards and inmates playing a soccer match as if it expressed such solidarity: Inga Clendinnen, *Reading the Holocaust*, Melbourne: Text, 1998, pp. 85–7. See also the discussion in Raimond Gaita, *A Common Humanity: Thinking About Love and Truth and Justice*, 2nd edn, London: Routledge, 2000, pp. 47–52.

8   Schlink, *op. cit.*, pp. 199–200.

The overall effect is hard to interpret definitively, but for just that reason I believe it is fair to say that *The Reader* to some extent fails fully to reveal Hanna's suffering and her victims' suffering *in their distinctively different lights*. In some degree it impairs the clear-sightedness necessary for moral judgement.

But even if I were wrong about this, what is certain is that Schlink manages to humanize Hanna only by depicting her as a victim of suffering, and by depicting her through Michael's love for her (and betrayal of her). These strategies are also present in *The Hand*, in the victim-status of the Kovalenko brothers, and in Fiona's love for them. The core problem with both novels (for my concerns in this essay) is that they do not face up to the really deep-rooted difficulty in humanizing evil-doers. What if the evil-doer has endured no suffering worth speaking of? And what if they are so repulsive we find ourselves quite unable to love them? Even if we can rest our humanization on these qualities in some cases, the humanization will be fragile, and vulnerable to fate (to discovering, for example, that the person's history is not what we thought, or to our affection for them drying up). *The Reader* is not anti-Semitic and it is not a piece of historical revisionism. But it does, in its attempt to humanize Hanna, fall into some of the same traps as *The Hand*. Both works (i) secure humanization in some degree at the expense of moral judgement, and (ii) make the task of humanization too easy by diluting in some way the evil of the evil-doer.[9]

III

I want to defend a form of humanization which is not at the expense of moral accountability, or of the evil of evil-doers, because it is unconnected to any kind of mitigation or release from punishment. Mitigation is a function of equitable judgement in particular cases. I take it as uncontroversial that discerning grounds for mitigation needs a certain sympathy with the perpetrator's life. But that is not the kind of humanization I am getting at. The humanization I am getting at is the understanding we have of evil-doers which makes them the subject of equitable justice at all, but it says nothing about what that justice should be, and it applies as much to the person for whom no grounds for leniency can be found as it does to the person for whom there are many. This is not to deny that of course the term 'humanization', and cognate language, cannot be applied to finding of grounds for mitigation. We do rightly humanize in this way. But it is not the sort of humanization that can reach to the very worst. What is needed is a humanization compatible with the full verdict that equitable justice would deliver on the *unqualified* evil-doer. What is needed is an appeal to a condition we share with the wicked that is *not*

_____

9   In Schlink's case it is understandable, perhaps essential, that he should present the evil-doer through the eyes of someone who loves her. He is giving a fictional form to the problem faced by his generation of Germans: how to come to terms with the fact that their parents, whom they naturally loved, could have done such things? Fiona's corresponding problem in *The Hand* is a fraud, the product of Darville assuming the false Ukrainian identity Demidenko.

moralistic and juridical, in the sense of constituting a ground for the mitigation of blame and desert. A condition which humanizes without exonerating, which is shared by everyone, even those for whom no attenuating condition can be found.

As a first stab, what might we make of the fact that though we are not all *equally* guilty, we are all guilty of *something*? Might reflection on this truth deter us from 'judgementalism' or 'moralism', which – in their ugliest incarnations, directed against serious evil-doers – are (among) the anti-humanizing attitudes which would exterminate evil-doers as vermin? Not by itself. There is nothing to prevent the severe moralist from insisting that even basic respect for someone's humanity – the respect that would save you from being exterminated like vermin, whatever you have done, whatever you are like – must be earned, and that if you sink low enough – if, say, you deliberately treat others as vermin – then you deserve to be treated like vermin yourself. It is a common enough sentiment, and it cannot be ruled out by anything like what philosophers call 'reason' (e.g. it is not internally inconsistent, does not contradict any patent fact, etc.). The severe moralist can be challenged as to whether he would be prepared to accept this extermination for himself, or those he loves, if he or they were to become guilty of the necessary evil. But I see no reason why the answer 'yes' *need* be lacking in full seriousness.

What is needed is not appeal to actions we are guilty of, nor ones our character makes us liable to. What is needed is our common *vulnerability* to evil. Not the vulnerability of our actual formed characters, but that of every baby or child with its future ahead of it. The guiding thought is not what I *have* done, or what I *am* liable to do given the sort of person I am – that to which juridical and moralistic concepts apply – but *what I might have been* and *might have done* had I had an entirely different upbringing and life – hypothetical things with which moralists and courts are not concerned. In a sense, this line of thought invites us to view human life *sub specie aeternitatis*, not from any individual perspective, but from a god-like one which sees the extent to which we are all subject to luck and fate, especially in the circumstances which go to form our characters in childhood and adolescence. From such a perspective one gains a sense of how narrowly one has avoided moral disaster that has overtaken others. Even if it is true that, given my character as it now is, and given yours, there are wrong choices you would make that I would not – a truth relevant to the moralist, and if you ever perform the corresponding actions, perhaps to a court – it also remains true of each and every one of us that different parents and upbringing from infancy on would have resulted in entirely different persons, of who knows what character. However much one believes in 'free will' – be it 'libertarian' or 'compatibilist' – no one thinks it extends back to the total authorship of our fate from the womb forwards. Even the libertarian must allow that 'contra-causal' freedom is not that extensive, that it must be exercised within conditions that are more or less favourable and some of which are highly unfavourable. Its exercise is not equally easy and sometimes not possible at all. Any of us might have been born to moral conditions that would have overwhelmed us. That we were not is sheer luck, and no merit on our own part. To fully, imaginatively realize this is to suffer a standing rebuke to pride in one's self-sufficiency, and to become more compassionate and less judgemental towards others.

It might be objected that while this may be the effect vis-à-vis those who were overwhelmed by unfavourable circumstances in their childhood and youth, it is much less likely to melt our hearts towards those evil-doers (the hard cases I have stressed all along) for whom no such mitigating conditions exist. So consider a case in which I compare myself to someone with a very similar background. That background is both materially and morally fortunate – one in which we would find no mitigating condition for a person who became evil. Yet, by his own decision, this person becomes evil, and I do not. Yet it is possible, when viewing his life and mine *sub specie aeternitatis*, to think: 'how easily I could have chosen the road he did'. For in the end we do not understand why one chooses one way and another differently. We cover our lack of understanding with concepts like 'determinism' or 'contra-causal freedom', but these are just labels covering the mystery (or desperate attempts to rationalize our response to the mystery, acknowledging it in the spirit of pity and compassion, or denying it in a spirit of judgementalism). The truth is that (absent empirical discoveries – e.g. that I chose some way because I had a brain tumour – which puts things back in the category of fate and luck) we only know *that* we chose as we did, not *why*. Faced with this enigma, this bald inexplicable fact that I went this way and he went that, it is possible (but not inevitable) that we will be impressed by how narrowly we escaped becoming evil ourselves, and this in turn can give birth to the compassionate and anti-judgemental thought: 'There but for the grace of God go I'.

Nothing in mere *logical consistency* prevents the moralist from standing his ground. But he can be pressed with challenges like: how can you be sure that, if you had his circumstances, you would not have turned out differently? And in the case where circumstances are comparable and favourable, he can still be asked: can you be sure, if you had your life over again, that you would not have chosen as he did? The questions are unanswerable. But just because they are unanswerable, any attempt to answer that you would not, can reasonably be viewed as arrogant, a pride-full over-estimation of your own invulnerability. Each of us has had good or bad luck, and each has made choices whose nature is unknown. To deny basic respect to others appears to be a denial of these truths, an assertion of an *inherent* superiority we do not possess.

This general idea receives subsidiary support from another hypothetical supposition. It is easy to underestimate the vulnerability of our actual characters. But each of us has his or her nemesis – possible experiences so profoundly disturbing that we fall apart morally. This was a common experience in the Nazi death camps and similar horrors: part of its suffering is what it reduced people to being morally. Again, anyone tempted to deny this susceptibility in their own case rightly attracts the suspicion of pharisaical self-righteousness. Does not the same suspicion rightly attach to anyone who tries to make too much of the claim that his 'breaking point' takes longer to reach than most others? Can he always be so confident of that? And even when he can (and there are such cases) does not the impulse to be so smack of an unsavoury self-promotion?

That point is particularly telling in the case of the Nazi death camps, where such moralism appears to take advantage of that suffering. But then the universe resembles such a camp to the extent that it hands out fates and reprieves capriciously and unyieldingly (like camp selections) but with a final fate, death itself, into which we are all eventually absorbed with relentless thoroughness. Not that one needs to look to such extremity. Secure as we may feel in such goodness as we may possess, who of us can be confident it will not be lost, when we are plunged into black despair and helplessness, by illness or injury, by grievous loss of those we love, or just by inexplicable melancholy? Perhaps for most of us it is enough simply to reflect that love eventually makes fools of all of us.

Against my whole line of argument it may be objected that I under-estimate the radical difference between *evil* and *ordinary wrong-doing*. Elizabeth Wolgast has argued powerfully that the latter concept leaves those to whom it applies within the reach of humanization.[10] We can identify with their frailties and vulnerability (including the effects of a traumatic upbringing), we can find mitigating circumstances, and our sympathy can be engaged. But, she argues, the whole point in characterizing someone as an evil-doer is to put them beyond the reach of such identification. Evil people tend to become just abstractions in our minds, emblems of evil, alien creatures the concrete details of their lives forgotten. (Perhaps, we might even add on her behalf, no mitigating circumstance seems adequate to account for their perversity. But that of course is just another reason why the humanization of evil-doers should not depend on such circumstances.) I have no doubt that the word 'evil' is often used in this way. For just this reason my account of humanization does not appeal to any actual weaknesses or failings we may share with evil-doers, but to a human condition – the vulnerability to evil – that is of the highest generality. I am attempting to dilute our sense of distance from evil-doers without diluting our sense of their evil. Admittedly, it may be true, as Raimond Gaita suggests, that only the (perhaps imagined) love of saints (or parents) may reveal to us the full humanity of some people.[11] But that is not a rival account to mine, for any elucidation of that love will appeal to its sense of our common vulnerability to evil (as well as other aspects of a shared human condition).

My claim is that the reflections I have sketched can constitute a sober check upon the attempt to set ourselves above evil-doers in the sort of moralistic judgementalism that would annihilate them from consideration at all, would reduce them to animals, able to be treated, as I keep saying, like vermin. The reflections should inspire a sense of a shared human condition, a condition demanding compassion and humility in our attitudes to one another. This compassion then naturally expresses itself in a fellowship of human beings, represented by drawing a *ring of immunity* around people into which morality (moral judgement – praise and blame, reward and

---

10 Elizabeth Wolgast 'Moral Paradigms', *Philosophy*, 70 (1995): 143–55.
11 Gaita, 'Goodness Beyond Virtue', in his *A Common Humanity*.

punishment) may not intrude. We express this immunity (in religious language) by saying that human beings are sacred. In struggling for secular equivalents we say that each individual human life is precious, irreplaceable, momentous, inviolable, and so on. In practical terms it is expressed in various restrictions on the way in which we may treat people, even those who deeds and characters are irredeemably foul. They may include, for example, that they cannot be tortured, or used as an example to deter others, that they must have a fair trial, that they cannot be subject to 'cruel and unusual' punishment, perhaps that they cannot be executed. More importantly perhaps is the 'spirit' in which they are treated – in particular that they cannot be wholly denied human company and support, left to rot or die alone. That companionship can be expressed (I do not say it always is) in the words 'may God have mercy on your soul', in the rituals of the disposal of the body, and so on. The guiding thought, variously expressed is: these are not vermin, but our brothers and sisters gone terribly wrong.

That is the kind of 'humanization' which can reach everyone, even the very worst. *The Hand* and *The Reader* both make humanization too easy by imagining their evil-doers to have mitigating circumstances or redeeming qualities. Moreover, they purchase their humanization at the price of a wholesale and explicit abandonment of moral judgement (in *The Hand*) or of a more ambiguous compromising or jeopardizing of it (in *The Reader*). But now, am I guilty of this too? Have I not authorized not merely a 'circle of immunity', but a wholesale exoneration from moral judgement? The answer – which I have space enough left barely to sketch – is that the notion of desert, of what we *deserve*, should be dissociated from a strict *distributive* justice. The difference is that a strict distributive justice will take into account the effects of 'moral luck', whereas ordinary moral judgement is designed (up to a point) to ignore moral luck. Praise and blame, reward and punishment, are reactions to what people have *done* and what their characters *are*, with relatively little regard to *how* they got to have those characters.

Doesn't that just show that 'ordinary moral judgement' is an unjust institution? Not if we think of it this way. Imagine praise and blame, and even reward and punishment, as a kind of *language*, as the way in which we recognize, in ourselves and one another, the nature of what we have done and what we are like. When an audience applauds a pianist or cheers an athlete they are *giving recognition* to his or her capacities and achievements. If they were to ignore or boo a great pianist or outstanding athlete they would (absent a special explanation) be *making a mistake*. So too if they were to give rapturous praise to a second-rate performance. This is why critics do (or should) try so hard to get their commentary *right* – and why it is a corruption of their vocation to be influenced by mere popularity, career interest, etc. In the same way to praise or be indifferent to wrong-doing is to fail to recognize, and certainly in the former case, to misrepresent, the acts and character of the wrong-doer. It is a species of either blindness or untruthfulness. (Think of how difficult it can be in words, tone and demeanour to be candid with someone about their behaviour.) Punishment is just the natural extension of this. Harsh words are already a form of sanction. In punishment one is further communicating to the wrong-doer one's assessment of the nature his actions and/or character. It is a mistaken view of the nature of language to object 'why couldn't you just tell him in words what you think'. Words get their meaning from their place in the context of human behaviour and practices – strip those away and one has merely marks and sounds. It is an illusion to think words of moral criticism can retain the same meaning while disconnecting them from the possibility of blame and punishment.

The crucial point is that such frankness and truthfulness about one another's behaviour and character, about what we deliberately and knowingly do, or are liable to do, requires overlooking history. The truth is no less the truth because it arises from unfairness, from circumstances beyond our control. It may help here to think of moral judgement and effort in one's own case. In considering my own wrong-doing, and the effort I need to make at reformation, I have to discount the circumstances, many beyond my control, that led me here. (If I do not, I will subvert my efforts, leaving me forever mired in grievance and self-pity.) It may be unjust, on a cosmic view of things, that the truth about me hurts so much. But then, no one said that life was always just. Would it be *better*, if on account of that distributive injustice, we hid from ourselves and one another the moral nature of our actions and characters? But if my claim about the non-dissociability of moral language from practices of praise and blame (etc.) is true, then there is no exposing that moral nature without those practices.

In practice we do make compromises between the strictness of moral judgements and compassion for the distributive injustice of moral luck. Thus it is that moralists and courts rightly make allowances for a wrong-doer's painful childhood and adolescence, especially when extreme. It gets counted as another mitigating circumstance. But only mitigation – it does not wholly release us from the need for the truthfulness of blame and punishment.

Thus it is that our normal practices of moral judgement are consistent with the humanization of wrong-doers, moral judgement going on *outside* the 'circle of immunity' which gives practical expression to humanization. That moral judgement sometimes includes counting a person's bad moral luck as a mitigating circumstance. The humanization I have described encourages a generous conception of such circumstances. Indeed morality needs this humanization if it is not to become inhuman. But most of all it affords all human beings a protection (the 'ring of immunity') against wholesale alienation from the human family. That is impossible under a moralistic regime where inclusion in humanity must be earned.[12] By contrast, the sense of a shared common condition bestows that protection as a grace.

I have given an account of humanization that secures for offenders protection against the severity of moralism, yet which does not surrender morality in the form of the equitable judgement. There are two alternatives. One can reject this shared

---

12 Just such a moralism seems to be advocated by John Kekes in *Facing Evil*, Princeton: Princeton University Press.

condition of humanity in the name of its perennial enemy, moralism. That will be a harsh world indeed. Or one can inflate the humanization into an antinomian obliteration of all moral distinctions. That will be hardly any less cruel.

Chapter 13

The Unbearable Space of Schlink's Persona

Richard H. Weisberg

Editor's Introduction

Rather than a philosophical piece, Richard Weisberg's is a literary commentary which explores a few ways of interpreting *The Reader*, but settles for one. Weisberg argues that *The Reader* does not, in fact, explore the tension between judging and understanding vis-à-vis Hanna's character and deeds. According to Weisberg, Hanna stands condemned from the moment in which her alleged deeds are revealed. We can try to understand Hanna, and feel sympathy for her, as Michael does to some extent, but the sympathy in question is not, according to Weisberg, a sympathy that condones. Rather than a literary defence of the idea that there is a tension between judging and understanding, the novel is primarily an invitation to feel sympathy for its 'anti-hero', Michael, the literary representative of the post-war generation in Germany, attempting, to the best of his abilities, to come to terms with the unspeakable, unforgivable, incomprehensible atrocities of his forebears; a group represented by the illiterate Hanna, but also by his father; the ethically impotent professor of philosophy who, when asked by his son for advice, recommends inaction. How can it be, Weisberg's Michael at some level thinks, that a culture, capable of producing 'the Goethe, the Kleist, the Keller' has been complicit in the deeds of 'Hitler and his gang'? The more Michael tries to understand his previous generation, which he increasingly associates metaphorically with Hanna's revealed illiterate brutality, the more he encounters the silence of the unspeakable. Hanna stands condemned and Michael is left to make sense of the atrocities and of his life in the face of these atrocities, but his efforts simply make him ever more incapable of having a proper life. He becomes a reasonably typical literary lawyer, trapped inside himself and incapable properly of having 'natural empathy'; an incapacity triggered by shame. Michael stands for Schlink's generation. He is Schlink's persona. The novel, viewed from Weisberg's prism, invites us to feel sympathy for Schlink, for he has inherited the 'language' that was debased by the Third Reich – the unspeakable legacy of death. So, *The Reader* is a novel about living with the weight of an unbearable legacy; a novel written in the language that was made into the language of blood, 'the language of the damned'.

* * *

My appreciation of *The Reader* now enters its fourth round. Several years ago, during a panel discussion that included Tina Rosenberger of the *New York Times* and Daniel Goldhagen – author of *Hitler's Willing Executioners* – I situated the novel's strengths within the genre of 'Law and Literature'. Schlink's anti-hero, Michael, belongs in the ranks of those I had called 'the lawyer as protagonist', a peculiar breed of leading men (mostly all men) whose legalistic proclivities lead them to favour complexity over simple human interaction. The result for other characters who need to deal with these lawyer-figures is usually disastrous. 'He goes to law school' I said of Michael. After that, the plot produces the usual inverse proportion of intellectual growth to natural empathy. Michael's marriage ends. He can make no affirmative choices at Hanna's trial. He feels numb when visiting the site of the death camp near Strasbourg. All that is left inside him is shame, his own and that of the country he lives in and the language he uses to speak and to write.

I meant for the novel no less than the praise implicit in the comparison of its leading figure to Hamlet, Mr. Jaggers, and Jean-Baptiste Clamence: protagonists who are either (like the latter two and Michael) formally trained in law or (like the Danish Prince) so trained to think like a lawyer that he might as well have received his Juris Doctor from Wittenburg. Hamlet's tests and tricks and verbal subtleties turn him from the crying needs not only of the people around him – Ophelia being the most poignant victim of traits he self-consciously later calls at her grave-side 'quiddities and quillities' – but of the entire state. Michael, too, becomes cold even as he becomes legalistic. Like these other characters, he lures people into a sense of dependency on their superior intellectual abilities; like them, too, he turns away at their keenest moments of need. Michael at Hanna's trial prefigures Michael meeting Hanna the day before she is to leave prison. He is there but not there. He is doubly absent for Hanna. Her suicide, like Ophelia's, bears the mark of the lawyer.

Several years after the panel discussion (which gained its 15 minutes of American fame by showing up from time to time on 'C-Span'), I participated in a written symposium on *The Reader* in the journal *Law and Literature*. Joined by such essayists as the editor of this present volume, I addressed the matter of forgiveness and memory. Does the novel 'intend' to render complex what seems most clear: the inexcusable culpability of Hanna's hideous war crimes? Although the focus of the inquiry seemed to shift from Michael to his paramour-camp guard, I responded by insisting, again, on Michael's double-absence for Hanna. I enlarged the screen, first, of Michael's failure to tell the judge that Hanna is illiterate and hence could not have organized the camp guards' collective iniquity. At the origin of this absence, which seals her fate, Michael seeks the advice of his father, another figure of estimable rational capacity unable to help others. He seems to want Michael to let the trial develop without a *deus ex machina*. The father does not believe in intervention. Michael does not intervene.

The episode hardly points to forgiveness of Hanna. Far from it! Michael lets the axe fall on his former lover. But it does extend the guilt for her crimes to other less overtly culpable members of her generation. She is old enough to be Michael's mother. Meanwhile, his real father (whose wartime record is surely not blemished by any 'active' wrongdoing) displays the fatal inability to act that characterized so many 'good' people during the Third Reich. Like the good philosopher he is, the father has evidently built this holding back into a veritable ethos. He has not been much of a father to Michael, making the boy line up for an appointment with him as though he were just another student waiting on line to see the great man; he does not want Michael to be much of a *mensch*, either. Michael's failure to speak up when he goes to see the judge assures Hanna's (justified) sentence.

During her long prison term, Michael sends her tapes that help her to learn to read. Does this mean he has forgiven her? Recall that he does not express anything of his feelings to her or to us. He just sends the tapes. We know this because the prison warden tells him how angry it made her that Hanna's 'benefactor' in this regard took no other friendly steps towards her as she was being rehabilitated. (Michael stands, again, in the Law and Literature tradition of lawyers like Mr. Jaggers: there but not really there for Pip and others whom he purports to be teaching.) When he finally comes to visit her, she 'reads' on his face the indifference he feels for her aging and lined face and body. He does not forgive her. Why should he? Why should we?^PThe sensitivity of very good interpreters such as Cynthia Ozick did not surprise me. Writing in *Commentary*, she took the novel to task for a perceived equivocation about Hanna's guilt. In the written symposium, story-teller Dan Stern elaborated by focusing on Hanna's statement to the court as it examines the guards' actions in leaving prisoners to die in the burning church: 'What would you have done?', she asked. Stern took this to be a more general rhetorical move made by Schlink: does any reader really know if he would have acted any differently? I liked the way Stern set up the problem, although I disagreed with his reading of the novel. Stern said that students in his seminar on the Holocaust through the years have also asked that question, as though to relativize the guilt of the actual perpetrators. What would *you* do? Stern answers: don't assume I (or you) would not do better! Good, I thought. But the novel leaves no doubt that Hanna's inquiry is a futile one, not meant to express the slightest narrative approbation for her question or for her actions in general.

My *Law and Literature* piece was called 'A Sympathy that Does Not Condone'. I felt the titular phrase marked the outside limit of the story's tolerance for Hanna. The lawyer who as a young man had been brutally hit in the face by the woman he now knows to have been a camp guard is not going to forgive her. But he is not without sympathy. This sympathy, and not Hanna's actions, needs *our* sympathetic understanding .

Because it takes work to understand Michael, while also comprehending the Ozick-Stern critique of *The Reader*, I organized yet a third discussion of the novel. This time a new group of panellists directly addressed the issue of 'The Limits on Imaginative Representation of the Holocaust'. Does an artist have some special obligation to cabin the creative urge, to restrict as he would not do about an ordinary subject the depiction of the Holocaust? Schlink is surely not the first story-teller to touch on the unthinkable (inexpressible?) horror of the Nazi camps. (While Schlink does not think his book is really a 'Holocaust-work' at all, it obviously is. Not only is Hanna's war-crimes trial perhaps the central scene of the story, but everything comes to pivot around it, including of course our understanding of the first part of the tale, in which Michael's sexual awakening at her hands foreshadows the later discovery only perhaps in her illiterate brutality towards him. There is also the highly significant scene at Strathof.) For some sensitivities, the tragic events are perhaps best left alone; silence ensures the requisite respect and words anyway fail us. For others, there is the threat of saturation; what for decades after the war amounted to a shameful taciturnity for the past 15 years has changed into a virtual obsession. For most others perhaps, representations are judged on a case-by-case basis. For me, as an example, Benigni's film 'Life is Beautiful' offends in its depiction of brass door-knobs and music in Auschwitz. For others, the film magnificently humanizes – I would say catholicizes – the genocide. Suffering is glorified. You either like that or you don't. But there is no absolute taboo on the subject. The problem, if any, lies in the specific artistic treatment.

The third group of panellists were well versed in the critical reactions to Schlink's story. Clayton Koelb, a distinguished professor of German Literature at the University of North Carolina in Chapel Hill, placed the work in the tradition not so much of Holocaust stories but of depictions of evil generally. He reminded us that almost all great villains (like Hanna?) have an attractive side. So Milton's fallen angel. So Richard III. But Koelb was deeply concerned that Schlink leaves ambiguous (as other writers do not) the specifics of his villain's wrong-doing. We never really find out for sure what, exactly, Hanna did or did not do as the church was burning with the Jewish victims inside it.

Schlink's story still unsettles. And that leads me to the present pass at his work, my fourth such effort. I find myself thinking of Schlink, of his desire to create of *us* the sympathetic reader, the oral advocate implied by his work's title. I am also more engaged now – in two senses – with the original meaning of *Der Vorleser*, which carries with it a sense of 'reading out loud'. My fourth public assessment of the text, my fourth try at stating 'out loud' my understanding of it might get me closer still to real 'literacy' about the novel, just as each oral reading of a story moves audiences closer to understanding or at least keeps people in touch with themselves, as the story grows on and with them each time it is read. Ironically here. However, each new reading carries with it greater *difficulty*, not greater understanding. Perhaps, I found myself thinking, the Ozick-Stern-Koelb view is right. After all, Schlink's persona – Michael – does consistently engage with the horrific past of a transgressor. Even before that past is revealed, she has beaten him, literally and figuratively. And, after he sees her convicted for the crimes he could not imagine during their earlier relationship (illiteracy and genocide), he continues their relationship and inculcates her into the great stories of the western tradition as though hers were still very much a soul worth saving for literate culture.

As I wrote in a prior examination of the story, Hanna's illiteracy is that of pre-war Germany generally. Steeped in culture, mainstream Germans – no more so than Hanna – could 'read' correctly the beast within. This much 'relativism' at least does emerge from the story: Hanna's failure is also Michael's father's, is also that of men and women educated in the classics who may not have been perpetrators but who had learned *indifference*. Michael's obsession with Hanna's literacy has less to do with any specific 'forgiveness' of her crimes as it has to do with *his* yearning to be situated humanely as he walks and talks among villains.

This is, finally, a tale about a second-generation post-war German's virtual inability to write and to be understood. His fate is to have been born and to have assimilated as his mother tongue the language of the Third Reich, a language debased by his own parents and their contemporaries as well (more obviously) as by Hitler and his gang. It is as though Schlink's persona wishes to revive through Hanna the Goethe, the Kleist, the Keller and the other writers whose medium he now adopts to tell her story. But this proves impossible. Hanna is still Hanna in the end, only older. Michael cannot escape, through her, his own destiny as a story-teller (legal or literary) doomed to use a language that had just recently visited Hell.

Schlink's persona is too much the detached lawyer to display overtly the anguish Schlink himself must feel. Michael's dominant mood at the end of the novel combines shame and numbness and abjures the passionate if negative irony of other such protagonists. But Schlink, despite a wonderful sense of humour (more on display in his terrific 'Selbst' stories than here), *is* desperate. He joins here a powerful post-war tradition begun by Günter Grass – re-read his chapter from *Blechtrommel* called 'Faith, Hope, Love'[1] – of German story-tellers overwhelmed by the task of using the debased tongue that is their craft's sole medium!

So I must try to 'condone' Schlink, not Hanna. I cannot put myself in the place of a writer whose every 'Du' and 'bist' must hurt, whose simplest syntactical creations must evoke for him the equally simple but brutal discourse of his father's generation: 'Die Juden sind unser Unglueck!', 'Arbeit macht Frei', 'Ich schwere bei Gott diese himmlische Eid: Adolf Hitler!. . .' Whatever force resides on the Ozick-Stern-Koelb critique, it yields to this understanding. Schlink's protagonist fails with Hanna; but each 'reading out loud' of Schlink's story leads us towards a consciousness of what it means to walk the soil and talk the language of the damned.

---

1 See my analysis of Grass' *Tin Drum* in *Poethics: and other Strategies of Law and Literature* (NY: Columbia U. Press, 1992).

Index